Das Verbot der Diskriminierung wegen Alters im australischen Recht

Europäische Hochschulschriften
Publications Universitaires Européennes
European University Studies

Reihe II
Rechtswissenschaft

Série II Series II
Droit
Law

Bd./Vol. 5280

PETER LANG
Frankfurt am Main · Berlin · Bern · Bruxelles · New York · Oxford · Wien

Daniel Welker

Das Verbot der Diskriminierung wegen Alters im australischen Recht

PETER LANG
Internationaler Verlag der Wissenschaften

Bibliografische Information der Deutschen Nationalbibliothek
Die Deutsche Nationalbibliothek verzeichnet diese Publikation in der Deutschen Nationalbibliografie; detaillierte bibliografische Daten sind im Internet über http://dnb.d-nb.de abrufbar.

Zugl.: Halle-Wittenberg, Univ., Diss., 2011

Gedruckt auf alterungsbeständigem, säurefreiem Papier.

3
ISSN 0531-7312
ISBN 978-3-631-63541-4

www.peterlang.de

Danksagung

Zuerst möchte ich mich bei meinem Doktorvater Herrn Prof. Dr. Wolfhard Kohte bedanken, der mir die Möglichkeit gab, das gewählte Thema wissenschaftlich zu bearbeiten und meine Dissertation an seinem Lehrstuhl zu erstellen.

Darüber hinaus möchte ich mich bei Herrn Associate Prof. Dr. Alex Ziegert von der Sydney Law School der University of Sydney für die sachkundige, erfahrene und wertvolle Unterstützung sowie den intensiven Gedankenaustausch bedanken. Gerade die Unterstützung in der Anfangsphase meiner Promotion hat wesentlich zum erfolgreichen Gelingen der Arbeit beigetragen.

Ebenfalls möchte ich mich an dieser Stelle für die unermüdliche, freundliche und geduldige Bereitschaft von Dr. Belinda Smith von der Sydney Law School an der University of Sydney sowie bei Juliet Bourke von der University of New South Wales bedanken. Sie haben mich nicht zuletzt fortlaufend über die neuesten Entwicklungen und Publikationen im australischen Antidiskriminierungsrecht informiert.

Bei Dr. Lenz Steinhauser bedanke ich mich für die gelegentlichen wissenschaftlichen Diskussionen und den gedanklichen Austausch zu aktuellen Fragen rund um das internationale Antidiskriminierungsrecht.

Ein ganz besonderer Dank geht an meine Familie, insbesondere an meine Ehefrau Dr. Sylvia Welker, die mir während der Anfertigung meiner Doktorarbeit immerzu unterstützend, geduldig, liebevoll und auch motivierend zur Seite stand.

Inhalt

Literaturverzeichnis

ABS (Australian Bureau of Statistics), Labour force projections, Australia (1999) cat. no. 6260.0.

ABS (Australian Bureau of Statistics), Population by age and sex, Australian states and territories (2004) cat. no. 3201.0.

ACCI, Age Discrimination Laws – Who benefits?, Age Discrimination Laws, April 2003, 3

Alexander, Family Mediation under the Microscope (1999) 10, Australasian Dispute Resolution Journal, 18

Alexander, Wirtschaftsmediation in Theorie und Praxis, 1999

Allen, Equal opportunity (1996) 5, Res Publica, 16

Andrews (Minister of Ageing), A Changing Workplace (2001) National Strategy for an Ageing Australia: An Older Australia, Challenges and Opportunities for All; abrufbar unter http://www.longevityinternational.com/assets/National%20Strategy%20for%20an%20Ageing%20Australia.pdf

Anti-Discrimination Board of New South Wales, Age Old Dilemmas (2004) 60 Equal Times 1

Arrowsmith/McGoldrick, Bridging The Theory And Practice Divide Through Collaborative Research – The Case of Ageism in Employment (1996)

Astor/Chinkin, Dispute Resolution in Australia, 1992

Attorney Generals Department of New South Wales, Age Discrimination – Options for New South Wales, A Discussion Paper (2000)

Australian Bureau of Statistics, Census of Population and Housing (1996)

Australian Bureau of Statistics, Successful and Unsuccessful Job Search Experience (2000)

Australian Bureau of Statistics, Job Search Experience of Unemployed Persons (2003)

Australian Bureau of Statistics, Australian Social Trends 2004: Mature Age Workers (2004)

Australian Council of Trade Unions and the Business Council of Australia; Senate Select Committee on Superannuation, Planning for Retirement (2003) Australian Parliament

Australian Employers Convention, The Human Resource Costs and Benefits of Maintaining an Age-Balanced Workforce (2001)

Australian Law Reform Commission, Report No. 89, 2000, Managing justice: continuity and change in the federal civil justice system

Bailey, Human Rights – Australia in an International Context, 1990

Bailey/Devereux, The Operation of Antidiscrimination Laws in Australia, in: *Kinley*, Human Rights in Australian Law, 1998

Baker, Access vs Process in Employment Discrimination: Why ADR suits the US but not the UK (2002) 31 Industrial Law Journal 113

Becker, The Economics of Discrimination, 1971

Beckett, Can Status Be A New Ground In Australian Discrimination Laws, (2004) AIAL FORUM No. 45, 40

Bennington, Age Discrimination: Converging Evidence From Four Australian Studies (2001) 13 Employee Responsibilities and Rights Journal 125

Bennington, Aiding and Abetting Employer Discrimination: the Job Applicant´s (2002) 14 Employee Responsibilities and Rights Journal 3

Bennington, Does the Secretarial Resume Open The Door to Age Discrimination? (2003) 22 Australasian Journal on Ageing 70

Bennington, Prime Age Recruitment: The Challenges for Age Discrimination Legislation (2004) Elder Law Review 8

Bennington/Tharenou, Older Workers: Myths, Evidence and Implications for Australian Managers (1996) 34 Asia Pacific Journal of Human Resources 21

Bennington/Wein, Anti-Discrimination Legislation in Australia: Fair, Effective, Efficient or Irrelevant? (2000) 21 International Journal of Manpower 21

Birren/Schiae, Handbook of the Psychology of Ageing, 1996

Boland, The Prospects for Mediation Having a Formal Role in Australia's Industrial Relations System, Alternative Dispute Resolution Bulletin, 1998

Boniface, Does anyone really know where we're going? Changes to the HREOC (1998) 4 Australian Journal of Human Rights 1

Bourke in: Australasian Diversity and Equality Survey (ADES) 2003

Bourke in: Australaisan Diversity and Equality Survey (ADES) 2005 abrufbar unter http://www.eeona.org/initiatives.html

Bourke, Age Discrimination and Human Resource Management in Practice, in: Baker & McKenzie, Age Discrimination: Mitigating Risk in the Workplace (2004)

Bourke, Are we having fun yet? Age discrimination in recruitment, abrufbar unter http://adage.com.au/Files/Are%20we%20having%20fun%20yet%20-%20CCH%2014.10.05.pdf

Bourke, Implementing flexibility in the legal profession: Myths and realities, (2005) 43 Law Society Journal 54

Bourke, Job redesign: A strategic approach to implementing flexible work practices (2001), August (121) CCH Australia and New Zealand Equal Opportunity Law and Practice 10

Bourke, Moving ahead on diversity and equality: Results from the 2005 Australasian Diversity and Equality Survey, in: *Davis/Pratt*, Making the Link. Affirmative Action and Employment Relations (2005)

Bourke, Moving ahead on diversity and equality: Results from the 2005 Australasian Diversity and Equality Survey, in: *Davis/Pratt*, Making the Link. Affirmative Action and Employment Relations (2005)

Bourke/Ronalds, Discrimination Laws – Striving For Equality, in: *Macken*, The Law of Employment, 2002

Bourke/Ronalds, Discrimination Laws – Striving Towards Equality, in Macken, The Law of Employment, 2002

Bryson, "And the leopard shall lie down with the kid": A Conciliation Model for Workplace Disputes (1998) 8 Australian Dispute Resolution Journal 245

Bryson, Mediator and Advocate: Conciliating Human Rights Complaints (1990) 1 Australian Dispute Resolution Journal 136
Bureau of Labour Market Research, Discrimination in the Labour – Force at older Ages (1983) Working Paper No 17
Burmester, Impact of Treaties and International Standards, (1995) 17 Sydney Law Review 127
Business Council of Australia, Age Can Work, 2003
Butler, Proposed amendments to the Anti-Discrimination Act 1977 (NSW) (1990) Australian Coporate Lawyer 32
Butterworths Australian Legal Dictionary, Sydney u.a., 1997

Cairns, Australian Civil Procedure, 2004
Cantanzariti, Federal discrimination claims after Brandy (1995) 33 Law Society Journal 16
Caroll/Mackie, International Mediation – The Art of Business Diplomacy, 2000
Catanzariti, Age and employment (1999) 4 Employment Law Bulletin 92
Catanzariti, WorkChoices – a rise in discrimination claims? (2006) 12 Employment Law Bulletin 25
Chan/Stevens, Job Loss and Employment Patterns of Older Workers (2001) 19 Journal of Labor Economics 484
Chapman, Sexuality and Workplace Oppression (1995) 20 Melbourne University Law Review 311
Charlesworth, The Australian Reluctance about Rights; in: *Alston*, Towards an Australian Bill of Rights, 1994
Charlton/Dewdney, The Mediator's Handbook: Skills and Strategies for Practicioners, 2004
Christian, Community Dispute Resolution: First Class-Process or Second-Class Justice? (1986) 14 NYU Review of Law & Social Change 771
Collins, Discrimination, Equality and Social Inclusion (2003) 66 Modern LR 16
Collins, Employment Law, Opportunity and Discrimination. 2003
Collins, Equality and Social Inclusion', (2003) 66 Modern Law Review 16
Colneric, Antidiskriminierung – quo vadis? – Europäisches Recht, NZA-Beilage 2008, Heft 2, 71
Colvin/Watson, The Workplace Relations Handbook – A guide to the Workplace Relations Act 1996 (Cth), Sydney 1998
Committee of Inquiry into Poverty in Australia (Henderson Report), Parliament of Australia, 1976
Crawford, Australian Courts of Law, 2004
Creigthon/Stewart, Australian Labour Law, 2005

Däubler/Bertzbach, Allgemeines Gleichbehandlungsgesetz, Handkommentar, 2. Auflage 2008
Department of the Treasury (2002), Intergenerational Report 2002-03, Budget Paper No 5 2002-03

Devereux, Human Rights by Agreement? (1996) 7, Australian Dispute Resolution Journal, 280

Drake Executive Survey National Findings in: House of Representatives Standing Committee on Employment, Education and Workplace Relations, Parliament of Australia, Age Counts, 2000

Drake Management Consulting (1999) Age Discrimination is Alive and Well, Submission to the House of Representatives Standing Committee on Employment, Education & Workplace Relations Inquiry into Issues Specific to Workers over 45 years, abrufbar unter: http://www.hreoc.gov.au/pdf/human_rights/age_report_2000.pdf

Dreyer, Race Relations Act 1976 und Rassendiskriminierung in Großbritannien, 2000

Drury, Older Workers in the European Community: Pervasive Discrimination, Little Awarness (1993) 20 Ageing International 12

Eastman, Exemptions and exceptions, in: Baker & McKenzie, Age Discrimination: Mitigating Risk in the Workplace, 2004

Eastman, Procedures, in: Baker & McKenzie, Age Discrimination: Mitigating Risk in the Workplace. 2004

Encel, Age Can Work: The Case for Older Australians Staying in the Workforce, 2003

Encel, Age Discrimination in Law and Practice, (2004) Elder Law Review 7

Encel, Age Discrimination in: *Patrickson/Hartmann*, Managing an Ageing Workforce (1998) 45

Encel, Age Discrimination

Encel, Ageing, Pensions and Employment in Australia: Recent Developments, (2004) 34 Geneva Association Newsletter 3

Encel, Older Workers-Can They Succeed in the Job Market?, (2004) 23 Australasian Journal of Ageing 34

Encel/Studencki, Over the Hill or Flying High? – An Analysis of Age Discrimination Complaint in NSW, 1998

Evatt, The Impact of International Human Rights on Domestic Law, in: *Hushcroft/Rishworth*, Litigatin Rights: Perspectives from Domestic and International Law, 2002

Explanatory Memorandum of the Age Discrimination Bill 2003 (Cth), abrufbar unter http://www.austlii.edu.au/au/legis/cth/bill_em/adb2003184/memo2.html

Fels, Now is the Time to Raise the Retirement Age (2003), abrufbar unter http://www.theage.com.au/articles/2003/12/25/1072308626614.html

Fiss, Against Settlement (1984) 93 The Yale Law Journal 1073

Foenander, Industrial Conciliation and Arbitration in Australia, 1959

Ford, Reconstructing Australian Labour Law: A Constitutional Perspective, (1997) 10 Australian Journal of Labour Law, 105

Ford, The Constitution and the Reform of Australian Industrial Relations, (1994) 7 Australian Journal of Labour Law 105

Foster, Towards a National Retirement Incomes Policy (Issue Paper, Social Security Review (Australia); no. 6 (1988) 17

Fozard/Gordon-Salant, Changes in Vision and Hearing with Age, in: *Birren/Schaie*, Handbook of the Psychology of Ageing, 1996
Fredman, Discrimination Law, 2002

Gardner, Liberals and Unlawful Discrimination (1989) 9 Oxford Journal of Legal Studies 1
Garth, The Movement toward Procedural Informalism in North American and Western Europe: A Critical Survey, in: Richard L. Abel, The Politics of Informal Justice, 1982
Gaze, The costs of Equal Opportunity (2000) 25 Alternative Law Journal 125
Goulding, The Law Handbook, 1995
Goward, The HREOC perspective – Age discrimination and its effects in the Australian community, in: Baker & McKenzie, Age Discrimination: Mitigating Risk in the Workplace, 2004
Gunningham, Industrial Law and the Constitution, 1988
Guthrie, Ageing – Discrimination and Workers Compensation, 2005

Hallier, Greenfield Recruitment and Selection: Implications for the Older Worker (2001) 30 Personnel Review 331
Hankins, Social Discrimination, in: *Seligman/Johnson*, Encyclopedia of Social Siences, Vol. 14, 1934
Harding, Age, The Road to Anti-Discrimination paved with good Intentions (1994) Law Society Journal 44
Hartmann, The Impact of Trends in Labour-Force Participation in Australia, 1998
Hemingway, Roadmap to ADA: The Age Discrimination Act 2004, 5 abrufbar unter http://www.hreoc.gov.au/age/roadmap_ADA.html
Hemingway, The Age Discrimination Act 2004
Henrich, Einführung in das Englische Privatrecht, 1993
Hirsch/MacPherson/Hardy, Occupational Age Structure and Access for Older Workers (2000) 53 Industrial and Labour Relations Review 401
Hofrichter, Neighbourhood Justice and the Social Control Problems of American Capitalism, in: Abel: The Politics of Informal Justice, Vol. 1, 1982
Honeyball/Bowers, Textbook on Labour Law
House of Representatives Standing Committee on Employment, Education and Workplace Relations, Parliament of Australia, Age Counts, 2000
Human Rights and Equal Opportunity Commission, Age matters? A discussion paper on age discrimination, 1999
Human Rights and Equal Opportunity Commission, Age Matters, 2000
Human Rights and Equal Opportunity Commission, Annual Report 1999 – 2000
Human Rights and Equal Opportunity Commission, Annual Report 2005 – 2006
Human Rights and Equal Opportunity Commission, Annual Report 2006 – 2007
Human Rights and Equal Opportunity Commission, Annual Report 2007 – 2008
Human Rights and Equal Opportunity Commission, Federal Discrimination Law 2009
Human Rights and Equal Opportunity Commission, Federal Discrimination Law 2005

Human Rights and Equal Opportunity Commission, Report of an Inquiry into a Complaint of Discrimination in Employment and Occupation, Discrimination on the Ground of Age, HRC Report No. 11

Human Rights and Equal Opportunity Commission, Report of inquiry into complaints of discrimination in employment and occupation, 1997

Human Rights and Equal Opportunity Commission, Submission to the Senate Legal and Constitutional Committee on the Age Discrimination Bill 2003, 2003, abrufbar unter http://www.humanrights.gov.au/legal/submissions/age_discrimination.html

Human Rights and Equal Opportunity Commission, An International Comparison of the Racial Discrimination Act 1975, Background Paper 1, 2008

Hunter, Indirect Discrimination in the Workplace, 1992

Ierodiaconou, Conciliation, Mediation and Federal Human Rights Complaints: Are Rights Compromised?, 2005

International Labour Conference, Equality in Employment and Occupation: General Survey by the Committee of Experts on the Application of Conventions and Recommendations, ILO Genf, 1996

Jones, How Redundancies Worsen Social Inequality (1999) International Journal of Sociology and Social Policy 57

Joseph, The International Covenant on Civil and Political Rights: Cases, Materials and Commentary, 2004

Ketchman/Stelmach, Age-Related Declines in Motor Control; in : *Birren/Schaie*, Handbook of the Psychology of Ageing, 1996

Kinley, Textbook on International Human Rights Law, 2006

Kohte, Zur Rechtmäßigkeit einer erneuten Änderung des § 14 Abs. 3 TzBfG im Gesetz zur Verbesserung der Beschäftigungschancen älterer Menschen v. 19.4.2007 (BGBl. I S. 538), AuR 2007, 168

Kohte, Bessere Beschäftigungschancen für ältere Arbeitnehmer - aber wie?, AuR 2008, 281

Kohte, Altersdiskriminierung von Universitätsprofessoren ("Georgiev"), EuGH, Urteil vom 18.11.2010, C-250/09, C-268/09, jurisPR-ArbR 2/2011, Anm. 7

Korac-Kakabadse/Reeves-Knyght/Konzmin, Inequality of Discourse and the Problem of Access to Justice, in: Social Justice Social Judgment, 1995

Kurland, The Impact of Legal Age Discrimination on Women in Professional Occupation (2001) 11 Business Ethic Quarterly 33

Landau, Conciliation as a mode of settlement of discrimination complaints (1988) 11 Adelaide Law Review 273

Laurent, Time to listen (1990) 86 Nursing Time 20

Lawrence, Organizational Age Norms: Why Is It So Hard To Know One When You See One? (1996) 36 The Gerontologist 209

Louw, Age Discrimination Act 2004 (Cth) – Application of the Act, in: Baker & McKenzie, Age Discrimination: Mitigating Risk in the Workplace, 2004

Lucas, Scrapheap Mentality Damages Businesses (2000) 13 Professional Engineering 26 *Ludeke*, The External Affairs Power: Another Province for Law and Order? (1993) 35 Journal of Industrial Relations 453

Lustgarten, Racial Inequality and the Limits of the Law (1986) 49 Modern Law Review 68

Mac Dermott, Age Discrimination and Employment Law: The Sky's the Limit, (1998) 11 AJLL 144

Mac Dermott, The Implications for Employment Law (1995) 8 Australian Journal of Labour Law 276

Macken/O'Grady/Sappideen/Warburton, The Law of Employment, 2002

Macnicol, Age Discrimination, An Historical and Contemporary Analysis, 2006

Madden, Speed and Timing of Behavioural Response, in: *Birren/Schaie*, Handbook of the Psychology of Ageing, 1996

Mason, The role of the Judiciary in developing Human Rights in Australian Law, in: Kinley, Human Rights in Australian Law, 1998

McEwan, Meeting the Challenges One Year On (2005), abrufbar unter http://www.hreoc.gov.au/age/workingage/speeches/mcewan.html

McGoldrick/Arrowsmith, Recruitment Advertising: Discrimination on the Basis of Age (1993) 15 Employee Relations 54

Montoya, Let's Mediate – a whole new ballgame at EEOC (1999) 24 Employee Relations Law Journal 53

Murray/Syed, Critical issues in managing age diversity in Australia (2005) 43(2) Asia Pacific Journal of Human Resources 210

Nand, Judicial Power and Administrative Tribunals: The Decision in Brandy v HREOC (1997) 14 Australian Institute of Administrative Law Forum 15

Nelson, The use of conciliation in Australia to resolve complaints of discrimination made under federal and state legislation, in: *Mugford*, Alternative Dispute Resolution, Australian Institute of Criminology, 1986

Neugarten, Age Distinctions and Their Social Functions, in: *Neugarten*, The Meanings of Age: Selected Papers of Bernice L. Neugarten, 1996

Neugarten/Moore/Lowe, Age Norms, Age Constraints and Adult Socialisation, in: *Neugarten*, The Meaning of Age: Selected Papers of Bernice L. Neugarten, 1996

O'Neill/Handley, Retreat from Injustice, Human Rights in Australian Law, 1994

Offenberger/Banks, Wind out of the sails – new federal structure for the administration of human rights legislation (2000) 6 Australian Journal of Human Rights 239

Omar, Darkness on the edge of town: the High Court and Human Rights in the Brandy case (1995) 2 Australian Journal of Human Rights 1

Opeskin, International Law and Federal States, in: *Opeskin/Rothwell*, International Law and Australian Federalism, 1997

Ozdowski, Adressing Age discrimination (2002) 81 Older People and the Law 12

Paddison, The Targeted Approach to Recruitment (1990) 22 Personnel Management 54
Patrickson/Hartmann, Managing an Ageing Workforce (1998) 55
Patterson, The Eradication of Compulsory Retirement and Age Discrimination in the Australian Workplace: A Cause for Celebration and Concern (2004) 3 Elder Law Review 7
Pearce/Geddes, Statutory Interpretation in Australia, 2006
Peetz, Retrechment and Labour Market Disadvantage: The Role of Age, Job Tenure and Casual Employment, in: Reflections and New Directions: AIRAANZ Conference 2003, Volume 2: Non-Refereed Papers, Association of Industrial Relations Academics of Australia and New Zealand
Pentony, Conciliation under the Racial Discrimination Act 1975, in: Human Rights Commission Occasional Paper No. 15, 1986
Perry/Bourhis, A Closer Look at the Role of Applicant Age in Selection Decisions (1998) 28 Journal of Applied Social Psychology 1670
Perry/Kulik/Bourhis, Moderating Effects of Personal and Contextual Factors in Age Discrimination (1996) 81 Journal of Applied Psychology 628
Pickersgill, Productivity of Mature and Older Workers: Employers´ Attitudes and Experiences (1996) ACIRRT, University of Sydney
Pickersgill/Briggs/Kitay/Keeffe/Gillezeau, Productivity of Mature and Older Workers: Employers´ Attitudes and Experiences (1996)
Priestley/Rabiee, Building Bridges: disability and old age (2001) ESRC resarch report

Ranzijn, Discrimination against older worker: psychology and economics (2005), abrufbar unter http://www.hreoc.gov.au/age/workingage/speeches/ranzijn.html
Ratnam, Federal Government´s proposed age discrimination legislation (2003) 9 Employment Law Bulletin 13
Redman/Matthews, Advertising for Effective Managerial Recruitment (1992) 18 Journal of General Management 29
Redman/Matthews, Getting Personal in Personnel Recruitment (1996) 18 Employee Relations 68
Rees/Lindsay/Rice, Australian Anti-Discrimination Law: Text, Cases and Materials, 2008
Regan, Dilemmas of Dispute Resolution Policy (1997) 8, Australian Dispute Resolution Journal 5
Resnik, Failing Faith, Adjudicatory Procedure in Decline (1986) 53 The University of Chicago Law Review 494
Revised Explanatory Memorandum, Age Discrimination Act (Cth) 2004
Risworth, The Rule of International Law, in: *Hushcroft/Rishworth*, Litigating Rights: Perspectives from Domestic and International Law, 2002
Roberts/Redman, Full service handling of Human Rights complaints (2000) Law Institute Journal 57
Ronalds, Discrimination – Law and Practice, 2004
Ronalds/Pepper, Discrimination Law and Practice, 2004

Schaie, Intellectual Development in Adulthood, in: *Birren/Schaie*, Handbook of the Psychology of Ageing, 1996

Schiae, The Impact of Longitudinal Studies on Understanding Development from Young Adulthood to Old Age (2000) 24 International Journal of Behavioural Development 257

Schlachter, Außergerichtliche Konfliktlösung im Arbeitsverhältnis, Verwirklichung von Chancengleichheit auf dem Verhandlungswege in Australien und Deutschland, 2002

Schlachter, Altersgrenzen angesichts des gemeinschaftlichen Verbots der Altersdiskriminierung, in: *Richardi/Reichhold*, Gedächtnisschrift Blomeyer, 2003, 373

Scholz, Lohngleichheit durch Verfahren, 2000

Schiek, Gleichbehandlungsrichtlinien der EU - Umsetzung im deutschen Arbeitsrecht, NZA 2004, 873

Schwartz/Kleiner, The Relationship Between Age and Emloyment Opportunities (1999) 18 Equal Opportunities International 105

Scutt, The Privatisation of Justice, in: *Mugford*, Alternative Dispute Resolution, Australian Institute of Criminology, 1986

Scutt, The Privatisation of Justice: Power Differentials, Inequality and the Palliative of Counselling and Mediation, in: *Mugford*, Alternative Dispute Resolution, 1986

Second Reading Speech, Anti Discrimination Bill, 23 November 1976, New South Wales Parliamentary Debates, Session 1976, Vol. 128, Third Series, 3337

Senate Employment, Education and Training References Committee, Commonwealth Parliament, Report on the inquiry into long term unemployment, 1995

Senate Legal and Constitutional Committee, Provisions of the Age Discrimination Bill 2003, 2003

Senne, Auswirkungen des europäischen Verbots der Altersdiskriminierung auf das deutsche Arbeitsrecht, 2006

Sheen, Older Australians: Working for the future, 1999

Shergold, Balancing Work and Family Conference – Different Lives, Different Needs, Key Note Adress (1999)

Smith, Australian Anti-Discrimination Laws – Framework, Developments and Issues, New Developments in Employment Discrimination Law – The 9 JILPT Comparative Labour Law Seminar (2008) 19

Smith, From *Wardley* to *Purvis*: How far has Australian anti-discrimination law come in 30 years? (2008) 21 Australian Journal of Labour Law 3

Smith, Harrassment and bullying in the workplace, (2005) 11 Employment Law Bulletin 1

Smith/Riley/Sarina, Industrial Legislation in 2004 (2005) 47 Journal of Industrial Relations 171

Sordo, The Lawyer's Role in Mediation (1996) 7 Australian Dispute Resolution Journal 20

Spriduso/MacRae, Motor Performance and Ageing, in: *Birren/Schiae*, Handbook of the Psychology of Ageing, 1996

Stein/Rocco/Goldenetz, Age and the University Workplace: a Case Study of Remaining, Retiring, Or Returning Older Workers (2000) 11 Human Resource Development Quarterly 61
Sternlight, In Search of the Best Procedure for Enforcing Employment Discrimination Laws: A Comparative Analysis (2004) 78 Tulane Law Review 1401
Stewart, Redefining Employment? Meeting the Challenge of Contract and Agency Labour (2002) Australian Journal of Labour Law 15
Steyn, The Intractable Problem of The Interpretation of Legal Texts (2003) 25 SydLRev 5
Stubbs, Feminism and Legal Positivism, in: *Weisberg*, Feminist Legal Theory: Foundations, 1993
Submission to the Senate Legal and Constitutional Legislation Committee on the Age Discrimination Bill 2003, abrufbar unter
www.humanrights.gov.au/legal/submissions/age_discrimination.html

Taqi, Older People, Work and Equal Opportunity (2002) 55 International Social Security Review 107
Taylor/Steinberg/Walley, Mature Age Employment: Recent Developments in Public Policy in Australia and The UK (2000) Australasian Journal of Ageing 125
The National Strategy for an Ageing Australia, Employment for Mature Age Workers, Issues Paper, 1999
Thew, Age discriminationn and the Human Rights and Equal Opportunity Commission Act 1986 (Cth), in: Baker & McKenzie, Age Discrimination: Mitigating Risk in the Workplace, 2004
Thornthwaite, The Operation of Anti-Discrimination Legislation in NSW in relation to Employment Complaints, (1993) 6 Australian Journal of Labour Law 31
Thornton, Antidiscrimination Remedies (1983) 9, The Adelaide Law Review, 235
Thornton, Equivocation of Conciliation: The Resolution of Discrimination Complaints in Australia (1989) 52 The Modern Law Review 733
Thornton, The Liberal Promise: Anti-Discrimination Legislation in Australia, 1990
Tyler, Why People Obey the Law, 1990

Ury/Brett/Goldberg, Getting disputes resolved – designing systems to cut the cost of conflict, 1989

Victorian, South Australian and Western Australian Equal Opportunity Commissioners, Age Limits: Age-Related Discrimination in Employment Affecting Workers Over 45, 2001

Walker, Age and Employment (1997) 17 Australasian Journal on Ageing 99
Waltermann, Alternde Arbeitswelt – Welche arbeits- und sozialrechtlichen Regelungen empfehlen sich?, NJW 2008, 2529.
Weisberg, Application of Feminist Legal Theory to Women's Live, 1996
Wheelwright, Butterworths Casebook Companions, Labour Law, 2002/2003
Williams, A Bill of Rights for Australia, 2000

Williams, Significant steps toward a Commonwealth Age Discrimination Act (2002) Older People and the Law 16
Williams/Gotting, (2001) 20 Australian Bar Review 264
Winckel, The Contextual Role of a Preamble in Statutory Interpretation (1999) 23 MULR 184

Yearta/Warr, Does Age Matter? (1995) 14 Journal of Management Development 28

Rechtsprechung

A School v Human Rights and Equal Opportunity Commission (No 2) [1998] FCA 145
AB v New South Wales Minister for Education and Training [2003] FMCA 16
Aldrige v Booth (1988) 80 ALR 1
Alexander v Home Office (1988) 1 WLR 968
Allders International Pty Limited v Anstee (1986) EOC 92-157 = 5 NSWLR 47
Allman v Australian Airlines Limited (1995) 60 IR 17
Ansett Transport Industries (Operations) Pty Ltd v Wardley (1979) 142 CLR 237
Ansett Transport Industries (Operations) Pty Ltd v Wardley (1984) EOC 92-002
Ardeshirian v Robe River Iron Associates (1993) 43 FCR 475
Australian Iron and Steel Pty Limited v Banovic (1989) 89 ALR 1, 15
Australian Iron and Steel v Banovic (1989) 168 CLR 165
Australian Liquor, Hospitality and Miscellaneous Workers Union, Queensland Branch, Union of Employees v Bark Australia Pty Ltd [2001] QIRComm 22
Australian Medical Council v Human Rights and Equal Opportunity Commission (1995) 68 FCR 46
Australian Mutual Provident Society Ltd v Chaplin (1978) 18 ALR 385
Australian Postal Commission v Dao (1985) 3 NSWLR 565
Australian Railways Union v Victorian Railways Commissioners (1930) 44 CLR 319
Awan v Minister for Immigration & Multicultural & Indigenous Affairs [2002] FCA 594

Ball v Morgan [2001] FMCA 127
Barghouthi v Transfield Services (2002) 122 FCR 19
Barnes v Northern Land Council & Ors [2002] FMCA 54
Bassanelli v QBE Insurance [2003] FMCA 412
Batzialas v Tony Davies Motors Pty Ltd [2002] FMCA 243
Bearings Inc (Australia) Pty Ltd v Treloar (1999) 95 IR 169
Beck v Leichhardt Municipal Council [2002] FCMA 331
Bender v Boris Lend Lease Pty Ltd (2003) 175 FLR 446
Bennett v Everitt (1988) EOC 92-157
Beu v PR Exhibitions Pty Ltd (1998) EOC 92-939
Blatchford v Qantas Airways Ltd (1997) EOC 92-888
Bloomfield v Westco Jeans Pty Ltd (2001) EOC 93-161 = [2001] ACTDT 4
Boehringer Ingelheim Pty Ltd v Reddrop [1984] 2 NSWLR 13
Borg v Commissioner, Department of Corrective Services (2002) EOC 93-198
Bowerman v Sinclair Halvorsen Pty Ltd [1999] NSWIRComm 21
Boyd v SCI Operations Pty Ltd (1996) EOC 92-853
Bradley v Commonwealth (1973) 128 CLR 557
Brandy v Human Rights and Equal Opportunity Commission (1995) EOC 2-662 = (1995) 183 Commonwealth Law Reports 245 = (1995) 127 Australian Law Report 1
Brandy v Human Rights and Equal Opportunity Commission (1995) EOC 2-662; 183 Commonwealth Law Reports 245

Brenner v First Artists' Management Pty Ltd [1993] 2 VR 221
Briginshaw v Briginshaw (1938) 60 CLR 336
Broadwater Taxation & Investment Services Pty Ltd v Hendriks (1993) 51 IR 221
Bropho v Western Australia [2004] FCA 1209
Bruch v Commonwealth of Australia [2002] FMCA 29
Burke v Tralaggan & Anor (1986) EOC 92-161
Burnett v MLA Holdings and Gavin Coulthard [1999] VCAT
Burrows v Coomonwealth of Police (1995) EOC 92-676
Buxton v Minister of Housing and Local Government (1961) 1 QB 278
Byrne Bros (Formwork) Ltd v Baird [2002] ICR 667

Calderbank c Calderbank (1975) 3 All ER 333
Cameron v Human Rights and Equal Opportunity Commission (1993) 46 FCR 509
Campbell v. FH Productions (1984) EOC 92 – 104
Capodicasa v Herald & Weekly Times Ltd & Ors (1999) EOC 92-969
Carr v Boree Aboriginal Corporation [2003] FMCA 408
Carr v Blade Repairs Australia Pty Ltd (No. 2) [2010] FCA 688
Catholic Education Office v Clarke [2004] FCAFC 197
CC v Djerrkura [2003] FMCA 372
Charles v Fuji Xerox Australia Pty Ltd (2000) 105 FCR 573
Christie v Qantas Airways Limited [1995] EOC 92-705; (1996) 60 IR 17
Christley v University of Newcastle (1992) EOC 92-474
Chung v University of Sydney [2001] FCMA 94
Chung v University of Sydney [2002] FCA 186
CIC Insurance Ltd v Bankstown Football Club Ltd (1997) 187 CLR 384
Clark v Evans (1989) 32 AILR 352
Clarke v Catholic Education Office (2003) 202 ALR 340
Clarke v. Eley (IMI) Kynoch Ltd [1982] IRLR 482
Coleman v Commission of Police [2001] NSWADT 32
Colgate-Palmolive v Cussons (1993) 46 FCR 225
Commonwealth *of Australia v Evans* [2004] FCA 654
Commonwealth of Australia v HREOC & Ors (1994) EOC 92-566
Commonwealth of Australia v Human Rights and Equal Opportunity Commission (1993) 119 ALR 133
Commonwealth of Australia v Human Rights and Equal Opportunity Commission [2000] FCA 1854
Commonwealth of Australia v Sex Discrimination Commissioner (1998) 90 FCR 179
Commonwealth v Bradley (1999) 95 FCR 218
Commonwealth v Evans [2004] FCA 654
Commonwealth v Hamilton (2000) 108 FCR 378
Commonwealth v Human Rights and Equal Opportunity Commission (1993) 46 FCR 191
Commonwealth v Tasmania (1983) 158 CLR 1
Computer Interchange Pty Ltd v Microsoft Corporation (1999) 88 FCR 438
Cooke v Plauen Holdings Pty Ltd [2001] FMCA 91

Corncare v A'Hearn (1993) 45 FCR 441
Creek v Cairns Post Pty Ltd [2001] FCA 293
Cretazzo v Lombardi (1975) 13 SASR 4
Croker v Sydney Institute of TAFE [2003] FMCA 181
Cuna Mutual Group Ltd v Bryant (2000) 102 FCR 270

Daghlian v Australian Postal Corporation [2003] FCA 759
Darlington v CASCO Australia Pty Ltd [2002] FMCA 176
De Alwis v Hair [2002] FMCA 357
De Silva v Ruddock [1998] 311 FCA
Dewan v Main Roads WA (2005) EOC 93-362
Dewan v. Main Roads WA (2005) EOC 93-362
Dietrich v The Queen (1992) 177 CLR 292
Director-General of Education v Atkins & Ors (1989) EOC 92-263
Dix v Crimes Compensation Tribunal (1993) 1 VR 297
Dixon J./Tiernan J./Reg v Davison (1954) 90, Commonwealth Law Reports, 353
Dobrovsak v AR Jamieson Investments Pty Ltd & Anor [1995] HREOCA 32
Donald v Campbell & Co v Pollack [1927] AC 732
Doyle v Chief of General Staff (1982) 42 ALR 283
Dranichinkov v Department of Immigration and Multicultural Affairs [2002] FMCA 72
Dunn-Dyer v ANZ Banking Group Ltd (1997) EOC 92-897

Elekwachi v Human Rights and Equal Opportunity Commission (1997) 79 FCR 271
Ellenbogen v Federated Municipal and Shire Council Employees Union of Australia & Ors [1989] HREOCA 3
Elliot v Nanda & Commonwealth [2001] FCA 418
Ermogenous v Greek Orthodox Community of SA Inc (2002) 187 ALR 92
Escobar v Rainbow Printing Pty Limited (No 3) [2002] FMCA 160
Escobar v Rainbow Printing Pty Ltd (No 2) [2002] FMCA 122
Esso Australian Resources Ltd v Commissioner of Taxation (1999) 201 CLR 49
Evans v National Crime Authority [2003] FMCA 375
Executive Council of Australian Jewry v Scully (1998) 79 FCR 537
Express & Echo Publications Ltd v Tanton [1999] ICR 693

Fares v Box Hill College of TAFE (1992) EOC 92-931
Fenwick v Beveridge Building Products Pty Ltd (1986) EOC 92-147
Ferneley v The Boxing Authority of New South Wales (2001) 115 FCR 306
Fetherston v Peninsula Health [2004] FCA 485
Fetherston v Peninsula Health (No 2) [2004] FCA 594
Firew v Busway Trust (No 2) [2003] FMCA 317
Font v Paspaley Pearls [2002] FMCA 142
Forbes v Commonwealth (No 2) [2003] FMCA 262
Forbes v Commonwealth of Australia [2003] FMCA 140
Forster v Farquhar (1893) 1 QB 564

Fortuity Pty Ltd v Barcza (1995) 32 IPR 517
Fothergill v Monarch Airlines Ltd [1981] AC 251, 294-5

Gardener v Norcott [2004] QADT 39
Gardner v National Netball League Pty Ltd (2001) 182 ALR 408
Gerhardy v Brown (1985) 159 CLR 70
Gilroy v Angelov (2000) 181 ALR 57
Goodworth v Marsden (No 2) (1996) EOC 92-846
Goodworth v Marsden Motors Pty Limited (1996) EOC 92-837
Groundwater v Territory Insurance Office [2004] FMCA 381
Grulke v KC Canvas [2000] FCA 1415
Gulliver v Council of City of Sydney (1987) EOC 92-185

Haines v Bendall (1991) 172 CLR 60
Haines v Leves [1987] 8 NSWLR 442
Hall v A & A Sheiban Pty Ltd (1989) 20 FCR 217
Hall v Sheiban (1989) 20 FCR 217
Harris v Caladine (1991) 99 ALR 193, Commonwealth Law Reports, 84
Hassan v Hume [2003] FMCA 476
Hassan v Smith Donaldson and Children's Hospital at Westmead [2001] FMCA 58
Hazan v Victorian Jewish Board of Deputies (1990) EOC 92-298
Herring v Benevolent Society of New South Wales (1992) EOC 92-408
Herring *v Benevolent Society of NSW* (1992) EOC 92-408, 78
Hickie v Hunt and Hunt (1998) EOC 92-910
Hill v University of New England (1990) EOC 92-291
Hills Grammar School v Human Rights and Equal Opportunity Commission (2000) 100 FCR 306
Hinchliffe v The University of Sydney [2004] FMCA 85
Hinchliffe v University of Sydney (No 2) [2004] FMCA 640
Ho v Regulator Australia Pty Ltd [2004] FMCA 62
Ho v Regulator Australia Pty Ltd (No 2) [2004] FMCA 402
Holdaway v Qantas Airways Limited (1992) EOC 92-430
Hollingdale v Northern Rivers Area Health Service [2004] FMCA 721
Horman v Distribution Group Limited [2001] FMCA 52
Horman v Distribution Group Limited [2002] FCA 219
Horne v Press Clough Joint Venture (1994) EOC 92-591
Howe v Qantas Airways Limited [2004] FMCA 242
Howe v Qantas Airways Ltd (No 2) [2004] FMCA 934
Huddart, Parker & Co. Proprietary Ltd. v Morrehead (1908) 8, Commonwealth Law Reports, 330
Hughes v Car Buyers Pty Ltd (2004) 210 ALR 645
Hughes v Western Australian Cricket Association (Inc) (1986) ATPR 40-748, 48-136
Human Rights and Equal Opportunity Commission v Mt Isa Mines (1993) 46 FCR 301 = 118 ALR 80

In re Sidebotham (1880) 14 ChD 458
Ivory v Griffith University [1997] QADT 4
IW v City of Perth (1997) 191 CLR 1 = 146 ALR 696

Jacomb v Australian Municipal, Administrative, Clerical and Services Union [2004] FCA 1600
Jamal v Secretary Department of Health (1988) 13 NSWLR 252, 271
Jandruwanda v Regency Park College of TAFE [2003] FCA 1455
Jandruwanda v University of South Australia [2003] FMCA 205
Jandruwanda v University of South Australia (No 2) [2003] FMCA 233
Johanson v Blackledge (2001) 163 FLR 58
Johanson v Michael Blackledge Meats [2001] FMCA 66
Johnson v Johnson (2000) 174 ALR 655
Jones v Scully (2002) 120 FCR 243
Jones v Toben [2002] FCA 1150
Jubber v Revival Centres International [1998] VADT 62
Jumbunna Coal Mine NL v Victorian Coalminers' Association (1908) 6 CLR 309

Kartinyeri v Commonwealth (1998) 195 CLR 337
Kennedy v ADI Ltd [2002] FCA 1603
Kinley v East Sydney Area Health Service & Anor (1994) EOC 92-559
Konrad v Victoria Police (1999) 91 FCR 95
Koowarta v Bjelke-Peterson (1982) 153 CLR 168
Korczak v Commonwealth of Australia (2000) EOC 92-056
Kowalski v Domestic Violence Crisis Service Inc (No 2) [2003] FMCA 210
Krenske-Carter v Minister of Education (2003) EOC 93-256

Langley v Niland [1981] 2 NSWLR 104
Latoudis v Casey (1990) 170 CLR 534
Lavery v Commissioner of Fire Brigades (2003) EOC 93-274
Lawrence v Clark (1993) EOC 92-539
Lawton v Lawson [2002] FMCA 68.
Leslie v Barrister's Sickness & Accident Fund Pty Limited [2003] NSWADT 216
Leslie v Graham [2002] FCA 32
Li v Minister for Immigration & Multicultural Affairs [2001] FCA 1414
Lorang v Mater Misericordiae Hospital & Anor (1994) EOC 92-602
Love v Australia, Communication No 983/2001, UN Doc CCPR/C/77/D/983/2001
Low v Australian Taxation Office [2000] FMCA 6
Low v Commonwealth of Australia [2001] FCA 702
Lucic v Nolan (1982) 45 ALR 411

Mabo v Queensland (No 2) (1992) 177 CLR 292
Masri v Nenny Santoso & Anor [2004] NSWIRComm 108
Mayer v ANSTO [2003] FMCA 209 = (2003) EOC 93-285
Mayer v Australian Nuclear Science and Technology Organisation [2003] FMCA 209

Mc Farlane v Glasgow City Council [2001] IRLR 7
McAlister v SEQ Aboriginal Corporation [2002] FMCA 109
McBride v Victoria [2003] FMCA 313
McBride v Victoria (No 1) [2003] FMCA 285
McBride v Victoria (No 2) [2003] FMCA 313
McGlade v Lightfoot (2002) 124 FCR 106
McIntosh v Australian Postal Corporation [2001] FCA 1012
McKenna v State of Victoria (1998) EOC 92-927
McKenzie v Department of Urban Services & Canberra Hospital (2001) 163 FLR 133
McLeod v Power [2003] FMCA 2
Merceica v Wade [2000] SACS 441
Midland Metals Overseas Ltd v Comptroller General of Customs (1991) 30 FCR 87
Mills v Meeking (1990) 169 CLR 214
Minister for Immigration and Ethnic Affairs v Teoh (1995) 128 ALR 53
Minister for Immigration and Multicultural and Indigenous Affairs v Al Masri (2003) 126 FCR 54
Minns v New South Wales [2002] FMCA 60
Minns v New South Wales (No 2) [2002] FMCA 197
Minogue v Human Rights and Equal Opportunity Commission (1999) 84 FCR 438
Mooney v Commissioner of Police (No 2) [2003] NSWADT 107
Morrison v Gallipoli Legion Club Newcastle Limited (1986) EOC 92-144
Murphy v Loper [2002] FMCA 310

Najdovska v Australian Iron & Steel Pty Ltd (1986) EOC 92-176
Neat Holdings Pty Ltd v Karajan Holdings Pty Ltd (1992) 110 ALR 449
Neilson v Maynard (1988) EOC 92-226 = (1988) 15 ALD 364
New South Wales (Department of Education) v Human Rights and Equal Opportunity Commission (2001) 186 ALR 69
Nizzari v Westpac Financial Services [2003] FMCA 255
North v City of Sydney Council (2001) EOC 93-149

O'Callaghan v Loder (No 2) [1983] 3 NSWLR 89; (1984) EOC 92-022
Oberoi v Human Rights and Equal Opportunity Commission [2001] FMCA 34
Oorloff v Lee [2004] FMCA 893
Oshlack v Richmond River Council (1998) 193 CLR 72

P & R (No 1) [2002] FMCA 65
Paramasivam v Grant [2001] FCA 882
Paramasivam v Shier [2001] FCA 545
Paramasivam v Wheeler & Ors [2001] FCA 231
Paramasivam v Wheeler [2000] FCA 1559
Parker v Swan Hill Police [2000] FCA 1688
Peacock v Human Rights and Equal Opportunity Commission [2005] FCAFC 45
Pham v Commonwealth of Australia [2002] FCA 669
Pham v University of Queensland [2002] FCAFC 40

Phillips v Australian Girls' Choir Pty Ltd [2001] FMCA 109
Physical Disability Council of NSW v Sydney City Council [1999] FCA 815
Polyukhovich v Commonwealth (1991) 172 CLR 501
Port Kembla Coal Terminal Limited v Braverus Maritime Inc. (No 2) [2004] FCA 1437
Port of Melbourne Authority v Anshun Pty (1981) 147 CLR 589
Precision Data Holdings Ltd. v Wills (1991) 173 Commonwealth Law Reports 167
Purvis v New South Wales (Department of Education and Training) [2003] HCA 62
Purvis v State of New South Wales (2003) 217 CLR 92

Qantas Airways Ltd v Christie (1998) 193 CLR 280
QBE Travel Insurance v Bassanelli [2004] FCA 396
Quarman v Burnett (1840) 6 M & W 499 = 151 ER 509
Queensland and Another v Commonwealth of Australia (1989) 167 CLR 232

R v Allan; Ex parte Australian Mutual Provident Society Ltd (1977) 16 SASR 237
R v Burgess; ex parte Henry (1936) 55 CLR 608
Rainsford v Group 4 Correctional Services [2002] FMCA 36
Rainsford v Victoria [2002] FMCA 266
Ralkon v Aboriginal Development Commission (1982) 43 ALR 535
Rana v University of South Australia [2003] FMCA 525
Rana v University of South Australia [2004] FCA 559
Re East; Ex parte Nguyen (1998) 196 CLR 354.
Re NSW Corporal Punishment in School Case (1986) EOC 92-160
Re Porter (1989) 34 IR 179
Rejfek v McElroy (1965) 112 CLR 517 = [1966] ALR 270
Richards v Webforge Australia Pty Ltd [2004] WAIRComm 13209
Richardson v Forestry Commission of Tasmania (1988) 164 CLR 261
Richardson v The Forestry Commission & Anor (1988) 77 ALR 237
Rispoli v Merck Sharpe & Dohme (Australia) Pty Ltd [2003] FMCA 160
Rispoli v Merck Sharpe & Dohme (Australia) Pty Ltd (No 2) [2003] FMCA 516
Ritter v Godfrey (1920) 2 KB 47
River Wear Commissioners v Adamson (1877) 2 AC 742
Rochas v The University of Sydney [2004] NSWADT 14 (21 January 2004)
Rose v Secretary, Department of Social Security (1990) 92 ALR 521
Ruddock v Vadarlis (No 2) (2001) 115 FCR 229
Ruddock v Vadarlis (2001) 188 ALR 143
Rural Press v Australian Competition and Consumer Commission (2003) 203 ALR 217
Ryan v Presbytery of Wide Bay Sunshine Coast and Pesbyterian Church of Queensland [2001] FMCA 12

Saddi v Active Employment Break Thru Personnel Inc, Care Employment and Commonwealth [2001] FMCA 73
Sammartino v Mayne Nickless (2000) 98 IR 168

Saraswati v The Queen (1991) 172 CLR 1
Schmitz-de-Jong v Netherlands, Communication No 855/1999, UN Doc CCPR/C/72/D/855/1999
Secretary, Department of Defence v Human Rights and Equal Opportunity Commission & Ors (1997) 78 FCR 208
Secretary, Department of Defence v Human Rights and Equal Opportunity Commission (1997) 78 FCR 208
Secretary, Department of Foreign Affairs and Trade v Styles (1988) EOC 92-39 und (1989) 23 FCR 251, 263 *(Styles)*
Series Cricket v Parish (1977) 16 ALR 181
Shaikh v Commissioner, NSW Fire Brigades (1996) EOC 92-808
Sharma v Legal Aid Queensland [2001] FCA 1699
Shell Company of Australia Ltd. v Federal Commissioner of Taxation (1930) 44, Commonwealth Law Reports, 530
Shiels v James [2000] FMCA 2
Shiels v Lipman [2000] FMC 2
Sivananthan v Commissioner of Police [2004] NSWADT 44
Sluggett v Human Rights and Equal Opportunity Commission [2002] FCA 1060
Smith v Leech Brain & Co. (1962) 2 QB 405
Somaghi v Minister for Immigration, Local Government and Ethnic Affairs (1991) 31 FCR 100
Song v Ainsworth Game Technology Pty Ltd [2002] FMCA 31
Soreng v Victorian State Director of Public Housing [2002] FMCA 124
Sparnon v Apand (1996) 68 FCR 322
Speirs v Darling Range Brewing Co Pty Ltd [2002] FMCA 126
Spencer v Dowling [1997] 2 VR 127
State of Victoria v Schou (2004) 8 VR 120 (Schou (No 2))
State of Victoria v Schou (2001) 3 VR 655
Stephenson v Human Rights and Equal Opportunity Commission (1995) 61 FCR 134
Stephenson v Human Rights and Equal Opportunity Commission (1996) 68 FCR 290
Stevens v Brodribb Sawmilling Co Pty Ltd (1986) 160 CLR 16; 63 ALR 513
Stokes v Royal Flying Doctor Service [2003] FMCA 164
Stokes v Royal Flying Doctor Service (No 2) [2003] FMCA 177
Stuart v Sanderson (2000) 100 FCR 150
Styles v Secretary, Department of Foreign Affairs and Trade & Anor (1988) 84 ALR 408
Sullivan v Department of Defence (1992) EOC 92-241

Tadawan v South Australia [2001] FMCA 25
Tate v Rafin [2000] FCA 1582
Tate v Rafin (2001) EOC 92-125
Taylor v Morrison [2003] FMCA 79
Teen Ranch Pty Ltd v Brown (1995) 87 IR 308
Textile, Clothing and Footwear Union of Australia v Givoni Pty Ltd [2002] FCA 1406

Tobacco Institute of Australia Ltd v Australian Federation of Consumer Organisations Inc (1992) 38 FCR 1
Tooheys Ltd v Minister for Business and Consumer Affairs (1981) 54 FLR 421
Transport Workers Union of Australia v Glynburn Contractors (Salisbury) Pty Ltd (1990) 34 IR 138
Travers v New South Wales (2000) FCA 1565
Travers v New South Wales (2001 163 FLR 99

Ugur v Police Service of NSW [2004] FCA 1032
University of Wollongong v Metwally (1984) 158 CLR 447
Upton v The Benevolent Society of New South Wales (1994) EOC 92-600

Vabu Pty Ltd v Commissioner of Taxation (1996) 81 IR 150
Vance v State Rail Authority [2004] FMCA 240
Victoria v Commonwealth (1996) CLR 416, 485
Victoria v Macedonien Teachers' Association (1999) 91 FCR 47
Victoria v McKenna (2000) EOC 93-080
Viskauskas v Niland (1983) 153 CLR 280

WAAD v Minister for Immigration and Multicultural Affairs [2002] FCAFC 399
Warramunda Village Inc v Pryde (2001) 105 FCR 437; [2004] FCA 654
Waterhouse v Bell (1991) 25 NSWLR 99
Waters v Public Transport Corporation (1991) 173 CLR 349
Waterside Workers' Federation of Australia v J. W. Alexander Ltd. (1918) 25, Commonwealth Law Reports, 434
Wattle v Kirkland (No 2) [2002] FMCA 135
Wedesweiler v Cole (1983) 47 ALR 528
Wesoky v Village Cinemas International Pty Ltd [2001] FCA 32
Wilcox, J., Maynard v Neilson (1988) EOC 92-226
Wills v Bigmac Pty Limited [2004] FCA 949
Wong v Sue [2001] FMCA 108
Wright v City of Brighton (1991) EOC 92-389

X v Commonwealth (1999) 200 CLR 177
X v McHugh (1994) 56 IR 248
Xiros v Fortis Life Assurance Ltd [2001] FMCA 15 = 162 FLR 433

Y v Australia Post (1997) EOC 92-865
Yat Tung Investment Co Ltd v Doo Heng Bank [1975] AC 581

A. Einführung

„A society for all ages is multi-generational. It is not fragmented, with youths, adults and older persons going their separate ways. Rather it is age-inclusive, with different generations recognizing – and acting upon – their commonality of interest.“[1]

I. Die Änderung der Altersstruktur in der australischen Bevölkerung und Arbeitswelt

Noch zum Ende des 19. Jahrhunderts waren nur nahezu 3 % der australischen Bevölkerung älter als 65 Jahre, so dass das fortgeschrittene Alter in der Gesellschaft kaum wahrnehmbar war. Bereits nur etwas mehr als 100 Jahre später, im Jahre 2001, waren dagegen mehr als 16 % der australischen Bevölkerung mindestens 65 Jahre alt. Im Jahr 2021 sollen es nach wissenschaftlichen Berechnungen 18 % der australischen Bevölkerung, in 2041 bereits 25 % und in 2051 sogar 30 % sein.[2] Der Rückgang der Geburtenrate sowie die gestiegene Lebenserwartung zeitigen ihre Wirkung und zeichnen keine positiven Trends.[3] Es ist unverkennbar, dass ältere Menschen in der Gesellschaft keine Ausnahme mehr darstellen und keine Rarität (mehr) sind. Die australische Bevölkerung wird unumkehrbar zusehends älter.[4]

Parallel zu dieser Veränderung ist seit den 1970iger Jahren – nicht nur in Australien, sondern weltweit – zu beobachten, dass der Anteil älterer Menschen im Alter ab 55 Jahren an der arbeitenden Bevölkerung (*labour-force participation rate – LFPR*) abnimmt.[5] Dennoch ist der Anteil älterer arbeitsloser Menschen an der australischen Gesamterwerbstätigenzahl erheblich höher und das durchschnittliche Renteneintrittsalter sinkt zunehmend.[6] Ebenso wird es aber jungen Bewerbern und Berufsanfängern deshalb nicht einfacher gemacht, den erfolgreichen Eintritt in die Arbeitswelt zu schaffen, so dass in der Gesamtschau keine Altersgruppe als Gewinner gelten kann und die – früher oftmals übliche – Durchmischung der Altersstruktur innerhalb eines Unternehmens nur noch selten zu finden ist.[7] Es scheint, als ob eine Zusammenarbeit zwi-

---

1 Human Rights and Equal Opportunity Commission, Age matters? A discussion paper on age discrimination (1999) 1.

2 The National Strategy for an Ageing Australia, Employment for Mature Age Workers, Issues Paper (1999) 5.

3 *Murray/Syed*, Critical issues in managing age diversity in Australia (2005) 43(2) Asia Pacific Journal of Human Resources 210; vgl. auch *ABS (Australian Bureau of Statistics)*, Labour force projections, Australia (1999) cat. no. 6260.0.; Australian Bureau of Statistics (ABS), Population by age and sex, Australian states and territories (2004) cat. no. 3201.0..

4 The National Strategy for an Ageing Australia, Employment for Mature Age Workers, Issues Paper (1999) 1; *Hartmann*, The Impact of Trends in Labour-Force Participation in Australia, 3.

5 *Encel*, Age Discrimination, 41.

6 *Encel*, Age Discrimination, 54.

7 *Perry/Bourhis*, A Closer Look at the Role of Applicant Age in Selection Decisions (1998) 28 Journal of Applied Social Psychology 1670; *Lucas*, Scrapheap Mentality Damages Businesses

schen den unterschiedlichen Altersgruppen und Generationen in der Beschäftigungspraxis immer schwerer umzusetzen und ein ausgewogenes Verhältnis zwischen der Anzahl junger und älterer Arbeitnehmer – sog. *age diversity* – zukünftig nur mit zusätzlichen Anstrengungen zu gewährleisten ist.

Mit der Alterung der australischen Gesellschaft entstehen neue Herausforderungen und Probleme im Bereich von Arbeit und Beschäftigung sowie auf vielen anderen gesellschaftlichen Ebenen, die es zu erkennen, aufzudecken, zu hinterfragen und aber auch zu lösen gilt. Ein nicht unerhebliches rechtliches Problem, welches sich dabei durch sämtliche Altersschichten zieht, ist die Diskriminierung aufgrund des persönlichen und individuellen Alters. Sie betrifft Beschäftigte jeden Alters – nicht nur ältere, sondern auch jüngere Arbeitnehmer.[8] Zusammen mit dem Geschlecht, der Rasse und der Herkunft stellt das Alter einen der Hauptgründe für diskriminierende Verhaltensweisen im gesellschaftlichen Leben und Miteinander dar.[9] So ist festzustellen, dass Beschwerden aufgrund Altersdiskriminierungen in Australien ein fester Bestandteil der Anti-Diskriminierungspraxis sind. Etwa fünf bis zehn Prozent aller pro Jahr bei der Human Rights and Equal Opportunity Commission erhobenen Beschwerden, werden mit einer Diskriminierung aufgrund des Alters begründet.[10] Dabei erscheint die Diskriminierung wegen Alters als eine besonders komplexe und schwierige Diskriminierungsform, weil trotz der Reichweite und Intensität Altersdiskriminierungen und eine damit verbundene ungleiche Behandlung in der modernen Gesellschaft als nicht ungewöhnlich und teilweise sogar als unabwendbar und zwangsläufig angesehen werden. Dadurch ist es schwierig, einen einheitlichen gesellschaftlichen Konsens zum wirksamen Vorgehen gegen Altersdiskriminierung in der täglichen Praxis herzustellen und eine ausgewogene und gerechte *age diversity* zu schaffen. Daher sowie auch aufgrund der Bipolarität wird die Altersdiskriminierung auch weiterhin als ein bestehendes grundsätzliches systematisches Problem wahrgenommen.[11]

Die Bedeutung von Altersdiskriminierung im Bereich von Arbeit und Beschäftigung lässt sich dabei sehr gut verdeutlichen, wenn man beachtet, dass 49 % aller Beschwerden gegen ein Diskriminierungsverbot aus dem Age Discrimination Act 2004 (Cth) in Verbindung mit der Arbeit und Beschäftigung stehen.[12] Als Beleg dafür, dass es insbesondere im Bereich der Arbeit und Beschäftigung immer wieder zu Diskriminierungen aufgrund des Alters kommt, dienen darüber hinaus zahlreiche wissenschaftliche Untersuchungen und Befragungen von Arbeitgebern über das Verhalten der Personalverantwortlichen und demografische Betrachtungen von arbeitslosen Beschäftig-

(2000) 13 Professional Engineering 26; *Stein/Rocco/Goldenetz*, Age and the University Workplace: A Case Study of Remaining, Retiring, Or Returning Older Workers (2000) 11 Human Resource Development Quarterly 61.

8 *Bennington*, Prime Age Recruitment: The Challenges for Age Discrimination Legislation (2004) Elder Law Review 8.

9 *Macnicol*, Age Discrimination, An Historical and Contemporary Analysis, 6.

10 Vgl. etwa Human Rights and Equal Opportunity Commission, Annual Report 2007 – 2008, 63 – Table 11: Complaints received and finalised by Act (Age Discrimination Act (ADA) 126 received, 114 finalised; Total 2077 received, 1883 finalised); ebenso aber auch bereits in den Annual Reports 2006 – 2007, 71 und 2005 – 2006, 76.

11 Human Rights and Equal Opportunity Commission, Annual Report 2007 – 2008, 140:

12 *Catanzariti*, WorkChoices – a rise in discrimination claims? (2006) 12 Employment Law Bulletin 25.

ten in Bezug auf deren Altersstruktur.[13] Zwar belegen derartige Begutachtungen, dass insbesondere bei älteren Beschäftigten die vorhandene Erfahrung und ein damit verbundenes ausgeprägtes Fachwissen sowie eine hohe Arbeitsmoral als positive Faktoren geschätzt werden, sie sich zugleich aber wegen des Vorwurfs der aufgrund ihres fortgeschrittenen Lebensalters mangelnden Anpassung und Affinität gegenüber technischen Neuerungen sowie unzureichender Flexibilität diskriminierenden Verhaltensweisen ausgesetzt sehen.[14] Darüber hinaus seien sie zwar in der Umsetzung von übergebenen Arbeitsanweisungen und Informationen besser als junge Beschäftigte, brauchen aber einen höheren Zeitaufwand für Weiterbildungsmaßnahmen.[15] So überrascht es nicht, dass in Australien der Anteil der männlichen Beschäftigten im Alter zwischen 60 und 64 Jahren allein im Zeitraum von 1966 und 1996 um ein Drittel zurückgegangen ist und sowohl männliche als auch weibliche Beschäftigte in diesem Alter vorzugsweise in Teilzeit beschäftigt werden, um einen Ausgleich der zuvor aufgezeigten (angeblichen) Vor- und Nachteile herbeizuführen.[16] Diese Maßnahmen ziehen in der

---

13 *Patrickson/Hartmann*, Managing an Ageing Workforce (1998), 54; mehr als die Hälfte der Beschäftigten über 45 Jahre gelten als Langzeitarbeitslose; vgl. The National Strategy for an Ageing Australia, Employment for Mature Age Workers, Issues Paper (1999); Australian Bureau of Statistics, Successful and Unsuccessful Job Search Experience (2000); vgl. auch *Yearta/Warr*, Does Age Matter? (1995) 14 Journal of Management Development 28; *Jones*, How Redundancies Worsen Social Inequality (1999) International Journal of Sociology and Social Policy 57; *Schwartz/Kleiner*, The Relationship Between Age and Emloyment Opportunities (1999) 18 Equal Opportunities International 105; *Hirsch/MacPherson/Hardy*, Occupational Age Structure and Access for Older Workers (2000) 53 Industrial and Labour Relations Review 401; *Chan/Stevens*, Job Loss and Employment Patterns of Older Workers (2001) 19 Journal of Labor Economics 484; vgl. insb. auch *Bourke*, Moving ahead on diversity and equality: Results from the 2005 Australasian Diversity and Equality Survey, in: *Davis/Pratt*, Making the Link. Affirmative Action and Employment Relations (2005).

14 *Becker*, The Economics of Discrimination (1971); *Pickersgill*, Productivity of Mature and Older Workers: Employers′ Attitudes and Experiences (1996) ACIRRT, University of Sydney; *Perry/Kulik/Bourhis*, Moderating Effects of Personal and Contextual Factors in Age Discrimination (1996) 81 Journal of Applied Psychology 628; The National Strategy for An Ageing Australia, Employment for Mature Age Workers, Issues Paper (1999) 31; Human Rights and Equal Opportunity Commission, Age matters? A discussion paper on age discrimination (1999) 12; House of Representatives Standing Committee on Employment, Education and Workplace Relations, Parliament of Australia, Age Counts (2000), 102; *Ozdowski*, Adressing Age discrimination (2002) 81 Older People and the Law 12; *Bennington*, Prime Age Recruitment: The Challenges for Age Discrimination Legislagtion (2004) Elder Law Review 8; vgl. auch Senate Employment, Education and Training References Committee, Commonwealth Parliament, Report on the inquiry into long term unemployment (1995) 53; Drake Management Consulting (1999) Age Discrimination is Alive and Well, Submission to the House of Representatives Standing Committee on Employment, Education & Workplace Relations Inquiry into Issues Specific to Workers over 45 years
(abrufbar unter http://www.hreoc.gov.au/pdf/human_rights/age_report_2000.pdf).

15 *Bennington/Tharenou* Older Workers: Myths, Evidence and Implications for Australian Managers (1996) 34 Asia Pacific Journal of Human Resources 21; Patrickson/*Hartmann*, Managing an Ageing Workforce (1998), 54.

16 *Patrickson/Hartmann*, Managing an Ageing Workforce (1998), 54 und 56ff.; Attorney Generals Department of New South Wales, Age Discrimination – Options for New South Wales, A

Regel vielfältige Konsequenzen nach sich. So wird der Einstieg und der Verbleib älterer Beschäftigter in der Arbeitswelt zunehmend erschwert und oftmals trifft sie ein erheblicher Einkommensverlust.[17] Der Anteil der Langzeitarbeitslosen im Alter von 45 bis 64 Jahren liegt bei 40 % der Erwerbslosenzahl, wobei innerhalb dieser Altersgruppe wiederum mehr als 50 % (60 % der über 55jährigen und 30 % der über 45jährigen Arbeitslosen) angeben, aufgrund der Erfolg- und Hoffnungslosigkeit in der Arbeitsplatzsuche entmutigt zu sein und sich als zu alt zu fühlen.[18] Nicht selten schreiben ältere Arbeitnehmer unzählige – erfolglose – Bewerbungen und sind aufgrund der langen Arbeitslosigkeit zwischenzeitlich bereit, bei der angestrebten Arbeit erhebliche Abstriche zu machen. Allein der Umstand wieder einer bezahlten Beschäftigung nachzugehen, wird oftmals das Hauptziel – unabhängig von der etwaigen Vergütungshöhe.[19] Es überrascht nicht, dass insbesondere ältere Personen durch diese Umstände zunehmend frustriert werden und sich zum Teil sogar als für die Gesellschaft nicht mehr nützliche und nicht mehr benötigte Arbeitskräfte charakterisieren.[20] Vor dem Hintergrund von bestehenden Rentenansprüchen wird älteren Arbeitnehmern und Beschäftigten darüber hinaus auch die Wahl über den Eintritt ins Rentenalter verwehrt, indem sie aufgrund Altersarbeitslosigkeit vorzugsweise ihre Rentenzahlung – unter Abzügen – früher als geplant (vorwiegend im Alter zwischen 55 und 65 Jahren) in Anspruch nehmen.[21]

Discussion Paper (2000) 8; *Bennington*, Prime Age Recruitment: The Challenges for Age Discrimination Legislagtion (2004) Elder Law Review 8.

17 *Stein/Rocco/Goldenetz*, Age and the University Workplace: a Case Study of Remaining, Retiring, Or Returning Older Workers (2000) 11 Human Resource Development Quarterly 61; House of Representatives Standing Committee on Employment, Education and Workplace Relations, Parliament of Australia, Age Counts (2000), 101; Bennington, Prime Age Recruitment: The Challenges for Age Discrimination Legislagtion (2004) Elder Law Review 8.

18 Australian Bureau of Statistics, Successful and Unsuccessful Job Search Experience (2000) und Job Search Experience of Unemployed Persons (2003) Catalogue No 6222.0; vgl. auch *Catanzariti*, Age and employment (1999) 4 Employment Law Bulletin 92; Human Rights and Equal Opportunity Commission, Age matters? A discussion paper on age discrimination (1999) 14; *McEwan*, Meeting the Challenges One Year On (2005), abrufbar unter http://www.hreoc.gov.au/age/workingage/speeches/mcewan.html.

19 House of Representatives Standing Committee on Employment, Education and Workplace Relations, Parliament of Australia, Age Counts (2000), 103.

20 Attorney Generals Department of New South Wales, Age Discrimination – Options for New South Wales, A Discussion Paper (2000) 9.

21 *Taylor/Steinberg/Walley*, Mature Age Employment: Recent Developments in Public Policy in Australia and The UK (2000) Australasian Journal of Ageing 125; *Taqi*, Older People, Work and Equal Opportunity (2002) 55 International Social Security Review 107; vgl. auch Anti-Discrimination Board of New South Wales, Age Old Dilemmas (2004) 60 Equal Times 1; zu einer konkreten Beispielrechnung zu den finanziellen Risiken einer Frühpensionierung vgl. The National Strategy for an Ageing Australia, Employment for Mature Age Workers, Issue Paper (1999) 19.

II. Rechtliche Fragestellung und Problemaufriss

Oftmals werden Altersdiskriminierungen in Bezug auf die eigene Person entweder nicht eingestanden oder bereits nicht in Betracht gezogen. Werden sie dagegen erkannt, eingestanden und wird versucht, die Altersdiskriminierung zu verhindern oder deren Ursachen zu beseitigen, so ist die Einzelperson jedoch mangels wirkungsvoller Rechtsinstrumente hilflos. Dem Opfer einer Altersdiskriminierung gelingt es daher nur selten, einen umfassenden Schutz seiner betroffenen Individualrechtsgüter zu erreichen und eine effektive Rechtsdurchsetzung herbeizuführen.

In der australischen Beschäftigungs- und Arbeitswelt wird dieser Umstand durch die von Arbeitgebern zur Regulierung der unternehmensinternen Alterstruktur und der damit beabsichtigten Verjüngung der Belegschaft praktizierten Zwangspensionierung von älteren Arbeitnehmern und die Aufstellung nahezu unüberwindbarer Einstellungshürden für junge Berufsanfänger und Absolventen verdeutlicht.

Der Gesetzgeber des australischen Commonwealth hat sich diesem grundsätzlichem Problem angenommen und den Age Discrimination Act 2004 (Cth) erlassen, um einen umfassenden Schutz gegen Altersdiskriminierungen herzustellen und zukünftig gewährleisten zu können.[22] Ob der Age Discrimination Act 2004 (Cth) den an ihn gestellten Anforderungen gerecht werden kann, wie er vor Altersdiskriminierungen schützt und welche Rechtsschutzinstrumente er der einzelnen Person an die Hand gibt, bedarf einer ausführlichen Betrachtung und Diskussion. Hierzu soll die vorliegende Arbeit einen Beitrag leisten, indem sie einerseits die Inhalte des Gesetzes im Hinblick auf den Schutz vor Altersdiskriminierungen aufzuzeigen versucht und zum anderen aber auch, die mit der Anwendung des noch jungen Gesetzes verbundenen Problem- und Fragestellungen durchleuchtet.

III. Gang der Arbeit

Die Arbeit besteht aus der Einführung und sieben weiteren Teilen neben einer gesonderten Schlussbetrachtung, wobei der Schwerpunkt der Arbeit insgesamt auf das Arbeitsrecht gerichtet ist. Der inhaltlichen Durchleuchtung des Age Discrimination Act 2004 (Cth) und seines materiellen Regelungsgehalts gehen Ausführungen zur historischen Entwicklung der Altersdiskriminierung in Australien und der verfassungsrechtlichen Legitimation für entsprechende gesetzliche Regelungen voraus. Dabei geht es vor allem um die Frage der verfassungsrechtlichen Verankerung des Age Discrimination Act 2004 (Cth), um die genaue Durchleuchtung des Anwendungsbereichs, des Schutzbereichs sowie der zahlreichen Diskriminierungsverbote wegen Alters sowie der ebenfalls gesetzlich normierten Ausnahmen bzw. Rechtfertigungen.

Im vierten Teil der Arbeit erfolgt eine Untersuchung typischer Frage- und Problemstellungen im Zusammenhang mit Altersdiskriminierung im Arbeits- und Beschäftigungsverhältnis unter ausführlicher Einbeziehung der Rechtsprechung. Hierbei werden verschiedene Phasen der Erwerbstätigkeit unter dem Einfluss von diskriminieren-

22 Der Age Discrimination Act 2004 (Cth) ist am 22. Juni 2004 in Kraft getreten.

den Faktoren – etwa die Bewerbungs- und Einstellungsphase sowie die Beendigungsphase und die altersbedingte Kündigung –durchleuchtet. Anschließend widmet sich der fünfte Teil der Arbeit den Rechtsfolgen eines Verstoßes gegen die zuvor aufgezeigten Diskriminierungsverbote wegen Alters.

Im sechsten und siebten Teil erfolgt sodann eine Auseinandersetzung mit den Rechtsschutzmöglichkeiten, die dem Einzelnen durch den Age Discrimination Act 2004 (Cth) zur Seite gestellt werden. Dabei wird insbesondere auf die Rolle der Human Rights and Equal Opportunity Commission sowie auf das conciliation-Verfahren und die damit verbundenen Probleme des effektiven Rechtsschutzes eingegangen, bevor eine nähere Auseinandersetzung mit dem gerichtlichen Verfahren gegen Altersdiskriminierungen, dessen Anforderungen und Ablauf erfolgt. Bevor in der Schlussbetrachtung die wesentlichen Ergebnisse der Arbeit zusammengefasst sowie ein Resümee zur Altersvielfalt in Bereich von Arbeit und Beschäftigung gezogen werden, widmet sich der achte Teil der Arbeit einigen Überlegungen und Strategien zur Vermeidung der Altersdiskriminierung in der arbeitsrechtlichen Praxis und hinterfragt, wie eine unternehmensinterne Personalpolitik ausgestaltet werden könnte.

B. Historische Entwicklung der Altersdiskriminierung im australischen Arbeitsrecht und der Gesetzgebung zum Age Discrimination Act 2004 (Cth)

In der australischen Verfassung fehlt ein ausdrücklicher Grund- bzw. Menschenrechtskatalog.[23] Um allerdings einen hinreichenden Schutzstandard in der Gesellschaft gewährleisten zu können, war der australische Gesetzgeber veranlasst, im Rahmen des Antidiskriminierungsrechts auf Maßnahmen der Einzelgesetzgebung zurück zu greifen, so dass heutzutage die Antidiskriminierungsgesetzgebung ein bedeutsames Beispiel für die gesetzgeberische Gewährleistung von Individualrechten darstellt.[24]

I. Geschichtlicher Abriss zur Altersdiskriminierung in Australien

Dem Diskriminierungsgrund des Alters wurde in der fernen Vergangenheit kaum Aufmerksamkeit geschenkt. So verwundert es nicht, dass das Bedürfnis nach einer gesetzlichen Regelung gegen Diskriminierungen aufgrund der Rasse und Herkunft, aufgrund des Geschlechts oder eine Behinderung in der Gesellschaft und beim australischen Gesetzgeber weitaus höher gewesen ist, als in Bezug auf den Diskriminierungsgrund des Alters.[25] In der historischen Betrachtung überrascht diese Entwicklung nicht. Denn Diskriminierungshandlungen, welche etwa aufgrund des Geschlechts oder der Rasse einer Person motiviert sind, treten in der Regel leicht erkennbar zu Tage und sind somit weniger schwierig zu verfolgen. Somit waren vor allem die Diskriminierungsgründe des Geschlechts und der Rasse die maßgeblich treibenden Kräfte in der Antidiskriminierungsgesetzgebung in Australien.

So ist seit den 70er Jahren des 20. Jahrhunderts das Antidiskriminierungsrecht aus der australischen Gesellschaft und der Jurisprudenz nicht mehr wegzudenken.[26] Zu diesem Zeitpunkt spielten aufgrund der vorangestellten Gründe vorwiegend Diskrimi-

---

23 Vgl. auf europäischer Ebene Art. 21 der Charta der Grundrechte der Europäischen Union.

24 *Encel*, Age Discrimination in Law and Practice, (2004) Elder Law Review 7.

25 *Encel/Studencki*, Over the Hill or Flying High? – An Analysis of Age Discrimination Complaint in NSW (1998), 28; vgl. auch *Dreyer*, Race Relations Act 1976 und Rassendiskriminierung in Großbritannien, 24 mit einer ähnlichen Betrachtung zur Gewichtung der verschiedenen Diskriminierungsgründe in Großbritannien.

26 *Bourke/Ronalds*, Discrimination Laws – Striving For Equality, in: *Macken*, The Law of Employment, 2002, 593; *Patrickson/Hartmann*, Managing an Ageing Workforce (1998), 55; *Encel*, Age Discrimination in Law and Practice, (2004) Elder Law Review 7 mit Bezug auf die Überlegungen des britischen Philosophen John Locke aus dem 17. Jahrhundert; vgl. auch *Smith*, Australian Anti-Discrimination Laws – Framework, Developments and Issues, New Developments in Employment Discrimination Law – The 9 JILPT Comparative Labour Law Seminar (2008) 18.

nierungen wegen des Geschlechts oder der Herkunft die Hauptrolle.[27] So wurde das erste Antidiskriminierungsgesetz vom *South Australian Parliamant* im Jahr 1966 gegen Diskriminierungen aufgrund der Rasse erlassen.[28] Auf der Ebene des Commonwealth war es ebenfalls die Rassendiskriminierung, gegen die mit dem Racial Discrimination Act 1975 (Cth) als eine der ersten Diskriminierungsformen wirksam vorgegangen werden sollte.[29] Denn mit der aufkommenden Migration und Zuwanderung nahmen die Rücksichtnahme auf die Rechte der australischen Ureinwohner (*„Indigenous Australians"*) und das Verständnis für ein gleichberechtigtes Nebeneinander der verschiedenen Bevölkerungsgruppen rasant ab.

Im Anschluss an verstärkte Diskussionen und die Einführung des Racial Discrimination Act 1975 (Cth) verlagerte sich der Blick auf die zahlreichen Benachteiligungen und ungerechtfertigten Beeinträchtigungen der Frauen in der Gesellschaft. Um eine angemessene Gleichbehandlung der Geschlechter herbeizuführen, wurde von den Vereinten Nationen das Jahr 1975 als das Internationale Jahr der Frauen begründet. Auch in der australischen Gesellschaft entwickelte sich zu dieser Zeit eine stark wachsende Frauenbewegung, deren Hauptanliegen die Gleichberechtigung von Frauen in der Gesellschaft, in Bildung und Beruf war. Dem sich immer stärker werdenden gesellschaftspolitischen Druck beugend, erließ die damalige australische Regierung 1984 den Sex Discrimination Act 1984 (Cth).[30]

Zur Durchsetzung der Diskriminierungsverbote aus den ersten Antidiskriminierungsgesetzen des Commonwealth und als Rechtsschutzinstitution wurde im Jahr 1981 die Human Rights Commission eingerichtet und sodann im Jahr 1986 durch die Human Rights and Equal Opportunity Commission – mit einem erheblichen erweiterten Aufgaben- und Kompetenzfeld – ersetzt.[31] Die Human Rights and Equal Opportunity Commission ist zuständig für das gesetzlich festgelegte Beschwerdeverfahren gegen Diskriminierungen wegen der Herkunft und Rasse, wegen des Geschlechts und wegen

---

27 *Encel/Studencki*, Over the Hill or Flying High? – An Analysis of Age Discrimination Complaint in NSW (1998), 28; *Encel*, Age Discrimination in Law and Practice, (2004) Elder Law Review 7.

28 Als Vorreiter erließ South Australia in kurzer zeitlicher Reihenfolge 1975 ein Gesetz gegen Diskriminierungen wegen des Geschlechts, 1981 gegen Diskriminierungen wegen Behinderungen und modifizierte bereits 1976 den Racial Discimination Act. Allerdings holten auch die anderen Bundesstaaten schließlich die entsprechende Gesetzgebung nach und deckten sogar weitaus mehr Diskriminierungsgründe mit ihren Gesetzen ab; vgl. überblicksartig zur Gesetzgebung der einzelnen Bundesstaaten die Darstellung in: *Ronalds/Pepper*, Discrimination Law and Practice, S. 5.

29 *Ronalds/Pepper*, Discrimination Law and Practice, S. 3.

30 *Ronalds/Pepper*, Discrimination Law and Practice, S. 4 mit weiterer ausführlicher Darstellung einiger Hintergründe zur Gesetzgebung zum Sex Discrimination Act 1984 (Cth).

31 Im Jahr 2008 wurde im Rahmen einer Strategiekampagne der Name in Australian Human Rights Commission geändert; nähere Informationen abrufbar unter http://www.hreoc.gov.au/about/strategic_plan.html; in Deutschland erfolgte die Gründung der Antidiskriminierungsstelle des Bundes erst im Jahre 2006, Details zur Arbeit, zu den Aufgaben und der Funktionsweise der Antidkiskriminierungsstelle des Bundes sind im Internet abrufbar unter http://www.antidiskriminierungsstelle.de/DE/Home/home_node.html.

einer Behinderung sowie wegen der Diskriminierungsgründe der Religion und des Alters.[32]

Im Jahr 1992 wurden nach einer Untersuchung zu Beschäftigungsmöglichkeiten von Menschen mit Behinderungen und einer breit angelegten Diskussion in der Gesellschaft sowie mit einzelnen Wirtschaftszweigen vom australischen Gesetzgeber auch die Behinderung als Diskriminierungsgrund im Disability Discrimination Act 1992 (Cth) kodifiziert und somit neue Rahmenbedingungen für Standards zur Bekämpfung und Beseitigung der Diskriminierung von behinderten Menschen geschaffen.

II. Entstehungsgeschichte des Age Discrimination Act 2004 (Cth)

Die gesetzgeberische Tätigkeit im Hinblick auf Diskriminierungen wegen der Rasse und Herkunft, wegen des Geschlechts bzw. wegen einer Behinderung verklären jedoch die bereits frühe Auseinandersetzung mit der Altersdiskriminierung in der australischen Gesellschaft. Denn ebenfalls bereits ab den 70er Jahren des 20. Jahrhunderts wurde der Diskriminierungsgrund des Alters Gegenstand zahlreicher wissenschaftlicher Studien und Untersuchungen zur Beschäftigung im Alter und zur sozialen Sicherung.[33] Trotz dieses frühen Bewusstseins um die Diskriminierung in der australischen Gesellschaft bedurfte es einer nicht unerheblichen Zeitdauer bis entsprechende Gesetze zum Verbot von Diskriminierungen wegen Alters – und aufgrund anderer Diskriminierungsgründe – erlassen worden sind.[34]

So wurde etwa im Parlament von New South Wales bereits 1977 versucht, ein Gesetzentwurf einzubringen, der das Alter als verbotenen Diskriminierungsgrund umfasste, welcher allerdings zu dieser Zeit noch ohne verbindliche Konsequenzen in der gesetzgeberischen Umsetzung blieb. Stattdessen wurde die Einführung des Diskriminierungsverbots wegen Alters durch die zuständige Antidiskriminierungsbehörde – Anti-Discrimination Board (ADB) – öffentlich befürwortet und entsprechend zu einer Kodifizierung angeregt.[35] Die beabsichtigte Wirkung zeigte sich in dann erst im Jahr 1993 mit Inkrafttreten des Anti-Discrimination Act 1977 und der entsprechenden Erfassung

32 *Ronalds/Pepper*, Discrimination Law and Practice, S. 4.

33 Committee of Inquiry into Poverty in Australia (Henderson Report), Parliament of Australia, (1976) 242; *C. Foster*, Towards a National Retirement Incomes Policy (Issue Paper, Social Security Review (Australia); no. 6.) (1988) 17.

34 Attorney Generals Department of New South Wales, Age Discrimination – Options for New South Wales, A Discussion Paper (2000) 17; *Beckett*, Can Status Be A New Ground In Australian Discrimination Laws, (2004) AIAL FORUM No. 45, 40; vgl. auch *Catanzariti*, Age and employment (1999) 4 Employment Law Bulletin 92.

35 Allerdings mit einer Empfehlung zum Ausschluss der Zwangspensionierung (altersbedingten Kündigungen wegen Erreichens eines bestimmten Alters); vgl. *Encel*, Age Discrimination in Law and Practice, (2004) Elder Law Review 7 mit Verweis auf den ADB`s Review, NSW Anti-Discrimination Board, Dicrimination and Age (1980).

des Alters als Diskriminierungsgrund.[36] Allerdings kam dem Bundesstaat New South Wales mit der Kodifizierung des Diskriminierungsverbots wegen Alters keine Vorreiterrolle im australischen Anti-Diskriminierungsrecht zu. Denn South Australia hatte sich schon 1984 mit Erlass des Equal Opportunity Act 1984 und einer tief greifenden Änderung im Jahr 1990 gegen Altersdiskriminierungen positioniert. Diese gesetzgeberischen Aktivitäten vollzogen sich in Queensland 1992, in Western Australia 1993, in New South Wales – wie erwähnt – 1994, im Northern Territory ebenfalls 1994, im Australian Capital Territory und in Victoria 1996 sowie in Tasmanien im Jahr 1999.[37]

Im Nachgang zu den einzelnen bundesstaatlichen Regelungen und den Gesetzen gegen Diskriminierungen wegen der Rasse und Herkunft, wegen des Geschlechts sowie wegen einer Behinderung sah sich der Gesetzgeber des australischen Commonwealth – nicht zuletzt auch wegen der Aktivität der einzelnen Bundesstaaten – zur Kodifizierung des Rechts gegen Altersdiskriminierung veranlasst.[38] So wurde die Altersdiskriminierung zum ersten Mal auf Ebene des Commonwealth im Workplace Relations Act 1996 für den Bereich der Arbeit und Beschäftigung aufgegriffen. Obwohl es nach dem Workplace Relations Act 1996 unrechtmäßig war, ein bestehendes Arbeitsverhältnis aufgrund des Alters des Beschäftigten zu beenden, waren zahlreiche Diskriminierungsformen nicht vom Regelungsbereich des Gesetzes erfasst, wie etwa für kurzzeitige und vorübergehende Beschäftigungen, befristete Arbeitsverträge und für Arbeitnehmer und Beschäftigte aus staatlichen Programmen und Arbeitsverhältnissen.[39]

Erst am 22. Juni 2004 trat mit dem Age Discrimination Act 2004 (Cth) ein komplett eigenständiges Anti-Diskriminierungsgesetz auf der Ebene des Commonwealth in Kraft, das sich gegen Diskriminierung wegen Alters richtet.[40] Dem endgültigen Erlass des Age Discrimination Act 2004 (Cth) gingen allerdings noch über einen Zeitraum

---

36 Zu den Änderungen im Überblick vgl. *Butler*, Proposed amendments to the Anti-Discrimination Act 1977 (NSW) (1990) Australian Coporate Lawyer 32; *Harding*, Age, The Road to Anti-Discrimination paved with good Intentions (1994) Law Society Journal 44.

37 *Hemingway*, Roadmap to ADA: The Age Discrimination Act 2004, 6 abrufbar unter http://www.hreoc.gov.au/age/roadmap_ADA.html; vgl. auch *Guthrie*, Ageing – Discrimination and Workers Compensation (2005) 1; vgl. auch den Überblick über die bundesstaatliche und territoriale Entwicklung der Anti-Diskriminierungsgesetzgebung in Bezug auf das Alter in: Attorney Generals Department of New South Wales, Age Discrimination – Options for New South Wales, A Discussion Paper (2000) 18ff..

38 *Beckett*, Can Status Be A New Ground In Australian Discrimination Laws, (2004) AIAL FORUM No. 45, 40; *Patterson*, The Eradication of Compulsory Retirement and Age Discrimination in the Australian Workplace: A Cause for Celebration and Concern (2004) 3 Elder Law Review 10.

39 Human Rights and Equal Opportunity Commission, Age Matters (2000), 58.

40 *Beckett*, Can Status Be A New Ground In Australian Discrimination Laws, (2004) AIAL FORUM No. 45, 40; ins Parlament wurde der Gesetzesentwurf im Januar 2003 durch den damaligen Justizminister („*Attorney-General*") Daryl Williams eingebracht, verkündet wurde der Age Discrimination Act 2004 (Cth) am 15. Juni 2004; vgl. auch *Smith/Riley/Sarina*, Industrial Legislation in 2004 (2005) 47 Journal of Industrial Relations 171; *Guthrie*, Ageing – Discrimination and Workers Compensation (2005) 13; *Smith*, Australian Anti-Discrimination Laws – Framework, Developments and Issues, New Developments in Employment Discrimination Law – The 9 JILPT Comparative Labour Law Seminar (2008) 19.

von fast zwei Jahren intensive gesonderte Betrachtungen und Überlegungen durch den Senat, die Human Rights and Equal Opportunity Commission, diverse Wirtschaftsorganisationen, Arbeitnehmer- und Arbeitgebervertretungen, Interessenvertretungen junger sowie älterer Menschen, des Gesundheitswesens sowie auch von zahlreichen sozialen und gemeinnützigen Verbänden voraus.[41] Die Kommission machte sich dabei insbesondere für eine größtmögliche Ausweitung des Anwendungsbereichs stark und empfahl dem Gesetzgeber neben den reinen Bereichen der Arbeit und Beschäftigung auch eine Berücksichtigung sonstiger arbeitsrechtsbezogener Sachverhalte, wie etwa die Tätigkeit von Arbeitsvermittlern und Bildungseinrichtungen, sowie darüber hinaus Problemkreise mit Bezug zur Gesundheitsfürsorge sowie zur Erbringung von Dienstleistungen und Waren.[42]

Gleichzeitig mit dem Age Discrimination Act 2004 (Cth) trat der Age Discrimination (Consequential Amendments) Act 2004 (Cth) in Kraft, der zahlreiche Änderungen für den Workplace Relations Act 1996 (Cth) und den Human Rights and Equal Opportunity Commissions Act 1986 (Cth) vorgenommen hat und eine Abstimmung zwischen dem Antidiskriminierungsrecht und dem Arbeitsrecht herstellen sollte.[43]

III. Bundesgesetzliche und territoriale Regelungen zur Diskriminierung wegen Alters

1. Die einzelnen bundesgesetzlichen und territorialen Antidis kriminierungsgesetze

Neben dem Age Discrimination Act 2004 (Cth) gibt es aber – wie zuvor bereits erwähnt – auch in den einzelnen Bundesstaaten und Territorien zwischenzeitlich zahlreiche Antidiskriminierungsgesetze, die eine große Zahl von Diskriminierungsverboten für verschiedenste Bereiche und Gründe umfassen.[44] Dies sind:

---

41 Vgl. Senate Legal and Constitutional Committee, Provisions of the Age Discrimination Bill 2003, 2003; Human Rights and Equal Opportunity Commission, Submission to the Senate Legal and Constitutional Committee on the Age Discrimination Bill 2003, 2003, abrufbar unter: http://www.humanrights.gov.au/legal/submissions/age_discrimination.html; *Smith*, Australian Anti-Discrimination Laws – Framework, Developments and Issues, New Developments in Employment Discrimination Law – The 9 JILPT Comparative Labour Law Seminar (2008) 19.

42 Human Rights and Equal Opportunity Commission, Age Matters (2000), 60f..

43 In Europa wurden nahezu zeitgleich im Zeitraum zwischen 2000 und 2004 mehrere Gleichbehandlungsrichtlinien (die Antirassismusrichtlinie 2000/43/EG, die Rahmenrichtlinie Beschäftigung 2000/78/EG, die „Gender-Richtlinie" 2002/73/EG und die Richtlinie zur Gleichstellung der Geschlechter auch außerhalb der Arbeitswelt 2004/113/EG) erlassen und sodann im Jahr 2006 auch in Deutschland in Form des Allgemeinen Gleichbehandlungsgesetzes in nationales Recht umgesetzt.

44 *Beckett*, Can Status Be A New Ground In Australian Discrimination Laws, (2004) AIAL FORUM No. 45, 40;
Hemingway, The Age Discrimination Act 2004, 6; Ronalds/*Pepper*, Discrimination Law and Practice, 9; *Goward*, The HREOC perspective – Age discrimination and its effects in the Australian community, in: Baker & McKenzie, Age Discrimination: Mitigating Risk in the Work-

New South Wales: Anti-Discrimination Act 1977 (NSW)

Queensland: Anti-Discrimination Act 1991 (Qld)

Western Australia: Equal Opportunity Act 1984 (WA)

South Australia: Equal Opportunity Act 1984 (SA)

Victoria: Equal Opportunity Act 1995 (Vic)

Tasmanien: Anti-Discrimination Act 1998 (Tas)

Australian Capital Territory: Discrimination Act 1991 (ACT)

Northern Territory: Anti-Discrimination Act 1992 (NT)

Das Diskriminierungsverbot aufgrund des Alters kennen dabei bis auf den Anti-Discrimination Act 1992 (NT) alle der aufgeführten bundesgesetzlichen und territorialen Antidiskriminierungsgesetze.[45] Bereits aus diesem Grund zeigt sich, dass zwischen den einzelnen bundesstaatlichen und territorialen Gesetzen sowie zur entsprechenden Regelung des Gesetzgebers des Commonwealth in Bezug auf die erfassten Diskriminierungsverbote ein hohes Maß an Ähnlichkeit besteht.[46] Daher stellt sich die Frage nach der Legitimation der zahlreichen Anti-Diskriminierungsgesetze, wenn zwischen den einzelnen Gesetzen ein solcher Gleichlauf besteht. Diese Frage lässt sich insbesondere mit Blick auf die Regelung des Art. 109 des Commonwealth of Australia Constitution Act 1901 beantworten, welche zum Widerspruch von Bundesrecht zu dem des Commonwealth wie folgt Stellung bezieht.

> „When a law of a State is inconsistent with a law of the Commonwealth, the latter shall prevail, and the former shall, to the extent of the inconsistency, be invalid."

Aufgrund dieser eindeutigen Formulierung schienen sämtliche Regelungen der einzelnen Bundesstaaten und Territorien zum Anti-Diskriminierungsrecht unwirksam zu sein, so dass wegen der damit verbundenen Unsicherheit über die Verbindlichkeit der entsprechenden Gesetze eine breite Diskussion ausbrach.[47] Erst als im Age Discrimination Act 2004 (Cth) in § 12 Abs. 3 und entsprechend in den anderen Anti-

---

place, S. 5; vgl. darüber hinaus zu den weiteren speziellen Diskriminierungsgesetzes des Commonwealth die Übersicht in *Bourke/Ronalds*, Discrimination Laws – Striving For Equality, in: *Macken*, The Law of Employment, 2002, 599; *Smith*, Australian Anti-Discrimination Laws – Framework, Developments and Issues, New Developments in Employment Discrimination Law – The 9 JILPT Comparative Labour Law Seminar (2008) 1ff. einschließlich Appendix A – Protected grounds under Australian Federal Anti-discrimination laws.

45 Vgl. die tabellarische Übersicht bei *Ronalds/Pepper*, Discrimination Law and Practice, Appendix A, 241 sowie bei Human Rights and Equal Opportunity Commission, Age matters? A discussion paper on age discrimination (1999) 6; *Smith*, Australian Anti-Discrimination Laws – Framework, Developments and Issues, New Developments in Employment Discrimination Law – The 9 JILPT Comparative Labour Law Seminar (2008) 3; zum Inhalt *Bourke/Ronalds*, Discrimination Laws – Striving For Equality, in: *Macken*, The Law of Employment, 2002, 603.

46 *Bourke/Ronalds*, Discrimination Laws – Striving For Equality, in: *Macken*, The Law of Employment, 2002, 601.

47 *Viskauskas v Niland* (1983) 153 CLR 280.

Diskriminierungsgesetzen des Commonwealth aufgenommen wurde, dass eine Begrenzung oder ein Ausschluss bundesstaatlicher bzw. territorialer Vorschriften nicht beabsichtigt wird und diese vielmehr nebeneinander bestehen, konnte eine Klärung herbeigeführt werden.[48] Gemäß § 12 Abs. 4 des Age Discrimination Act 2004 (Cth) besteht ein Wahlrecht, um sich auf das bundesstaatliche oder auf das Recht des Commonwealth zu berufen.[49]

Daneben hat auch die Politik einen nicht unerheblichen Teil dazu beigetragen, dass die Bundesstaaten und Territorien im Vergleich zum Anti-Diskriminierungsrecht des Commonwealth sehr ähnliche Regelungen getroffen haben. Denn somit lässt sich gegenüber der Gesellschaft der praktische Beweis erbringen, dass die jeweilige Regierung den Schutz der Menschenrechte und die Bekämpfung von Diskriminierungen ernst nimmt und mit Ernsthaftigkeit verfolgt. Dies zeigt sich etwa an einem Auszug einer Rede eines früheren australischen Premierministers:

> „The protection of fundamental rights and freedoms of the individual is of paramount importance to governments. The principle that all human beings are born equal, have a right to be treated with equal dignity, and a right to expect equal treatment in society is a firmly upheld principle of my government.“[50]

Auch lässt sich somit der durch bestimmte Interessenvereinigung und Organisationen der Politik gegenüber aufgebaute Druck zum Vorgehen gegen Diskriminierungen effektiv abbauen.

All die vorgenannten Gründe dienen demnach zur Legitimation des Wechselspiels zwischen den Antidiskriminierungsgesetzen der einzelnen Bundesstaaten und Territorien und dem Commonwealth. Dieses stellenweise Nebeneinander der einzelnen Antidiskriminierungsgesetze ist dabei zugleich als eines der Hauptmerkmale des australischen Anti-Diskriminierungsrechts hervorzuheben.

2. Das Spannungsverhältnis zwischen dem Antidiskriminic rungsrecht des Commonwealth und dem der Bundesstaaten und Territorien

a. Der lokale Anwendungsbereich des Age Discrimination Act 2004 (Cth)

Der Age Discrimination Act 2004 (Cth) stellt das Herzstück der australischen Gesetzgebung des Commonwealth im Bereich der Altersdiskriminierung dar und spielt des-

48 Vgl. auch § 6A RDA, § 10 Abs. 3, 4 und 5 SDA, § 13 DDA.

49 *Louw*, Age Discrimination Act 2004 (Cth) – Application of the Act, in: Baker & McKenzie, Age Discrimination: Mitigating Risk in the Workplace, S. 13; Explanatory Memorandum of the Age Discrimination Bill 2003 (Cth), Annexure C, Clause 12, Operation of State and Territory laws.

50 Vgl. Second Reading Speech, Anti Discrimination Bill, 23 November 1976, New South Wales Parliamentary Debates, Session 1976, Vol. 128, Third Series, 3337.

halb eine nicht unbedeutende Rolle in der täglichen Rechtspraxis im australischen Antidiskriminierungsrecht. Als Gesetz des Commonwealth gilt der Age Discrimination Act 2004 (Cth) in allen sechs Bundesstaaten (New South Wales, Victoria, Queensland, South Australia, Western Australia, Tasmanien) und den zwei Territorien Australiens (Northern Territory, Australian Capital Territory).[51] Ebenso findet der Age Discrimination Act 2004 (Cth) mit seinen Verboten der Altersdiskriminierung immer dort Anwendung, wo diskriminierende Maßnahmen innerhalb Australiens vorgenommen werden und diese sich auf Menschen, Sachen oder Ereignisse sowohl innerhalb als auch außerhalb Australiens auswirken, §§ 9 Abs. 2 und Abs. 3, 10 Abs. 5 ADA.[52]

b. Das Anwendungsverhältnis zwischen dem Age Discrimination Act 2004 (Cth) und den Antidiskriminierungsregelungen der einzelnen Bundesstaaten und Territorien

Wie bereits angesprochen verbieten zwar nahezu alle – teilweise schon seit mehreren Jahrzehnten existierenden – antidiskriminierungsrechtlichen Regelungen der einzelnen Bundesstaaten und der Territorien die Diskriminierung wegen Alters.[53] Sie stehen aber zugleich in einem Konkurrenzverhältnis zum Age Discrimination Act 2004 (Cth). Denn sobald eine Klage wegen einer Altersdiskriminierung auf der rechtlichen Grundlage einer bundesstaatlichen oder territorialen Regelung erhoben wird, ist es dem Anspruchsinhaber gemäß § 12 Abs. 3 ADA verwehrt, Rechte aus dem Age Discrimination Act 2004 (Cth) geltend zu machen. Andererseits ist es einem Kläger aber zugleich aufgrund der gesetzlichen Regelung in § 12 Abs. 4 ADA ausdrücklich nicht verwehrt, zuerst seine Rechte aus dem Age Discrimination Act 2004 (Cth) gerichtlich geltend zu machen und erst dann eine nachrangige Klage auf der Grundlage einer bundesstaatlichen oder territorialen Regelung anzustrengen.[54]

§ 12 Abs. 5 und Abs. 6 regelt darüber hinaus, dass eine Person aufgrund einer diskriminierenden Handlung zwar sowohl auf der Grundlage des Age Discrimination Act 2004 (Cth) als auch aufgrund von bundesstaatlichen oder territorialen Antidiskriminierungsgesetzen gerichtlich verfolgt und verurteilt werden kann, sie aber nicht mehrmals bestraft werden darf.[55]

---

51 *Ratnam*, Federal Government's proposed age discrimination legislation (2003) 9 Employment Law Bulletin 13; Human Rights and Equal Opportunity Commission, Federal Discrimination Law 2005, 12; *Hemingway*, The Age Discrimination Act 2004, 6.

52 Explanatory Memorandum of the Age Discrimination Bill 2003 (Cth), Annexure C, Clause 9, Geographical application of Bill.

53 *Ratnam*, Federal Government's proposed age discrimination legislation (2003) 9 Employment Law Bulletin 13; *Hemingway*, The Age Discrimination Act 2004, 6 m.w.N..

54 *Louw*, Age Discrimination Act 2004 (Cth) – Application of the Act, in: Baker & McKenzie, Age Discrimination: Mitigating Risk in the Workplace, S. 13; Explanatory Memorandum of the Age Discrimination Bill 2003 (Cth), Annexure C, Clause 12, Operation of State and Territory laws.

55 Explanatory Memorandum of the Age Discrimination Bill 2003 (Cth), Annexure C, Clause 12, Operation of State and Territory laws.

Zwischen dem Recht des Commonwealth – dem Age Discrimination Act 2004 (Cth) – und den einzelnen bundesgesetzlichen und territorialen Regelungen kann es aber trotz dieser gesetzlichen Regelungen im Age Discrimination Act 2004 (Cth) zum Wechselspiel zwischen den einzelnen Anti-Diskriminierungsgesetzen der Bundesstaaten und Territorien sowie dem Commonwealth in Einzelfällen dennoch zu Konflikten kommen, da die jeweiligen Definitionen und der Wortlaut zwar gleichartig, aber nicht absolut identisch sind. Denn meistens diente das Antidiskriminierungsrecht des Commonwealth als Vorlage für die Gesetzgebung der einzelnen Bundesstaaten und Territorien, wobei dann insbesondere die Diskriminierungsverbote modifiziert worden sind.[56]

Um zusätzlich dazu beizutragen, mögliche Konflikte und Spannungen zu vermeiden, bestimmt – wie bereits zuvor angesprochen – Art. 109 des Commonwealth of Australia Constitution Act 1901 für den Fall, dass Gesetze des Commonwealth und der einzelnen Bundesstaaten und Territorien nicht übereinstimmen, dass das Recht des Commonwealth maßgebend sein soll. Allerdings soll nach Ansicht der Rechtsprechung zugleich berücksichtigt werden, ob das jeweilige Gesetz des Commonwealth darauf bedacht ist, den konkreten Anwendungsbereich allumfassend abzudecken oder ob es eine Möglichkeit gibt, bundesstaatlichem oder territorialem Recht dennoch zur Geltung zu verhelfen.[57] So kann sich jede Gesetzgebung eine nötige Flexibilität hinsichtlich der Gesetzesanwendung, der Auslegung und der Schaffung von Präzedenzfällen bewahren, ohne das Nebeneinander der einzelnen Anti-Diskriminierungsgesetze der Bundesstaaten und Territorien sowie des Commonwealth zu gefährden.[58]

56 *Ronalds/Pepper*, Discrimination Law and Practice, 11.

57 *Ansett Transport Industries (Operations) Pty Ltd v Wardly* (1979) 142 CLR 237; *University of Wollongong v Metwally* (1984) 158 CLR 447.

58 *Ronalds/Pepper*, Discrimination Law and Practice, 12.

C. Verfassungsrechtliche Grundlagen für gesetzliche Regelungen zur Altersdiskriminierung in Australien

Das grundlegende Problem in der Bestimmung der verfassungsrechtlichen Grundlagen für eine Antidiskriminierungsgesetzgebung – im Besonderen für das Recht der Altersdiskriminierung – ist das Fehlen von geschriebenen Gesetzgebungskompetenzen zur Verwirklichung von einheitlichen Grundrechtsstandards im australischen Commonwealth.[59] Auch der Versuch der Eingliederung geschriebener Grundrechte in Form einer *„Bill of Rights"* in die Verfassung des australischen Commonwealth scheiterte, weil sich keine verfassungsändernde Mehrheit finden ließ.[60] Somit bedarf es einer umfassenden Beleuchtung und Klärung der Gesetzgebungskompetenz für die Regelungen zum Age Discrimination Act 2004 (Cth), um zu einer verfassungsrechtlichen Absicherung zu gelangen.

I. Verfassungsrechtliche Verankerung des Age Discrimination Act 2004 (Cth)

1. Gesetzgebungskompetenz des Parlaments des Common wealth

a. Art. 51 des Commonwealth of Australia Constitution Act 1901 als Gesetzgebungskompetenz für den Age Discrimination Act 2004 (Cth)

aa. Allgemeine Kompetenz des australischen Commonwealth zur Gesetzgebung

Die Verfassung des australischen Commonwealth gesteht dem Parlament des Commonwealth zwar grundsätzlich in Art. 122 des Commonwealth of Australia Constitution Act 1901 die allgemeine Gesetzgebungshoheit für das gesamte Gebiet und für alle Regierungen des australischen Commonwealth zu. Im Speziellen wird dem Parlament des Commonwealth aber nur für die in Art. 51 des Commonwealth of Australia Constitution Act 1901 aufgeführten Bereiche die Befugnis zur gesetzlichen Regelung überlassen, ohne diese aber genauer zu bezeichnen. Jedoch muss sich das Parlament des Commonwealth aufgrund dieser Regelung strikt an die verfassungsrechtlich zugewiesene allgemeine Gesetzgebungsbefugnis halten und sich im Rahmen jeglicher Gesetzgebung durch das Parlament des Commonwealth versichern, dass die Gesetzge-

59 *Opeskin*, International Law and Federal States, in: *Opeskin/Rothwell*, International Law and Australian Federalism, 1997, 1; *Bailey/Devereux*, The Operation of Antidiscrimination Laws in Australia, in: *Kinley*, Human Rights in Australian Law, 1998, 292.

60 *Charlesworth*, The Australian Reluctance about Rights; in: *Alston*, Towards an Australian Bill of Rights, 1994, 21; *Williams*, A Bill of Rights for Australia, 2000.

bungsbefugnis aus Art. 51 des Commonwealth of Australia Constitution Act 1901 im konkreten Fall gegeben ist.

bb. Begrenzung der allgemeinen Gesetzgebungskompetenz

Unter Berücksichtigung der Menschenrechte, von möglicherweise entstehenden oder bereits existierenden Diskriminierungen und unter Beachtung einer beabsichtigten Gleichbehandlung gesteht dabei Art. 51 Abs. xxix des Commonwealth of Australia Constitution Act 1901 dem Parlament des Commonwealth aufgrund der Gesetzgebungskompetenz in außenpolitischen Angelegenheiten (*„external affairs power"*) für den Bereich der Altersdiskriminierung und somit für den Age Discrimination Act 2004 (Cth) die Regelungsbefugnis zu.

Die Verankerung und Ausgestaltung der Gesetzgebungsbefugnis für den Age Discrimination Act 2004 (Cth) in Art. 51 Abs. xxix des Commonwealth of Australia Constitution Act 1901 mag auf den ersten Blick nur wenig eindeutig und nicht recht nachvollziehbar erscheinen. Denn worin soll ein direkter Zusammenhang zwischen einer Diskriminierung wegen Alters und den *„external affairs"*, den außenpolitischen Angelegenheiten, bestehen? Beleuchtet man jedoch die hinter dieser Gesetzgebungskompetenz stehende Intention des Gesetzgebers, dann wird die vorliegende Regelungssystematik nachvollziehbar und es stellt sich heraus, dass diese Gesetzgebungskompetenz die einzige Möglichkeit bietet, um eine für das gesamte Commonwealth einheitliche Lösung zu finden und für das Parlament des Commonwealth eine Annexkompetenz für den Bereich der Altersdiskriminierung zu schaffen.[61]

b. Die Gesetzgebungskompetenz der außenpolitischen Angelegenheiten

Vorab gilt es deshalb die Gesetzgebungskompetenz der *„external affairs power"* etwas genauer zu betrachten, um so ihren Wirk- und Geltungsbereich einzugrenzen und zu verstehen.

aa. External affairs power

Art. 51 Abs. xxix des Commonwealth of Australia Constitution Act 1901 lautet:

> "The Parliament shall, subject to this Constitution, have power to make laws for the peace, order, and good government of the Commonwealth with respect to ... external affairs."

Auf der Grundlage dieser *„external affairs power"* steht dem australischen Commonwealth demnach die Kompetenz zur Gesetzgebung zu, wenn internationale Abkommen oder Völkerrechtsverträge geschlossen werden, die in nationales australisches Recht

61 *Bourke/Ronalds*, Discrimination Laws – Striving For Equality, in: *Macken*, The Law of Employment, 2002, 597 mit Verweis auf *Commonwealth v Tasmania* (1983) 158 CLR 1.

umgesetzt werden müssen.[62] Folglich sind das in der Regel diejenigen Abkommen und Verträge, die mangels einer Ratifizierung (noch) nicht in australisches Recht transformiert worden sind.

bb. Auslegung der „external affairs power"

(1) Die Grundsätze der Gesetzesauslegung

Vorrangige Bedeutung kommt im Australischen Recht grundsätzlich immer der Wortlautauslegung zu, so dass zuerst der ausdrücklich verwendete Wortlaut und die gewöhnliche Bedeutung der Wörter betrachtet werden muss. Dabei ergibt sich unweigerlich, dass bei den Worten *„the doing of an act"* nicht von einem Unterlassen die Rede ist. Fraglich erscheint jedoch, ob nicht auf der Grundlage der wichtigsten Hauptregeln der *„Interpretation of Statutes"* von diesem Ergebnis abgewichen werden kann oder sogar abgewichen werden muss.

(a) Literal Rule

So besagt die *„Literal Rule"*, dass der Wortlaut des Gesetzes in der Regel so zu verstehen sein sollte, wie er von der Allgemeinheit der von dem entsprechenden Gesetz betroffenen Personen verstanden wird.[63] Wegen der deutlichen Wortwahl erscheint es als nahe liegend, dass die durch den Age Disrimination Act 2004 (Cth) betroffenen Personen, die Formulierung *„the doing of an act"* nicht automatisch und ohne besondere zusätzliche Umstände mit einem Unterlassen verbinden werden. Folglich hilft die Anwendung der *„Literal Rule"* zur Präzisierung nicht weiter.

(b) Golden Rule

Im Rahmen der Gesetzesauslegung muss eine logische Interpretation gewährleistet sein. Daher darf bei der Auslegung eines Gesetzes von dem grammatikalischen und gewöhnlichen Sinn einer Formulierung nur dann abgewichen werden, wenn dieser sich als widersprüchlich darstellt und somit mit anderen Gesetztesteilen bzw. –regelungen nicht vereinbar ist.[64] Zwar ist ein Widerspruch der Formulierung *„the doing of an act"* zu anderen Teilen des Age Discrimination Act 2004 (Cth) nicht offen erkennbar. Es erscheint jedoch als nicht unwahrscheinlich, dass eine Ausgrenzung des Unterlassens zu Rechtsschutzlücken führen kann und sich die besagte Formulierung als im Verhältnis zum weit gefassten Zweck des Age Discrimination Act 2004 (Cth) widersprüchlich darstellt.

(2) Die Auslegung durch den High Court of Australia

Der High Court of Australia legt in seiner Rechtsprechung im Lichte der zuvor beschriebenen Auslegungsregeln Art. 51 Abs. xxix des Commonwealth of Australia

---

62 *Smith*, Australian Anti-Discrimination Laws – Framework, Developments and Issues, New Developments in Employment Discrimination Law – The 9 JILPT Comparative Labour Law Seminar (2008) 3.

63 *Henrich*, Einführung in das Englische Privatrecht, S. 21.

64 *Henrich*, Einführung in das Englische Privatrecht, S. 20.

Constitution Act 1901 in Bezug auf die Regelungen zur Diskriminierung wegen Alters im Age Discrimination Act 2004 (Cth) im Ergebnis weit aus, so dass danach dem Parlament des Commonwealth die Kompetenz zur Gesetzgebung immer dann zukommt, soweit Regelungsbereiche internationaler Abkommen oder völkerrechtlicher Verträge einbezogen werden.[65] Denn nur so könne eine engere Verbindung zwischen den verschiedenen Nationen hergestellt werden.[66] Bei der Auslegung orientiert sich die australische Rechtsprechung an den oben dargestellten klassischen Auslegungsregelungen des *common law*. Dies führt im Ergebnis dazu, dass grundsätzlich der Wortlautauslegung eine maßgebliche und vor allem vorrangige Bedeutung zugemessen wird.[67]

Weiterhin führt der High Court in seiner Rechtsprechung nahezu wörtlich aus:

> „... es ist nicht weiter möglich zu behaupten, dass es irgendeinen Bereich gibt, der erforderlicherweise von der Liste der möglichen Themen internationaler Verhandlungen, internationaler Streitigkeiten oder internationaler Übereinkünfte ausgeschlossen werden müsste. Im Wege der Veranschaulichung müssen wir beachten, dass bereits Teil 13 des Versailler Vertrages erklärt, dass sich ein die ganze Welt umfassender Frieden nur dann herstellen lässt, wenn er auf einer sozialen Gerechtigkeit basiert und dass Arbeitskämpfe, die durch nicht zufrieden stellende Bedingungen verursacht werden, auch den Frieden in der Welt gefährden. Im Angesicht dieser Aussagen und der Gründung der International Labour Organisation muss jetzt wahrgenommen werden, dass die Aufrechterhaltung bzw. die Verbesserung der Arbeitsbedingungen ein geeignetes Thema einer internationalen Übereinkunft darstellt. Aufgrund der Unterschiede in den Arbeitsbedingungen kann sich die Zahl der Reibungen zwischen den verschiedenen Nationen selbst dann erhöhen, wenn der Handelswettbewerb für sie sonst unter den gleichen Bedingungen stattfindet.“[68]

In einer anderen Entscheidung aus dem Jahre 1982 geht der High Court of Australia ebenfalls auf die sich stetig weiterentwickelnden Bereiche von internationalem Belang ein. Er stellt insoweit erweiternd fest:

> „Solche Bereiche, die ausschließlich inländischen Bezug haben, sind regelmäßig begrenzt und solche mit internationalem Bezug breiten sich weiter ständig aus. Trotzdem lässt die Qualität der internationalen Bezüge einen rechtsverbindlichen Maßstab übrig, auf dessen Grundlage eine spezielle Materie einen Teil der „external affairs“ eines Staates bilden kann. Eine solche Materie mit internationalem Bezug besitzt erforderlicherweise die Kapazität, um auf die Beziehungen eines Landes zu einer anderen Nation Einfluss zu nehmen und bereits dieses Qualitätsmerkmal ist ausreichend, um einen Regelungsbereich zum Gegenstand der „external affairs“ zu machen...“[69]

Nochmals erweiternd führte der High Court einige Jahre später in der Entscheidung *Polyukhovich v Commonwealth* aus, dass:

---

65 *R v Burgess; ex parte Henry* (1936) 55 CLR 608; *Commonwealth v Tasmania* (1983) 158 CLR 1.

66 *R v Burgess; ex parte Henry* (1936) 55 CLR 608; *Evatt/McTiermann*, S. 680-681.

67 Zu den Grundsätzen der Gesetzesauslegung im Common Law *Henrich*, Einführung in das Englische Privatrecht, 20f..

68 *R v Burgess; ex parte Henry* (1936) 55 CLR 608; *Evatt/McTiermann*, S. 680-681.

69 *Koowarta v Bjelke-Petersen* (1982) 153 CLR 168.

„...the grant of the legislative power with respect to external affairs should be construed with all generality that the words admit and that, so construed, the power extends to matters and things, as well as relationships outside Australia.“[70]

cc. *Begrenzung der „external affairs power“*

Unter Berücksichtigung der Ausführung der inländischen Gesetzgebung, darf sich aber nicht zu präzise an den Bedingungen und Regelungsinhalten der internationalen Verträge orientiert werden. Denn für die Rechtsgültigkeit der internationalen Verträge genügt letztlich bereits eine vernünftige und geeignete Erweiterung.[71] Allerdings ist es trotz dieser bewusst weiten Auslegung der *„external affairs power“* problematisch, dass es kaum einen nicht von internationalen Abkommen und Völkerrechtsverträgen betroffenen Regelungsbereich gibt und deshalb die Gefahr einer Gesamtzuständigkeit des australischen Commonwealth in allen internationalen Angelegenheiten ohne eine Änderung der Verfassung besteht.[72]

Entgegen einigen Stimmen in der Literatur, die sich für eine Einschränkung der Umsetzung internationaler Vereinbarungen einsetzen, befürwortet vor allem die Rechtsprechung eine weite Auslegung des Art. 51 Abs. xxix des Commonwealth of Australia Constitution Act 1901.[73] So hat eine Minderheit der Richter des High Court bereits frühzeitig die Auffassung vertreten, dass dem Parlament des Commonwealth die Kompetenz zustehe, alle internationalen Abkommen und Völkerrechtsverträge in nationales Recht umzusetzen, wobei jedoch noch einschränkend verlangt wurde, dass ein unbestreitbarer internationaler Einschlag gegeben sein müsse.[74] In der dieser Entscheidung nachfolgenden Rechtsprechung verfestigte sich zunehmend die Ansicht, dass das Commonwealth of Australia unter Bezugnahme auf die *„external affairs power“* internationale Abkommen und völkerrechtlicher Verträge ohne Einschränkungen umsetzen dürfe.[75]

Nach aufkommenden Zweifeln über die Verfassungsmäßigkeit der Gesetzgebungskompetenz der *„external affairs power“* und deren weiten Anwendungsbereich wurde von der australischen Bundesregierung eine Verfassungskommission mit der Prüfung beauftragt. Diese stellte jedoch keinerlei Bedenken gegen die Verfassungsmäßigkeit fest, so dass der High Court konsequent an seiner Meinung festhielt und nach-

---

70 *Polyukhovich v Commonwealth* (1991) 172 CLR 501.

71 *Richardson v The Forestry Commission & Anor* (1988) 77 ALR 237; *Aldridge v Booth* (1988) 80 ALR 1.

72 *Commonwealth v Tasmania* (1983) 158 CLR 1; *Colvin/Watson*, The Workplace Relations Handbook – A guide to the Workplace Relations Act 1996 (Cth), Sydney 1998, 31.

73 *Ford*, Reconstructing Australian Labour Law: A Constitutional Perspective, (1997) 10 Australian Journal of Labour Law, 105.

74 Vgl. die Ausführungen der Richter Evatt und McTeirnan in *R v Burgess; Ex parte Henry* (1936) 55 CLR 608, 696.

75 *Koowarta v Bjelke-Petersen* (1982) 153 CLR 168; *Commonwealth v Tasmania* (1983) 158 CLR 1; *Richardson v Forestry Commission of Tasmania* (1988) 164 CLR 261; *Queensland and Another v Commonwealth of Australia* (1989) 167 CLR 232; *Polyukhovich v Commonwealth* (1991) 172 CLR 501; vgl. auch *Ludeke*, The External Affairs Power: Another Province for Law and Order?, (1993) 35 Journal of Industrial Relations, 453.

folgend entschied, dass die außenpolitischen Angelegenheiten so weit auszulegen sind, wie es der Wortlaut gerade noch zulässt:

> „...the phrase „external affairs“ is to be construed with all the generality which the words admit.”[76]

Durch dieses aufgrund der Rechtsprechung begründete weite Verständnis der *„external affairs power“* scheint tatsächlich eine Gefahr der Gesamtzuständigkeit des australischen Commonwealth in allen internationalen Angelegenheiten entstanden zu sein. Der High Court war sich in seinen Entscheidungen dieser Gefahr jedoch bewusst und beschränkt die weite Auslegung. Die Rechtsprechung verlangt deshalb, dass eine internationale Vereinbarung tatsächlich verhältnismäßig geeignet und zur Umsetzung angemessen und passend ist:

> „To be a law with respect to „external affairs“, the law must be reasonably capable of being considered appropriate and adapted to implementing the treaty.”[77]

Somit bleibt im Ergebnis festzustellen, dass der Anwendungsbereich der *„external affairs power“* gemäß Art. 51 Abs. xxix des Commonwealth of Australia Constitution Act 1901 zwar sehr weit gefasst ist, aber trotzdem keine Gesamtzuständigkeit des australischen Gesetzgebers in außenpolitischen Angelegenheiten schafft.[78] Denn die Kompetenz für diese dient allein der Umsetzung von internationalen Abkommen und völkerrechtlichen Vereinbarungen, so dass sich aus diesem Sinn und Zweck eine immanente verfassungsmäßige Einschränkung ergibt.

c. Einbeziehung internationaler Abkommen und Verträge in die Bundesgesetzgebung

Folglich konstituiert die Gesetzgebungskompetenz aus Art. 51 Abs. xxix des Commonwealth of Australia Constitution Act 1901 nicht per se die unbeschränkte Befugnis zur gesetzlichen Regelung der Altersdiskriminierung. Vielmehr wird lediglich die grundsätzliche Möglichkeit eröffnet, existierende und für mehrere Staaten verbindliche – sowie auch von Australien ratifizierte – internationale Abkommen und völkerrechtliche Verträge – insbesondere zur Beachtung der Menschenrechte und zum Ausschluss von Diskriminierungen im inländischen australischen Recht – umzusetzen und somit in die Gesetzgebung zur Altersdiskriminierung einfließen zu lassen. Demnach müssen internationale Abkommen entsprechend in inländisches australisches Recht im Rahmen einer Transformation umgewandelt, integriert und präzisiert werden.[79] Durch die-

---

76 *Victoria v Commonwealth* (1996) CLR 416, 485.

77 *Victoria v Commonwealth* (1996) CLR 416, 485.

78 *Ford*, The Constitution and the Reform of Australian Industrial Relations, (1994) 7 Australian Journal of Labour Law, 105.

79 *R v Burgess; ex parte Henry* (1936) 55 CLR 608 at 644; *Koowarta v Bjelke-Petersen* (1982) 153 CLR 168 at 193; *Colvin/Watson*, The Workplace Relations Handbook – A guide to the Workplace Relations Act 1996 (Cth), Sydney 1998, 31; *Williams/Gotting*, (2001) 20 Australian

sen Akt der Ratifizierung sollen die subjektiven Rechte der australischen Bevölkerung gestärkt und weiter ausgebaut werden.[80]

aa. Einbeziehungsregelungen zu Regelungen aus internationalen Abkommen

Aus diesem Grund werden sog. „Einbeziehungsregelungen“ (*„the introduction of domestic legislation“*) im australischen Bundesrecht aufgenommen.[81] Auf der Grundlage der Rechtsprechung des High Court of Australia sind sie mittlerweile als übliche Regelungsmechanismen anerkannt und in zahlreichen Gesetzen enthalten. So enthält auch der Age Discrimination Act 2004 (Cth) eine ausdrückliche „Einbeziehungsregelung“ mehrerer international verbindlicher Regelungen in § 10 Abs. 7 ADA. Zu den einzubeziehenden Regelungen zählen die Discrimination (Employment and Occupation) Convention, 1958, der International Labour Organisation (ILO 111, § 10 Abs. 7 lit. a) ADA), das International Covenant on Civil and Political Rights (ICCPR, § 10 Abs. 7 lit. b) ADA), das International Covenant on Economic, Social and Cultural Rights (ICESCR, § 10 Abs. 7 lit. c) ADA), die Convention on the Rights of the Child (CROC, § 10 Abs. 7 lit. d) ADA), außerhalb von Australien geltende Regelungen (§ 10 Abs. 7 lit. e) ADA) sowie weitere Regelungen von internationaler Bedeutung (§ 10 Abs. 7 lit. f) ADA). Die vorgenannten Übereinkommen verpflichten zur Beseitigung verschiedener Diskriminierungen, allerdings nennen sie nicht ausdrücklich die Diskriminierung wegen Alters. In der australischen Diskussion gelingt jedoch durch den Rückgriff auf das Verbot der Diskriminierung wegen „des sonstigen Statuts“ auch ein Bezug zur Diskriminierung wegen Alters. Wie zuvor anhand der Rechtsprechung aufgezeigt, konnte somit in Australien das Diskriminierungsverbot wegen Alters frühzeitig als völkerrechtlicher Grundsatz anerkannt werden.[82]

Bar Review, 264; *Bourke/Ronalds*, Discrimination Laws – Striving For Equality, in: *Macken*, The Law of Employment, 2002, 595 m.w.N.; vgl. zur Konformität inländischen Rechts ohne Transformation internationaler Abkommen *Minister for Immigration and Ethnic Affairs v Teoh* (1995) 128 ALR 53.

80 *Bourke/Ronalds*, Discrimination Laws – Striving For Equality, in: *Macken*, The Law of Employment, 2002, 597.

81 *Bourke/Ronalds*, Discrimination Laws – Striving For Equality, in: *Macken*, The Law of Employment, 2002, 595 m.w.N.; vgl. auch *Bradley v Commonwealth* (1973) 128 CLR 557; Zugleich besteht gegenüber den internationalen Organisationen (ILO etc.) eine Berichtspflicht Australiens über die Umsetzung ratifizierten Abkommen in innerstaatliches Recht, vgl. hierzu z.B. Report of the Committee of Experts on the Application of Conventions and Recommendations, Direct Request 2000 to Australia, 71st Session on ILO 156, abrufbar unter http://webfusion.ilo.org/public/db/standards/normes/appl/index.cfm?lang=EN.

82 Aus der Rechtsprechung des EuGH in Sachen *Mangold* findet die – insbesondere in der deutschen Diskussion nicht unerheblich kritisierte – Anerkennung des Verbotes der Diskriminierung wegen Alters als allgemeiner Grundsatz des Gemeinschaftsrechts hier eine bemerkenswerte Bestätigung; vgl. EuGH, Urteil vom 22.11.2005 – C-144/04 = NJW 2005, 3695 = NZA 2005, 1345; vgl. auch BVerfG, Beschluss vom 6.7.2010 – 2 BvR 2661/06 = NJW 2010, 3422 = NZA 2010, 995; vgl. im Zusammenhang mit dem Mangold-Urteil des EuGH und der damit verbundenen Neuregelung des § 14 Abs. 3 TzBfG die Bedenken von Kohte in AuR 2007, 168; vgl. weiter zum Verbot der Altersdiskriminierung als allgemeinen Grundsatz des Gemeinschaftsrechts die Entscheidung des EuGH in Sachen *Kücükdeveci* EuGH, Urteil vom 19.01.2010 – C-555/07 = NJW 2010, 427 = NZA 2010, 85.

(1) Die Discrimination (Employment and Occupation) Convention – ILO 111

Im Übereinkommen 111 (Übereinkommen über die Diskriminierung in Beschäftigung und Beruf) hat die Allgemeine Konferenz der Internationalen Arbeitsorganisation ein ausdrückliches Vorgehen gegen und die Beseitigung von Diskriminierungen im Bereich von Arbeit und Beschäftigung aufgrund der Rasse, der Hautfarbe, des Geschlechts, des Glaubensbekenntnisses, der politischen Meinung, der nationalen Abstammung oder der sozialen Herkunft verbindlich geregelt, Art. 1 Abs. 1 lit. a) ILO 111. Darüber hinaus hat sie den einzelnen Vertragsstaaten erlaubt, weitere Diskriminierungsverbote mit nationalem Bezug hinzuzufügen, Art. 1 Abs. 1 lit. b) ILO 111. Im Jahr 1989 hat die australische Regierung zahlreiche weitere Motive – wie Nationalität, Familienstand, Gewerkschaftszugehörigkeit, physische sowie psychische Behinderung und auch das Alter – hinzugefügt, § 4 Human Rights and Equal Opportunity Regulations 1989 (Cth). Die einzelnen Regelungen des Übereinkommens sind dabei jedoch nicht Bestandteil des inländischen australischen Rechts, sondern vielmehr in vergleichbarer Form Inhalt des Human Rights and Equal Opportunity Act 1986 (Cth) geworden; § 31 lit. b) HREOCA.[83]

(2) Art. 2 und 26 des International Covenant on Civil and Political Rights

Im Internationalen Pakt über bürgerliche und politische Rechte hat sich gemäß Art. 2 jeder einzelne Vertragsstaat verpflichtet, die anerkannten Rechte zu achten und sie allen in seinem Gebiet befindlichen und seiner Herrschaftsgewalt unterstehenden Personen ohne Unterschied, wie insbesondere der Rasse, der Hautfarbe, des Geschlechts, der Sprache, der Religion, der politischen oder sonstigen Anschauung, der nationalen oder sozialen Herkunft, des Vermögens, der Geburt oder des sonstigen Status zu gewährleisten. Darüber hinaus regelt Art. 26 für alle Vertragsstaaten verbindlich, dass alle Menschen vor dem Gesetz gleich sind und ohne Diskriminierung einen Anspruch auf gleichen Schutz durch das Gesetz haben. In dieser Hinsicht hat das Gesetz jede Diskriminierung zu verbieten und allen Menschen gegen jedwede Diskriminierung, wie insbesondere wegen der Rasse, der Hautfarbe, des Geschlechts, der Sprache, der Religion, der politischen oder sonstigen Anschauung, der nationalen oder sozialen Herkunft, des Vermögens, der Geburt oder des sonstigen Status, gleichen und wirksamen Schutz zu gewährleisten, Art. 26 S. 2. Obwohl trotz des umfangreichen Schutzbereichs das Alter als Diskriminierungsgrund keine ausdrückliche Erwähnung findet, soll mit der Formulierung des „sonstigen Status" auch das Alter einer Person bzw. Personengruppe erfasst sein.[84] Wie bereits die zuvor aufgezeigten Regelungen aus ILO 111 finden die betreffenden Vorschriften aus dem Internationalen Pakt über bürgerliche und politische Rechte über die innerstaatliche Regelung im Human Rights and Equal Opportunity Commission Act 1986 (Cth) Anwendung im australischen Recht, § 31 lit. b) HREOCA.

83 Revised Explanatory Memorandum, Age Discrimination Act 2004, 40.

84 *Schmitz-de-Jong v Netherlands*, Communication No 855/1999, UN Doc CCPR/C/72/D/855/1999; *Love v Australia*, Communication No 983/2001, UN Doc CCPR/C/77/D/983/2001.

(3) Art. 2 des International Covenant on Economic, Social and Cultural Rights

Weiter enthält der Internationale Pakt über wirtschaftliche, soziale und kulturelle Rechte in Art. 2 die Verpflichtung für die einzelnen Vertragsstaaten zu gewährleisten, dass die verkündeten Rechte ohne Diskriminierung hinsichtlich der Rasse, der Hautfarbe, des Geschlechts, der Sprache, der Religion, der politischen oder sonstigen Anschauung, der nationalen oder sozialen Herkunft, des Vermögens, der Geburt oder des sonstigen Status ausgeübt werden können. Auch insoweit wird das Alter wieder über den Begriff des „sonstigen Status" als einbezogen angesehen. Für die Einbeziehung in inländisches australisches Recht gilt das zuvor Gesagte.[85]

(4) Die Convention on the Rights of the Child

Im Übereinkommen über die Rechte des Kindes ist ebenfalls in Art. 2 die Verpflichtung der Vertragsstaaten zur Achtung und Gewährleistung der festgelegten Rechte zugunsten des Kindes, ohne jede Diskriminierung unabhängig von der Rasse, der Hautfarbe, dem Geschlecht, der Sprache, der Religion, der politischen oder sonstigen Anschauung, der nationalen, ethnischen oder sozialen Herkunft, des Vermögens, einer Behinderung, der Geburt oder des sonstigen Status des Kindes, seiner Eltern oder seines Vormunds geregelt und wieder entsprechend über § 31 lit. b) HREOCA im inländischen australischen Recht anwendbar.

bb. Weitere Regelungen von internationaler Bedeutung

Neben dem Bezug auf die vorgenannten internationalen Übereinkommen strebt insbesondere auch die gesetzliche Regelung des § 10 Abs. 7 lit. f) ADA danach, eine Gesetzgebungsbefugnis aus Art. 51 Abs. xxix des Commonwealth of Australia Constitution Act 1901 auf formelle Gesetzes auszuweiten, indem sie versucht eine Beziehung zu einer Frage mit internationalem Bezug herzustellen. Um dieses Ziel zu erreichen, bedarf es eines weiten Verständnisses. Denn als Fragen mit internationalem Bezug werden bereits allgemeine Bereiche mit international praktischem Bezug bezeichnet.[86]

Um die Rechtsgültigkeit und die bestmögliche Wirkkraft des Age Discrimination Act 2004 (Cth), auch in Bezug auf internationale Bereiche, zu gewährleisten, wird demzufolge mit der gesetzlichen Regelung des § 10 ADA versucht, die gesetzgebende Gewalt des Commonwealth zur Unterstützung anzuhalten und gleichzeitig vorzugeben, dass das Parlament des Commonwealth keinerlei gesetzliche Regelungen treffen solle, zu denen ihm die Gesetzgebungskompetenz fehlt.

Weitere vergleichbare „Einbeziehungsregelungen" finden sich etwa in § 9 Abs. 10 des Sex Discrimination Act 1984 (Cth)[87], in § 7 des Racial Discrimination Act 1975

---

85 Vgl. auch *Hemingway*, Roadmap to ADA: The Age Discrimination Act 2004, 5 abrufbar unter http://www.hreoc.gov.au/age/roadmap_ADA.html.

86 *Polyukhovich v Commonwealth* (1991) 101 ALR 545.

87 Bezug zur International Convention on the Elimination of All Forms of Discrimination Against Women (CEDAW).

(Cth)[88], in § 12 Abs. 8 des Disability Discrimination Act 1992 (Cth)[89] und sind darüber hinaus in § 3 des Human Rights and Equal Opportunity Commission Act 1986 (Cth)[90] enthalten.

d. Weitere Gesetzgebungskompetenzen des Art. 51 des Commonwealth of Australia Constitution Act 1901

Ebenfalls begründen auch Art. 51 Abs. i, xiii, xiv und xx des Commonwealth of Australia Constitution Act 1901 eine allgemeine Gesetzgebungsbefugnis, aus welcher das Parlament des Commonwealth eine Kompetenz zur Regelung der Alterdiskriminierungsgesetzgebung in Form des Age Discrimination Act 2004 (Cth) ableiten konnte.

Art. 51 Abs. i nimmt Bezug auf die Gesetzgebungskompetenz für Wirtschaft und Handel, Art. 51 Abs. xiii auf die Gesetzgebungskompetenz für den privaten Bankenbereich, Art. 51 Abs. xiv auf die Gesetzgebungskompetenz für den Bereich der nichtstaatlichen Versicherungen und Art. 51 Abs. xx letztlich auf die Gesetzgebungskompetenz im Bereich ausländischer juristischer Personen.

Diese Verfassungsnorm strebt folglich danach, der Gesetzgebung zum Age Discrimination Act 2004 (Cth) Rechtsverbindlichkeit in Bezug auf verschiedenartige Diskriminierungen und Anwendungsbereiche zu eröffnen. Hierzu gehören etwa Diskriminierungen von einer ausländischen juristischen Person gemäß § 10 Abs. 8 lit. a) ADA, von einer Person im Rahmen einer Verpflichtung als Amtsinhaber oder Arbeitnehmer einer solchen juristischen Person gemäß § 10 Abs. 8 lit. b) ADA, von einer inländischen juristischen Person gemäß § 10 Abs. 9 lit. a) ADA, von einer Person im Rahmen einer Verpflichtung als Amtsinhaber oder Arbeitnehmer einer solchen juristischen Person gemäß § 10 Abs. 9 lit. b) ADA, Diskriminierungen während der Fortführung eines Bankgeschäftes gemäß § 10 Abs. 10 lit. a) ADA, eines Versicherungsgeschäftes gemäß § 10 Abs. 10 lit. b) ADA sowie Diskriminierungen im Rahmen oder in Verbindung mit Wirtschaft und Handel gemäß § 10 Abs. 11 ADA zwischen Australien und einem Ort außerhalb Australiens oder zwischen den Bundesstaaten oder zwischen den Bundesstaaten und einem Territorium oder zwischen zwei Territorien.

2. Einfluss der Discrimination (Employment and Occupation) Convention, 1958, der International Labour Organisation

Der im Umfang erheblichste Einfluss auf die Gesetzgebung zum Age Discrimination Act 2004 (Cth) kommt im Ergebnis wohl aber der Discrimination (Employment and

88 Bezug zur International Convention on the Elimination of All Forms of Racial Discrimination (CERD).

89 Bezug zur Discrimination (Employment and Occupation) Convention, 1958, of the International Labour Organisation (ILO 111), zum International Covenant on Civil and Political Rights (ICCPR) und International Covenant on Economic, Social and Cultural Rights (ICESCR).

90 Bezug zur UN Declaration of the Rights of the Child, UN Declaration on the Rights of Mentally Retarded Persons und zur UN Declaration on the Rights of Disabled Persons.

Occupation) Convention, 1958, der International Labour Organisation (ILO 111) zu, obwohl in ihr kein ausdrückliches Verbot der Altersdiskriminierung enthalten ist. Vielmehr werden in Art. 1 lit. a) ILO 111 ausdrücklich „nur“ Diskriminierungen aufgrund der Rasse, der Hautfarbe, des Geschlechts, der Religion, der politischen Meinung und der nationalen Abstammung oder sozialen Herkunft verboten.

Aber darüber hinaus dehnt Art. 1 lit. b) ILO 111 die Bedeutung des Begriffs Diskriminierung auch auf solche Unterschiede, Ausschlüsse und Bevorzugungen aus, aufgrund derer eine Chancengleichheit oder eine gleichartige Behandlung in der Beschäftigung oder im Beruf beeinträchtigt oder beseitigt wird. Folglich muss auch das Alter hierunter subsumiert werden und somit zu Recht eine Verbindung zwischen dem Age Discrimination Act 2004 (Cth) und der Discrimination (Employment and Occupation) Convention, 1958, der International Labour Organisation (ILO 111) hergestellt werden.[91]

Erhebliche Bedeutung kommt in dieser Hinsicht vor allem der Auslegung von Gesetzen durch die Rechtsprechung zu.[92] Zwar wird den Gerichten insbesondere eine weite Wortlautauslegung zugebilligt, aber nur solange sie die Grenzen und Regeln internationalen Rechts und internationaler Verpflichtungen bzw. Abkommen Australiens beachten sowie die dort aufgestellten Befreiungen und Ausnahmen angemessen berücksichtigen.[93] Nicht selten wird für die australische Rechtsprechung zur Interpretation und Auslegung des eigenen Rechts und der internationalen Abkommen zusätzlich auf die Empfehlungen der entsprechenden internationalen Ausschüsse hingewiesen. Jedoch handelt es sich dabei lediglich um unverbindliche Empfehlungen, an deren Einhaltung die Gerichte grundsätzlich nicht gebunden sind.[94] Gleichwohl hat sich in der Rechtsprechung eine hohe Akzeptanz der Entscheidungen und der Autorität derartiger Ausschüsse und Komitees herausgebildet. So fließen vor allem die Entscheidungen der Menschenrechtskomitees der Vereinten Nationen ohne weiteres in die Verfahren über Diskriminierungen wegen Alters und auch anderer Faktoren ein.[95]

---

91 International Labour Conference, *Equality in Employment and Occupation: General Survey by the Committee of Experts on the Application of Conventions and Recommendations,* ILO Genf, 1996, S. 246.

92 Vgl. allgemein *Pearce/Geddes*, Statutory Interpretation in Australia, 5.14.

93 *Jumbunna Coal Mine NL v Victorian Coalminers' Association* (1908) 6 CLR 309; *Koowarta v Bjelke-Peterson* (1982) 153 CLR 168; *Minister for Immigration and Ethnic Affairs v Teoh* (1995) 183 CLR 273; *Kartinyeri v Commonwealth* (1998) 195 CLR 337; *Qantas Airways Limited v Christie* (1998) 193 CLR 280.

94 *Burmester*, Impact of Treaties and International Standards, (1995) 17 Sydney Law Review 127.

95 *Evatt*, The Impact of International Human Rights on Domestic Law, in: *Hushcroft/Rishworth*, Litigatin Rights: Perspectives from Domestic and International Law (2002), 258; *Risworth*, The Rule of International Law, in: *Hushcroft/Rishworth*, Litigating Rights: Perspectives from Domestic and International Law (2002), 267; *Joseph*, The International Covenant on Civil and Political Rights: Cases, Materials and Commentary (2004) 24 [1.51]; vgl. auch die Rspr. *Fothergill v Monarch Airlines Ltd* [1981] AC 251, 294-5; *Chan v Minister for Immigration and Ethnic Affairs* (1989) 169 CLR 379; *Somaghi v Minister for Immigration, Local Government and Ethnic Affairs* (1991) 31 FCR 100; *Dietrich v The Queen* (1992) 177 CLR 292; *Mabo v Queensland (No 2)* (1992) 177 CLR 292; *Commonwealth v Bradley* (1999) 95 FCR 218; *Commonwealth v Hamilton* (2000) 108 FCR 378.; *Johnson v Johnson* (2000) 174 ALR 655; *Minister for Immigration and Multicultural and Indigenous Affairs v Al Masri* (2003) 126 FCR 54.

Während die Discrimination (Employment and Occupation) Convention, 1958, der International Labour Organisation (ILO 111) die Mitgliedsstaaten zur Beseitigung von Diskriminierung in Beschäftigung und Beruf wegen verschiedener Umstände verpflichtet, unterstützt der Age Discrimination Act 2004 (Cth) demnach mit dieser verfassungsrechtlichen Grundlage (scheinbar) nur die Verbote von Altersdiskriminierung im Bereich der Arbeit und nur das International Covenant on Economic, Social and Cultural Rights (ICESCR), das International Covenant of Civil and Political Rights (ICCPR) und die Convention on the Rights of the Child (CROC) unterstützen die Beseitigung von Altersdiskriminierung in anderen Bereichen des öffentlichen Lebens.

II. Die Rechtsprechung der Bundesgerichte und ihr Einfluss auf die Gesetzgebungskompetenz des Parlament des Commonwealth

Wie ebenfalls noch zu zeigen sein wird, ist die Gesetzgebungshoheit des Parlament des Commonwealth in Australien aufgrund des „*case law*" ständig einer wesentlichen Beeinflussung durch die Rechtsprechung ausgesetzt. Ebenso gibt es starke Beeinflussungen und Wechselwirkungen innerhalb der Rechtsprechung zu den einzelnen Diskriminierungsgründen. Die Sensibilisierung für einen Blick über den Tellerrand hinaus und eine Betrachtung der Entscheidungen anderer australischen Gerichte zu den jeweiligen Anti-Diskriminierungsrechten, aber auch für die Arbeit, Stellungnahmen und die Ergebnisse aus den *conciliation*-Verfahren der Human Rigths and Equal Opportunity Commission, ist daher in der australischen Rechtswelt stark ausgeprägt.[96]

96 *Bourke/Ronalds*, Discrimination Laws – Striving For Equality, in: *Macken*, The Law of Employment, 2002, 601.

D. Der Age Discrimination Act 2004 (Cth) und sein materieller Regelungsgehalt

In den Jahren 2044/45 wird einer von vier Menschen in Australien älter sein als 65 Jahre. Das bedeutet eine Verdopplung des heute bestehenden Verhältnisses in der australischen Altersstruktur.[97]

> „In 2002, the aged to working-age ratio (the proportion of people aged over 65 to people of traditional labour force age, 15 to 64) is 19 per cent. This is projected to rise to almost 41 per cent by 2042.“98

Die erwartete Entwicklung der australischen Altersstruktur bringt diverse gesellschaftliche aber auch rechtliche Probleme mit sich. Im Fokus der rechtlichen Betrachtung stehen dabei insbesondere die negativen Auswirkungen der Altersdiskriminierung. Denn ohne gegensteuernde Maßnahmen des australischen Gesetzgebers wird sich das Problem der Diskriminierung älterer aber auch junger Menschen verstärken.[99] Deshalb hat sich der australische Gesetzgeber der Bekämpfung von Altersdiskriminierung verschrieben und insbesondere die Unterstützung von älteren Arbeitskräften als ein wichtiges (gesetzgeberischeres) Anliegen hervorgehoben.[100]

Als Antwort auf die alternde Gesellschaft in Australien und die damit verbundenen rechtlichen Probleme im Bereich der Altersdiskriminierung hat der Gesetzgeber des Commonwealth den Age Discrimination Act 2004 (Cth) erlassen. Ob dadurch allerdings in allen Bereichen des öffentlichen Lebens eine Besserung im Umgang mit dem Alter per se eingetreten ist und eintreten wird, ist fraglich, würde den Rahmen der vorliegenden Arbeit sprengen und daher nicht ihr Gegenstand. Vielmehr soll der Schwerpunkt der Arbeit neben den konkreten Zielen des Age Discrimination Act 2004 (Cth) und unter Herausarbeitung des Schutzbereiches, der einzelnen Diskriminierungsverbote sowie auch der zahlreichen Ausnahmen auf den Bereich der Arbeit und Beschäftigung und die dort bestehenden Problemfelder gelenkt werden.

Neben den alltäglichen Problemen mit Bezug zu einer Altersdiskriminierung in der Arbeitswelt, die bereits in der Bewerbungs- und Einstellungsphase beginnen und bekannt sind, existieren darüber hinaus weitere, aber nicht weniger erhebliche Schwie-

---

97 Department of the Treasury (2002), Intergenerational Report 2002-03, Budget Paper No 5 2002-03, 23; *Goward*, The HREOC perspective – Age discrimination and its effects in the Australian community, in: Baker & McKenzie, Age Discrimination: Mitigating Risk in the Workplace, 2; *Ozdowski*, Adressing Age discrimination (2002) 81 Older People and the Law 12.

98 Department of the Treasury (2002), Intergenerational Report 2002-03, Budget Paper No 5 2002-03, 23.

99 Revised Explanatory Memorandum, Age Discrimination Act (Cth) 2004, 5.

100 Revised Explanatory Memorandum, Age Discrimination Act (Cth) 2004, 10; *Smith*, Australian Anti-Discrimination Laws – Framework, Developments and Issues, New Developments in Employment Discrimination Law – The 9 JILPT Comparative Labour Law Seminar (2008) 19.

rigkeiten, die allerdings (noch) nicht im gleichen Maße die Beachtung der Öffentlichkeit finden.[101]

I. Gesetzeszweck und Anwendungsbereich

1. Gesetzeszweck und Aufbau

a. Der Gesetzeszweck

Der Age Discrimination Act 2004 (Cth) soll vor allem helfen, Altersdiskriminierungen zu beseitigen (§ 3 lit. a) ADA) und das Bewusstsein, dass Menschen jeden Alters dieselben Rechte haben, zu stärken (§ 3 lit. b) ADA). Auch sollen im konkreten Einzelfall für Menschen eines bestimmten Alters Vorteile und Unterstützungen gewährt (§ 3 lit. c) ADA), die Wahrnehmung und Akzeptanz der fundamentalen Rechte der Menschen jeden Alters innerhalb der Gesellschaft unterstützt (§ 3 lit. d) ADA) und die Grenzen und Hindernisse von Beteiligungsmöglichkeiten älterer Menschen innerhalb der Gesellschaft beseitigt sowie vorhandene Klischees und Vorurteile gegenüber älteren Menschen ausgeräumt werden (§ 3 lit. e) ADA):[102]

Demnach will dieses Gesetz erreichen, dass eine Diskriminierung aufgrund des Alters – unabhängig davon, ob sie wegen eines hohen oder eines jungen Alters geschieht – in allen Bereichen des öffentlichen Lebens verhindert wird und zugleich soll somit auf Australiens alternde Bevölkerungsstruktur und die damit verbundenen Probleme reagiert werden.[103]

Folglich sind gemäß § 3 lit. a) und b) ADA zwei maßgebliche Ziele hervorzuheben – einerseits die Beseitigung jeglicher Diskriminierung wegen Alters und andererseits die Sicherstellung, dass jedermann trotz unterschiedlichen Alters dieselben Chancen und Rechte innerhalb einer Gemeinschaft haben kann und tatsächlich hat.[104] In der Gesamtschau steht die Gleichstellung („*equality*") von Menschen unterschiedlichen Alters bzw. verschiedener Altersgruppen im Vordergrund.[105]

---

101 Mit Verweis auf die Pflege im Alter und den damit verbundenen Kostenanstieg *Goward*, The HREOC perspective – Age discrimination and its effects in the Australian community, in: Baker & McKenzie, Age Discrimination: Mitigating Risk in the Workplace, S. 2; vgl. auch *Williams*, Significant steps toward a Commonwealth Age Discrimination Act (2002) Older People and the Law 16.

102 Human Rights and Equal Opportunity Commission, Federal Discrimination Law 2009, 1; Human Rights and Equal Opportunity Commission, Federal Discrimination Law 2005, 11.

103 *Goward*, The HREOC perspective – Age discrimination and its effects in the Australian community, in: Baker & McKenzie, Age Discrimination: Mitigating Risk in the Workplace, S. 2, 5; *Smith*, Australian Anti-Discrimination Laws – Framework, Developments and Issues, New Developments in Employment Discrimination Law – The 9 JILPT Comparative Labour Law Seminar (2008) 2.

104 *Louw*, Age Discrimination Act 2004 (Cth) – Application of the Act, in: Baker & McKenzie, Age Discrimination: Mitigating Risk in the Workplace, S. 14.

105 *Smith*, From *Wardley* to *Purvis*: How far has Australian anti-discrimination law come in 30 years? (2008) 21 Australian Journal of Labour Law 3 mit Ausführungen zur *formal* und *sub-*

b. Der Aufbau des Age Discrimination Act 2004 (Cth)

Der Age Discrimination Act 2004 (Cth) stellt die Diskriminierungsformen der direkten und indirekten Diskriminierung zusammen mit zahlreichen Definitionen gleich zu Beginn heraus, bevor der Gesetzgeber aufzeigt, in welchen Bereichen des Lebens eine Diskriminierung wegen Alters unrechtmäßig ist. Insoweit gleicht der Age Discrimination Act 2004 (Cth) der Struktur des Disability Discrimination Act 1992 (Cth) und des Sex Discrimination Act 1984 (Cth).[106]

2. Anwendungsbereich

Nicht nur der noch näher zu betrachtende Kreis der von den zahlreichen Diskriminierungsverboten des Age Discrimination Act 2004 (Cth) betroffenen Normadressaten ist in seinem Umfang sehr weit. Auch die durch die Diskriminierungsverbote konkret zu schützenden Personen und Personengruppen sind zahlreich. Der Age Discrimination Act 2004 (Cth) enthält jedoch keinen gesondert aufgeführten Katalog aller vom persönlichen Schutzbereich erfassten Personen und Personengruppen. Es finden sich nur vereinzelt Regelungen zum geschützten Personenkreis in den jeweiligen Vorschriften über die entsprechenden Diskriminierungsverbote.

Ausgehend von der sehr klar und deutlich umrissenen Zwecksetzung des Age Discrimination Act 2004 (Cth) – Beseitigung jeglicher Diskriminierung wegen Alters und Sicherstellung einer für jedes Alter geltenden Chancengleichheit – sowie der sehr detaillierten Regelung der Diskriminierungsverbote könnte man annehmen, dass auch die Normadressaten deutlich erkennbar bestimmt sind. Zwar finden sich einige der Normadressaten und einzelne sie betreffende Begriffe in den gesetzlichen Regelungen des Age Discrimination Act 2004 (Cth) wieder, aber die konkrete Inhaltsbestimmung überlässt der australische Gesetzgeber der Rechtssprechung.

Feststeht allerdings, dass der Age Discrimination Act 2004 (Cth) gemäß § 3 lit. a) ADA die Diskriminierung wegen Alters nicht nur in den Bereichen der Beschäftigung und des Berufs, sondern in vielerlei Gebieten des öffentlichen Lebens verbietet.[107]

Dorthin gehören grundsätzlich zwar auch die Arbeit und die Beschäftigung, aber zugleich ebenso diejenigen Bereiche der Bildung, der Unterkunft und Unterbringung, des Zugangs zu Gütern, der Dienstleistungen und Einrichtungen, der Veräußerung von

---

stantive equality; vgl. auch *Smith*, Australian Anti-Discrimination Laws – Framework, Developments and Issues, New Developments in Employment Discrimination Law – The 9 JILPT Comparative Labour Law Seminar (2008) 10.

106 Human Rights and Equal Opportunity Commission, Federal Discrimination Law 2009, 2; Human Rights and Equal Opportunity Commission, Federal Discrimination Law 2005, 12.

107 Im Vergleich hierzu ist in Europa der Anwendungsbereich der Rahmenrichtlinie Beschäftigung RL 2000/78/EG begrenzt auf Beruf und Beschäftigung; allerdings hat die Kommission der Europäischen Gemeinschaften am 2. Juli 2008 einen Vorschlag für eine ergänzende Richtlinie zur Anwendung des Grundsatzes der Gleichbehandlung und der damit verbundenen Erfassung von Diskriminierungen in sämtlichen Bereichen außerhalb von Beruf und Beschäftigung vorgelegt (dieser Vorschlag wurde im April 2009 innerhalb des Europäischen Parlaments angenommen, wobei abschließende Erörterungen im Rat noch ausstehen).

Land, der Verwaltung und Ausübung des Rechts und von Programmen des Commonwealth und der Nachfrage nach Informationen. Der Age Discrimination Act 2004 (Cth) hat somit aufgrund des weiten sachlichen Anwendungsbereichs nicht nur, aber insbesondere auch, Auswirkungen auf die Vorsorge und mögliche Vorkehrungen gegen Altersdiskriminierungen im Rahmen der Arbeit und Beschäftigung.[108]

Der Anwendungsbereich des Age Discrimination Act 2004 (Cth) ist auch dann eröffnet, wenn Diskriminierungen aufgrund verschiedener Motivationen vorgenommen werden, aber zumindest eine Diskriminierung wegen Alters eine maßgebliche Rolle spielt. Heutzutage kommt es hierfür auf die Betrachtung der im konkreten Einzelfall vorliegenden Diskriminierungen und ihrer Qualität an. Bis zum Jahre 1990 gab es – nach dem Vorbild des Racial Discrimination Act 1975 (Cth) – ein vorgeschriebenes Testverfahren (*„dominant purpose test"*), welches nach Ansicht des Senate Legal and Constitutional Legislation Committee als zu streng, zu unpraktisch und im Ergebnis zu wenig einzelfallorientiert kritisiert wurde und deshalb von der weiteren Anwendung abgesehen wird.[109] Wie allerdings nachfolgend zu zeigen ist, wird beim Vorliegen mehrerer Diskriminierungsgründe noch immer versucht anhand des sog. *„dominant reason test"* ein Anwendungsvorrang zu erreichen.

Zwar enthält der Age Discrimination Act 2004 (Cth) eine Fülle von Diskriminierungsverboten und sogar Straftatbeständen, diese gelten aber in der Regel nicht absolut. Vielmehr existieren im Age Discrimination Act 2004 (Cth) auch zahlreiche, entweder in den einzelnen Diskriminierungsverboten oder gesondert geregelte, Ausnahmen.110 Darüber hinaus ist festzuhalten, dass nicht per se jede Altersdiskriminierung eine Straftat im Sinne des Age Discrimination Act 2004 (Cth) darstellt, § 49 ADA.

a. Das Arbeits- und Beschäftigungsverhältnis und sein weites Ver ständnis im Sinne des Age Discrimination Act 2004 (Cth)

Grundlegende Bedeutung zur Bestimmung des persönlichen Schutzbereichs sowie der Normadressaten kommt dabei dem Begriff des Arbeitsverhältnisses und der Beschäftigung (*„employment"*) zu. Der Gesetzgeber hat in § 5 ADA die Beschäftigung wie folgt definiert:

> „...employment includes:
> part-time and temporary employment; and
> work under a contract for services; and
> work as a Commonwealth employee; and
> work as an employee of a State or an instrumentality of a State."

108 Nicht erfasst wird jedoch der Bereich der ehrenamtlichen Tätigkeit und der Tätigkeit im privaten Haushalt, § 18 Abs. 3 ADA.

109 *Louw*, Age Discrimination Act 2004 (Cth) – Application of the Act, in: Baker & McKenzie, Age Discrimination: Mitigating Risk in the Workplace, S. 17.

110 *Smith*, Australian Anti-Discrimination Laws – Framework, Developments and Issues, New Developments in Employment Discrimination Law – The 9 JILPT Comparative Labour Law Seminar (2008) 4.

Danach wird deutlich, dass dem Beschäftigungsbegriff des Age Discrimination Act 2004 (Cth) ein weites Verständnis zu Grunde gelegt werden muss. Denn er umfasst nahezu jegliche denkbare Form der Arbeit.[111] So zählt eine abhängige Beschäftigung – egal ob als Teilzeitbeschäftigung oder in Form einer befristeten Anstellung – ebenso wie eine selbständige Tätigkeit als Beschäftigung im Sinne von § 5 ADA. Die in § 5 ADA enthaltene Definition zum Begriff der Beschäftigung erfasst zudem die Teilzeitarbeit genauso wie eine befristete berufliche Tätigkeit, die Arbeit aufgrund eines Arbeitsvertrages, die Arbeit als Angestellter im öffentlichen Dienst des Commonwealth sowie eines Bundesstaates oder seiner Institutionen.[112] Obwohl in § 5 ADA nicht alle Bedeutungen ausdrücklich erwähnt werden, herrscht Einigkeit darüber, dass insbesondere auch die berufliche Tätigkeit und Beschäftigung im privaten Bereich eingeschlossen sein soll.[113] Denn vielmehr sollte mit dieser gesetzlichen Regelung bezweckt werden, dass spezielle Beschäftigungsbereiche erfasst und ausdrücklich dem Geltungsbereich des Age Discrimination Act 2004 (Cth) zugeordnet werden, anstatt eine als abschließend zu verstehende Regelung aufzustellen, die somit zahlreiche weitere Beschäftigungsbereiche ausschließen würde.[114]

Allerdings erscheint die Begriffsdefinition des Gesetzgebers etwas ungenau. Dies hat er erkannt und führt daher in der Gesetzesbegründung erläuternd aus, dass die Definitionsbeispiele keinen abschließenden Charakter haben, sondern vor allem Spezialbereiche ausdrücklich erfasst werden sollen und daher auch nicht erwähnte Tätigkeitsbereiche umfasst sein müssten.[115] Folglich fällt daher auch die zuvor erwähnte Beschäftigung im privaten Bereich nach Ansicht des Gesetzgebers in den Anwendungsbereich des Age Discrimination Act 2004 (Cth).[116]

Die Notwendigkeit einer weiten Auslegung wird dabei auch durch die Einbeziehung der Discrimination (Employment and Occupation) Convention, 1958, der International Labour Organisation (ILO 111) zusätzlich hervorgehoben. Denn durch die Einbeziehung und den Rückgriff auf die internationalen Instrumente im australischen Altersdiskriminierungsrecht, hier Art. 1 Abs. 3 ILO 111, zählen zur Beschäftigung im Sinne des § 5 ADA auch die Bewerbungs- und Trainingsphasen sowie im konkreten Einzelfall aufgestellte Bedingungen und Anforderungen:[117]

---

111 *Bourke/Ronalds*, Discrimination Laws – Striving For Equality, in: *Macken*, The Law of Employment, 2002, 618; *Ratnam*, Federal Government's proposed age discrimination legislation (2003) 9 Employment Law Bulletin 15.

112 *Ratnam*, Federal Government's proposed age discrimination legislation (2003) 9 Employment Law Bulletin 16.

113 Explanatory Memorandum of the Age Discrimination Bill 2003 (Cth), Annexure C, Clause 5, Definitions.

114 *Louw*, Age Discrimination Act 2004 (Cth) – Application of the Act, in: Baker & McKenzie, Age Discrimination: Mitigating Risk in the Workplace, S. 19.

115 *Louw*, Age Discrimination Act 2004 (Cth) – Application of the Act, in: Baker & McKenzie, Age Discrimination: Mitigating Risk in the Workplace, S. 19.

116 Explanatory Memorandum of the Age Discrimination Bill 2003 (Cth), Annexure C, Clause 5, Definitions.

117 *Thew*, Comparisons between the Australian jurisdictions, in: Baker & McKenzie, Age Discrimination: Mitigating Risk in the Workplace, S. 56.

„...the terms employment and occupation include access to vocational training, access to employment and particular occupations, and terms and conditions of employment.“

Zwar sollte zuerst der Bereich der unbezahlten Tätigkeit, wie sie im Rahmen von Praktika erbracht wird, nicht vom Beschäftigungsbegriff des Age Discrimination Act 2004 (Cth) erfasst werden.[118] Vor dem Hintergrund, dass der Age Discrimination Act 2004 (Cth) aber einen sehr weiteren Schutzbereich aufweist und in der Literatur und Rechtsprechung darüber hinaus zu einer weiten (Begriffs-)Auslegung tendiert wird sowie Art. 1 Abs. 3 ILO 111 auch die unbezahlte Arbeit – wie etwa ein Praktikum – umfasst, sollte konsequenterweise der Beschäftigungsbegriff erweitert werden. Auch wenn der Wortlaut des § 5 ADA hierzu keine Aussage trifft, da die Entgeltlichkeit der Tätigkeit nicht erwähnt wird, spricht vor allem auch der hinter dem Gesetzeszweck stehende Schutzgedanke für die hier vertretene Auffassung.[119]

b. Die einzelnen Beschäftigungsformen im Anwendungsbereich des Age Discrimination Act 2004 (Cth)

aa. *Entgeltliche Beschäftigung im Rahmen einer unselbständigen Tätigkeit*

(1) Arbeitnehmer und Angestellte

Auch im Common Law wird zwischen einer unselbständigen und selbständigen Tätigkeit unterschieden. Dabei setzt das Arbeitsverhältnis im Rahmen einer unselbständigen Tätigkeit ein Über- und Unterordnungsverhältnis sowie einen bestehenden Arbeitsvertrag zwischen der Person voraus, die für die Arbeit bezahlt – Arbeitgeber – und derjenigen Person, welche die jeweilige Arbeit ausführt – Arbeitnehmer.[120] Somit sind im Common Law zwar diverse Bereiche vom Begriff des Arbeitsverhältnisses und der Beschäftigung grundsätzlich ausgeschlossen. Nicht umfasst werden demnach alle unentgeltlichen Arbeitverhältnisse, die gewöhnlich ohne Vergütung stattfinden, wie etwa ein Praktikum oder eine ehrenamtliche Tätigkeit.[121] Aufgrund der Gleichrangigkeit zwischen dem Arbeitgeber und einem freiem unabhängigen Mitarbeiter ist die Mitarbeit im Rahmen eines solchen freien Beschäftigungsverhältnisses grundsätzlich ebenfalls nicht erfasst.[122]

Diese Unterscheidung ist auf das Prinzip der Haftung für fremdes Verschulden („*vicarious liability*“) zurückzuführen.[123] Denn seit dem 19. Jahrhundert hat sich im

---

118 Vgl. die Darstellung bei *Ratnam*, Federal Government's proposed age discrimination legislation (2003) 9 Employment Law Bulletin 16.

119 Vgl. auch zum Begriff der Beschäftigung („*employment*“) und der Einbeziehung der unentgeltlichen Tätigkeit *Stewart*, Redefining Employment? Meeting the Challenge of Contract and Agency Labour (2002) 15 Australian Journal of Labour Law 235.

120 *Stewart*, Redefining Employment? Meeting the Challenge of Contract and Agency Labour, Australian Journal of Labour Law (2002) 15.

121 *Teen Ranch Pty Ltd v Brown* (1995) 87 IR 308.

122 *Clark v Evans* (1989) 32 AILR 352.

123 *Bourke/Ronalds*, Discrimination Laws – Striving For Equality, in: *Macken*, The Law of Employment, 2002, 640.

Common Law das Grundprinzip herausgebildet, dass ein Arbeitgeber im Außenverhältnis nur für das Verhalten und die Handlung eines in seinem Schutz- und Einflussbereich stehenden Arbeitnehmers verantwortlich sein kann. Dagegen übernimmt er keinerlei Verantwortung für jegliches Verhalten eines zwar für ihn Arbeit verrichtenden, aber vertraglich vollständig unabhängigen Vertragspartner.[124] In der Rechtspraxis ist – wie nachfolgend noch aufgezeigt wird – die Unterscheidung zwischen einem unselbständig beschäftigten Arbeitnehmer und einem Selbständigen jedoch grundsätzlich schwierig, da der Arbeitgeber beide Personengruppen oftmals gleich behandelt.[125]

Um eine verlässliche Abgrenzung zwischen der nichtselbständigen und somit weisungsgebundenen und der selbständigen Tätigkeit vornehmen zu können, fehlt (auch) im australischen Arbeitsrecht die Rückgriffsmöglichkeit auf eine allgemeingültige Definition im Gesetz.[126] Vielmehr existieren lediglich von der Rechtsprechung zur Abgrenzung zu beachtende Kriterien.[127] So ist anhand eines von der Rechtsprechung aufgestellten Tests herauszufinden, in welchem Umfang der Arbeitgeber Einfluss und Kontrolle auf den Arbeitnehmer hat:[128]

Kriterium	Nichtselbständige Tätigkeit	Selbständige Tätigkeit
Ist die Person in die Arbeitsorganisation eingebunden?	Ja	
Hat die Person Werkzeug oder Ausrüstung bereitzustellen?		Ja
Wird die Person bei Abschluss der Arbeit oder nach Zeit bezahlt?		Ja
Trägt die Person ein finanzielles oder wirtschaftliches Risiko oder profitiert sie vom Gewinn?		Ja

124 *Quarman v Burnett* (1840) 6 M & W 499; 151 ER 509.

125 *Broadwater Taxation & Investment Services Pty Ltd v Hendriks* (1993) 51 IR 221; *Fortuity Pty Ltd v Barcza* (1995) 32 IPR 517.; *Wesoky v Village Cinemas International Pty Ltd* [2001] FCA 32.

126 *R v Allan; Ex parte Australian Mutual Provident Society Ltd* (1977) 16 SASR 237; *Australian Mutual Provident Society Ltd v Chaplin* (1978) 18 ALR 385; *Sammartino v Mayne Nickless* (2000) 98 IR 168; *Ermogenous v Greek Orthodox Community of SA Inc* (2002) 187 ALR 92.

127 Vgl. etwa *Stevens v Brodribb Sawmilling Co Pty Ltd* (1986) 160 CLR 16; 63 ALR 513.

128 *Stewart*, Redefining Employment? Meeting the Challenge of Contract and Agency Labour, Australian Journal of Labour Law (2002) 15.

Steht es der Peron frei, zur gleichen Zeit auch für jemand anderen zu arbeiten?		Ja
Kann die Person die Arbeit weiterdelegieren oder weiter geben?		Ja
Wird vom Entgelt der Person eine Steuer direkt vom Arbeitgeber abgeführt?	Ja	
Ist die Person für die Absicherung des Arbeitsrisikos verantwortlich?		Ja
Wird der Person Urlaub oder bei Krankheit Entgeltfort-Zahlung gewährt?	Ja	

Je mehr demnach eine Person in den Organisationsbereich und die Weisungsebene eingebunden ist, umso wahrscheinlicher ist seine rechtliche Charakterisierung als Arbeitnehmer. Zwar ist fraglich, wie sich das Zusammentreffen von mehreren der vorgenannten Kriterien auswirkt. Aufgrund der zahlreichen Rechtsprechung steht aber fest, dass der persönlichen Erbringung der Arbeitsleistung wesentliche Bedeutung zukommt.[129]

Danach ist beispielsweise die Tätigkeit eines Fahrers etwa dann als selbständige Tätigkeit und gerade nicht als abhängige Beschäftigung einzuordnen, wenn es dem Fahrer erlaubt ist, bei Verhinderung oder Krankheit einen Ersatz zu benennen. Hier fehlt es an der persönlichen Erbringung der geschuldeten Tätigkeit:

> „The fact that any substitute driver had to be approved by the companyy does not give the respondent control over the delegation. In terms of the contract I don't believe approval of an appropriate person was such an unreasonable condition, the company surely had the right to be confident that any substitute driver was competent to do the work and maintain the integrity of the company as Mr Coombs [the company's State Manager] put it. What must not be forgotten is that it would have been Mr Bowerman's responsibility to seek a replacement if necessary (or indeed have someone else do part of his work on a permanent basis and take a reduced profit). This is not the action of an employee.“[130]

129 *Express & Echo Publications Ltd v Tanton* [1999] ICR 693; *Bowerman v Sinclair Halvorsen Pty Ltd* [1999] NSWIRComm 21.

130 *Bowerman v Sinclair Halverson Pty Ltd* {1999] NSWIRComm 21.

In Einzelfällen kann die Arbeitnehmereigenschaft aber selbst dann noch bejaht werden, wenn die Arbeit nicht persönlich erbracht werden muss, als Ersatz aber nur eine Person nach Wahl des Arbeitgebers – etwa aufgrund einer von diesem aufgestellten internen Personalliste – erlaubt und diese vom Arbeitgeber direkt bezahlt wird.[131]

Trotz der teilweise schwierigen Abgrenzung zwischen Arbeitnehmer und Selbständigem ist es für die Einordnung gänzlich unerheblich, wie die Parteien die Art der Beschäftigung tatsächlich im Vertrag bezeichnen.[132]

> „...The parties cannot create something which has every feature of a rooster, but call it a duck and insist that everybody else recognise it as a duck.“[133]

Denn würde man diese – zugegebenermaßen sehr einfache Lösung – ohne weiteres zulassen, so wären zahlreiche aus der nichtselbständigen Tätigkeit resultierende Rechte ausgeschlossen und somit etwa ein Anspruch auf Urlaub etc. verwehrt. Allerdings wird von der australischen Rechtsprechung häufig gegen diesen Grundsatz verstoßen, indem sich die Gerichte vorwiegend an den Formulierungen, Begriffen und Vereinbarungen im jeweiligen Arbeitsvertrag anstatt an der tatsächlichen Ausgestaltung des Beschäftigungsverhältnisses orientieren.[134] Aber gerade die wirtschaftliche Abhängigkeit vom Arbeitgeber und deren konkrete Ausgestaltung kann nur dann hinreichend berücksichtigt werden, wenn die tatsächlichen und nicht lediglich die im Vertrag vereinbarten Gegebenheiten in die Beurteilung einbezogen werden.

> „Some difficulty my arise where the practical constraints on a party conflict with the express stipulations in the contract. For instance, a party may be described as an independent contractor, and the contract may even provide expressly that he or she is at liberty to provide service to other persons, outside the contract. The reality may be that economic considerations dictate the work will only be accepted from the other party to the contract... In such circumstances, there is no particular reason why a court should ignore the pracitcal circumstances, and cling to the theoretical niceties. The level of economic dependence of one party upon another, and the manner in which that economic dependence may be exploited, will always be relevant factors in the determination whether a particular contract is one of employment.“ [135]

---

131 *Mc Farlane v Glasgow City Council* [2001] IRLR 7; vgl. auch *Byrne Bros (Formwork) Ltd v Baird* [2002] ICR 667.

132 *Australian Mutual Provident Society Ltd v Chaplin (1978) 18 ALR 385*; *Konrad v Victoria Police* (1999) 91 FCR 95; *Bearings Inc (Australia) Pty Ltd v Treloar* (1999) 95 IR 169; *Merceica v Wade* [2000] SACS 441; *Textile, Clothing and Footwear Union of Australia v Givoni Pty Ltd* [2002] FCA 1406.

133 *Re Porter* (1989) 34 IR 179; ebenso *Transport Workers Union of Australia v Glynburn Contractors (Salisbury) Pty Ltd* (1990) 34 IR 138.

134 *Vabu Pty Ltd v Commissioner of Taxation* (1996) 81 IR 150; *Australian Liquor, Hospitality and Miscellaneous Workers Union, Queensland Branch, Union of Employees v Bark Australia Pty Ltd* [2001] QIRComm 22.

135 *Re Porter* (1989) 34 IR 179; ebenso *Transport Workers Union of Australia v Glynburn Contractors (Salisbury) Pty Ltd* (1990) 34 IR 138.

Aufgrund des oben angesprochenen weiten Verständnisses des Begriffs des Arbeits- und Beschäftigungsverhältnis im Sinne von § 5 ADA ist eine genaue Abgrenzung im Einzelfall jedoch nicht erforderlich.[136] Denn feststeht, dass die unselbständig und weisungsgebundenen Beschäftigten – Arbeitnehmer und Angestellte – in den Anwendungsbereich des Age Discrimination Act 2004 (Cth) fallen. Zwar wird aus der gesetzlichen Regelung des umfassenden Diskriminierungsverbotes des § 18 Abs. 1 und Abs. 2 ADA für den Bereich der Beschäftigung und der Arbeit allein aus dem Wortlaut nicht deutlich, welchen konkreten Rahmen der persönliche Schutzbereich erfahren soll. Denn dort ist allgemein nur von einer Person die Rede *(„against a person")*. Die Begriffe des Arbeitnehmers bzw. Angestellten werden nicht ausdrücklich aufgegriffen. Da das Diskriminierungsverbot des § 18 Abs. 1 und Abs. 2 ADA letztlich aber den Bereich der Beschäftigung und der Arbeit gezielt und umfassend betrifft, müssen Arbeitnehmer und Angestellte von seinem persönlichen Schutzbereich erfasst werden, um die Vorschrift nicht leer laufen zu lassen. Demnach ist insbesondere die nichtselbständige und somit arbeitsvertraglich weisungsgebundene Beschäftigung erfasst.

Gemäß § 18 Abs. 1 ADA ist es für einen Arbeitgeber oder eine andere Person, die wie ein Arbeitgeber handelt oder dazu befugt ist, rechtswidrig, jemanden aufgrund seines Alters schon während der Vorbereitungen über die Festlegung oder bei der Bestimmung selbst (§ 18 Abs. 1 lit. a) ADA), wem eine bestimmte berufliche Tätigkeit angeboten werden soll (§ 18 Abs. 1 lit. b) ADA) oder aber durch die Festlegung von bestimmten mit dem Beschäftigungsangebot verbundenen Bedingungen und Anforderungen (§ 18 Abs. 1 lit. c) ADA) zu diskriminieren.

Dabei kommt vor allem den Begriffen der Bedingungen und Anforderungen ein umfassender Anwendungsbereich zu, da dadurch jegliche Bereiche des Beschäftigungsverhältnisses betroffen sein können und nicht auf bestimmte Formulierungen im Arbeitsvertrag beschränkt werden.[137] Umfasst sind demnach auch die vertragliche Vereinbarung von besonderen mit der jeweiligen Beschäftigung verbundenen Leistungen und Vergünstigungen sowie aus dieser resultierenden Ansprüchen und Auflagen.

Darüber hinaus ist es einem Arbeitgeber oder einer anderen Person, die wie ein Arbeitgeber handelt oder dazu befugt ist, gemäß § 18 Abs. 2 ADA untersagt, jemanden aufgrund seines Alters durch bestimmte Beschäftigungsbedingungen und – anforderungen (§ 18 Abs. 2 lit. a) ADA), durch die Weigerung dem Arbeitnehmer den Zugang zu Ausbildungs- und Weiterbildungsmöglichkeiten und anderen mit der Beschäftigung in Verbindung stehenden Unterstützungen zu verwehren (§ 18 Abs. 2 lit. b) ADA), durch eine Entlassung des Arbeitnehmers (§ 18 Abs. 2 lit. c) ADA) oder durch jegliche andere Nachteilszufügung (§ 18 lit. d) ADA) zu diskriminieren.

(2) Überlassene Arbeitnehmer

Ausdrücklich aufgrund der vertraglichen Regelung in § 20 Abs. 1 und Abs. 4 ADA vom persönlichen Schutzbereich erfasst, werden die Vertragsarbeiter (*„contract workers"*). Dabei handelt es sich, wie bereits dargestellt, gemäß der Definition des § 20

---

136 *Stewart*, Redefining Employment? Meeting the Challenge of Contract and Agency Labour (2002) 15 Australian Journal of Labour Law 235.

137 *Allders International Pty Ltd v Anstee* (1986) 5 NSWLR 47.

Abs. 4 ADA um Personen, die für einen Arbeitgeber tätig sind und von diesem aufgrund eines Vertrages an eine weitere Person zur Arbeit vermittelt und überlassen werden. Ein typische Beispiel eines Vertragsarbeiters im Sinne von § 20 ADA ist der seitens einer (privaten) Arbeitsvermittlung tätige Arbeitnehmer.[138]

Auch die Altersdiskriminierung von Vertragsarbeitern ist unter vergleichbaren Voraussetzungen wie in den § 18 Abs. 1 und 2 sowie § 19 Abs. 1 und 2 ADA untersagt, § 20 Abs. 1 ADA. So ist es dem Geschäftsherrn (*„principal"*) nicht erlaubt, einen Vertragsarbeiter aufgrund seines Alters zu diskriminieren, indem er wegen Alters bestimmte Bedingungen und Anforderungen festsetzt, unter denen der Vertragsarbeiter für ihn arbeiten soll (§ 20 Abs. 1 lit. a) ADA), er es dem Vertragsarbeiter untersagt zu arbeiten oder seine Arbeit fortzusetzen (§ 20 Abs. 1 lit. b) ADA), sich weigert dem Vertragsarbeiter den Zugang zu Ausbildungs- und Weiterbildungsmöglichkeiten und anderen mit der Beschäftigung in Verbindung stehenden Unterstützungen zu gewähren (§ 20 Abs. 1 lit. c) ADA) oder er dem Vertragsarbeiter auf sonstige Art und Weise Nachteil zufügt (§ 20 Abs. 1 lit. d) ADA). Gemäß § 20 Abs. 4 ADA ist der Geschäftsherr im Verhältnis zum Vertragsarbeiter diejenige Person, für die der Vertragsarbeiter aufgrund einer vertraglichen Vereinbarung zwischen seinem Arbeitgeber und der als Geschäftsherr auftretenden Person tätig wird.

(3) Bewerbungs- und Vorstellungsphase als Beschäftigung

Zum Bereich der Beschäftigung und der Arbeit gehört zudem auch der Bereich im Vorfeld dieser, also die Bewerbungs- und Vorstellungsphase. Aufgrund der eindeutig in § 18 Abs. 1 und Abs. 2 ADA definierten Diskriminierungshandlungen wird ersichtlich, dass auch die Bewerber zum geschützten Personenbereich zählen müssen.[139]

Besondere Bedeutung kommt hinsichtlich der Bewerbungs- und Vorstellungsphase für eine Arbeits- und Beschäftigungstätigkeit dem Diskriminierungsverbot des § 32 ADA zu, wonach es rechtswidrig ist, Personen eines bestimmten Alters Fragen zu stellen, die anderen Personen eines anderen Alters nicht gestellt worden wären (*„request for information"*). Denn nicht selten sehen sich zukünftige Arbeitnehmer rechtlich unzulässigen Fragen ausgesetzt und müssen bei der Verweigerung einer wahrheitsgemäßen Antwort um die Anstellung fürchten.

Nicht immer auf der Hand liegend, aber dennoch von praktischer Relevanz ist die Problematik der unzulässigen Fragestellungen darüber hinaus insbesondere in Bezug auf die Gesundheit und mögliche Erkrankungen von älteren Arbeitnehmern.[140] Allerdings soll nach der gesetzgeberischen Absicht das Diskriminierungsverbot des § 32 ADA nicht nur im Bereich von Arbeit und Beschäftigung gelten, sondern vielmehr umfassend wirken und somit alle Bereiche erfassen, in denen sich eine Person Fragen

138 Explanatory Memorandum of the Age Discrimination Bill 2003 (Cth), Annexure C, Clause 19, Discrimination against commission agents.

139 Vgl. auch Explanatory Memorandum of the Age Discrimination Bill 2003 (Cth), Annexure C, Clause 18, Discrimination in employment.

140 Explanatory Memorandum of the Age Discrimination Bill 2003 (Cth), Annexure C, Clause 32, Requests for information.

ausgesetzt sieht, die ihr gerade aufgrund ihres Alters gestellt werden und die möglicherweise eine Wirkung auf zukünftige Umstände haben können.[141]

bb. Die Erwerbstätigkeit außerhalb eines unselbständigen Beschäftigungsverhält nisses

(1) Selbständige und Freiberufler

In der Abgrenzung zu den weisungsgebundenen Arbeitnehmern und Angestellten stellt sich die Frage, ob auch Selbständige, Freiberufler und Gewerbetreibende aufgrund einer (weiteren) ausdrücklichen gesetzlichen Regelung des Age Discrimination Act 2004 (Cth) vom persönlichen Schutzbereich erfasst werden.[142] Für eine solche Annahme könnte vor allem das Diskriminierungsverbot des § 22 Abs. 1 ADA sprechen. Denn die gesetzliche Regelung des § 22 Abs. 1 ADA soll gerade vor einer Altersdiskriminierung schützen, die dadurch erfolgt, dass die Ausübung eines bestimmten Berufs, die Errichtung einer zur Berufsausübung erforderlichen Praxis oder die Errichtung und der Betrieb eines Gewerbes nicht stattfinden können, weil die dafür vorausgesetzte Einwilligung oder Berechtigung nicht erteilt, nicht erneuert, nicht im begehrten Maße erweitert oder sogar aufgehoben oder zurückgenommen wird.[143] Zwar kann die Frage der grundsätzlichen Berufsausübung auch einen Arbeitnehmer oder Angestellten betreffen, aber die typischerweise vom Regelungsbereich des § 22 Abs. 1 ADA geschützte Person, arbeitet in der Regel selbständig oder freiberuflich.

(2) Arbeitgeber und arbeitgeberähnliche Personen

Zwar enthält das Diskriminierungsverbot des § 18 Abs. 1 ADA für den Bereich der Beschäftigung und Arbeit den Begriff des Arbeitgebers („*employer*"). Aber aus der bloßen Begriffsnennung ist es nicht möglich eine Schlussfolgerung vorzunehmen, um feststellen zu können, welche Personen im konkreten Fall als Arbeitgeber angesehen werden können. Zur Präzisierung des Arbeitgeberbegriffs bedarf es daher – wie so oft im Common Law – des Rückgriffs auf die Rechtsprechung. Gemäß § 8 ADA kann das Commonwealth zumindest für beim Commonwealth beschäftigte Personen als Arbeitgeber angesehen werden. Folglich unterliegen somit neben den privaten Arbeitgebern auch große Teile der öffentlichen Hand in ihrer Eigenschaft als Arbeitgeber dem Diskriminierungsverbot des § 18 Abs. 1 ADA, so dass auch sie als Normadressat verpflichtet werden können.

Gleiches gilt für die Personen im Sinne des § 18 Abs. 1 ADA, die wie ein Arbeitgeber handeln oder zu einem solchen Handeln befugt sind, sog. arbeitgeberähnliche Personen („*person acting or purporting to act on behalf of an employer*").

---

141 Explanatory Memorandum of the Age Discrimination Bill 2003 (Cth), Annexure C, Clause 32, Requests for information.

142 Vgl. zur weiten Auslegung des Begriffs des Arbeits- und Beschäftigungsverhältnisses im Sinne von § 5 ADA die Ausführungen unter D. I. 2. a.

143 Explanatory Memorandum of the Age Discrimination Bill 2003 (Cth), Annexure C, Clause 22, Qualifying bodies.

(3) Geschäftsherr

Die Diskriminierungsverbote der §§ 19 Abs. 1 und Abs. 2, 20 Abs. 1 ADA verwenden den Begriff des Geschäftsherrn (*„prinicpal"*), erläutern ihn aber nicht näher. Eine Definition findet sich einerseits aber in § 19 Abs. 5 ADA wieder, nach welcher der Geschäftsherr diejenige Person ist, für die ein Vertreter oder Bevollmächtigter der Human Rights and Equal Opportunity Commission (*„commission agent"*) – eine Definition hierzu ist ebenfalls in § 19 Abs. 5 ADA enthalten – tätig ist. Darüber hinaus findet sich eine weitere Definition – wie auch für den Begriff des Vertragsarbeiters (*„contract worker"*) – in § 20 Abs. 4 ADA.

Ebenso findet sich der Begriff des Geschäftsherrn noch in weiteren Diskriminierungsverboten wieder. So spricht etwa auch § 30 Abs. 1 ADA vom Geschäftsherrn, ohne dass in dieser gesetzlichen Regelung aber eine nähere Definition vorgenommen wird. Unter Berücksichtigung der vorgenannten Begriffsbestimmungen in den §§ 19 Abs. 5 und 20 Abs. 4 ADA kann zusammenfassend aber festgestellt werden, dass ein Geschäftsherr im Grunde immer diejenige Person ist, die für eine andere Person – der Geschäftsführer – ein Geschäft führt.

c. Weitere verwandte Anwendungsbereiche mit Bezug zu einen Ar beits- und Beschäftigungsverhältnis

aa. Gewerkschaften, Arbeitgeber- und Berufsverbände, ihre Organe und Mitglieder

Durch das Diskriminierungsverbot des § 23 Abs. 1 ADA werden bestimmte Organisationen und Vereinigungen sowie auch ihre Leitungsorgane als Normadressaten deutlich herausgestellt und folglich verpflichtet.

Zu den Organisationen und Vereinigungen im Sinne von § 23 Abs. 1 ADA zählen gemäß § 23 Abs. 3 ADA all diejenigen, die in der Auflistung Nr. 1 B des Workplace Relations Act 1996 (Cth) abschließend genannt werden. Insbesondere und für das Arbeitsrecht besonders bedeutend sind dabei Gewerkschaften und Arbeitgebervertretungen. Als Leitungsorgan wird aufgrund der Definition in § 23 Abs. 3 ADA diejenige Gruppe oder dasjenige Gremium angesehen, dass die Angelegenheiten der betreffenden Organisation bzw. Vereinigung im Einzelfall leitend ausführt.

Weiterhin zählen gemäß § 23 Abs. 1 und Abs. 2 ADA zukünftige und aktuelle Mitglieder von den in der Auflistung Nr. 1 B des Workplace Relations Act 1996 (Cth) genannten Organisationen und Vereinigungen zum geschützten Personenbereich.

Gemäß § 23 Abs. 1 ADA sind die zuvor in Bezug genommenen Organisationen und Vereinigungen, ihre Leitungsorgane und auch die einzelnen Mitglieder der Leitungsorgane verpflichtet, Diskriminierungen anderer Personen aufgrund deren Alters zu unterlassen. Denn Handlungen und Verhaltensweisen, die einer Person aufgrund ihres Alters den Zugang zur Mitgliedschaft verwehren (§ 23 Abs. 1 lit. a) ADA) oder die aufgrund dessen bestimmte Bedingungen und Anforderungen an eine Mitgliedschaft stellen (§ 23 Abs. 1 lit. b) ADA), sind wegen Altersdiskriminierung rechtswidrig.

bb. Öffentlich-rechtliche Einrichtungen des Commonwealth

Darüber hinaus wendet sich der Age Discrimination Act 2004 (Cth) mit dem in § 31 Abs. 1 ADA enthaltenen speziellen Diskriminierungsverbot auch an die öffentliche Hand des Commonwealth (*„Administration of Commonwealth Laws and Programs"*). Genauer betrachtet wird als Normadressat aber derjenige Mitarbeiter des Commonwealth verpflichtet, der gemäß § 31 Abs. 1 lit. a) ADA eine Funktion innerhalb des Commonwealth bekleidet oder dem gemäß § 31 Abs. 1 lit. b) ADA in sonstiger Weise Verantwortung bei der Verwaltung oder Durchführung des Rechts des Commonwealth zukommt.

In diesem Zusammenhang bedeutsam ist das Diskriminierungsverbot des § 31 Abs. 1 ADA, wonach es jedem Mitarbeiter, der innerhalb der Reichweite des Rechts des Commonwealth oder von Programmen des Commonwealth eine Funktion bekleidet (§ 31 Abs. 1 lit. a) ADA) oder dem in sonstiger Weise Verantwortung bei der Verwaltung oder Durchführung des Rechts des Commonwealth zukommt (§ 31 Abs. 1 lit. b) ADA), verboten ist, in diesem Bereich eine Person aufgrund ihres Alters zu diskriminieren. Als Programme des Commonwealth gelten dabei solche Programme, welche durch oder zugunsten der Regierung des Commonwealth durchgeführt werden, § 31 Abs. 2 ADA.

Des Weiteren zählen auch die Vertreter und Beschäftigten der Human Rights and Equal Opportunity Commission zum vom Age Discrimination Act 2004 (Cth) geschützten Personenkreis. Aufgrund der klaren Definition in § 19 Abs. 5 ADA, werden unter diesem Begriff alle Personen verstanden, die für eine andere Person – den Geschäftsherrn – als deren Vertreter und Bevollmächtigter arbeiten und entweder ganz oder zum Teil von der Human Rights and Equal Opportunity Commission für ihre Tätigkeit entschädigt werden.

Unter den gleichen Voraussetzungen wie bei der Altersdiskriminierung von Arbeitnehmern und Angestellten im Arbeits- und Beschäftigungsverhältnis ist eine Diskriminierung wegen Alters von Vertretern und Bevollmächtigten der Human Rights and Equal Opportunity Commission gemäß § 19 Abs. 1 und 2 ADA ebenfalls untersagt. Unter Vertretern und Beschäftigten der Human Rights and Equal Opportunity Commission sind gemäß der Definition in § 19 Abs. 5 ADA die Personen zu verstehen, die für eine andere Person als Vertreter und Bevollmächtigter einer weiteren Person arbeiten und entweder ganz oder zum Teil von der Human Rights and Equal Opportunity Commission für ihre Tätigkeit entschädigt werden.

cc. Berufszulassung und –anerkennung

Behörden oder Körperschaften (*„authority or body"*), die ermächtigt sind, eine für die Ausübung eines Berufs, für die Errichtung einer zur Berufsausübung erforderlichen Praxis oder für die Errichtung und den Betrieb eines Gewerbes, vorausgesetzte Einwilligung oder Berechtigung zu erteilen, zu erneuern, zu erweitern, aufzuheben oder zurückzunehmen, gelten gemäß § 22 Abs. 1 ADA ebenfalls als Normadressaten des Age Discrimination Act 2004 (Cth).

Solche Behörden oder Körperschaften (*„qualifying bodies"*), die ermächtigt sind, eine, für die Ausübung eines Berufs, für die Errichtung einer zur Berufsausübung erforderlichen Praxis oder für die Errichtung und den Betrieb eines Gewerbes, vorausgesetzte Einwilligung oder Berechtigung zu erteilen, zu erneuern, zu erweitern, aufzuheben oder zurückzunehmen, dürfen gemäß § 22 ADA ebenso wenig altersdiskriminierende Handlungen vornehmen. Dabei ist es ihnen insbesondere untersagt, eine Person aufgrund ihres Alters zu diskriminieren, indem sie die Erteilung, Erneuerung oder Erweiterung einer begehrten Einwilligung oder Berechtigung ablehnen oder scheitern lassen (§ 22 Abs. 1 lit. a) ADA), indem sie die Bedingungen und Anforderungen für die Erteilung, Erneuerung oder Erweiterung der Einwilligung oder Berechtigung in einer bestimmten Art und Weise festlegen (§ 22 Abs. 1 lit. b) ADA) oder die Einwilligung oder Berechtigung aufheben oder zurücknehmen oder die Bedingungen und Anforderungen an diese abändern (§ 22 Abs. 1 lit. c) ADA).

dd. Arbeitsvermittlungseinrichtungen

Unter den Begriff der Arbeitsvermittlungen („*employment agencies*") fallen gemäß § 24 Abs. 4 ADA alle Personen oder Unternehmen, die entgeltlich oder unentgeltlich andere Personen darin unterstützen, eine Beschäftigung oder andere Arbeit zu finden oder die an Arbeitgeber Arbeitnehmer vermitteln. Diese Definition ist sehr weit gefasst und versucht dadurch einen weit reichenden Schutz vor Altersdiskriminierungen durch Arbeit vermittelnde Personen oder Unternehmen zu gewährleisten. Somit werden öffentliche und auch private Arbeitsvermittlungseinrichtungen gleichermaßen verpflichtet.

Allerdings bedarf die Begriffsbestimmung des § 24 Abs. 4 ADA einer einschränkenden Auslegung, um eine zu weite Ausuferung des Adressatenkreises zu vermeiden und eine hinreichende Bestimmtheit herbeizuführen. Demzufolge sollten nur die Arbeitsvermittlungen verpflichtet werden, bei denen diese Vermittlungen regelmäßig durchgeführt werden und bei denen die Vermittlung somit zu einem dauernden Bestandteil ihrer ausgeübten Tätigkeit geworden ist. Im Einzelfall muss aber auch die mit Absicht einer dauerhaften Tätigkeit vorgenommene Vermittlung als vom § 24 Abs. 4 ADA erfasst angesehen werden, um andererseits zugleich eine drohende und zu umfangreiche Begrenzung des Adressenkreises zu vermeiden.

Unternehmen, deren Geschäftsbereich die Arbeitsvermittlung ausmacht, ist es nicht erlaubt eine Person aufgrund ihres Alters zu diskriminieren, indem sie ihr deshalb ihre Vermittlungstätigkeit verweigern (§ 24 Abs. 1 lit. a) ADA), indem sie bestimmte Bedingungen und Anforderungen für die Vermittlung festlegen (§ 24 Abs. 1 lit. b) ADA) oder indem sie einer Person aufgrund ihres Alters die Dienste nur in einer besonderen Art und Weise bereitstellen (§ 24 Abs. 1 lit. c) ADA). So ist es Arbeitsvermittlungen etwa untersagt, eine Vorauswahl potentieller Arbeitnehmer allein auf der Grundlage des Alters zu treffen, solange keine dafür rechtfertigenden Ausnahmen vorliegen.[144]

144 Explanatory Memorandum of the Age Discrimination Bill 2003 (Cth), Annexure C, Clause 24, Employment agencies.

ee. Arbeitsorientierte Bildung

(1) Bildungseinrichtungen

Innerhalb der gesetzliche Regelung des Diskriminierungsverbotes des § 26 Abs. 1 und Abs. 2 ADA wird lediglich der Begriff der Bildungsbehörde (*„educational authority"*) als verpflichteter Normadressat genannt. Eine Definition wird in § 26 Abs. 4 ADA vorgenommen. Danach werden vom Begriff einer Bildungsbehörde alle Organe und Personen umfasst, die eine Bildungseinrichtung verwalten. Der Begriff der Bildungseinrichtung wird ebenfalls im § 26 Abs. 4 ADA näher erläutert und als Schulen, Fach- und Hochschule, Universitäten oder andere Einrichtungen, an denen eine Aus- oder Weiterbildung angeboten wird, definiert. Der Anwendungsbereich des § 26 ADA erstreckt sich dabei auf jede Art von Schulen, Fach- und Hochschulen, Universitäten oder anderen Bildungseinrichtungen, in denen eine Aus- oder Weiterbildung angeboten wird.[145]

Die gesetzliche Regelung des § 26 ADA untersagt einer Bildungseinrichtung, eine Person aufgrund ihres Alters zu diskriminieren, indem sie deshalb eine Bewerbung für eine Aufnahme ablehnt oder eine Aufnahme versagt wird (§ 26 Abs. 1 lit. a) ADA) oder wegen des Alters des Bewerbers bestimmte Bedingungen und Anforderungen an eine Aufnahme als Schüler, Student etc. festlegt (§ 26 Abs. 1 lit. b) ADA). Ebenso ist es rechtswidrig wegen des Alters, Begünstigungen zu versagen oder zu beschränken (§ 26 Abs. 2 lit. a) ADA), den Schüler, Studenten etc. von der Bildungseinrichtung auszuschließen (§ 26 Abs. 2 lit. b) ADA) oder ihn in sonstiger Art und Weise zu benachteiligen (§ 26 Abs. 2 lit. c) ADA).

(2) Schüler, Auszubildende und Studenten

Aus den das Diskriminierungsverbot des § 26 Abs. 1 und Abs. 2 ADA treffenden Normadressaten kann zwangsläufig – mangels eindeutiger gesetzlicher Bestimmung – der persönliche Schutzbereich geschlussfolgert werden. Zu diesem zählen die an den Bildungseinrichtungen im Sinne von § 26 Abs. 4 ADA lernenden Personen, folglich also Schüler, Auszubildende, Studenten und auch sich weiterbildende Personen, wobei eine klare Begrenzung des Umfangs des persönlichen Schutzbereichs aufgrund der Vielzahl der verschiedenartigen Bildungseinrichtungen kaum möglich erscheint.

d. Schuldrechtliche und schuldrechtsähnliche Annexe als weitere An wendungsbereiche außerhalb eines Arbeits- und Beschäftigungsver hältnisses

aa. Personengesellschaften und ihre Gesellschafter

Die einzelnen Gesellschafter, der in § 21 Abs. 1 ADA verpflichteten Gesellschaft, werden nicht nur durch die Vorschrift des § 21 Abs. 2 ADA selbst zu den Normadressaten hinzugerechnet. Sie gehören gemäß § 21 Abs. 3 ADA gleichzeitig auch zum per-

---

145 Explanatory Memorandum of the Age Discrimination Bill 2003 (Cth), Annexure C, Clause 26, Education.

sönlichen Schutzbereich des Age Discrimination Act 2004 (Cth). Damit nehmen sie folglich eine Doppelstellung ein. Folglich werden durch das in § 21 Abs. 1 ADA statuierte Diskriminierungsverbot personengeführte Gesellschaften mit mindestens sechs oder mehr Partnern („*partnership*") sowie auch ihre Gesellschafter („*partner*") als Normadressaten des in § 21 Abs. 2 ADA an sie gerichteten Diskriminierungsverbotes verpflichtet.

In diesem Bereich ist insbesondere die Diskriminierung einer Person wegen ihres Alters durch personengeführte Gesellschaften mit mindestens sechs oder mehr Partnern gemäß § 21 ADA untersagt. Die gesetzliche Regelung des § 21 Abs. 1 ADA ordnet deshalb diskriminierende Entscheidungen der Gesellschaft darüber, wer in die Gesellschaft aufgenommen werden soll (§ 21 Abs. 1 lit. a) ADA) oder über Festsetzungen von diskriminierenden Bedingungen und Anforderungen in Bezug auf eine solche Aufnahme (§ 21 Abs. 1 lit. b) ADA) als rechtswidrig ein, wenn sie aufgrund des Alters der die Aufnahme begehrenden Person getätigt worden sind. Gleiches gilt auch für Handlungen eines einzelnen oder mehrerer der an der Gesellschaft beteiligten Personen, § 21 Abs. 2 ADA.

Ebenfalls ist aber auch jede auf das Alter eines anderen Teilhabers bezogene diskriminierende Handlung durch die anderen an der Gesellschaft beteiligten Personen rechtswidrig, wenn dadurch dem einzelnen Teilhaber der Zugang zu Begünstigungen, die aus der Partnerschaft resultieren, verwehrt oder er nur den anderen an der Gesellschaft beteiligten Personen gewährt wird (§ 21 Abs. 3 lit. a) ADA), der andere Teilhaber aus der Gesellschaft ausgeschlossen wird (§ 21 Abs. 3 lit. b) ADA) oder ihm in sonstiger Art und Weise Nachteile zugefügt werden (§ 21 Abs. 3 lit. c) ADA).

bb. Eigentümer und Besitzer

Das umfassende Diskriminierungsverbot des § 27 ADA, das die Altersdiskriminierung wegen Verwehrung des Zugangs und des Zutritts zu Räumlichkeiten („*access to premises*") im Sinne von § 5 ADA umfasst, enthält keinerlei Regelungen zum Begriff des Schädigers. Vielmehr spricht der Gesetzgeber allgemein von einer Person, so dass der Kreis der Normadressaten anscheinend sehr weit gezogen werden soll. Für eine solche Auslegung spricht insbesondere auch, dass sich in der Gesetzesbegründung keinerlei einschränkende Feststellungen des Gesetzgebers finden lassen. Denn dort wird nahezu ausschließlich auf die diskriminierenden Handlungen und auf die Definition des Begriffs der Räumlichkeit im Sinne von § 27 ADA eingegangen.[146] Um aber auch hier den Kreis der Normadressaten nicht unendlich ausufern zu lassen und eine Feststellung dessen zu ermöglichen, sollte er auf Eigentümer und Besitzer der jeweils betreffenden Räumlichkeiten sowie auf die darüber zur Verfügung Ermächtigten begrenzt werden. Nach Auffassung des Gesetzgebers ist dagegen hinreichend definiert, dass als Räumlichkeiten im Sinne des § 27 ADA nicht nur Gebäude, sondern auch Flugzeuge, Fahrzeuge und Schiffe, Plätze und Teile dieser Räumlichkeiten gelten.[147]

---

146 Vgl. insb. Explanatory Memorandum of the Age Discrimination Bill 2003 (Cth), Annexure C, Clause 27, Access to premises.

147 Explanatory Memorandum of the Age Discrimination Bill 2003 (Cth), Annexure C, Clause 27, Access to premises.

In diesem Zusammenhang ist eine Diskriminierung wegen Alters im Hinblick auf den Zugang und den Zutritt zu diesen Räumlichkeiten durch das Diskriminierungsverbot des § 27 ADA untersagt.

cc. *Dienstleister und Dienstnehmer*

Darüber hinaus werden aufgrund des in § 28 ADA enthaltenen Diskriminierungsverbotes auch Dienstleister als Normadressaten vom Age Discrimination Act 2004 (Cth) verpflichtet. Zwar enthält auch § 28 ADA keinerlei Definitionen, aber in § 5 ADA findet sich ein ausführlicher Katalog zur Eingrenzung des § 28 ADA zugrunde gelegten Dienstleistungsbegriffs („*services*"). Der Begriff der Dienstleistung umfasst nach der Definition des Age Discrimination Act 2004 (Cth) dabei all jene, die im Bereich der Bank- und Versicherungswirtschaft, des Rentenwesen und der Versorgung mit Genehmigungen, Darlehen oder Finanzierungen erbracht werden oder die den Bereich der Unterhaltung und der Freizeit oder des Transports und der Reise oder der Telekommunikation oder einen Berufsstand, ein Handwerk oder den öffentlichen Bereich betreffen, § 5 ADA.

Folglich kann als Dienstleister diejenige Person angesehen werden, die im Sinne des sehr weit gefassten § 5 ADA im Bereich der Bank- und Versicherungswirtschaft, des Rentenwesen und der Versorgung mit Genehmigungen, Darlehen oder Finanzierungen oder im Bereich der Unterhaltung und der Freizeit oder des Transports und der Reise oder der Telekommunikation oder im Bereich eines bestimmten Berufsstands, eines Handwerks oder des öffentlichen Bereichs Dienste erbringt.

Es stellt einen Verstoß gegen § 28 ADA dar, wenn eine Person, die entgeltlich oder unentgeltlich Güter oder Dienstleistungen anbietet, eine andere Person aufgrund ihres Alters diskriminiert. So ist es rechtswidrig, wenn die andere Person deshalb nicht mehr mit Gütern und Dienstleistungen versorgt wird (§ 28 Abs. 1 lit. a) ADA), bestimmte Bedingungen und Anforderungen an die Leistungserbringung aufgestellt (§ 28 Abs. 1 lit. b) ADA) oder die Güter und Dienstleistungen nur in einer bestimmte Art und Weise erbracht werden (§ 28 Abs. 1 lit. c) ADA).

Darüber hinaus entfaltet in zahlreichen der zuvor genannten Bereiche das Diskriminierungsverbot des § 50 ADA seine Wirkung. Danach ist es untersagt ein Inserat oder eine Werbung in der Zeitung oder in einer anderen Publikation (§ 50 Abs. 1 lit. b) i) ADA), im Radio oder Fernsehen (§ 50 Abs. 1 lit. b) ii) ADA), in Mitteilungen, auf Schildern und Etiketten (§ 50 Abs. 1 lit. b) iii) ADA), durch das Verteilen von Mustern und Proben, von Postwurfsendungen, Katalogen, Preislisten oder anderem Material (§ 50 Abs. 1 lit. b) iv) ADA), durch das Ausstellen von Bildern, Modellen oder Filmen (§ 50 Abs. 1 lit. b) v) ADA) oder auf andere Art und Weise (§ 50 Abs. 1 lit. b) vi) ADA) zu veröffentlichen oder Anlass für die Veröffentlichung zu geben (§ 50 Abs. 1 lit. a) ADA). Zusätzlich muss die Werbung oder das Inserat als eine Aufforderung zu einer Handlung verstanden werden (§ 50 Abs. 1 lit. c) ADA), die im Sinne des 4. Teils des Age Discrimination Act 2004 (Cth) rechtswidrig ist (§ 50 Abs. 1 lit. d) ADA). Demnach ist beispielsweise eine Stellenanzeige, in welcher die Eignung auf eine bestimmte Altersgruppe ohne erkennbare Ausnahmen beschränkt wird ebenso altersdiskriminierend, wie beispielsweise eine Annonce für die Besetzung einer Stelle eines Call Center Agents mit dem deutlichen Hinweis, dass sich Personen, die älter als 40 Jahre sind, nicht bewerben brauchen. Etwas anderes wäre nur dann denkbar, wenn eine gerechtfertigte Ausnahme vorliegen würde, wie etwa bei einem Inserat, in welchem ein Barkeeper für den Verkauf von Alkohol gesucht wird und dieser ausdrücklich älter als 18 Jahre sein solle.[148]

Aufgrund der offenen Regelung der Verbreitungsmöglichkeiten sind die in § 50 Abs. 1 lit. b) ADA genannten nicht abschließend und eröffnen somit die Möglichkeit neuartige Medien und Technologien einzubeziehen.[149]

Das Diskriminierungsverbot des § 50 ADA findet sich aufgrund der enthaltenden Strafdrohung nicht bei den vorgenannten Diskriminierungsverboten wider und erscheint somit als etwas versteckt im Gesetz angeordnet. Das Verbot der Altersdiskriminierung in der Werbung und in Inseraten gemäß § 50 ADA, dass gesetzessystematisch als Vergehen ausgestaltet ist, ist nicht allein aufgrund seiner strafrechtlichen Bedeutung für viele Bereiche der Altersdiskriminierung relevant.

dd. Vermieter und Mieter

Das Diskriminierungsverbot des § 29 Abs. 1 und Abs. 2 ADA betreffend, ist festzustellen, dass auch diese gesetzliche Regelung keine einschränkende Definition enthält. Vielmehr wird lediglich vom Geschäftsherrn und dessen Vertreter gesprochen. Folglich kann einerseits der Eigentümer und Vermieter sowie der zur Verfügung Berechtigte verpflichtet sein.

Um jedoch eine konkrete Bestimmung des Kreises der Normadressaten vornehmen zu können, muss auf den Anwendungsbereich des Diskriminierungsverbotes des § 29 Abs. 1 und Abs. 2 ADA in Bezug auf Unterkunft und Unterbringung („*accomodation*") abgestellt werden. Die Begriffe der Unterkunft und Unterbringung im Sinne von § 29 Abs. 1 und Abs. 2 ADA erfassen aufgrund der Definition des § 29 Abs. 4 ADA sowohl den Bereich des privaten Wohnraums als auch den gewerblichen Bereich („*residential or business accomodation*"). Folglich gilt der diesem Bereich zuzuordnende Eigentümer und Vermieter sowie der zur Verfügung Berechtigte als Normadressat.

Hier darf eine Person nicht wegen ihres Alters diskriminiert werden, indem aus diesem Grund ihr Begehren nach einer bestimmten Unterkunft abgelehnt wird (§ 29 Abs. 1 lit. a) ADA), bestimmte Bedingungen und Anforderungen, unter denen die Unterkunft angeboten wird, aufgestellt werden (§ 29 Abs. 1 lit. b) ADA) oder die Person aufgrund ihres Alters innerhalb mehrerer Bewerber nachrangig behandelt wird (§ 29 Abs. 1 lit. c) ADA). Ebenso ist es rechtswidrig, den Zugang zu einer mit der Unterkunft zusammenhängenden Begünstigung zu verwehren oder zu beschränken (§ 29 Abs. 2 lit. a) ADA), eine Zwangsräumung durchzuführen (§ 29 Abs. 2 lit. b) ADA) oder in sonstiger Art und Weise einen Nachteil zuzufügen (§ 29 Abs. 2 lit. c) ADA).

---

148 Explanatory Memorandum of the Age Discrimination Bill 2003 (Cth), Annexure C, Clause 50, Advertisments.

149 Explanatory Memorandum of the Age Discrimination Bill 2003 (Cth), Annexure C, Clause 50, Advertisments.

Eine vergleichsweise sehr ähnliche Regelung zum Verbot der Altersdiskriminierung in Bezug auf das Eigentum an einem Grundstück oder den Erwerb und den Verkauf einer Liegenschaft enthält das Diskriminierungsverbot des § 30 ADA.

II. Diskriminierungsarten

Aufgrund seiner weiten und klaren Formulierung im dritten Teil verbietet der Age Discrimination Act 2004 (Cth) die direkte und zugleich auch die indirekte Diskriminierung wegen Alters, §§ 14 und 15 ADA. Hierin gleicht der Age Discrimination Act 2004 (Cth) im Allgemeinen all den Gesetzen, die eine Benachteiligung oder Ungleichbehandlung – unabhängig von ihrer Art und Weise – beseitigen wollen.[150]

Die Begriffe der direkten und indirekten Diskriminierung (*„direct/indirect discrimination"*) sind allein technisch zu verstehen und nicht gleichbedeutend mit der Unterscheidung zwischen einem offenkundigen und einem verdeckten Verhalten einer Person.[151] Sie sollten dabei vor allem in Verbindung mit dem Begriff der formalen Gleichstellung von Personen gesehen werden, bei welcher der Gedanke einer Gleichbehandlung ohne Beeinflussung durch bestimmte persönliche Eigenschaften (und Diskriminierungsgründe) im Vordergrund steht.[152]

1. Direkte Diskriminierung

a. Charakteristika der direkten Diskriminierung

Die direkte Diskriminierung tritt immer dann auf, wenn eine Person im Vergleich zu einer anderen, auch hypothetischen, Person bei Vorliegen der identischen Begleitumstände nachteilig behandelt wird.[153] Nach dem Wortlaut des Age Discrimination Act 2004 (Cth) liegt deshalb eine direkte Diskriminierung immer dann vor, wenn eine Person – der *„discriminator"* – eine andere Person – die *„aggrieved person"* – aufgrund des Alters nachteilig behandelt oder beabsichtigt nachteilig zu behandeln.

---

150 Bourke/Ronalds, Discrimination Laws - Striving Towards Equality, in Macken, The Law of Employment, 609.

151 Bourke/Ronalds, Discrimination Laws - Striving Towards Equality, in Macken, The Law of Employment, 609; vgl. zu Beispielen für direkte und indirekte Diskriminierungen wegen Alters *Harding*, Age, The Road to Anti-Discrimination paved with good intentions, (1994) Law Society Journal 44.

152 *Collins*, Equality and Social Inclusion', (2003) 66 Modern Law Review 16; vgl. zum Begriff *„Equality"* ausführlich *Fredman*, Discrimination Law, 92ff.; *Goulding*, The Law Handbook, 520.

153 Bourke/Ronalds, Discrimination Laws - Striving Towards Equality, in Macken, The Law of Employment, 609; *Sullivan v Department of Defence* (1992) EOC 92-241; *Commonwealth of Australia v Human Rights and Equal Opportunity Commission* (1993) 119 ALR 133; *Human Rights and Equal Opportunity Commission v Mt Isa Mines Ltd* (1993) 118 ALR 80; *Honeyball/Bowers*, Textbook on Labour Law, 245; *Collins*, Discrimination, Equality and Social Inclusion (2003) 66 Modern Law Review 16.

Zusätzlich ist es ebenso erforderlich, dass der *„discriminator"* eine andere Person eines anderen Alters, unter denselben oder nicht grundlegend anderen Umständen, im Vergleich zur *„aggrieved person"* ungleich behandeln würde oder beabsichtigen würde zu behandeln (§ 14 lit. a) ADA) und der *„discriminator"* entweder aufgrund des Alters der diskriminierten Person (§ 14 lit. b) i) ADA), wegen einer Eigenschaft, die gewöhnlich bei Personen im Alter des Geschädigten auftritt (§ 14 lit. b) ii) ADA) oder wegen einer Eigenschaft, die gewöhnlich Personen im Alter des Geschädigten zugeschrieben wird (§ 14 lit. b) iii) ADA), diskriminierend handelt.[154]

Folglich beinhaltet der Nachweis einer direkten Diskriminierung ein *„comparator"*-Element (Ungleichbehandlung trotz gleicher Umstände) und ein *„causation"*-Element (Ungleichbehandlung aufgrund des Alters).[155]

Im Bereich des Arbeitsrechts und der damit verbundenen beruflichen Tätigkeit und Beschäftigung gibt es keinen Bereich, in dem eine direkte Diskriminierung wegen Alters nicht denkbar wäre. Vielmehr kann sie nahezu in jeder Beschäftigungs- und Arbeitssituation auftreten, so dass auch die Bereiche der Bewerbung, der Ausbildung und Schulung für eine bestimmte Tätigkeit sowie die Phase der Auflösung und Beendigung eines Arbeitsverhältnisses von einer direkten Diskriminierung wegen Alters beeinflusst werden können.[156]

Eine direkte Diskriminierung wegen Alters liegt etwa dann vor, wenn Altersgrenzen für den Zugang zu einer bestimmten Beschäftigung aufgestellt werden oder sich ein Arbeitgeber ausdrücklich aufgrund des jüngeren Alters eines Mitbewerbers gegen eine Einstellung des älteren Arbeitnehmers entscheidet.[157] Ebenso sind aber auch Fälle denkbar, in denen jüngere Beschäftigte gegenüber bereits älteren Personen nachteilig behandelt werden, ohne dass ein ersichtlicher Grund zur Rechtfertigung gegeben wäre.[158]

b. Die nachteilige Behandlung als Diskriminierungshandlung

Grundsätzlich ist demnach immer eine Handlung in Form einer Behandlung einer Person in einer bestimmten Art und Weise erforderlich. Der Age Discrimination Act 2004 (Cth) spricht in § 7 ADA selbst von *„the doing of an act"*, also ausdrücklich nur von einer Handlung, so dass sich insbesondere die Frage stellt, ob die verwendete Gesetzesformulierung von *„the doing of an act"* auch ein Unterlassen erfasst.

---

154 *Commonwealth v Human Rights and Equal Opportunity Commission* (1993) 46 FCR 191.

155 *Smith*, From *Wardley* to *Purvis*: How far has Australian anti-discrimination law come in 30 years? (2008) 21 Australian Journal of Labour Law 3.

156 Bourke/Ronalds, Discrimination Laws - Striving Towards Equality, in Macken, The Law of Employment, 611 mit Verweis auf die unveröffentlichte Entscheidung *Bloomfoeld v Westco Jeans Pty Ltd.*

157 *Harding*, The Road to Anti-Discrimination paved with good intentions, (1994) Law Society Journal, 44.

158 Attorney Generals Department of New South Wales, Age Discrimination – Options for New South Wales, A Discussion Paper (2000) 3.

aa. Die Auslegung des Begriffs der nachteiligen Behandlung im Rahmen der „In terpretation of Statutes"

Um diese Frage verbindlich beantworten zu können, bedarf es – nicht zuletzt wegen des sehr klaren Wortlauts von § 7 ADA – der im Common Law (überaus) bedeutsamen Auslegung des Gesetzes (*„Interpretation of Statutes"*). Im Lichte der bereits zuvor erläuterten Hauptregeln der Gesetzesauslegung führt die Auslegung hier zu keinem eindeutigen Ergebnis. Jedoch läßt sich die Tendenz erkennen, dass ein Unterlassen konsequenter Weise von der Formulierung *„the doing of act"* umfasst werden sollte. Denn nur so kann dem Diskriminierungsopfer ein Höchstmaß an Rechtsschutz gewährt und ein Ausgleich dafür, dass die Art und Weise des diskriminierenden Verhaltens nicht in seinem Einflussbereich liegt, geschaffen werden.

bb. Die Auslegung des Begriffs der nachteiligen Behandlung unter Berücksichti gung der Erwägungen der Rechtsprechung

Dieser Umstand spiegelt sich auch in den von der Rechtsprechung entwickelten allgemeinen Prinzipien zur Bedeutung der Begriffsbestimmung der Behandlung wider:

(1) Grundprinzipien der Rechtsprechung zur nachteiligen Behandlung

- Der Begriff der Behandlung umfasse demnach die herkömmliche Bedeutung im Sinne von sich gegenüber einer Person in einer bestimmten Art und Weise verhalten, ihr gegenüber in einer bestimmten Art und Weise handeln und sie somit auch in einer bestimmten Art und Weise zu behandeln.[159]
- Der Begriff der Behandlung umfasst deshalb aber nicht jede Entscheidung und wird auch nicht solche Entscheidungen erfassen, die niemanden gegenüber bekannt gegeben werden oder die keine praktische Auswirkung in der realen Welt haben können. So werden weder philosophische, metaphysische, theoretische, präventive, private oder semantische Entscheidungen berücksichtigt.[160]
- Eine Behandlung meint nicht notwendigerweise zugleich auch eine ungerechte, ungleiche oder verschiedenartige Behandlung, denn eine andersgeartete Behandlung muss nicht immer zugleich nachteilig sein.[161]

(2) Der Fall Krenske-Carter v Minister of Education und die nachteilige Behand lung durch Unterlassen

Überaus betrachtenswert ist in diesem Zusammenhang der Fall *Krenske-Carter v Minister of Education*, in dem eine Schülerin, die von einer Auto-Immunkrankheit, die sich vor allem durch Stress, Bewegung und Sonneneinwirkung verschlimmert, betroffen war, wegen einer ihrer Meinung nach nachteiligen und für sie somit diskriminierenden Behandlung durch ihre Lehrer geklagt hatte.[162] In dieser Entscheidung wird von der Rechtsprechung zwar primär auf eine indirekte Diskriminierung abgestellt, aber

---

159 *Capodicasa v Herald & Weekly Times Ltd & Ors* (1999) EOC 92-969.

160 *Capodicasa v Herald & Weekly Times Ltd & Ors* (1999) EOC 92-969.

161 *Capodicasa v Herald & Weekly Times Ltd & Ors* (1999) EOC 92-969.

162 *Krenske-Carter v Minister of Education* (2003) EOC 93-256.

zugleich das Problem der nachteiligen Behandlung durch Unterlassen aufgeworfen und – zumindest indirekt – diskutiert.

Die Schülerin trug vor, dass die Lehrer der Warnboro Senior High School es u.a. unterlassen hätten, sie vor den wegen ihrer Krankheit getätigten Tyrannisierungen und Schikanierungen der Mitschüler zu schützen – diese behaupteten, die Schülerin sei an AIDS erkrankt und drohten ihr, sie zu töten. Weiterhin sollen die Lehrer es ebenso unterlassen haben, sie während ihrer krankheitsbedingten Abwesenheit mit Schul- und Lernaufgaben zu versorgen und sie während des Sportunterrichts vor übermäßiger Sonneneinstrahlung zu schützen sowie ihr ausreichend zu trinken zu geben, weil sie vergessen hatte ihre Sportkleidung mitzubringen. Darüber hinaus sei es der Schülerin nicht erlaubt worden, die Krankenschwester der Schule aufzusuchen.[163]

Der den Fall zu entscheidende Equal Opportunity Tribunal of Western Australia konnte in seiner Entscheidung aber für die Schülerin keine nachteilige Behandlung im Sinne einer direkten Diskriminierung feststellen, auch wenn die Schülerin aufgrund ihrer Krankheit einen Nachteil erlangt haben soll. Denn nach Auffassung der Rechtsprechung des Equal Opportunity Tribunal of Western Australia sei die Schülerin von ihren Lehrern genauso wie die anderen Schüler behandelt worden. Folglich habe erst diese Gleichbehandlung zu Nachteilen für die Schülerin geführt. Aus diesem Grund lag nach Ansicht der Rechtsprechung in diesem Fall keine direkte Diskriminierung vor.[164]

Das Gericht hat seine Entscheidung aber zum Anlass genommen eine indirekte Diskriminierung zu prüfen und eine solche im Ergebnis bejaht, weil zu seiner Überzeugung bewiesen werden konnte, dass die Lehrer es unterlassen hätten, sich ausreichend über die Krankheit der Schülerin zu informieren, um so ihren besonderen Bedürfnissen gerecht werden und die Schülerin angemessen behandeln zu können. Dieses Verhalten sei ursächlich für eine Verschlimmerung der Krankheit gewesen und habe zu einer vermehrten krankheitsbedingten Abwesenheit und zu einem Absinken des Niveaus der von der betroffenen Schülerin erbrachten schulischen Leistungen geführt.[165]

Auch wenn das Equal Opportunity Tribunal of Western Australia vorliegend eine direkte Diskriminierung verneint und nicht weiter zur Diskriminierung durch Unterlassen und seinen Voraussetzungen ausgeführt hat, so gelang es ihm aber, ausdrücklich erkennen zu lassen, dass eine nachteilige Behandlung auch dann angenommen werden könne, wenn sie durch ein Unterlassen des Schädigers verursacht worden ist.[166]

Anhand des konkreten Verhaltens der verantwortlichen Lehrer, welches das Gericht als ursächlich für die nachteilige Behandlung hat ausreichen lassen, lässt sich somit erkennen, dass das Unterlassen dem aktiven Handeln im konkreten Einzelfall in seiner Wertigkeit gleichkommen muss.

---

163 *Krenske-Carter v Minister of Education* (2003) EOC 93-256; vgl. auch die zusammenfassende Darstellung des Sachverhalts im Commissioner for Equal Opportunity Newsletter, Discrimination matters, December 2002, 4.

164 *Krenske-Carter v Minister of Education* (2003) EOC 93-256.

165 *Krenske-Carter v Minister of Education* (2003) EOC 93-256.

166 Vgl. auch *Purvis v New South Wales (Department of Education and Training)* [2003] HCA 62.

(3) Der Fall Purvis v New South Wales (Department of Education and Training)

Die Problematik des Unterlassens spielte – neben weiteren, im Anschluss noch zu betrachtenden und zu klärenden Fragen der Bildung von Vergleichsgruppen – auch im Fall *Purvis v New South Wales (Department of Education and Training* eine nicht unerhebliche Rolle.[167]

In dieser Entscheidung klagte Daniel Hoggan, vertreten durch seinen Vater Mr. Purvis, wegen Diskriminierungen aufgrund dessen Behinderung, die er im Alter von zwölf Jahren an der Grafton Primary School erleiden musste und die aufgrund nachfolgender Ereignisse und Reaktionen zum wiederholten Ausschluss von Daniel Hoggan von der Schule führten. Daniel Hoggan hatte als Kleinkind im Alter von sieben Monaten eine irreparable Schädigung seines Gehirns erlitten, die später nachweislich zu unsozialem, aggressiven und gewalttätigem Verhalten gegenüber anderen Personen führte.[168]

Dieses Verhalten hätte zur Überzeugung des Gerichts aber durch die Versetzung in eine spezielle Klasse und eine damit verbundene intensive Betreuung von fachlich besonders gebildeten Lehrern reguliert oder gar verhindert werden können. Darin, dass ihm eine solche gesonderte Unterstützung aber verwehrt wurde, mithin gerade nicht die im konkreten Fall erforderlichen Maßnahmen ergriffen worden sind, lag in diesem Fall eine für ihn nachteilige Behandlung und folglich eine direkte Diskriminierung durch Unterlassen.[169] Eine derartige direkte Diskriminierung durch Unterlassen ist demnach auch in Fällen denkbar, in welchen es der Arbeitgeber unterlässt, durch präventive Maßnahmen zum Schutz vor Benachteiligungen dafür zu sorgen, dass in seinem Unternehmen altersgerechte Arbeitsbedingungen herrschen und sich weder durch Arbeitskollegen oder Dritte noch durch den Arbeitgeber selbst Benachteiligungen aufgrund des Alters realisieren.[170] Dadurch wird nicht zuletzt die Initiative des Arbeitgebers gefördert, indem vorbeugende Maßnahmen sowie auch eine Aufklärung über die

---

167 *Purvis v New South Wales (Department of Education and Training)* [2003] HCA 62, vgl. zu den vorherigen Entscheidungen auch *Purvis v New South Wales (Department of Education and Training)* (2001) 186 ALR 69, (2002) 190 ALR 588; insb. *Ansett Transport Industries (Operations) Pty Ltd v Wardley* (1984) EOC 92-002; vgl. im Überblick *Smith*, From *Wardley* to *Purvis*: How far has Australian anti-discrimination law come in 30 years? (2008) 21 Australian Journal of Labour Law 3.

168 *Purvis v New South Wales (Department of Education and Training)* [2003] HCA 62.

169 *Purvis v New South Wales (Department of Education and Training)* [2003] HCA 62.

170 Vgl. auf europäischer Ebene auch Art. 5 der Richtlinie 2000/78/EG des Rates vom 27. November 2000 zur Festlegung eines allgemeinen Rahmens für die Verwirklichung der Gleichbehandlung in Beschäftigung und Beruf, wonach der Arbeitgeber die geeigneten und im konkreten Fall erforderlichen Maßnahmen ergreifen muss, um den Menschen mit Behinderung den Zugang zur Beschäftigung, die Ausübung eines Berufes, den beruflichen Aufstieg und die Teilnahme an Aus- und Weiterbildungsmaßnahmen zu ermöglichen, es sei denn, diese Maßnahmen würden den Arbeitgeber unverhältnismäßig belasten; vgl. auch ErfK/*Schlachter*, § 12 AGG Rn. 1ff. m.w.N. zu den einzelnen Maßnahmen nach deutschem Antidiskriminierungsrecht; auch Däubler/Bertzbach-*Buschmann*, § 12 Rn. 3ff.; umfassend zur Richtlinie 2000/78/EG *Senne*, Auswirkungen des europäischen Verbots der Altersdiskriminierung auf das deutsche Arbeitsrecht, 129ff..

Unzulässigkeit von Benachteiligungen und damit verbundenen Altersdiskriminierungen verlangt werden.[171]

(4) Schlussfolgerungen für den Begriff der nachteiligen Behandlung unter Berück sichtigung der Erwägungen der Rechtsprechung

(a) Handlung

Unter Berücksichtigung der vorgenannten Grundprinzipien der Rechtsprechung kann eine nachteilige Behandlung im Sinne des Age Discrimination Act 2004 (Cth) folglich in verschiedenartigen Erscheinungsformen auftreten. So kann sie gerade in der Verweigerung der Erlaubnis für die Teilnahme an einer Weiterbildungsmaßnahme für einen Arbeitnehmer oder in einer Entlassung eines Arbeitnehmers liegen, wenn der Arbeitgeber sein Verhalten damit begründet, dass der Arbeitnehmer zu alt sei, um sich weiterzubilden oder um einen Ertrag für das Unternehmen zu erwirtschaften.[172] Dabei kommt es bei einer Weiterbildungsmaßnahme nicht auf deren Ausgestaltung an, so dass es völlig unerheblich ist, ob es um die Teilnahme an einer internen Fortbildung, um die Teilnahme an einer externen Maßnahme oder gar um den Ersatz der dadurch angefallenen Kosten geht.[173] Ebenfalls ist auch die Weigerung, eine Person einzustellen, weil sie zu entweder zu jung oder aber zu alt sei, oder ihr den Zutritt oder die Mitgliedschaft zu einer Vereinigung aus diesen Gründen zu verwehren, als nachteilige Behandlung gemäß § 14 lit. a) ADA einzustufen.[174]

(b) Unterlassen

Zwar lassen sich aus der Rechtsprechung im Einzelnen kaum genauere Voraussetzungen einer nachteiligen Behandlung durch ein Unterlassen entnehmen. Auch ist eine trennscharfe Abgrenzung zwischen den insbesondere im Bereich der Diskriminierungen wegen Behinderung vom Arbeitgeber geforderten angemessenen Vorkehrungen und etwaigen allgemeinen Organisationspflichten bereits deshalb nicht möglich, weil sich Diskriminierungen wegen Alters und Behinderung überlagern können.[175] Im Ergebnis erkennt sie das Unterlassen, sofern es dem aktiven Handeln in seiner Wirkungsweise gleich gesetzt werden kann und es ursächlich für die Diskriminierung ist, aber ebenfalls als für eine Diskriminierung erforderliche nachteilige Behandlung ausreichend an, um eine bestmögliche Erreichung des Gesetzeszwecks erzielen zu können

171 Zur Frage der Erforderlichkeit der Maßnahmen sowie zum Beurteilungsmaßstab vgl. Däubler/Bertzbach-Buschmann, § 12 Rn. 11ff..

172 Bourke/Ronalds, Discrimination Laws - Striving Towards Equality, in Macken, The Law of Employment, 628, 631.

173 *Boyd v SCI Operations Pty Ltd* (1996) EOC 92-853.

174 *Thew*, Discrimination under the Age Discrimination Act, in: Baker & McKenzie, Age Discrimination: Mitigating Risk in the Workplace, S. 37.

175 Vgl. zu den angemessenen Vorkehrungen im Gemeinschaftsrecht mit Bezug auf das Verbot der Diskriminierung wegen Behinderung *Schiek* NZA 2004, 873.

und ein hohes Maß an rechtlichem Schutz und Abwehr gegenüber Diskriminierungen zu gewährleisten.[176]

cc. Eigene Stellungnahme

Die aufgezeigte Ausweitung der nachteiligen Behandlung im Sinne von § 7 ADA, die dort allgemein mit der Formulierung *„the doing of an act"* vom Gesetzgeber geregelt wird, ist unter Rechtsschutzgesichtspunkten gerechtfertigt und interessengerecht.

Zwar besteht im Common Law eine überaus starke Bindung an die vom Gesetzgeber gewählte Formulierung; selbst dann, wenn die Auffassung besteht, dass der Gesetzgeber die Regelung mit ihren Auswirkungen so nicht gewollt oder nicht bedacht hat. Aber auch wenn grundsätzlich eine Korrektur – etwa durch die Rechtsprechung – nicht in der Form vorgenommen werden darf, als dass die ratio der Bestimmung über den Wortlaut gestellt wird, so ist die hier favorisierte Ausweitung anhand des vom Gesetzgeber verfolgten Gesetzeszwecks zulässig. Denn der australische Gesetzgeber hat mit § 15AA des Acts Interpretation Act 1901 (Cth) selbst die Möglichkeit geschaffen, eine Gesetzesauslegung dahingehend vorzunehmen, als dass der Zweck des jeweiligen Gesetzes in der bestmöglichen Art und Weise erreicht werden kann:[177]

> „In the interpretation of a provision of an Act, a construction that would promote the purpose or object underlying the Act (whether that purpose or object is expressly stated in the Act or not) shall be preferred to a construction that would not promote that purpose or object."

Der Gesetzeszweck kann also selbst dann Berücksichtigung finden, wenn die gesetzliche Regelung in sich nicht widersprüchlich, sondern nur zu unpräzise formuliert ist und mehrere Auslegungsmöglichkeiten gegeben sind.[178]

Nur wenn folglich auch das Unterlassen als Diskriminierungshandlung als direkte Diskriminierung erfasst wird, kann der in § 3 ADA statuierte Gesetzeszweck – Beseitigung jeglicher Diskriminierung wegen Alters und Sicherstellung, dass jedermann trotz unterschiedlichen Alters dieselben Chancen und Rechte innerhalb einer Gemeinschaft haben kann und tatsächlich hat – erreicht werden, da somit eine erhebliche Vielzahl an diskriminierenden Verhaltensweisen von § 7 ADA erfasst werden können.

Zudem widerspräche eine ausschließliche Fokussierung auf den tatsächlichen Wortlaut dem Gesetzeszweck. Denn erst die Einbeziehung des mit der entsprechenden gesetzlichen Regelung verfolgten gesetzgeberischen Zwecks sowie der Gesamtumstände des Einzelfalls kann die Gesetzesauslegung mit Leben füllen und die betroffenen Interessen konkret berücksichtigen.[179] Meines Erachtens sollte zur Gewährleistung

---

176 *Krenske-Carter v Minister of Education* (2003) EOC 93-256; *Purvis v New South Wales (Department of Education and Training)* [2003] HCA 62.

177 Vgl. zu § 15AA auch *Winckel*, The Contextual Role of a Preamble in Statutory Interpretation (1999) 23 MULR 184.

178 *Mills v Meeking* (1990) 169 CLR 214; *Saraswati v The Queen* (1991) 172 CLR 1; *CIC Insurance Ltd v Bankstown Football Club Ltd* (1997) 187 CLR 384.

179 *River Wear Commissioners v Adamson* (1877) 2 AC 742; vgl. auch *Steyn*, The Intractable Problem of The Interpretation of Legal Texts, (2003) 25 SydLRev 5.

eines umfassenden Schutzes gegen Altersdiskriminierung die Frage sodann lauten, ob im Bereich von Beschäftigung und Beruf der Arbeitgeber angemessene Vorkehrungen zum Schutz vor Benachteiligungen wegen Alters in seinem Unternehmen getroffen hat, z.B. durch das Vorhalten und den Zugang zu Weiterbildungsmaßnahmen, durch altersgerechte Arbeitsbedingungen, Arbeitszeiten und –belastung.[180]

c. Das Alter der geschädigten Person

aa. Der Begriff des Alters im Sinne des Age Discrimination Act 2004 (Cth)

Der Age Discrimination Act 2004 (Cth) verlangt für das Vorliegen einer unrechtmäßigen direkten Diskriminierung, dass sie entweder aufgrund des Alters der geschädigten Person (§ 14 lit. b) i) ADA), wegen einer Eigenschaft, die gewöhnlich bei Personen im Alter des Geschädigten auftritt (§ 14 lit. b) ii) ADA) oder wegen einer Eigenschaft, die gewöhnlich Personen im Alter des Geschädigten zugeschrieben wird (§ 14 lit. b) iii) ADA), vorgenommen wird.

Unter dem Begriff des Alters wird aufgrund des klaren Wortlauts der in § 5 ADA enthaltenen Definition neben einem bestimmten Alter auch eine bestimmte Altersgruppe bzw. Altersklasse verstanden:

> „...age includes age group."

Da eine direkte Diskriminierung nicht zwangsweise immer wegen eines bestimmten Alters erfolgen muss, sondern auch wegen der Zugehörigkeit zu einer bestimmten Altersklasse geschehen kann, beabsichtigt der Age Discrimination Act 2004 (Cth) folglich auch ihre Einbeziehung.[181]

> "Age is defined to include age group, so that an act of discrimination needs not be linked to a specific age but can, as is often the case, be related to the age group of a person."[182]

Diese weite Auslegung ist konsequent, da es nur so möglich sein kann, den gesetzgeberischen Zweck zu erfüllen und die Bipolarität der Altersdiskriminierung zu erfassen.

> „Legislation which does not specify an age limit is based on the principle that the three major stages of childhood, work and retirement should occur during a person´s life when the circumstances for that individual warrant is rather than when they have reached a particular chronological age as well as on the principle that people should not be treated less favoura-

180 Vgl. hierzu auch § 15 Abs. 1 lit. b) ADA und die Bezugnahme auf gerechte bzw. ungerechte Bedingung, Anforderung oder Praktiken.

181 Explanatory Memorandum of the Age Discrimination Bill 2003 (Cth), Annexure C, Clause 5, Definitions; *Hemingway*, The Age Discrimination Act 2004, 9; vgl. auch *Guthrie*, Ageing – Discrimination and Workers Compensation (2005) 13.

182 Explanatory Memorandum of the Age Discrimination Bill 2003 (Cth), Annexure C, Clause 5, Definitions; *Hemingway*, The Age Discrimination Act 2004, 9.

> bly in employment, provision of goods and services or accommodation because of their chronological age."[183]

Dieser Zielsetzung hat sich – wie nachfolgend aufgezeigt wird – mittlerweile die Rechtsprechung in ihren Entscheidungen angeschlossen.[184]

bb. Berücksichtigung der Individualität der geschädigten Person

Die Begriffe der Eigenschaften, die einerseits üblicherweise zu Personen im Alter des Geschädigten gehören (§ 14 lit. b) ii) ADA) und die andererseits üblicherweise Personen im Alter des Geschädigten zugeschrieben werden (§ 14 lit. b) iii) ADA) beziehen sich auf spezielle Merkmale. So wird in der Gesetzesbegründung als Beispiel für ein Merkmal im Sinne von § 14 lit. b) ii) ADA, dass gewöhnlich bei älteren Personen auftritt, die graue Haarfarbe und als Beispiel für ein Merkmal im Sinne von § 14 lit. b) iii) ADA, dass gewöhnlich älteren Personen zugeschrieben wird, mangelnde Kenntnis im Umgang mit Computern genannt.[185]

(1) Der Fall Boehringer Ingelheim Pty Ltd v Reddrop

Insbesondere der New South Wales Court of Appeal hat in der Entscheidung *Boehringer Ingelheim Pty Ltd v Reddrop* ausführlich zu diesem Bereich Stellung genommen.[186] So soll es nicht erforderlich sein, dass der Arbeitgeber spezielle persönliche Eigenschaften ignoriert, die der Kläger für gewöhnlich nur aufgrund seines Familienstandes aufweisen kann oder die nur einer Person mit einem bestimmten Familienstand zugeschrieben werden können. Vielmehr ist der Arbeitgeber einerseits verpflichtet, beim Umgang mit dem Arbeitnehmer solche speziellen Merkmale zu berücksichtigen und zugleich ist er aber auch berechtigt, auf diese speziellen Merkmale im Rahmen der die Arbeitnehmer treffenden Behandlung einzugehen.[187] Denn bei jeder einzelnen Person sollten sich die individuelle Persönlichkeit und die sie kennzeichnenden Merkmale in ihrer Behandlung widerspiegeln. Demzufolge sei es nicht erforderlich, dass jemand so behandelt wird, als wenn er durch andere, im konkreten Fall aber nicht vorliegende, Eigenschaften zu charakterisieren sein würde.[188]

(2) Der Fall Waterhouse v Bell

Seine Rechtsprechung erweiternd hat sich der New South Wales Court of Appeal im Fall *Waterhouse v Bell* erneut mit § 14 lit. b) ii) und iii) ADA auseinandergesetzt.[189] Dieser Entscheidung lag dabei folgender Sachverhalt zugrunde: Eine Bewerberin klag-

---

183 Attorney Generals Department of New South Wales, Age Discrimination – Options for New South Wales, A Discussion Paper (2000) 4.

184 *Dewan v Main Roads WA* (2005) EOC 93-362.

185 Explanatory Memorandum of the Age Discrimination Bill 2003 (Cth), Annexure C, Clause 14, Discrimination on the ground of age – direct discrimination.

186 *Boehringer Ingelheim Pty Ltd v Reddrop* [1984] 2 NSWLR 13.

187 *Boehringer Ingelheim Pty Ltd v Reddrop* [1984] 2 NSWLR 13.

188 *Boehringer Ingelheim Pty Ltd v Reddrop* [1984] 2 NSWLR 13, 21-22.

189 *Waterhouse v Bell* (1991) 25 NSWLR 99.

te wegen einer Diskriminierung, weil ihr vom Australian Jockey Club Committee die Trainerlizenz versagt und als Begründung dafür angeführt wurde, dass ihr Ehemann bereits von allen dem Australian Jockey Club Committee unterstehenden Galopprennbahnen verwiesen worden sei.[190] Hierin sah die Bewerberin, als Beschwerdeführerin im genannten Rechtsstreit, eine Diskriminierung aufgrund eines speziellen Umstandes, der sie nur wegen ihres Familienstandes berühren konnte.[191]

Der Court of Appeal war in diesem Fall einstimmig der Auffassung, dass das Urteil in Sachen *Boehringer Ingelheim Pty Ltd v Reddrop* so zu verstehen sei, dass mit den in § 14 lit. b) ii) und iii) ADA Bezug gemeinten persönlichen Eigenschaften und Merkmalen, für alle Personen gemeinsam, nur die sie speziell treffenden maßgeblich sein können und weniger die alle Personen zugleich und allgemein treffenden Eigenschaften und Merkmale.[192]

(3) Schlussfolgerungen zu den Eigenschaften und Merkmalen im Sinne von § 14 lit. b) ii) und iii) ADA

Denknotwendig sind mit jeder einzelnen Person individuelle Eigenschaften und Merkmale verbunden, die auch einen besonderen Bezug zum Alter der Person haben können. Da nur durch sie eine umfassende Beurteilung der jeweiligen Persönlichkeit stattfinden kann, ist eine grundsätzlich weite Auslegung und ein allgemeines Rückgriffsverbot im Rahmen der Behandlung der Person nicht per se förderlich. Denn so könnte die Gefahr entstehen, dass im Wege einer individuellen Abwägung zu Gunsten einer schematischen Betrachtungsweise die Gerechtigkeit im Einzelfall leidet. Ein umfassender Opferschutz lässt sich sicher auch dann erreichen, wenn Merkmale und Eigenschaften, die vorwiegend mit einem bestimmten Alter zusammenhängen oder für eine bestimmte Altersgruppe charakteristisch sind, ausreichend und interessengerecht berücksichtigt werden und auch die hinter einem konkreten Verhalten stehende Motivation in angemessenem Umfang Beachtung findet.

d. Bestimmung der Vergleichspersonen und Vergleichsgruppen

Damit eine Feststellung getroffen werden kann, ob sich die Behandlung im konkreten Einzelfall aber tatsächlich als nachteilig darstellt, bedarf es eines Vergleichs mit anderen Personen bzw. Personengruppen.

Fraglich ist, wie ein solcher Vergleich vorgenommen werden soll. Sinnvoll erscheint dafür die Bestimmung eines konkreten und vor allem einheitlichen Vergleichsmaßstabs. Um einen einheitlichen Vergleichsmaßstab bestimmen und sodann auch anwenden zu können, stellt die Rechtsprechung in den von ihr zahlreich ent-

---

190 *Waterhouse v Bell* (1991) 25 NSWLR 99, 101.

191 Das Verfahren kam zum New South Wales Court of Appeal, weil eine Entscheidung dahingehend beantragt worden war, dass das Equal Opportunity Tribunal aufgrund des Urteils in Sachen *Boehringer Ingelheim Pty Ltd v Reddrop* nicht zur Abweisung der Beschwerde verpflichtet sei.

192 *Waterhouse v Bell* (1991) 25 NSWLR 99, 115.

schiedenen Fällen im Grundsatz auf das Alter bzw. auf eine bestimmte Altersgruppe im Sinne von § 5 ADA ab.

aa. Der Fall Purvis v New South Wales (Department of Education and Training)

Die Entscheidung des High Court of Australia im Rechtsstreit *Purvis v New South Wales (Department of Education and Training)* zeigt dabei sehr deutlich, dass es in der Praxis schwierig sein kann, allein auf das Alter bzw. eine Altersgruppe als Vergleichsmaßstab abzustellen.[193]

Wie zuvor bereits dargestellt, lag der Entscheidung der folgende Sachverhalt zugrunde: Ein Schüler hatte geklagt, weil er sich aufgrund seiner geistigen Behinderung vom New South Wales Department of Education and Training nachteilig behandelt fühlte. Seine geistige Behinderung wirkte sich dabei u.a. durch aggressives und gewalttätiges Verhalten aus, das zum wiederholten Ausschluss von der Schule führte, welches nach Ansicht der Rechtsprechung aber durch eine besondere Betreuung durch fachlich gebildete Lehrer hätte reguliert werden können.

Darin, dass ihm eine gesonderte Unterstützung jedoch verwehrt wurde und er von der Schule verwiesen worden ist, liege zur Überzeugung des High Court of Australia eine für ihn nachteilige Behandlung und folglich eine direkte Diskriminierung. Gleichfalls wies die Rechtsprechung aber auch darauf hin, dass ein derartiges aggressives und gewalttätiges Verhalten die Bildung und die Sicherheit der Schüler und Lehrer an einer Schule beeinträchtige, aber gleichwohl grundsätzlich die Schule für den Schutz der anderen Schüler und der Lehrer verantwortlich ist und folglich für jegliche Reaktionen gegenüber dem betreffenden Schüler die alleinige Verantwortung tragen müsse. Jede aufgrund der Behinderung getätigte nachteilige Behandlung des – von der Schule verwiesenen – Schülers stelle eine Diskriminierung dar.[194]

(1) Entscheidung und Argumentation der Mehrheit

Der High Court of Australia entschied mit einer Mehrheit von fünf zu zwei Stimmen, dass als Vergleichsperson ein Schüler betrachtet werden müsse, der zwar nicht dieselbe Behinderung aufweisen, aber das gleiche Verhaltensmuster erfüllen müsse und dass demnach nicht primär auf die zu der aggressiven und gewalttätigen Verhaltensweise führende geistige Behinderung abgestellt werden könne.[195] Zu dieser Ansicht gelangte die Mehrheit der Richter deshalb, weil sie in § 4 lit. f) und g) DDA eine Trennung zwischen der Behinderung und dem daraus resultierenden Verhalten enthalten sahen. Folglich musste also eine Trennung zwischen der Behinderung und der durch sie verursachten Verhaltensweise des Schülers vorgenommen werden.[196]

---

193 *Purvis v New South Wales (Department of Education and Training)* [2003] HCA 62.

194 *Purvis v New South Wales (Department of Education and Training)* [2003] HCA 62.

195 *Purvis v New South Wales (Department of Education and Training)* [2003] HCA 62 unter Zustimmung der Richter *Gleeson CJ, Callinan, Gummow, Hayne, Heydon JJ.*

196 Vgl. auch *Tate v Rafin* (2001) EOC 92-125; *Waterhouse v Bell* (1991) 25 NSWLR 99; *Boehringer Ingelheim Pty Ltd v Reddrop* [1984] 2 NSWLR 13.

(2) Abweichende Meinungen

Die eine abweichende Meinung vertretenden Richter, waren dagegen der Auffassung, dass der Focus primär auf die Behinderung gelenkt werden müsse, um eine geeignete Vergleichsperson zu finden. Denn jemand ohne diese Behinderung hätte sich nur aufgrund einer autonomen Entscheidung gleichfalls aggressiv und gewalttätig verhalten und wäre nicht durch außerhalb seiner Einflussmöglichkeiten liegenden Umstände zu derartiger Verhaltensweise veranlasst worden.[197] Nach dieser Auffassung könne die Behinderung gerade nicht von der durch sie verursachten Verhaltensweise in der Betrachtung getrennt werden, da sie denknotwendig miteinander verbunden sind.[198]

(3) Schlussfolgerung und eigene Stellungnahme

Im vorliegend betrachteten Fall spielt das Alter bei der Bildung des Vergleichsmaßstabes allerdings keine hervorgehobene Rolle, da hier die Behinderung und das durch sie verursachte Verhalten im Vordergrund standen. Aber unabhängig davon, ob man hier der Mehrheitsentscheidung folgt oder sich der davon abweichenden Meinung anschließt, das Alter der diskriminierten Person und der zur vergleichsweisen Beurteilung herangezogenen anderen Personen oder Personengruppen muss auf jeden Fall berücksichtigt werden. Denn nur so können weitere in den Vergleich einfließende Faktoren, wie z.B. der Entwicklungsstand und die geistige Entwicklung, angemessen berücksichtigt und – sofern erforderlich – nur abgestuft in die Bewertung eingestellt werden.

Diese Entscheidung verdeutlicht darüber hinaus, dass, wie bereits zuvor festgestellt, eine direkte Diskriminierung einerseits durch ein aktives Handeln – hier durch das Verweisen des Schülers von der Schule – und andererseits aber auch durch ein Unterlassen – hier durch das Verwehren einer besonderen Betreuung durch fachlich geschultes Personal – erfolgen kann.

bb. Der Fall Lightning Bolt Co Pty Limited v Skinner & Anor

Demgegenüber stellte der Supreme Court of Queensland im Rechtsstreit *Lightning Bolt Co Pty Limited v Skinner & Anor* in seiner Rechtsprechung fest, dass die Begründung des Arbeitgebers, er habe die betroffenen Arbeitnehmer entlassen, weil er die Meinung vertrete, dass jüngere Arbeitnehmer in der Regel leistungsstärker seien, unerheblich sein müsse und er die betroffenen Arbeitnehmer demnach ausschließlich mit jüngeren Arbeitnehmern vergleichen könne.[199] Entgegen der Rechtsprechung im Fall *Purvis v New South Wales (Department of Education and Training)* und entgegen der Entscheidung der Vorinstanz stellte der Supreme Court of Queensland allein auf das

197 *Purvis v New South Wales (Department of Education and Training)* [2003] HCA 62 mit abweichender Meinung der Richter *Kirby* und *McHugh JJ*. Vgl. auch das obiter dictum in *IW v City of Perth & Ors* (1997) 191 CLR 1; *Mooney v Commissioner of Police (No 2)* [2003] NSWADT 107; *Commonwealth of Australia v HREOC & Ors* (1994) EOC 92-566.

198 Vgl. auch *X v McHugh* (1994) 56 IR 248; *Human Rights and Equal Opportunity Commission v Mt Isa Mines* (1993) 46 FCR 301, 118 ALR 80; *IW v City of Perth* (1997) 191 CLR 1, 146 ALR 696; *Y v Australia Post* (1997) EOC 92-865.

199 *Lightning Bolt Co Pty Limited v Skinner & Anor* [2002] QSC 062.

Alter bzw. auf Altersgruppen als Vergleichsmaßstab ab und ließ mögliche weitere Umstände, wie die Leistungsfähigkeit der Arbeitnehmer, unberücksichtigt. Denn der Supreme Court sowie auch die Vorinstanz werteten das Verhalten des Arbeitgebers als direkte Diskriminierung. Eine indirekte Diskriminierung hätte nach Ansicht der Rechtsprechung allenfalls dann vorgelegen, wenn sich der Arbeitgeber etwa aufgrund mangelnder Leistungsfähigkeit zur Kündigung der Arbeitnehmer entschieden hätte und durch diesen Kündigungsgrund eine größere Zahl von älteren Beschäftigten betroffen gewesen wäre. Dies jedoch war vorliegend nicht der Fall.[200]

cc. Der Fall Boehringer Ingelheim Pty Ltd v Reddrop

In der Entscheidung des Court of Appeal in Sachen *Boehringer Ingelheim Pty Ltd v Reddrop*, in der es um eine Altersdiskriminierung in Bezug auf den Familienstand ging, vertrat die Rechtsprechung eine sich der überwiegenden Richtermeinung im Fall *Purvis v New South Wales (Department of Education and Training)* annähernde Auffassung. Denn es wurde die Ansicht vertreten, um feststellen zu können, ob eine nachteilige Behandlung des Klägers vorgelegen habe, müsse seine Behandlung mit der einer charakteristisch identischen, aber einen anderen Familienstand aufweisenden Person verglichen werden.[201] Im Ergebnis sollte zwar wiederum auch das Alter der Vergleichsperson erheblich sein, aber darüber hinaus wurde ein weiterer Umstand, der Familienstand, als Vergleichsmaßstab herangezogen.

dd. Schlussfolgerung zur Bestimmung der Vergleichspersonen und Vergleichsgruppen

Aus den angeführten Urteilen und vor allem aus der Entscheidung im Fall *Purvis v New South Wales (Department of Education and Training)* wird deutlich, dass das Alter der Vergleichsperson oder aber die etwaige Altersgruppe in der Regel nicht allein als Vergleichsmaßstab zur weiteren Beurteilung der nachteiligen Behandlung geeignet ist. Vielmehr müssen häufig weitere, mit dem Alter meistens zwangsläufig zusammenhängende Umstände, wie etwa die altersbedingte Leistungsfähigkeit, vom Gericht betrachtet werden. Ist eine verminderte Leistungsfähigkeit etwa ein typisches Symptom für ein bestimmtes Alter, dann muss als Vergleich eine Person anderen Alters, aber mit dem gleichen Leistungsniveau, herangezogen und gefragt werden, ob für sie ebenfalls eine Diskriminierung vorliege bzw. vorliegen würde.[202]

e. Die Diskriminierung wegen einer Behinderung

Grundsätzlich nicht in den Anwendungsbereich des Age Discrimination Act 2004 (Cth) fallen jedoch jegliche Diskriminierungen wegen einer Behinderung. Denn für

---

200 *Lightning Bolt Co Pty Limited v Skinner & Anor* [2002] QSC 062.

201 *Boehringer Ingelheim Pty Ltd v Reddrop* [1984] 2 NSWLR 13.

202 Tritt eine solche Streitfrage auf, dann muss an § 6 ADA und das Verhältnis von Diskriminierung wegen einer Behinderung und einer Diskriminierung wegen Alters gedacht werden

solche Fälle ist ausschließlich die spezialgesetzliche Regelung des Disability Discrimination Act 1992 (Cth) anzuwenden, § 6 ADA.[203]

aa. Überschneidungen der Diskriminierung wegen einer Behinderung und der Dis kriminierung wegen Alters

Allerdings können trotz der eindeutigen gesetzlichen Regelung des § 6 ADA dennoch Überschneidungen der Anwendungsbereiche des Age Discrimination Act 2004 (Cth) und des Disability Discrimination Act 1992 (Cth) auftreten. Das ist vor allem in den Fällen denkbar, in welchen Behinderungen vorliegen, die mit einem bestimmten Alter zusammenhängen oder zusammenhängen können. Zu denken ist dabei etwa an Schwerhörigkeit. Eine erhebliche Bedeutung kommt darüber hinaus insbesondere auch einer körperlichen und somit bewegungseinschränkenden Behinderung oder aber auch einer Beeinträchtigung der Sehfunktion zu.[204]

Solche möglichen Überschneidungen wurden vom Gesetzgeber frühzeitig erkannt und bereits in der Erklärung zur Gesetzesvorlage zum Age Discrimination Act 2004 (Cth) – Age Discrimination Bill 2003 (Cth) – herausgearbeitet. In der Begründung zu dieser wird ausdrücklich darauf hingewiesen, dass neben dem Disability Discrimination Act 1992 (Cth) keine zweite oder alternative Rechtsschutzmöglichkeit geschaffen werden soll und dass Streitfragen in Bezug auf Diskriminierungen mit behinderungsrelevanten Sachbezug gerade dann unter die spezialgesetzlichen Regelungen des Disability Discrimination Act 1992 (Cth) fallen, wenn ihre Ursache in der Behinderung angelegt ist und sie nicht aufgrund des Alters erfolgt sind.[205] Eine Behinderung im Sinne des Disability Discrimination Act 1992 (Cth) wird in § 4 wie folgt definiert:[206]

„...(a) total or partial loss of the person's bodily or mental functions; or
(b) total or partial loss of a part of the body; or
(c) the presence in the body of organisms causing disease or illness; or
(d) the presence in the body of organisms capable of causing disease or illness; or
(e) the malfunction, malformation or disfigurement of a part of the person's body; or
(f) a disorder or malfunction that results in the person learning differently from a person without the disorder or malfunction; or

---

203 Vgl. überblicksartig *Bourke/Ronalds*, Discrimination Laws – Striving For Equality, in: *Macken*, The Law of Employment, 2002, 615.

204 Human Rights and Equal Opportunity Commissionn, Federal Discrimination Law 2009, 7; Human Rights and Equal Opportunity Commissionn, Federal Discrimination Law 2005, 17; Explanatory Memorandum of the Age Discrimination Bill 2003 (Cth), Annexure C, Clause 6, Age discrimination not to include disability discrimination.

205 Explanatory Memorandum of the Age Discrimination Bill 2003 (Cth), Annexure C, Clause 6, Age discrimination not to include disability discrimination; *Louw*, Age Discrimination Act 2004 (Cth) – Application of the Act, in: Baker & McKenzie, Age Discrimination: Mitigating Risk in the Workplace, S. 17.

206 Vgl. zur Definition des Begriffs der Behinderung im Kontext von Beschäftigung und Beruf nach europäischem Recht und zur Rechtsprechung des EuGH in der Rechtssache Chacón Navas *Colneric*, Antidiskriminierung – quo vadis? – Europäisches Recht, NZA-Beilage 2008, Heft 2, 72.

(g) a disorder, illness or disease that affects a person's thought processes, perception of reality, emotions or judgment or that results in disturbed behaviour;
and includes a disability that:
(h) presently exists; or
(i) previously existed but no longer exists; or
(j) may exist in the future (including because of a genetic predisposition to that disability); or
(k) is imputed to a person."

Besteht zwischen der Diskriminierung wegen einer Behinderung und der Diskriminierung wegen Alters kein zwingender Zusammenhang, dann sind sowohl der sachliche Anwendungsbereich des Disability Discrimination Act 1992 (Cth) und der des Age Discrimination Act 2004 (Cth) eröffnet. Folglich können dann nebeneinander Klagen wegen einer Diskriminierung wegen Behinderung und wegen einer Diskriminierung wegen Alters erhoben werden, ohne das eine gesetzliche Sperrwirkung eintritt.

bb. Anwendungsvorrang des Age Discrimination Act 2004 (Cth) – der dominant reason test

Erfolgt die Diskriminierung wegen einer Behinderung aber primär aufgrund des Alters einer Person, obwohl mehrere Diskriminierungen vorliegen, dann kann der Age Discrimination Act 2004 (Cth) gemäß § 16 ADA Anwendungsvorrang genießen. Dazu muss einer der Diskriminierungsgründe das Alter der betroffenen Person erfassen und gegenüber dem weiteren Diskriminierungsgrund muss die Diskriminierung wegen des Alters überwiegen. Ob die Diskriminierung wegen Alters aber tatsächlich überwiegt, ist anhand des sog. *„dominant reason test"* festzustellen.[207] Deshalb ist eine konkrete Einzelfallbetrachtung zur zutreffenden Bewertung des Charakters der Diskriminierung unerlässlich.

Mit dieser Vorrangregelung sollen nach Ansicht des Gesetzgebers insbesondere das Aufkommen sowie die Ausweitung von Hindernissen für eine positive Entwicklung der Beschäftigung älterer (australischer) Arbeitnehmer minimiert und eingedämmt werden.[208] Diese Zielsetzung und Argumentation überrascht deshalb, weil in den anderen Antidiskriminierungsgesetzen kein derartiger *„dominant reason test"* enthalten ist. Vielmehr soll es dort für die Eröffnung des sachlichen Anwendungsbereichs beim Vorliegen mehrerer unterschiedlicher Diskriminierungsgründe genügen, wenn einer der Diskriminierungsgründe dem Anwendungsbereich des jeweiligen Antidiskriminierungsgesetzes zugeordnet werden kann.[209] Tatsächlich besteht aber die Gefahr, dass durch den *„dominant reason test"* der Rechtsschutz gegen Altersdiskriminierungen gerade erschwert anstatt erleichtert wird.

---

207 *Esso Australian Resources Ltd v Commissioner of Taxation* (1999) 201 CLR 49; insofern weicht der Age Discrimination Act von allen anderen Anti-Diskriminierungsgesetzen auf Commonwealth-Ebene ab.

208 Explanatory Memorandum of the Age Discrimination Bill 2003 (Cth), Annexure C, Clause 16, Act done because of age and for other reason.

209 *Hemingway*, The Age Discrimination Act 2004, 11; vgl. § 8 SDA, § 18 RDA, § 10 DDA.

Gegen die gesetzliche Ausgestaltung des § 16 ADA und den daraus erneut resultierenden Vorrangtest („*dominant reason test*") wandte sich auch die Human Rights and Equal Opportunity Commission bereits in ihrem Antrag an das Senate Legal and Constitutional Committee im Rahmen des Gesetzgebungsverfahrens für den Entwurf des Age Discrimination Act 2004 (Cth). Denn nach ihrer Ansicht werde es den Geschädigten durch das gesetzliche Erfordernis, dass bei mehreren Diskriminierungen zuerst geklärt werden müsse, aus welcher primären Motivation eine Diskriminierung vorgenommen wurde, unnötig erschwert, erfolgreich eine Klage auf der Grundlage des Age Discrimination Act 2004 (Cth) wegen einer Altersdiskriminierung zu erheben und zugleich werde der Eindruck erweckt, dass der Altersdiskriminierung als im Vergleich zur Diskriminierung wegen der Rasse, des Geschlechts oder einer Behinderung weniger Bedeutung beizumessen ist.[210] Damit der positive Nutzen der Gesetzgebung auf der Grundlage der Altersdiskriminierung nicht verloren geht, solle dieser Vorrangtest, wie etwa im Gesetzesentwurf des Law and Justice Legislation Amendment Bill 1990 vorgesehen und mit dem „*dominant purpose test*" im Bereich der Diskriminierung wegen der Rasse im Jahr 1990 geschehen, nunmehr endgültig und auch tatsächlich abgeschafft werden.

Für die Auffassung der Human Rights and Equal Opportunity Commission spricht vor allem auch die zuvor angesprochene gesetzgeberische Ausgestaltung des Anwendungsvorrangs im Sex Discrimination Act 1984 (Cth), im Racial Discrimination Act 1975 (Cth) und im Disability Discrimination Act 1992 (Cth). Denn dort genügt für die Anwendung des jeweiligen Gesetzes, dass eine Diskriminierung aus dem Anwendungsbereich des jeweiligen Gesetzes vorliegt. Es spielt dabei keine Rolle, ob sie die überwiegende Diskriminierung ist und damit den maßgeblichen Diskriminierungsgrund darstellt oder nicht.[211] Die mit dem „*dominant reason test*" erfolgte Einschränkung beim Age Discrimination Act 2004 (Cth) erscheint demnach nicht konsequent.[212]

Allerdings muss dennoch berücksichtigt werden, dass es im Grundsatz möglich ist, eine Klage wegen einer Diskriminierung wegen Alters zu erheben und zugleich auch gerichtlich gegen eine Diskriminierung wegen einer Behinderung vorzugehen.[213]

210 *Esso Australian Resources Ltd v Commissioner of Taxation* (1999) 201 CLR 49; *Sparnon v Apand* (1996) 68 FCR 322; vgl. auch Submission to the Senate Legal and Constitutional Legislation Committee on the Age Discrimination Bill 2003, abrufbar unter www.humanrights.gov.au/legal/submissions/age_discrimination.html.

211 Vgl. § 8 SDA, § 18 RDA, § 10 DDA.

212 So auch *Smith*, Australian Anti-Discrimination Laws – Framework, Developments and Issues, New Developments in Employment Discrimination Law – The 9 JILPT Comparative Labour Law Seminar (2008) 19; im Ergebnis wurde aufgrund der Kritik § 16 ADA entsprechend angepasst und der *"dominant reason test"* im Jahr 2010 beseitigt; auch im deutschen Allgemeinen Gleichbehandlungsgesetz soll der Kausalitätszusammenhang zwischen der nachteiligen Behandlung und dem Diskriminierungsgrund bereits bei einer Anknüpfung an einen der in § 1 AGG genannten Gründe gegeben sein; gemäß der Rechtsprechung des deutschen Bundesarbeitsgerichts genügt es, dass der Diskriminierungsgrund des Alters Bestandteil eines Motivbündels ist (vgl. BAG, Urteil vom 22.01.2009 - 8 AZR 906/07 = NZA 2009, 945).

213 Human Rights and Equal Opportunity Commission, Federal Discrimination Law 2009, 8 Human Rights and Equal Opportunity Commission, Federal Discrimination Law 2005, 17; Explanatory Memorandum of the Age Discrimination Bill 2003 (Cth), Annexure C, Clause 16, Act done because of age and for other reason.

Denn vielmehr soll der Rechtsschutz gegen Diskriminierungen nicht eingeschränkt, sondern ausgeweitet werden. Somit wird letztlich in der Praxis über einen Umweg dennoch ein umfassender Schutz versucht zu gewähren.[214]

cc. *Die Abgrenzung der Diskriminierung wegen einer Behinderung von der Dis kriminierung wegen Alters im Einzelfall*

Gerade in der Praxis zeigen sich aber immer wieder erhebliche Probleme in der eindeutigen Abgrenzung einer Diskriminierung wegen einer Behinderung von der Diskriminierung wegen Alters, da rechtsverbindliche Maßstäbe und Kriterien fehlen.

Einigkeit besteht allerdings dahingehend, dass es für eine Diskriminierung wegen einer Behinderung nicht auf die Kenntnis des Diskriminierenden von der Behinderung ankommt. Denn ansonsten würde eine ungewollte Begrenzung des Diskriminierungsschutzes herbeigeführt, indem einer wegen einer Behinderung diskriminierten Person der Anwendungsbereich des Disability Discrimination Act 1992 (Cth) verschlossen bliebe.[215] Darüber hinaus sollte berücksichtigt werden, dass sich die konkrete Wahrnehmung von diskriminierenden Maßnahmen und Verhaltensweisen für jeden Menschen subjektiv unterschiedlich gestaltet und dadurch abweichende komplexe und multidimensionale Erfahrungen entstehen.[216]

Da oftmals altersbedingte physische und/oder psychische Defizite vom jeweiligen Betroffenen nicht als eine Behinderung im eigentlichen Sinn aufgefasst, sondern als „normale" Alterserscheinungen charakterisiert werden, sollte dieser Umstand für eine Abgrenzung zwischen einer altersbedingten Diskriminierung und einer Diskriminierung wegen einer Behinderung genutzt werden.

> „I would not necessarily say an older person had a disability if they have got age related hearing loss. I would say well that's something that happens with age. It is like your hair going grey."[217]

Darüber hinaus erscheint die Einbindung der medizinischen Definitionskomponente für den Begriff der Behinderung und somit die Fokussierung auf medizinische oder funktionelle Beeinträchtigungen als hilfreich für eine trennscharfe Abgrenzung. Daher werden sich im Ergebnis immer die Fragen stellen, was kann ein älterer Mensch im Vergleich zu einer Person mit einer Behinderung und liegt der Schwerpunkt allein beim konkreten Alter oder haben die Beeinträchtigen weitergehende physische oder psychische Ursachen.

---

214 Revised Explanatory Memorandum, Age Discrimination Act 2004 (Cth), 39.

215 *Tate v Rafin* [2000] FCA 1582; *New South Wales (Department of Education) v Human Rights and Equal Opportunity Commission* (2001) 186 ALR 69.

216 *Hemingway*, The Age Discrimination Act 2004, 11.

217 *Priestley/Rabiee*, Building Bridges: disability and old age (2001) ESRC resarch report R000223581, 10.

2. Indirekte Diskriminierung

Nicht selten führt eine umfassende Gleichbehandlung mehrerer Personen zu einer im Ergebnis ungleichen und somit benachteiligenden Behandlung, wenn die jeweiligen persönlichen Umstände und Situationen eines Einzelfalles nicht angemessen berücksichtigt werden.[218] Dies gilt auch im Bereich des Alters. So tritt im Gegensatz zur direkten Diskriminierung eine indirekte Diskriminierung meistens in der Form auf, dass die mit ihr verbundenen Bedingungen und Anforderungen neutral und gerecht erscheinen, aber dennoch eine bestimmte Altersgruppe unzumutbar benachteiligen.[219]

So liegt eine indirekte Diskriminierung nach dem Wortlaut des Gesetzes deshalb immer dann vor, wenn eine Person – *„discriminator"* – eine andere Person – *„aggrieved person"* – aufgrund des Alters durch die Verwendung von Bedingungen, Anforderungen oder Praktiken missbraucht oder beabsichtigt zu missbrauchen (§ 15 Abs. 1 lit. a) ADA), die Bedingungen, Anforderungen oder Praktiken unter den gegebenen Umständen nicht gerecht sind (§ 15 Abs. 1 lit. b) ADA) und diese Bedingungen, Anforderungen oder Praktiken für den Geschädigten im Vergleich mit Personen gleichen Alters eine benachteiligende Wirkung haben oder haben können (§ 15 Abs. 1 lit. c) ADA). In der Regel handelt es sich dabei also immer um Bedingungen, Anforderungen und Praktiken, die in ihrer Wirkung eigentlich neutral erscheinen, aber dann in der praktischen Anwendung bestimmte Personen oder Personengruppen benachteiligen.

In der Praxis tritt eine indirekte Diskriminierung etwa dann hervor, wenn Stellenanzeigen besondere Berufserfahrung ausdrücklich als Voraussetzung für den zu besetzenden Job nennen, da hierdurch vor allem jüngere Mitbewerber, denen eine solche Erfahrung zwangsläufig fehlt, durch die unzulässige Implementierung einer Altersgrenze benachteiligt werden.[220] Gleiches gilt auch für besondere Weiterbildungsmaßnahmen, für deren Teilnahme eine bestimmte Berufserfahrung in der jeweiligen Tätigkeit als Erfordernis aufgestellt wird.[221]

In der Diskriminierungsrechtspraxis wird von dem nachfolgend näher erörterten Begriff der indirekten Diskriminierung wegen Alters nur wenig Gebrauch gemacht, da er scheinbar von den meisten Klägern nicht hinreichend genug verstanden wird. Denn für den Laien scheint auf den ersten Blick tatsächlich eine Gleichbehandlung gegeben zu sein.[222] Nichtsdestotrotz muss aufgrund der Antidiskriminierungsgesetzgebung und der mit dieser verbundenen und sehr weit gefassten Ziele, Diskriminierungen wegen Alters bereits im Vorfeld zu verhindern oder aber zumindest wirksam zu beseitigen, davon ausgegangen werden, dass eine Diskriminierung selbst dann vorliegen kann,

---

218 *Fredman*, Discrimination Law, 106.

219 Bourke/Ronalds, Discrimination Laws - Striving Towards Equality, in Macken, The Law of Employment, 611; *Collins*, Employment Law, 59; *Honeyball/Bowers*, Textbook on Labour Law, 245.

220 *Collins*, Employment Law, Opportunity and Discrimination, 56; *Goulding*, The Law Handbook, 517; Attorney Generals Department of New South Wales, Age Discrimination – Options for New South Wales, A Discussion Paper (2000) 3.

221 *Harding*, The Road to Anti-Discrimination paved with good intentions, (1994) Law Society Journal, 44.

222 Bourke/Ronalds, Discrimination Laws - Striving Towards Equality, in Macken, The Law of Employment, 613.

wenn sie nicht sofort und ohne weiteres erkennbar ist. Gleiches gilt unabhängig davon, ob der *„discriminator"* die Altersdiskriminierung bewusst oder unbewusst vorgenommen hat oder er seiner Ansicht nach, sogar zum Vorteil der betreffenden Person zu handeln geglaubt hat.[223] Die Motivation für das diskriminierende Verhalten ist demnach unerheblich.

a. Grundprinzipien der indirekten Diskriminierung

aa. Bedingungen, Anforderungen oder Praktiken

Die Gerichte legten bereits im Rahmen ihrer früher zur Antidiskriminierung ergangenen Rechtsprechung einen weiten Maßstab an, um bestimmen zu können, was unter die Begriffe der Bedingungen, der Anforderungen oder der Praktiken (*„conditions, requirements, practices"*) zu subsumieren ist.[224] Damit sollte insbesondere eine vorteilhafte und günstige Gestaltung einer Antidiskriminierungsgesetzgebung erreicht werden.[225]

(1) Der Fall Australian Iron and Steel Pty Limited v Banovic

Unter Beachtung des Zwecks und des Ziels der Gesetzgebung zur Antidiskriminierung muss es nach Ansicht der Rechtsprechung grundsätzlich klar sein, dass den Begriffen der Anforderungen und Bedingungen nur ein weites Verständnis entgegengebracht werden kann, um somit jegliche Erscheinungsformen einer durch den Arbeitgeber von einem Arbeitnehmer verlangten Voraussetzung zu erfassen.[226] Trotzdem soll es aber erforderlich sein, in jedem konkreten Fall die aktuellen Anforderungen und Bedingungen präzise zu formulieren und hinreichend zu substantiieren.[227] Zur Bewertung betrachten die Gerichte insbesondere die Vereinbarung, die zu der Aufstellung der konkreten Anforderungen und Bedingungen geführt hat.[228]

(2) Der Fall State of Victoria v Schou (No 2)

In der Entscheidung in Sachen *State of Victoria v Schou (No 2)* legte der Victorian Court of Appeal seiner Rechtsprechung eine eingeschränktere Auslegung der Begriffe Anforderungen und Bedingungen zugrunde.[229] Die Mehrheit der Richter war in diesem Verfahren der Ansicht, dass die Anforderungen und Bedingungen selbst, ohne Berücksichtigung möglicher anderer Alternativen, wie etwa der sie hervorrufenden Vereinba-

---

223 *Water v Public Transport Corporation* (1991) 173 CLR 359.

224 *Bourke/Ronalds*, Discrimination Laws – Striving For Equality, in: *Macken*, The Law of Employment, 2002, 625.

225 *Clarke v. Eley (IMI) Kynoch Ltd* [1982] IRLR 482; *Styles v Secretary, Department of Foreign Affairs and Trade & Anor* (1988) 84 ALR 408.

226 *Australian Iron and Steel Pty Limited v Banovic* (1989) 89 ALR 1, 15; *Clarke v. Eley (IMI) Kynoch Ltd* [1982] IRLR 482.

227 *Australian Iron and Steel Pty Limited v Banovic* (1989) 89 ALR 1, 15.

228 *Australian Iron and Steel Pty Limited v Banovic* (1989) 89 ALR 1, 15.

229 *State of Victoria v Schou* (2004) 8 VR 120 (Schou (No 2)).

rung, für die Betrachtung maßgeblich seien.[230] Denn das Gesetz gebe keine Anhaltspunkte dafür, dass mögliche Veränderungen der Anforderungen, Bedingungen oder Praktiken berücksichtigt werden sollen, die gerechterweise vorgenommen werden könnten, um die speziellen Bedürfnisse einer Person aufzunehmen.[231]

(3) Der Fall Waters v Public Transport Corporation

Im Zusammenhang mit dem Zugang zu Gütern und Dienstleistungen ist der High Court im Fall *Waters v Public Transport Corporation* der etwas weitergehenden Auffassung, dass eine Anforderung und Bedingung all das umfasst, was den Gütern und Dienstleistungen notwendigerweise innewohnt.[232] Denn in diesem Fall ging es um die Einführung sog. *„scratch-tickets"* für den öffentlichen Straßenbahnverkehr, bei denen ein bestimmtes Feld zur Entwertung freigekratzt werden muss. Hierin sah die Rechtsprechung eine indirekte Diskriminierung von behinderten Menschen, weil diese nicht in der Lage sein können, diese Anforderung an die Entwertung der Straßenbahnfahrkarte ohne fremde Hilfe zu erfüllen und folglich vom Gebrauch derartiger Fahrscheine ausgeschlossen werden.[233]

(4) Schlussfolgerungen zu Bedingungen, Anforderungen und Praktiken

Die vorangestellten Beispiele aus der Rechtsprechung zur Klärung, was genau unter die Begriffe der Bedingungen, Anforderungen oder Praktiken im Sinne von § 15 Abs. 1 lit. a) ADA zu subsumieren sei, zeigen die vielfältigen Erscheinungsformen. So können insbesondere Anforderungen in Stellenanzeigen, aufgrund derer Absolventen gesucht werden, die erst vor kurzer Zeit ihren Studienabschluss oder einen Abschluss einer vergleichbaren Ausbildungseinrichtung erlangt haben, bereits als indirekt diskriminierende Bedingungen, Anforderungen oder Praktiken angesehen werden.[234] Gleiches gilt darüber hinaus für Anforderungen an einen Bewerber, dass er ehrgeizig, dynamisch und kreativ sein solle oder er sich nur durch die Teilnahme an einem Fitnesstest für eine bestimmte Stelle qualifizieren könne, denn ältere Bewerber können somit indirekt diskriminiert werden, weil sie aus altersbedingten Gründen diese Anforderungen und Bedingungen gegebenenfalls nicht mehr erfüllen könnten. Das gilt auch für die Bedingungen, nach denen der Bewerber älter und reifer sein müsse.

Im Ergebnis muss, um einen ausreichenden Schutz vor (versteckter) indirekter Altersdiskriminierung gewährleisten zu können, trotz einschränkender Versuche der Rechtsprechung ein weiter Maßstab angelegt werden.

---

230 *State of Victoria v Schou* (2004) 8 VR 120 (Schou (No 2)) unter Zustimmung der Richter *Phillips, Callaway* und *Buchanan JJA*.

231 *Thew*, Discrimination under the Age Discrimination Act, in: Baker & McKenzie, Age Discrimination: Mitigating Risk in the Workplace, S. 43.

232 *Waters v Public Transportation Corporation* (1991) 103 ALR 513, 521.

233 *Waters v Public Transportation Corporation* (1991) 103 ALR 513, 556.

234 *Dewan v. Main Roads WA* (2005) EOC 93-362.

bb. Gerechte Bedingungen, Anforderungen oder Praktiken

Im Gegensatz zu anderen australischen Antidiskriminierungsgesetzen (wie etwa zum Sex Discrimination Act 1984 (Cth), Equal Opportunity Act 1995 (Vic), Anti-Discrimination Act 1991 (Qld) oder zum Discrimination Act 1991 (ACT)) enthält der Age Discrimination Act 2004 (Cth) keinerlei gesetzgeberische Formeln dazu, wann eine Bedingung, Anforderung oder Praxis nicht als gerecht im Sinne von § 15 Abs. 1 lit. b) ADA gilt.[235] Anstatt der Gesetzgebung kommt auch in diesem Bereich der Rechtsprechung eine maßgebliche Bedeutung zur Klärung und Auslegung des Begriffes der gerechten Bedingung, Anforderung oder Praxis gemäß § 15 Abs. 1 lit. b) ADA zu, wobei ein erster Eindruck auch durch einen vergleichenden Blick in die eben genannten Gesetze gewonnen werden kann.[236]

(1) Mangels gesetzlicher Begriffsbestimmung erforderliche Abwägung

So soll nach der einschlägigen Rechtsprechung die bloße Existenz von alternativen Vereinbarungen, die auf Veranlassung des Arbeitgebers getätigt worden sind, die Bedingungen, Anforderungen oder Praktiken noch nicht automatisch gerecht werden lassen.[237] Vielmehr müsse eine Abwägung dieser einzelvertraglichen Vereinbarung mit der in jedem Einzelfall konkret herauszustellenden Diskriminierung vorgenommen werden, um deren Gerechtigkeit und Zumutbarkeit feststellen zu können.[238]

Um zwischen den verschiedenen und miteinander konkurrierenden Faktoren eine ausgewogene Abwägungsbewertung vornehmen zu können, müsse nach Ansicht der Rechtsprechung deshalb vor allem untersucht werden, ob logische und nachvollziehbare Gründe für die aufgestellten Bedingungen und Anforderungen erkennbar und ob sie geeignet und erforderlich sind, das gesetzte Ziel bzw. den beabsichtigten Zweck zu erreichen und dies auch tatsächlich beabsichtigt sei.[239] Darüber hinaus bedürfen aber auch die finanzielle Belastung des Beklagten mit der Durchführung einer alternativen Änderung und Vereinbarung der Bedingungen und Praktiken im Vergleich mit der aktuellen Situation, die ihm zur Verfügung stehenden finanziellen Mittel, die Zweckmäßigkeit und die Effektivität der Aufrechterhaltung der aktuellen Bedingungen, Anforderungen und Praktiken sowie der Einfluss von Konkurrenten auf die Möglichkeit der Herbeiführung alternativer Vereinbarungen im Rahmen der Abwägung einer umfassenden Betrachtung.[240]

---

235 Human Rights and Equal Opportunity Commission, Federal Discrimination Law 2009, 8; Human Rights and Equal Opportunity Commission, Federal Discrimination Law 2005, 15.

236 Vgl. vor allem die Entscheidung zum Disability Discrimination Act 1992 (Cth): *Clarke v Catholic Education Office* (2003) 202 ALR 340; *Catholic Education Office v Clarke* [2004] FCAFC 197.

237 *State of Victoria v Schou (No 2)* (2004) 8 VR 120 *(Schou (No 2))* mit Verweis auf *Commonwealth Bank v HREOC* (1997) 80 FCR 78, 88.

238 *Secretary, Department of Foreign Affairs and Trade v Styles* (1988) EOC 92-39 und (1989) 23 FCR 251, 263 *(Styles).*

239 *State of Victoria v Schou (No 2)* (2004) 8 VR 120 *(Schou (No 2))*; *Waters v Public Transportation Corporation* (1991) 173 CLR 349, 379.

240 *Secretary, Department of Foreign Affairs and Trade v Styles* (1988) EOC 92-39 und (1989) 23 FCR 251, 263 *(Styles).*

Des Weiteren dürfen die vom Kläger erlittenen Nachteile nicht unberücksichtigt bleiben. Vielmehr müssen sie mit den allgemein durch alternative Vereinbarungen der Bedingungen, Auflagen und Praktiken hervorgerufenen Nachteilen verglichen werden. Darüber hinaus müssen auch die Art und Weise sowie die Angemessenheit von Unterstützungsleistungen gegenüber dem Geschädigten bei der Vereinbarung von Auflagen und Bedingungen in die Abwägung einfließen.[241]

(2) Beweislastverteilung

Gemäß § 15 Abs. 2 ADA wird lediglich für den Nachweis, dass die Bedingungen, Anforderungen und Praktiken gerecht im Sinne von § 15 Abs. 1 lit. b) ADA sind, die Beweislast auf den *„discriminator"* (den Diskriminierende) verlagert. Denn derjenige der eine Anforderung oder Bedingung einführt oder einzuführen beabsichtigt, ist aufgrund der praktischen Bezugsnähe in der Regel am besten in der Lage die im Einzelfall ausschlaggebenden Gründe umfassend darzulegen, zu erklären oder zu rechtfertigen.[242] So versteht der Arbeitgeber, dessen Unternehmen für eine ausreichende Wettbewerbsfähigkeit verschiedene Produktivitätsanforderungen stellt oder externen Anforderungen entsprechen muss, am besten, warum dies erforderlich ist und er ist deshalb auch am besten in der Lage zu zeigen, dass die gestellten Anforderungen gerecht sind.[243]

b. Schlussfolgerungen zu den Grundprinzipien der indirekten Diskriminierung

Im Vergleich mit der direkten Diskriminierung ist die Bewertung eines Verhaltens als indirekte Diskriminierung nicht einfacher. Denn im Rahmen einer solchen indirekten Diskriminierung kann insbesondere die zu § 15 Abs. 1 lit. b) ADA vorzunehmende Einzelfallabwägung zahlreiche Schwierigkeiten zu Tage fördern. Trotz der Hürden sollte in jedem erforderlichen Fall eine hinreichende Abwägung vorgenommen werden, um sicher feststellen zu können, ob eine mit der Gleichbehandlung verbundene indirekte Diskriminierung gerechtfertigt ist. Denn das erstrebte Fernziel sollte zwar eine umfassende Gleichbehandlung jedweder Altersgruppen sein. Sofern aber besondere Anforderungen und Bedingungen mit gewichtigen – gleich ob unternehmerischen oder gesellschaftspolitischen – Argumenten eine Abweichung im Einzelfall erforderlich werden lassen, kann es zulässig sein, eine solche – sonst beabsichtigte – gleiche Behandlung ausnahmsweise nicht vorzunehmen.[244]

---

241 *Hinchliffe v The University of Sydney* [2004] FMCA 85.

242 Explanatory Memorandum of the Age Discrimination Bill 2003 (Cth), Annexure C, Clause 15, Discrimination on the ground of age – indirect discrimination.

243 Explanatory Memorandum of the Age Discrimination Bill 2003 (Cth), Annexure C, Clause 15, Discrimination on the ground of age – indirect discrimination.

244 *Fredman*, Employment Law, 115.

3. Das Verhältnis von direkter und indirekter Diskriminierung

Die Diskriminierungsarten der direkten und indirekten Diskriminierung schließen sich aufgrund ihres Charakters gegenseitig aus.[245] Folglich kann eine direkte Diskriminierung niemals zugleich eine indirekte Diskriminierung sein.[246]

Das bedeutet jedoch nicht zwangsläufig, dass eine diskriminierende Behandlung im Wege des gerichtlichen Verfahrens nicht alternativ als direkte oder indirekte Diskriminierung verfolgt werden kann.[247] Denn oftmals wird es für den von einer Altersdiskriminierung Betroffenen nicht ohne weiteres auf Anhieb rechtlich zutreffend festzustellen sein, ob es sich um eine direkte oder eine indirekte Diskriminierung gehandelt hat. Deshalb sollten die Anforderungen nicht überspannt werden und eine alternative rechtliche Wertung zugestanden werden. Vor allem soll diese Möglichkeit in solchen Fällen ohne weiteres offen stehen, wenn es rechtlich vertretbar erscheint für das Vorliegen einer direkten Diskriminierung zu argumentieren und sich aber zugleich auch in vertretbarer Weise alternativ eine indirekte Diskriminierung belegen ließe.[248]

Sofern mehrere Diskriminierungen behauptet und angegriffen werden, wird der Grundsatz der Exklusivität der direkten und indirekten Diskriminierung jedoch nicht berührt, so dass der Kläger sich einerseits auf eine direkte Diskriminierung und daneben – wegen eines anderen Diskriminierungsverhaltens – auf eine indirekte Diskriminierung berufen kann. Würde man ihm dieses Recht abschneiden, so entstünde der Zwang zu einem weiteren kostenpflichtigen Verfahren und zugleich würde auch die effiziente Rechtsverfolgung und –durchsetzung nicht unerheblich leiden.

> „There is, in my view, no obligation upon an applicant to make an election between mutually exclusive direct and indirect disability claims. If both claims are arguably open upon the facts, they may be pleaded in the alternative. The fact that they are mutually exclusive would almost inevitably lead to a disadvantageous costs outcome for an applicant, but that is the applicant's choice."[249]

4. Belästigungen und Schikanierungen wegen Alters

Vor allem im Bereich von Arbeit und Beschäftigung spielen Belästigungen und Schikanierungen („*harassment*") wegen des Alters einer Person eine bedeutende Rolle, da sie Auswirkungen in mehrere Richtungen mit sich bringen. Nicht nur der betroffene Arbeitnehmer bzw. Mitarbeiter wird persönlich diskriminiert, sondern wie Untersuchungen zeigen, leidet oftmals auch die Produktivität und somit gleichzeitig die Ren-

---

245 *Waters v Public Transport Commission* (1991) 173 CLR 349; *Australian Medical Council v Human Rights and Equal Opportunity Commission* (1995) 68 FCR 46; *Mayer v Australian Nuclear Science and Technology Organisation* [2003] FMCA 209.

246 *Hemingway*, The Age Discrimination Act 2004, 9 m.w.N..

247 *Minns v New South Wales* [2002] FMCA 60.

248 *Waters v Public Transport Commission* (1991) 173 CLR 349 at 393; *Australian Medical Council v Human Rights and Equal Opportunity Commission* (1995) 68 FCR 46; *Mayer v ANSTO* [2003] FMCA 209; (2003) EOC 93-285; *Hollingdale v Northern Rivers Area Health* [2004] FMCA 721.

249 *Hollingdale v Northern Rivers Area Health* [2004] FMCA 721 m.wN..

tabilität der Arbeit unter derartigen Verhaltensweisen.[250] Darüber hinaus werden in der Regel die Kosten eines Unternehmens durch den nicht selten verursachten Personalausfall erhöht, die Gefahr des Verlustes qualifizierter Fachkräfte steigt und oftmals leidet auch das öffentliche Ansehen eines Unternehmens.

a. Belästigungen wegen Alters

Im Gegensatz zu den Definitionen der direkten und der indirekten Diskriminierung findet sich im Age Discrimination Act 2004 (Cth) keine ausdrückliche Regelung eines Verbots von Belästigungen wegen Alters. Allerdings hat die Rechtsprechung sexuelle und rassistische Belästigungen als zu den Diskriminierungen wegen des Geschlechts oder wegen einer Rasse gehörend eingestuft, ohne dass in diesen Fällen eine ausdrückliche gesetzliche Regelung gegeben ist.[251] Denn nach Ansicht der Rechtsprechung des Federal Court, sei z.B. eine sexuelle Belästigung einer Arbeitnehmerin durch ihren Arbeitgeber dann eine Diskriminierung der Frau am Arbeitsplatz aufgrund des Geschlechts, wenn eine andere Person des anderen Geschlechts nicht in der gleichen Art und Weise vom Arbeitgeber behandelt worden wäre oder wird.[252]

Aufgrund der vergleichbaren Interessenlage für die geschädigten Personen können wegen des Sachbezugs – unter Beachtung des konkreten Einzelfalles und einer weiten Wortlautauslegung – unter die Begriffe der direkten oder indirekten Diskriminierung auch Belästigungen wegen Alters subsumiert werden.[253] Trotz dieser vorwiegend rechtspraktischen Lösung besteht Handlungsbedarf des Gesetzgebers, denn erst eine klare gesetzliche Regelung würde eindeutig aufzeigen, dass auch eine derartige Verhaltens- und Handlungsweise unrechtmäßig ist und deshalb nicht toleriert werden kann.[254]

b. Schikanierungen wegen Alters

Wie der Sexual Discrimination Act 1984 (Cth) und der Disability Discrimination Act 1992 (Cth) enthält auch der Age Discrimination Act 2004 (Cth) in den §§ 51 ADA gesetzliche Regelungen zu Schikanierungen wegen Alters und zu schikanierenden Drohungen („*victimisation*") mit einem Nachteil für das Opfer. In § 51 ADA werden

---

250 *Bourke/Ronalds*, Discrimination Laws – Striving For Equality, in: *Macken*, The Law of Employment, 2002, 615; *Smith*, Harrassment and bullying in the workplace, (2005) 11 Employment Law Bulletin 1.

251 *O'Callaghan v Loder (No 2)* [1983] 3 NSWLR 89; (1984) EOC 92-022; *Aldridge v Booth* (1988) 80 ALR 1.

252 *Aldridge v Booth* (1988) 80 ALR 1, 16.

253 Der Vergleich mit der bisherigen deutschen Judikatur zeigt, dass die Belästigung im Sinne des § 3 Abs. 3 AGG als spezifische Form der Diskriminierung noch recht blass geblieben; vgl. aber BAG NZA 2010, 387.

254 *Louw*, Age Discrimination Act 2004 (Cth) – Application of the Act, in: Baker & McKenzie, Age Discrimination: Mitigating Risk in the Workplace, S. 16.

schikanierende Verhaltens- und Handlungsweisen und Drohungen als Vergehen charakterisiert und mit einer Freiheitsstrafe von sechs Monaten geahndet.[255]

aa. Schikanierendes Verhalten und schikanierende Behandlungen

Um aber zu einer Bestrafung zu gelangen, bedarf es zuerst der Auseinandersetzung mit dem Begriff der Schikanierung wegen Alters. Insbesondere erscheint zur Klarstellung eine Abgrenzung zur (bloßen) Belästigung erforderlich zu sein.

Die Aufnahme der Schikanierung wegen Alters in eine ausdrückliche gesetzliche Regelung und der damit verbundenen Pönalisierung im Age Discrimination Act 2004 (Cth) könnte dabei vermuten lassen, dass eine Schikanierung wegen Alters schwerer wiegen und deshalb zwangsläufig konkretere Verhaltensformen voraussetzen wird, als es bei einer (bloßen) Belästigung wegen Alters der Fall sein könnte.

Der Age Discrimination Act 2004 (Cth) fasst jede Verhaltensweise einer Person (*„the first person"*), die zu Lasten eines anderen (*„the second person"*) einen Nachteil herbeiführt oder mit der beabsichtigt wird, einen Nachteil herbeizuführen, als Schikanierung auf, wenn sie ohne Zustimmung der anderen Person (*„the second person"*) und aufgrund einer in § 51 Abs. 1 lit. e) i)-vii) ADA aufgeführten Überzeugungen vorgenommen wird.

Dabei werden von § 51 Abs. 1 lit. e) i)-vii) ADA insbesondere Handlungen des Täters umfasst, die er vornimmt, weil die andere Person eine Klage auf der Grundlage des Human Rights and Equal Commission Act 1986 eingereicht hat oder beabsichtigt einzureichen (§ 51 Abs. 1 lit. e) i) ADA), weil die andere Person ein Verfahren auf der Grundlage des Human Rights and Equal Commission Act 1986 angestrengt hat oder beabsichtigt anzustrengen (§ 51 Abs. 1 lit. e) ii) ADA), weil die andere Person Informationen oder Dokumente an eine Person weitergegeben hat oder beabsichtigt weiterzugeben, die auf der Grundlage des Human Rights and Equal Commission Act 1986 zu Untersuchungen oder Handlungen berechtigt ist (§ 51 Abs. 1 lit. e) iii) ADA), weil die andere Person an einer Konferenz, die auf der Grundlage des Human Rights and Equal Commission Act 1986 abgehalten wird, teilnimmt oder beabsichtigt teilzunehmen (§ 51 Abs. 1 lit. e) iv) ADA), weil die andere Person in einem Verfahren auf der Grundlage des Human Rights and Equal Commission Act 1986 als Zeuge auftritt oder aufzutreten beabsichtig (§ 51 Abs. 1 lit. e) v) ADA), weil die andere Person in gerechtfertigter Weise Rechte von einer oder mehreren Personen auf der Grundlage des Human Rights and Equal Commission Act 1986 geltend macht oder beabsichtigt geltend zu machen (§ 51 Abs. 1 lit. e) vi) ADA) oder die andere Person behauptet, dass jemand eine im Sinne des 4. Teils des Age Discrimination Act 2004 (Cth) gesetzeswidrige Handlung vorgenommen hat (§ 51 Abs. 1 lit. e) vii) ADA).

Zusammenfassend kommt es hier demnach grundsätzlich immer auf die Absicht des Täters und die fehlende Zustimmung des Opfers an.

---

255 Das identische Strafmaß enthält auch § 42 Abs. 1 DDA. In § 94 Abs. 1 SDA reicht die Strafdrohung dagegen für natürliche Personen von einer Geldstrafe in Höhe von 2.500 AUD bis zu einer Freiheitsstrafe von drei Monaten und für juristische Personen beträgt das Strafmaß Geldstrafe in Höhe von 10.000 AUD.

bb. Schikanierende Drohungen mit Nachteilen

Gleichfalls werden aber auch schikanierende Drohungen mit einer Nachteilszufügung durch § 51 Abs. 2 ADA unter Strafe gestellt. Droht eine Person („*the first person*") einer anderen Person („*the second person*"), um für diese oder einen Dritten einen Nachteil zu verursachen (§ 51 Abs. 2 lit. a) ADA) und beabsichtigt sie („*the first person*") zugleich, dass die andere Person („*the second person*") die Durchführung der Drohung fürchtet (§ 51 Abs. 2 lit. b) i) ADA) oder verursacht sie („*the first person*") in rücksichtsloser Art und Weise, dass die andere Person die Durchführung der Drohung befürchtet (§ 51 Abs. 2 lit. b) ii) ADA) und nimmt sie („*the first person*") die Drohungen aufgrund einer Überzeugung im Sinne von § 51 Abs. 1 lit. e) i)-vii) ADA vor, dann droht ihr – ebenfalls wie bei § 51 Abs. 1 ADA – eine Freiheitsstrafe von sechs Monaten. Dabei können die Drohungen ausdrücklich oder stillschweigend erfolgen (§ 51 Abs. 3 lit. a) ADA) oder bedingt oder unbedingt sein (§ 51 Abs. 3 lit. b) ADA).

Gemäß § 51 Abs. 4 ADA ist es aber unter Opferschutzgesichtspunkten im Rahmen der Strafverfolgung nicht erforderlich, dass für ein Vergehen gegen § 51 Abs. 2 ADA die andere Person („*the second person*") tatsächlich die Durchführung der Drohung befürchtet hat. Die bloße Absicht eine solche herbeizuführen genügt für die Strafbarkeit.

cc. Schlussfolgerung zu Belästigungen und zu Schikanierungen wegen Alters

Aufgrund der Pönalisierung wiegen Schikanierungen wegen Alters und die Drohung mit solchen im Gegensatz zu (bloßen) Belästigungen für den Täter schwerer. Aber auch für das Opfer stellt sich eine andere Wirkung ein. Denn durch Schikanierungen oder Drohungen will der Täter in der Regel verhindern, dass jemand die ihm auf der Grundlage des Age Discrimination Act 2004 (Cth) gesetzlich zustehenden Rechte gegen Diskriminierungen wegen Alters wahrnimmt. Somit unterscheiden sich Belästigungen von den Schikanierungen wegen Alters und den Drohungen mit solchen dadurch, dass bei ersteren die Wahrnehmung der Rechte aus dem Age Discrimination Act 2004 (Cth) nicht beeinträchtigt werden, sondern vielmehr die physische und psychische Beeinträchtigung im Vordergrund steht.[256]

III. Befreiungen und Ausnahmen von den Diskriminierungsverboten

Das Recht aufgrund seines Alters nicht diskriminiert zu werden, stellt trotz der zahlreich im Age Discrimination Act 2004 (Cth) geregelten Diskriminierungsverbote kein „absolutes" Recht dar. So finden sich eine Vielzahl spezieller, aber zum Teil auch sehr allgemein gehaltener, Befreiungen und Ausnahmen im Gesetz, die entweder bestimm-

256 Explanatory Memorandum of the Age Discrimination Bill 2003 (Cth), Annexure C, Clause 51, Victimisation.

te Verhaltensweisen oder aber besondere Normadressaten erfassen.[257] Diese können demnach grundsätzlich nicht unter die einzelnen Diskriminierungsverbote subsumiert werden, wobei die Rechtsprechung die Ausnahmen aber grundsätzlich sehr eng auslegt, um einen maximalen Schutz vor Diskriminierungen wegen Alters zu gewährleisten.[258] Allerdings bestehen – wie noch zu zeigen sein wird – infolge der bereits ergangenen Rechtsprechung einige zum Teil erhebliche Erweiterungen der Befreiungen. Dadurch wird es oftmals nicht unproblematisch, die mit der gesetzlichen Regelung der Diskriminierungsverbote verbundenen Ziele gerade nicht zu unterlaufen und dennoch eine umfassende Bekämpfung der Altersdiskriminierung zu erreichen.[259]

Nicht ausdrücklich vom Age Discrimination Act 2004 (Cth) erfasst werden allerdings die allgemein in der Gesellschaft – aufgrund spezialgesetzlicher Regelung – tolerierten Diskriminierungen wegen Alters, so dass sich zu diesen auch keine Ausnahmen oder Rechtfertigungen im Age Discrimination Act 2004 (Cth) finden lassen. Hierher gehören etwa das gesetzlich vorgeschriebene Alter zum Führen eines Fahrzeugs, für den legalen Konsum von Alkohol, zur Heirat, für das aktive und passive Wahlrecht etc..[260]

1. Spezielle Befreiungen und Ausnahmen im Bereich von Be schäftigung und Arbeit

a. Die der Beschäftigung anhaftenden Voraussetzungen bzw. Anforde rungen

Wird jemandem eine bestimmte Beschäftigung verwehrt, indem er als Bewerber abgelehnt wird, oder wird ihm gekündigt, weil er aufgrund seines Alters nicht den speziellen der konkreten Tätigkeit anhaftenden Anforderungen („*inherent requirements*") entsprechen kann, so soll darin gerade keine Altersdiskriminierung begründet sein.[261] Diese Ausnahmeregelung in Form eines gesetzlichen Verteidigungsmittels („*statutory defence*") findet sich an zahlreichen Stellen im Age Discrimination Act 2004 (Cth) – §§ 18 Abs. 4, 19 Abs. 3, 20 Abs. 2, 21 Abs. 4, 22 Abs. 2 und 24 Abs. 2 ADA und zeigt deutlich die besondere Rechtfertigungsstruktur von Diskriminierungen wegen Al-

257 *Bourke/Ronalds*, Discrimination Laws - Striving Towards Equality, in Macken, The Law of Employment, 638.

258 *Rose v Secretary, Department of Social Security* (1990) 92 ALR 521; vgl. auch zur Kritik an den Ausnahmen *Encel*, Age Discrimination in Law and Practice, (2004) Elder Law Review 7; *Thornton*, The Liberal Promise (1990) 114; *Thornthwaite*, The Operation of Anti-Discrimination Legislation in NSW in relation to Employment Complaints, (1993) 6 Australian Journal of Labour Law 31.

259 *Hemingway*, The Age Discrimination Act 2004 (Cth), 25.

260 *Goulding*, The Law Handbook, 517; *Bourke/Ronalds*, Discrimination Laws – Striving For Equality, in: *Macken*, The Law of Employment, 2002, 593.

261 *Ratnam*, Federal Government's proposed age discrimination legislation, (2003) 9 Employment Law Bulletin 16; *Smith*, Australian Anti-Discrimination Laws – Framework, Developments and Issues, New Developments in Employment Discrimination Law – The 9 JILPT Comparative Labour Law Seminar (2008) 12.

ters.[262] Denn zur Rechtfertigung ist zu prüfen, ob überhaupt spezielle und vor allem der konkreten Tätigkeit anhaftende Anforderungen vorliegen und ob es dem Arbeitnehmer nicht möglich ist, diese Anforderungen zu erfüllen.[263] Dabei gilt es jedoch zu beachten, dass sie ausschließlich und ausdrücklich für die Bewerbung und Kündigung eines Arbeitnehmers einschlägig ist.[264] Demnach ist während des Beschäftigungsverhältnisses aber jegliches Verhalten verboten, welches zu einer Diskriminierung wegen Alters führen kann.[265]

Der Begriff der einer Beschäftigung anhaftenden Anforderungen wird dabei an die Discrimination (Employment and Occupation) Convention, 1958, der International Labour Organisation (ILO 111) angelehnt und von den Gerichten versucht einheitlich auszulegen, um nicht zuletzt eine internationale Übereinstimmung zu erreichen.[266] So wird eine Voraussetzung bzw. Anforderung als der Beschäftigung anhaftend charakterisiert, wenn sie für die bestimmte Beschäftigung von erheblicher Bedeutung (*„essential element"*) ist.[267] Ob eine solche erhebliche Bedeutung gegeben ist, hängt dabei nicht zuletzt von der Organisation der Beschäftigung durch den Arbeitgeber ab. Denn um diese Bestimmung vornehmen zu können, soll es erforderlich sein, nicht nur die Bedingungen und Konditionen, welche den Arbeits- und Beschäftigungsbereich und die damit verbundenen Aufgaben festlegen und beschreiben, zu betrachten, sondern auch die weiteren Umstände, unter denen die bestimmte Beschäftigung ausgeführt wird.[268] Dazu können der Ort der Arbeit oder eine mit dieser verbundene Gefahr zählen. Allerdings ist gleichzeitig zu berücksichtigen, dass die Anforderungen nicht überspannt werden dürfen. Denn einem Arbeitgeber kann keine bestimmte Unternehmensorganisation vorgeschrieben werden und zudem kann er nicht verpflichtet werden, den Beschäftigungsbetrieb so auszugestalten und zu überwachen, dass keinerlei Diskriminierungsmöglichkeiten mehr entstehen können.[269]

Der Age Discrimination Act 2004 (Cth) bezieht sich im Gegensatz zu anderen Bundesgesetzen demnach auf die spezielle Beschäftigung (*„inherent requirement of*

---

262 *Hemingway*, The Age Discrimination Act 2004, 13.

263 Nach dem Wortlaut der RL 2000/78/EG liegt dann keine Diskriminierung vor, wenn das an sich verbotene Differenzierungsmerkmal eine wesentliche und entscheidende berufliche Voraussetzung ist, soweit der verfolgte Zweck rechtmäßig und die Anforderung angemessen ist. Dieser Wortlaut wird von § 8 Abs. 1 AGG aufgegriffen.

264 Der Rechtfertigungsgrund der beruflichen Anforderungen im Sinne von Art. 4 RL 2000/78/EG sowie § 8 Abs. 1 AGG fokussiert nicht auf bestimmte Phasen des Berufs und der Beschäftigung; vgl. auch die aktuelle Rechtsprechung des EuGH in Sachen *Wolf*, EuZW 2010, 142.

265 *Smith*, From *Wardley* to *Purvis*: How far has Australian anti-discrimination law come in 30 years? (2008) 21 Australian Journal of Labour Law 3 m.w.N..

266 *Commonwealth of Australia v Human Rights and Equal Opportunity Commission* [2000] FCA 1854.

267 *Qantas Airways Limited v Christie* (1998) 193 CLR 280; *X v Commonwealth* (1999) 200 CLR 177; *Catanzariti*, (1999) 4 Employment Law Bulletin 92.

268 *Qantas Airways Limited v Christie* (1998) 193 CLR 280; *X v Commonwealth* (1999) 200 CLR 177; vgl. auch Human Rights and Equal Opportunity Commission, Federal Discrimination Law 2009, 14; Human Rights and Equal Opportunity Commission, Federal Discrimination Law 2005, 19.

269 *Hemingway*, The Age Discrimination Act 2004, 14 m.w.N..

the particular employment") und nicht etwa wie bei § 659 Abs. 3 WR Act[270] auf einen ganz speziellen Arbeitsplatz (*„the particular position concerned"*).[271] Dieser Fokus resultiert aus der Ansicht des Gesetzgebers, nach welcher der Age Discrimination Act 2004 (Cth) eine umfassende Möglichkeit zur Verteidigung gegen Altersdiskriminierungen gewährleisten soll. Folglich soll bei der Beurteilung einer etwaigen Befreiung von einem Diskriminierungsverbot auf die jeweilige Beschäftigung im Allgemeinen abgestellt und dadurch die Beantwortung der Frage erleichtert werden, ob eine Rechtfertigung für das diskriminierende Verhalten gegeben ist. Die Vornahme einer Einzelfallbetrachtung und somit einer Beurteilung des konkreten Arbeitsplatzes würde die Grenzen der Rechtfertigung aufweichen und zugleich erweitern, ohne dass eine allgemeingültige Regelung – welcher Art und Weise auch immer – aufgestellt werden könne.[272]

In diesem Zusammenhang wird in der Praxis nicht selten die Frage nach vorurteilsbehafteten Erfahrungssätzen über die nachlassenden Fähigkeiten älterer Arbeitnehmer diskutiert.[273] Die Schwierigkeit besteht in der Regel darin, dass weder ausschließlich positive Aussagen über die Leistungsfähigkeit junger Arbeitnehmer gerechtfertigt, noch rein negativ verallgemeinernde Aussagen über das Nachlassen der Leistungsfähigkeit von älteren Arbeitnehmern zutreffend sind. Daher darf nicht aufgrund der allgemeinen Lebenserfahrung auf eine verringerte Leistungsfähigkeit älterer Arbeitnehmer geschlossen werden. Auch kann eine Rechtfertigung nicht bereits durch die verallgemeinernde Behauptung, dass die Leistungsfähigkeit des Arbeitnehmers im Alter generell schwinde und mit dem Eintritt eines bestimmten Lebensalters sogar die Arbeits- bzw. Dienstunfähigkeit drohe, bejaht werden. Vielmehr muss der Arbeitgeber den angenommenen und behaupteten Leistungsabfall empirisch belegen.[274] Allerdings werden Beschäftigungschancen älterer Arbeitnehmer nicht zuletzt durch ihren Gesundheitszustand und die durch diesen beeinflusste Leistungsfähigkeit geprägt. Einen maßgeblichen Beitrag an der Minderung der Krankheitsanfälligkeit der Arbeitnehmer kann dabei grundsätzlich der Arbeitgeber durch präventive Maßnahmen zur Anpassung und Verbesserung des Arbeitsplatzes mit Blick auf das jeweilige Alter des Arbeitnehmers leisten. Zu denken ist hierbei etwa an die Unterstützung durch technische Hilfen beim Heben von schweren Gegenständen oder die Einschränkung ergonomisch ungünstiger Bewegungsabläufe.[275]

---

270 Zuvor § 170CK Abs. 2 WR Act.

271 *MacDermott*, Age Discrimination and Employment Law: The Sky's the Limit, (1998) 11 AJLL 144.

272 Anders aber die Rechtsprechung, vgl. hierzu *Qantas Airways Limited v Christie* (1998) 193 CLR 280; vgl. auch die nachfolgenden Ausführungen unter E. IV. 2.

273 Aus der deutschen Rechtsprechung kritisch BAG NZA 2010, 327, 330; vgl. auch Kohte AuR 2008, 281ff..

274 Däubler/Bertzbach-*Buschmann*, § 8 Rn. 25, 30.

275 Kohte AuR 2008, 281ff..

b. Unterschiedliche Bezahlung für Jugendliche unter 21 Jahren

Eine weitere wichtige Befreiung enthält § 25 Abs. 1 ADA, wonach eine Diskriminierung wegen Alters dann nicht vorliegt, wenn sie gemäß § 25 Abs. 2 ADA im Zusammenhang mit dem Arbeitslohn für Jugendliche unter 21 Jahren steht (*„youth wages"*). Dadurch kann der Arbeitgeber Beschäftigte, die jünger sind als 21 Jahre selbst dann anders – in der Regel geringer – bezahlen, wenn sie dieselbe Arbeit verrichten, wie Personen die älter als 21 Jahre sind.[276] Die *„youth wages"* stellen bereits deshalb ein interessantes Beispiel der Befreiungen und Ausnahmen vom Verbot der Diskriminierung wegen Alters dar, weil es sich zugleich um einen Fall von im Gesetz angelegter direkter Diskriminierung handelt. Zur Begründung dieser direkten Diskriminierung von jungen Arbeitnehmern und der damit verbundenen Ausnahmeregelung führt der australische Gesetzgeber den beabsichtigten Schutz der Wettbewerbsposition jüngerer Personen auf dem Arbeitsmarkt an.[277] Allerdings erscheint dieser äußerst fraglich, wenn somit eine generell geringere Lohnpolitik für Arbeitskräfte unter 21 Jahren begründet werden soll.[278] Zweckmäßiger wäre etwa eine Begrenzung der Ausnahmevorschrift auf bestimmte und gezielte Beschäftigungsprogramme für Jugendliche, da somit eine generelle Benachteiligung in Bezug auf unterschiedliche Bezahlung verhindert werden könnte.[279] Allerdings zeigt diese Ausnahmevorschrift deutlich, dass sich die Altersdiskriminierung nicht zwangsläufig gegenüber älteren Menschen vor dem Hintergrund einer bevorzugten Behandlung von Jüngeren niederschlagen muss. Die Diskriminierung wegen Alters ist kein einheitliches Problem. Vielmehr gestaltet sich die Diskriminierung von älteren Menschen aufgrund ihres Alters als gesondertes Phänomen. Denn jüngere Menschen, die etwa durch *youth wages* benachteiligt werden, werden die Gruppe der betroffenen Personen zwangsläufig mit fortschreitendem Lebensalter verlassen. Dagegen ist es Menschen mit einem höheren Alter nicht möglich, dieser Gruppe zu entkommen – sie werden immer älter, sehen sich weiterhin wegen ihres Alters Vorverurteilungen ausgesetzt und erfahren im schlimmsten Fall einen zu-

---

276 *Ratnam*, Federal Government's proposed age discrimination legislation, (2003) 9 Employment Law Bulletin 16; *Goulding*, The Law Handbook, 517.

277 *Hemingway*, The Age Discrimination Act 2004, 18; in § 8 Abs. 2 AGG wird die Vereinbarung einer geringeren Vergütung für gleiche oder gleichwertige Arbeit selbst beim Vorliegen besonderer Schutzvorschriften nicht als zulässige unterschiedliche Behandlung wegen beruflicher Anforderungen und somit als Rechtfertigung anerkannt; vgl. auch die Vorlage des BAG (Beschluss vom 20.05.2010 – 6 AZR 319/09) an den EuGH zur Frage ob im öffentlichen Dienst die Staffelung der Grundvergütung nach Lebensaltersstufen gegen das Verbot der Altersdiskriminierung verstoße.

278 Human Rights and Equal Opportunity Commission, Age Matters, 2000, 114.

279 Human Rights and Equal Opportunity Commission, Age matters? A discussion paper on age discrimination (1999) 37; Revised Explanatory Memorandum, Age Discrimination Act 2004 (Cth), 12; vgl. auch die Entscheidungen des EuGH vom 08.09.2011 C-297/10 und C-298/10 auf zwei verbundene Vorlagen des BAG zur Frage, ob (fortwirkende) Lebensaltersstufen in den Tarifvertragswerken des öffentlichen Dienstes eine verbotene Diskriminierung wegen des Alters darstellen; der EuGH hat die Regelungen im Tarifvertrag, nach denen sich innerhalb der jeweiligen Vergütungsgruppe die Grundvergütung eines Angestellten im öffentlichen Dienst bei dessen Einstellung nach dessen Alter bemisst, verworfen und die Ersetzung durch ein auf objektive Kriterien gestütztes Vergütungssystem verlangt.

nehmenden sozialen Ausschluss aus der Gesellschaft.[280] Darüber hinaus sind für ältere Menschen die Gefahren auch aufgrund ihres Alters Opfer von Diskriminierungen wegen einer Behinderung zu werden nicht unerheblich. Denn oftmals sind die Grenzen zwischen altersbedingten körperlichen bzw. geistigen Defiziten mit denen, die auf das hohe Alter der betreffenden Person zurückzuführen sind, fließend.[281] Vor diesem Hintergrund scheint eine Ausnahmeregelung zu Lasten jüngerer Arbeitnehmer und Beschäftigten als verhältnismäßig und nicht in unangemessener Form benachteiligend.

c. Befreiungen durch die Erfüllung von bestimmten Verpflichtungen

Es liegt kein Verstoß gegen ein Diskriminierungsverbot vor, wenn gemäß § 39 Abs. 8 lit. a) ADA ein Auftrag oder eine Weisung eines Gerichts, eine amtlich beglaubigte Einigung gemäß § 39 Abs. 8 lit. b) ADA oder eine Einigung im Sinne einer *„Australian workplace agreement"* gemäß § 39 Abs. 8 lit. c) ADA befolgt wird.[282]

d. Befreiungen bei Tätigkeiten im Haushalt

Bei einer Beschäftigung im Haushalt des Arbeitgebers (*„domestic duties"*) ist es diesem von Gesetzes wegen grundsätzlich erlaubt, einen Arbeitnehmer aufgrund seines Alters abzulehnen, vgl. § 18 Abs. 3 ADA. Zwar definiert der Age Discrimination Act 2004 (Cth) den Begriff der *„domestic duties"* nicht näher, aber nach seiner gewöhnlichen und ursprünglichen Bedeutung dürfte er alle Tätigkeiten umfassen, die annähernd im häuslichen Bereich ausgeführt werden.[283]

2. Weitere spezielle Befreiungen und Ausnahmen

Neben den insbesondere auf den Bereich der Arbeit und Beschäftigung bezogenen Befreiungen von den Diskriminierungsverboten des Age Discrimination Act 2004 (Cth) existieren zahlreiche weitere Ausnahmen. Denn nur durch sachgerechte und ordnungsgemäße Ausnahmeregelungen kann in hinreichendem Maße verhindert werden, dass sich nicht sämtliche Verhaltens- und Handlungsweisen des Vorwurfes einer Diskriminierung wegen Alters ausgesetzt sehen müssen.[284]

a. Bildung

Entgegen der Diskriminierungsverbote des § 26 Abs. 1 und Abs. 2 ADA lässt § 26 Abs. 3 ADA eine Beschränkung im Zugang zu Bildungseinrichtungen auf der Basis

280 *Fredman*, Discrimination Law (2002), 60.

281 *Fredman*, Discrimination Law (2002), 60.

282 *Eastman*, Exemptions and exceptions, in: Baker & McKenzie, Age Discrimination: Mitigating Risk in the Workplace, S. 78.

283 *Masri v Nenny Santoso & Anor* [2004] NSWIRComm 108; Explanatory Memorandum of the Age Discrimination Bill 2003 (Cth), Annexure C, Clause 18, Discrimination in employment.

284 ACCI, Age Discrimination Laws – Who benefits?, Age Discrimination Laws, April 2003, 3.

des Alters zu. So ist es einer Bildungseinrichtung, die hauptsächlich oder überwiegend für Schüler bzw. Studenten eines bestimmten Alters eingerichtet wurde, erlaubt, die Aufnahme eines Schülers bzw. Studenten zu verweigern, wenn er älter als die vorgesehene Altersgruppe ist, § 26 Abs. 3 ADA.[285]

b. Unterkunft und Unterbringung

§ 29 Abs. 3 ADA nimmt Klagen wegen Altersdiskriminierung in Bezug auf die Unterkunft und Unterbringung von Personen vom Anwendungsbereich des Age Discrimination Act 2004 (Cth) aus, wenn der Vermieter ein Familienangehöriger bzw. Verwandter ist, im gleichen Gebäude lebt und die vermieteten Räumlichkeiten für nicht mehr als drei Personen geeignet sind. Damit soll eine Trennung zwischen dem öffentlichen Lebensbereich und der Privatsphäre realisiert werden, in welcher der Staat eine umfassendere persönliche Handlungsmöglichkeit gewährleisten möchte.[286]

c. Grundstücke

Wo von einer vermeintlichen Diskriminierungshandlung wegen Alters die Übertragung von Grund und Boden betroffen sein könnte, gewährt der Age Discrimination Act 2004 (Cth) ebenfalls eine Ausnahme von der Anwendung des Diskriminierungsverbotes in § 30 Abs. 1 ADA. So werden bei der Veräußerung von Grundstücken die Schenkung sowie die Verfügung von Todes wegen durch § 30 Abs. 2 ADA vom Anwendungsbereich des Diskriminierungsverbotes ausgenommen. Allerdings ist diese Befreiung sehr weit gefasst, da sie keinerlei Definitionen und somit Einschränkungen sowie Konfliktpotential enthält. Weder wird klargestellt, welche rechtlichen Handlungen als Schenkung und als Verfügung von Todes wegen definiert werden können, noch erfolgt eine Eingrenzung des Veräußerungsbegriffs.[287] So bleibt die Auslegung und Einschränkung ein weiteres Mal der Rechtsprechung überlassen.

3. Allgemeine Befreiungen und Ausnahmen

Neben den an die einzelnen Abschnitte des Age Discrimination Act 2004 (Cth) angepassten Ausnahmevorschriften hat sich der Gesetzgeber des Commonwealth of Australia veranlasst gesehen, weitere allgemeine Befreiungen und Ausnahmen von den das Alter betreffenden Diskriminierungsverboten aufzustellen. Diese sind deshalb

285 Explanatory Memorandum of the Age Discrimination Bill 2003 (Cth), Annexure C, Clause 26, Education.

286 Explanatory Memorandum of the Age Discrimination Bill 2003 (Cth), Annexure C, Clause 29, Accomodation.

287 *Eastman*, Exemptions and exceptions, in: Baker & McKenzie, Age Discrimination: Mitigating Risk in the Workplace, S. 80.

vorwiegend an bestimmte Adressaten und Verhaltens- bzw. Handlungsweisen gebunden.[288]

a. Positive Diskriminierungen

Erfolgt eine Altersdiskriminierung infolge der Bevorzugung einer bestimmten Altersgruppe, so liegt eine positive Diskriminierung vor, die ausdrücklich vom Anwendungsbereich des Age Discrimination Act 2004 (Cth) ausgenommen und somit in diesem Sinne nicht gesetzeswidrig ist, § 33 ADA.[289] In diesem Zusammenhang ist insbesondere an vergünstigte Eintrittspreise zu Veranstaltungen für Schüler oder Senioren, den Zugang zu speziellen sozialen Einrichtungen für Jugendliche etc. zu denken.[290] Denn durch derartige Maßnahmen und Vergünstigungen soll gerade keine Benachteiligung oder ein Ausschluss einer bestimmten Altersgruppe erzielt werden.[291] Darüber hinaus besteht etwa im Hinblick auf Preisnachlässe für bestimmte Altersgruppen eine breite gesellschaftliche Akzeptanz. Vor allem jedoch sind hier die zahlreichen arbeitsrechtlichen Senioritätsprivilegien, wie etwa die Staffelung des Arbeitslohns und die Erhöhung des Urlaubsanspruchs mit zunehmendem Alter, die etwaige Verkürzung der Arbeitszeit von älteren im Vergleich zu jüngeren Arbeitnehmern oder aber auch Zusatzleistungen für die Länge der Zugehörigkeit zu einem Unternehmen, aufzuführen. Diese können aufgrund der in Australien ebenfalls üblichen gewerkschaftlichen Organisation und der damit verbundenen betriebsübergreifenden und branchenweiten Tarifverträge unterschiedlich geregelt werden und nicht ganz unerheblich voneinander abweichen.

Diese Befreiung resultiert aus der Zielsetzung des Gesetzgebers, eine umfassende Gleichheit und Gleichberechtigung herbeizuführen, zu der es seiner Ansicht nach auch gehört, in der Vergangenheit geschehene Benachteiligungen auszugleichen.[292] Folglich soll – auch nach Ansicht der Rechtsprechung – ausnahmsweise die aus einer ungleichen und benachteiligenden Behandlung einer bestimmten Alters- und Personengruppe resultierende Bevorzugung dazu dienen, im Ergebnis zu einer umfassenden Gleichheit und Gleichberechtigung der Altersgruppen zu führen.[293]

Aus dem vorgenannten Grund ist es nicht als Verstoß gegen ein Diskriminierungsverbot des Age Discrimination Act 2004 (Cth) anzusehen, wenn gemäß § 33 lit.

---

288 *Hemingway*, The Age Discrimination Act 2004, 16.

289 *Ratnam*, Federal Government's proposed age discrimination legislation, (2003) 9 Employment Law Bulletin 16.; Human Rights and Equal Opportunity Commission, Federal Discrimination Law 2009, 14; Human Rights and Equal Opportunity Commission, Federal Discrimination Law 2005, 22; zur Kritik vgl. u.a. *Fredman*, Employment Law, 126ff..

290 *Hemingway*, The Age Discrimination Act 2004, 16; Revised Explanatory Memorandum, Age Discrimination Act 2004 (Cth), 50.

291 Vgl. die Beispiele im Newsletter of the NSW Anti-Discrimination Board, Age discrimination affects

292 *Eastman*, Exemptions and exceptions, in: Baker & McKenzie, Age Discrimination: Mitigating Risk in the Workplace, S. 85; vgl. auch die Vorlagen in § 7D SDA, § 8 RDA, § 45 DDA.

293 *Wright v City of Brighton* (1991) EOC 92-389; Human Rights and Equal Opportunity Commission, Federal Discrimination Law 2009, 14; Human Rights and Equal Opportunity Commission, Federal Discrimination Law 2005, 23.

a) ADA einer Person eines bestimmten Alters eine finanzielle Unterstützung gewährt wird oder gemäß § 33 lit. b) ADA ein aufgrund eines bestimmten Alters entstehendes Bedürfnis befriedigt wird oder gemäß § 33 lit. c) ADA ein sonstiger altersbedingter Nachteil ausgeglichen wird. Vielmehr wird vom Gesetzgeber ein Ausnahmekatalog geschaffen, der eine positive Diskriminierung wegen Alters für zulässig erklärt. Denn die erlaubten Maßnahmen stellen im Grunde dennoch Diskriminierungen dar, die aber von den entsprechenden Diskriminierungsverboten ausgenommen sind, um einer benachteiligten Person zur Gleichberechtigung bzw. Gleichstellung zu verhelfen. In diesem Zusammenhang erscheint allerdings fraglich, ob die durch § 33 ADA vorgenommene gesetzliche Eingrenzung der positiven Diskriminierung aufgrund des Alters einer Person anhand bestimmter Fallgruppen oder Rechtfertigungstatbestände als abschließend angesehen werden muss.

Im Lichte der hinter dem Age Discrimination Act 2004 (Cth) stehenden gesetzgeberischen Absicht, wird aber jedenfalls – obwohl nähere Erläuterungen weder vom Gesetzgeber noch von der Rechtsprechung geliefert werden – deutlich, dass, dass der Gesetzgeber zwingend eine Einzelfallbetrachtung wünscht. Um also die erforderlichen Grenzen ziehen zu können, hat er in der gesetzlichen Regelung des § 33 ADA gleichzeitig zur gesetzlichen Regelung konkrete Beispiele aufgeführt.[294] Da der Gesetzgeber hierbei selbst die Bezeichnung als Beispiele gewählt hat, fällt die Gewichtung zwar zugunsten eines nicht abschließenden Katalogs aus. Einerseits erscheint diese Gestaltung im Ergebnis wenig hilfreich, weil somit eine nicht unerhebliche Rechtsunsicherheit geschaffen werden könnte. Es ist anhand der im Gesetz nur spärlich gelieferten Beispiele praktisch kaum verbindlich subsumierbar, ob eine positive Diskriminierung im jeweiligen Einzelfall zulässig ist. Andererseits eröffnet der nicht abschließende Charakter der Regelung des § 33 ADA eine Erfassung all jener Maßnahmen, die eine völlige Gleichstellung anstreben. Somit erscheint es fraglich, welche Anforderungen an positive Diskriminierungen als Ausnahme vom Verbot der Diskriminierung wegen Alters gestellt werden. Zu dieser Grundsatzfrage zum Age Discrimination Act 2004 (Cth) schweigt der australische Gesetzgeber. Auch finden sich in der australischen Rechtsprechung (noch) keine konkreten Fallbeispiele zu den Anforderungen an positive Diskriminierungen im Bereich der Diskriminierung wegen Alters.[295] Allerdings lässt sich zusammenfassend feststellen, dass positive Diskriminierungen als Ausnahme vom Diskriminierungsverbot zu verstehen sind und diese Ausnahme zwar dem Anschein nach diskriminierend sind, aber am Ende in der Praxis bestehende faktische Ungleichbehandlungen beseitigen bzw. zumindest verringern sollen. Vor diesem Hintergrund sollte meines Erachtens der eröffnete Raum bestmöglich genutzt werden, ohne den Bedenken einer etwaigen Rechtssicherheit Vorrang einzuräumen. Unter Berücksichtigung der durch den Gesetzgeber ausdrücklich gewünschten Einzelfallbetrachtung sollte jedoch einzig ein automatischer Vorrang einer benachteiligten Person

294 Explanatory Memorandum of the Age Discrimination Bill 2003 (Cth), Annexure C, Clause 33, Positive discrimination; *Eastman*, Exemptions and exceptions, in: Baker & McKenzie, Age Discrimination: Mitigating Risk in the Workplace, S. 86.

295 In der Rechtsprechung zum Racial Discrimination Act 1975 (Cth) werden zur Gewährleistung der völligen Gleichstellung spezifische Maßnahmen (*special measures)* verlangt; vgl. *Gerhardy v Brown* (1985) 159 CLR 70; *Bruch v Commonwealth* [2002] FMCA 29.

als nicht zulässig eingestuft werden. Diese Einschränkung würde sodann im Einklang stehen mit den durch die Rechtsprechung zum Racial Discrimination Act 1975 (Cth) entwickelten Anforderungen an positive Diskriminierungen. Denn auch dort wird eine Einzelfallbetrachtung gefordert:

> „...A special measure (1) confers a benefit on some or all members of a class, (2) ..., (3) for the sole purpose of securing adequate advancement of the beneficiaries in order that they meay enjoy and exercise equally with others human rights and fundamental freedom, (4) in circumstances where the protection given to the beneficiaries by the special measure is necessary in order that they may enjoy and exercise equally with others human rights and fundamental freedoms.“[296]

Basis für diese Rechtsprechung ist einmal mehr der Rückgriff auf den völkerrechtlichen Grundsatz der Gleichbehandlung und auf internationale Abkommen. Eine entscheidende Rolle kommt bei positiven Diskriminierungen insbesondere dem Art. 5 Abs. 2 vom Übereinkommen 111 (Übereinkommen über die Diskriminierung in Beschäftigung und Beruf) der Internationalen Arbeitsorganisation zu:

> Jedes Mitglied kann nach Anhörung der maßgebenden Arbeitgeber- und Arbeitnehmerverbände, soweit solche bestehen, erklären, dass auch andere Sondermaßnahmen nicht als Diskriminierung gelten sollen, sofern diese auf die Berücksichtigung der besonderen Bedürfnisse von Personen abzielen, die aus Gründen des Geschlechts, des Alters, der Behinderung, der Familienpflichten oder der sozialen oder kulturellen Stellung anerkanntermaßen besonders schutz- oder hilfsbedürftig sind.

b. Die Vergabe wohltätiger Leistungen

Von jeglichen Diskriminierungsverboten ausgenommen ist die Vergabe von wohltätigen Leistungen (*„charities“*), § 34 Abs. 1 ADA. Danach ist es rechtmäßig, wenn die Vergabe derartiger Leistungen an ein bestimmtes Lebensalter gebunden wird und die Zahlung deshalb verweigert wird, weil die betroffene Person das vorausgesetzte Alter noch nicht erreicht oder die Altersgrenze bereits überschritten hat, § 34 Abs. 1 lit. a) ADA. Gleiches gilt auch für die Unterstützung solcher Verhaltensweisen, § 34 Abs. 1 lit. b) ADA.

c. Die Betätigung religiöser Vereinigungen und ihrer Glaubensanhän ger

aa. Der Anwendungsbereich des § 35 ADA

Gemäß § 35 ADA sind sämtliche religiösen Handlungen und Verhaltensweisen vom Anwendungsbereich des Age Discrimination Act 2004 (Cth) und somit von der Einwirkung von Diskriminierungsverboten ausgenommen. Allerdings gilt diese Befreiung nur, sofern die religiös motivierte Handlung mit dem Glaubensbekenntnis gemäß § 35

---

296 *Gerhardy v Brown* (1985) 159 CLR 70.

lit. a) ADA konform ist oder gemäß § 35 lit. b) ADA erforderlich ist, die Verletzung persönlicher Belange und Empfindlichkeiten der Glaubensanhänger zu verhindern.[297]

bb. Die Einschränkung der Ausnahmevorschrift des § 35 ADA

(1) Unklare Grenzen

Jedoch erscheint auch diese Ausnahmevorschrift in ihrem Anwendungsbereich nahezu grenzenlos zu wirken, da etwa nicht ohne weiteres ersichtlich ist, wann persönliche Belange und Empfindlichkeiten eines Gläubigen verletzt sein können. Deshalb bietet sich einerseits eine einschränkende Einzelfallbetrachtung an. Darüber hinaus geht die Rechtsprechung, in der Absicht eine weitere Einschränkung von der Ausnahme des § 35 ADA zu erreichen, davon aus, dass § 35 ADA nur innerhalb einer religiösen Vereinigung und zwischen ihren Glaubensanhängern zur Anwendung gelangen kann. Die Rechtsprechung führt als Begründung ins Feld, dass bei einer gegenteiligen Behandlung die Bindung an die weltliche Rechtsordnung gefährdet wäre.

(2) Der Fall Burke v Tralaggan & Anor

Der New South Wales Equal Opportunity Tribunal setzte ausdrücklich Grenzen für die weite Auslegung einer derartigen Ausnahme.[298] Zwar erging die Entscheidung im Fall *Burke v Tralaggan & Anor* zu einer bundesstaatlichen Vorschrift. Diese ist aber nahezu mit § 35 ADA identisch.

Ein nicht verheiratetes Paar begehrte Rechtsschutz, weil es sich um eine Wohnung beworben hatte, diese ihm aber seitens des Eigentümers mit dem Hinweis auf ihre außereheliche Lebensgemeinschaft nicht gewährt wurde. Der Wohnungseigentümer und Klagegegner berief sich dabei auf die mit § 35 ADA vergleichbare Bundesvorschrift, da es seinem Glauben und seinem Weltbild nach essentiell sei, dass sich die Lebenspartner verheiraten und in einer rechtlich anerkannten Ehe miteinander leben.

Das Gericht lehnte es in ausdrücklicher Form ab, dass Glaubensanhänger – unabhängig welcher Religion sie sich zugehörig fühlen – ihren Glauben und ihre Weltanschauung auf die weltliche Gesellschaft übertragen, um so die Geltung deren Rechtsordnung für sich zu umgehen.[299] Somit kann es für einen Glaubensanhänger einer religiösen Vereinigung, deren Glaubenslehre die Ehe als einzig anerkannte Verbindung von Mann und Frau betrachtet, nicht erlaubt sein, dieses Kriterium bei der Vergabe von Wohnraum auf die Bewerber anzuwenden. Denn eine solche Ausnahmeregelung soll vor allem die Glaubensanhänger und die Ausübung ihrer Religion untereinander schützen.[300]

---

297 *Hazan v Victorian Jewish Board of Deputies* (1990) EOC 92-298; *Jubber v Revival Centres International* [1998] VADT 62.

298 Vgl. etwa *Burke v Tralaggan & Anor* (1986) EOC 92-161.

299 *Burke v Tralaggan & Anor* (1986) EOC 92-161.

300 *Burke v Tralaggan & Anor* (1986) EOC 92-161.

d. Das Verhalten gemeinnütziger Vereinigungen

Auch gemeinnützige Vereinigungen („*voluntary bodies*“) werden durch eine Ausnahmevorschrift von den Diskriminierungsverboten des Age Discrimination Act 2004 (Cth) ausgenommen, § 36 Abs. 1 ADA. Dies gilt aber nur dann, wenn es gemäß § 36 Abs. 1 lit. a) ADA um die Aufnahme eines neuen Mitglieds oder gemäß § 36 Abs. 1 lit. b) ADA um die Gewährung von Leistungen an Mitglieder geht. Darüber hinaus unterliegt jedes Handeln einer gemeinnützigen Vereinigung, wie etwa der Ausschluss eines Mitglieds und das Verhalten gegenüber Nichtmitgliedern, den Vorschriften und Diskriminierungsverboten des Age Discrimination Act 2004 (Cth).

Als gemeinnützig zählt eine Vereinigung gemäß § 36 Abs. 2 ADA insbesondere dann, wenn sie nicht mit der Absicht Gewinn zu erzielen arbeitet, wobei jedoch in § 36 Abs. 2 lit. a) bis c) ADA zahlreiche Vereinigungen, wie etwa Gewerkschaften und Arbeitgeber- und Arbeitnehmerverbände, vom Anwendungsbereich der Befreiung des § 36 Abs. 1 ADA ausgenommen sind.[301]

e. Handlungen von Pensionskassen, Versicherungen und Darlehensgebern

Der Age Discrimination Act 2004 (Cth) gestattet Altersdiskriminierungen in engen Grenzen durch Handlungen von Pensionskassen, Versicherungen und Darlehensgebern, sofern diese gemäß § 37 Abs. 2 ADA in Beziehung zum Angebot oder zur Ablehnung einer Rente bzw. Pension, einer Versicherung oder eine Darlehens stehen und gemäß § 37 Abs. 3 ADA verlässliche versicherungsmathematische oder statistische Daten bzw. vergleichbaren Faktoren die Grundlage bilden und deren Beachtung angemessen ist.[302] Dabei muss das zugrunde gelegte Datenmaterial aufgrund der Vorgaben des Privacy Act 1988 (Cth) und der Information Privacy Principles sowie der National Privacy Principles allgemeingültig und anonymisiert sein.[303] Denn oftmals zeigt sich in der Praxis, dass die Vertragsbedingungen in Abhängigkeit zum Alter des Versicherten individuell ausgestaltet werden müssen, um eine hinreichende Leistungsgerechtigkeit vor allem im Bezug auf die Höhe der Beitragszahlungen und der Prämien erreichen zu können.[304]

---

301 Explanatory Memorandum of the Age Discrimination Bill 2003 (Cth), Annexure C, Clause 36, Voluntary bodies.

302 Explanatory Memorandum of the Age Discrimination Bill 2003 (Cth), Annexure C, Clause 37, Superannuation, insurance and credit - actuarial data etc..

303 Explanatory Memorandum of the Age Discrimination Bill 2003 (Cth), Annexure C, Clause 37, Superannuation, insurance and credit - actuarial data etc..

304 So im Ansatz auch Explanatory Memorandum of the Age Discrimination Bill 2003 (Cth), Annexure C, Clause 37, Superannuation, insurance and credit - actuarial data etc. mit konkreten Beispiel zur Kfz-Versicherung bei jüngeren Versicherungsnehmern; vgl. darüber hinaus *Leslie v Barrister's Sickness & Accident Fund Pty Limited* [2003] NSWADT 216; *QBE Travel Insurance v Bassanelli* [2004] FCA 396.

f. Diskriminierungen infolge der Beachtung gesetzlicher Regelungen

Eine bedeutende und in ihrem Geltungsbereich sehr umfassende Ausnahme von den Diskriminierungsverboten des Age Discrimination Act 2004 (Cth), die von der Rechtsprechung jedoch nur sehr beschränkt herangezogen wird, stellt die Vorschrift des § 39 ADA dar.[305] Ist die behauptete Altersdiskriminierung nachweislich auf der Grundlage und in Beachtung einer gesetzlichen Regelung (*„direct compliance"*) im Sinne von § 39 Abs. 1 lit. a) oder b) ADA vorgenommen worden, so soll darin kein Verstoß gegen ein Diskriminierungsverbot des Age Discrimination Act 2004 (Cth) begründet werden können.

Folglich ist zwischen der diskriminierenden Handlung und der beachteten gesetzlichen Regelung ein kausaler Zusammenhang erforderlich. Demzufolge ist es nach Ansicht der Rechtsprechung Voraussetzung, dass die Diskriminierungshandlung tatsächlich notwendig gewesen ist, um eine gesetzliche Regelung im Sinne von § 39 Abs. 1 ADA beachten zu können. Sollte aufgrund einer solchen gesetzlichen Regelung aber ein Ausübungsermessen zur konkreten Art und Weise der Vornahme einer Handlung, die eine Diskriminierung wegen Alters verursacht, eingeräumt sein, so lehnt die Rechtsprechung die Anwendung von § 39 ADA ab. Denn in einem solchen Fall fehle es an einer *„direct compliance"*.[306]

Bis zum 23. Juni 2006 räumte § 39 Abs. 2 ADA eine zusätzliche – generalklauselartige – Befreiung ein, die nicht nur eine Befreiung hinsichtlich der gesetzlichen Regelungen im Sinne von § 39 Abs. 1 ADA erteilte, sondern sämtliche Bundesgesetze als Rechtfertigung gelten ließ. Da § 39 Abs. 2 ADA jedoch nur für die Dauer von 2 Jahren nach Inkrafttreten des Age Discrimination Act 2004 (Cth) gelten sollte, ist seine Geltung inzwischen entfallen.[307]

Darüber hinaus enthalten die §§ 40 bis 43 ADA weitere gesetzliche Regelungen, deren Beachtung nach dem Willen des Gesetzgebers nicht zu einer im Sinne des Age Discrimination Act 2004 (Cth) gesetzeswidrigen Diskriminierung wegen Alters führt. Allerdings gilt auch dort, dass die Einhaltung der in §§ 40 bis 43 ADA aufgeführten Gesetze und Vorschriften tatsächlich erforderlich und absolut notwendig sein muss. Ob dieser Zusammenhang vorliegt lässt sich meistens nicht allgemeingültig feststellen, sondern nur anhand einer konkreten und genauen Einzelfallbetrachtung erkennen.

---

305 *Gulliver v Council of City of Sydney* (1987) EOC 92-185; *Waters v Public Transport Corporation* (1991) 173 CLR 349; *McBride v Victoria (No 1)* [2003] FMCA 285; *Howe v Qantas Airways Limited* [2004] FMCA 242.

306 *Eastman*, Exemptions and exceptions, in: Baker & McKenzie, Age Discrimination: Mitigating Risk in the Workplace, S. 83.

307 Explanatory Memorandum of the Age Discrimination Bill 2003 (Cth), Annexure C, Clause 39, Direct compliance with laws, orders, etc.; vgl. aber die nachfolgende Regelung in § 39 Abs. 1a ADA aufgrund des Age Discrimination Amendment Act 2006 (Cth); Human Rights and Equal Opportunity Commission, Annual Report 2005 – 2006, 155.

In diesem Zusammenhang ist zugleich auch zu berücksichtigen, dass eine solche, die Altersdiskriminierung rechtfertigende, gesetzliche Regelung nicht per se und nicht alleiniger Streitgegenstand einer Klage nach dem Age Discrimination Act 2004 (Cth) sein kann.[308]

308 *Gerhardy v Brown* (1985) 159 CLR 70; *Secretary, Department of Defence v Human Rights and Equal Opportunity Commission & Ors* (1997) 78 FCR 208.

E. Besondere Fragestellungen und Probleme bei der Altersdiskriminierung im Arbeits- und Beschäftigungsverhältnis

Im Bereich von Arbeit und Beschäftigung ist das Antidiskriminierungsrecht im Allgemeinen darauf angelegt, dass grundsätzlich niemand daran gehindert wird, eine bestimmte Tätigkeit auszuüben bzw. einer konkreten Beschäftigung nachzugehen. Ein Arbeitnehmer bzw. Angestellter soll folglich nicht aufgrund seiner Eigenschaften, Leistungsmerkmale und persönlichen Charakteristika im Vergleich zu anderen benachteiligt und diesen gegenüber ungleich behandelt werden.[309] Dieser allgemeingültige und weit gefasste Gesetzeszweck der Gleichbehandlung lässt dem Arbeitgeber aber anhand zulässiger und objektiv nachprüfbarer Kriterien, wie etwa Bildung, Kompetenz, Fachwissen und Berufserfahrung, die Möglichkeit, gerechtfertigte Differenzierungen der einzelnen Arbeitsverhältnisse vorzunehmen – sofern hierfür nicht das Alter der jeweiligen Person das tatsächliche Motiv des Arbeitgebers darstellt. Denn der Gesetzeszweck soll nicht nur die öffentliche Hand als Arbeitgeber treffen, sondern insbesondere auch die Entscheidungen privater Arbeitgeber und Unternehmer beeinflussen.[310]

In zahlreichen Bestimmungen verbietet der Age Discrimination Act 2004 (Cth) – wie zuvor aufgezeigt – die Diskriminierung wegen Alters im Bereich der Arbeit und Beschäftigung und charakterisiert somit bestimmte Handlungen und Verhaltensweisen von personengeführten Gesellschaften, besonders berechtigten Behörden und Körperschaften sowie bestimmter Organisationen (§§ 21-23 ADA) und Arbeitsvermittlungen (§ 24 ADA) gegenüber Arbeitnehmern, Angestellten, Vertretern und Bevollmächtigten der Human Rights and Equal Opportunity Commission sowie von Vertragsarbeitern (§§ 18ff. ADA) als rechtswidrig.

Da Diskriminierungen wegen Alters nicht auf einen bestimmten Bereich der Beschäftigung bzw. eine konkrete Phase der beruflichen Tätigkeit beschränkt sind, werden vor allem im Arbeitsrecht sämtliche Stationen und Formen eines Arbeits- und Beschäftigungsverhältnisses von den speziellen Diskriminierungsverboten des Age Discrimination Act 2004 (Cth) erfasst.[311] Zu denken ist dabei insbesondere an den Bewerbungs- und Einstellungsprozess, die Bedingungen und Konditionen der Beschäftigung, die Aus- und Weiterbildung sowie die Förderung von Arbeitnehmern und Beschäftigten, die Bezüge und Leistungen des Arbeitgebers, die Beendigung des Arbeitsverhältnisses sowie aber auch das Arbeitsumfeld und die Arbeitsumgebung. Bereits diese Vielfalt an potentiellen Diskriminierungsfeldern im Bereich von Arbeit und Beschäftigung verdeutlicht, dass die Altersdiskriminierung hier ein nicht unbedeutendes Wir-

309 *Collins*, Employment Law, Opportunity and Discrimination (2003), 54.

310 *Gardner*, Liberals and Unlawful Discrimination (1989) 9 Oxford Journal of Legal Studies 1.

311 *Bourke/Ronalds*, Discrimination Laws – Striving For Equality, in: *Macken*, The Law of Employment, 2002, 620; *Ozdowski*, Adressing age discrimination, (2002) 81 Older People and the Law 11; *Ratnam*, Federal Government's proposed age discrimination legislation, (2003) 9 Employment Law Bulletin 15.

kungsfeld abdeckt und drastische Folgen verursachen kann.[312] Denn die Diskriminierung wegen Alters im Bereich von Arbeit und Beschäftigung zeitigt sowohl für junge als auch für Menschen fortgeschrittenen Alters Auswirkungen auf den täglichen Lebensablauf, die finanzielle Lage sowie auf die Teilnahme und Teilhabe an bestimmten Leistungen.[313]

Zusätzlich wird auch durch die Rechtsprechung versucht, einen umfassenden Diskriminierungsschutz zu gewährleisten, indem die jeweiligen Diskriminierungsverbote weit ausgelegt werden.[314] Die Betrachtung der aktuellen Situation in der Praxis der australischen Arbeits- und Beschäftigungswelt lehrt die Erforderlichkeit, die gesetzlich statuierten Diskriminierungsverbote zur effektiven Wirkung nicht unnötig zu beschränken.[315] Die Benachteiligung und Diskriminierung wegen Alters im Bereich von Arbeit und Beschäftigung und die damit verbundene Verhinderung der Durchmischung der Altersstruktur führt in der Praxis zu nicht unerheblichen Gewinn- und Profiteinbußen für die Wirtschaft, da wertvolle Ressourcen ungenutzt bleiben.[316] Neben dieser betriebswirtschaftlichen Komponente treten in Verbindung mit Altersdiskriminierungen im Betrieb nicht selten interstrukturelle Konflikte hinzu, da aufgrund einer fehlenden Vielfalt des Alters der beschäftigten Menschen nur schwerlich soziale Kontakte und ein entsprechender Zusammenhalt geschaffen werden können. Erst der Zugang zu einem von Gleichbehandlung geprägten Arbeitsverhältnis mit einer ausgewogenen Altersstruktur (*„age diversity"*) schafft für viele junge als auch ältere Menschen die Möglichkeit, sich angemessen in die Gesellschaft und das soziale Gefüge zu integrieren.[317]

Die Altersdiskriminierung tritt zwar sowohl aufgrund jungen als auch wegen älteren Lebensalters auf.[318] Aufgrund der zuvor aufgezeigten – sich insbesondere für ältere Beschäftigte stellenden – Probleme, ist der Begriff des älteren Beschäftigten vorrangig klärungsbedürftig, wobei sich in der Rechtspraxis und Literatur unterschiedliche Beurteilungen und Eingrenzungen finden lassen und darüber hinaus nicht selten zwischen

---

312 Bureau of Labour Market Research, Discrimination in the Labour – Force at older Ages (1983) Working Paper No 17, 7; Attorney Generals Department of New South Wales, Age Discrimination – Options for New South Wales, A Discussion Paper (2000) 25; *Guthrie*, Ageing – Discrimination and Workers Compensation (2005) 14.

313 Attorney Generals Department of New South Wales, Age Discrimination – Options for New South Wales, A Discussion Paper (2000) 25.

314 Vgl. nur *Australian Iron and Steel Pty Ltd v Banovic* (1989) 168 CLR 165; *Waters v Public Transport Corporation* (1992) 173 CLR 349.

315 *Encel*, Age Discrimination in Law and Practice, (2004) Elder Law Review 7; House of Representatives Standing Committee on Employment, Education and Workplace Relations, Parliament of Australia, Age Counts (2000), 101ff..

316 *Collins*, Employment Law, Opportunity and Discrimination (2003), 54.

317 *Collins*, Discrimination, Equality and Social Inclusion (2003) 66 Modern LR 16.

318 *McGoldrick/Arrowsmith*, Recruitment Advertising: Discrimination on the Basis of Age (1993) 15 Employee Relations 54; *Patrickson/Harmann*, Managing An Ageing Workforce (1998), 56; *Bennington/Wein*, Anti-Discrimination Legislation in Australia: Fair, Effective, Efficient or Irrelevant? (2000) 21 International Journal of Manpower 21; vgl. Australian Bureau of Statistics, 1991 Census of Population and Housing (1996).

Männern und Frauen unterschieden wird.[319] Denn arbeitsmarkttypisch gibt es bestimmte – vor allem von Frauen – bekleidete Berufe, bei denen es maßgeblich auf Jugendlichkeit bzw. jugendliches Aussehen ankommt. Zu denken sei hier etwa an Tätigkeiten als Model, Friseuse etc., bei denen die Grenze der Einordnung als älterer Beschäftigter sehr niedrig ist und vor allem im Vergleich mit einigen Männerberufen, wie Bauarbeiter, Fabrikarbeiter, Monteur oder Manager, gravierend abweichen kann.[320] Wissenschaftliche Untersuchungen jedoch haben gezeigt, dass Beschäftigte und Arbeitnehmer bereits in einem recht jungen Alter als ältere Beschäftigte angesehen werden.[321] Bereits 15 % der Arbeitgeber sehen Beschäftigte in der Altersgruppe von 41 bis 45 Jahren als ältere Arbeitnehmer an, wobei die Mehrheit der Arbeitgeber (62 %) die Altersgruppe über 55 Jahren als alt einordnet.[322] Erstaunlich ist, dass immerhin 7 % der Arbeitgeber bereits die Altersgruppe von 36 bis 40 Jahren dem Bereich der älteren Beschäftigten zuordnen.[323] Aufgrund dieser Verteilung können im Ergebnis Arbeitnehmer und Beschäftigte ab einem Alter von 45 Jahren als ältere Arbeitnehmer im Sinne des Antidiskriminierungsrechts – insbesondere auch im Lichte international verwendeter Definitionen – angesehen werden.[324]

I. Altersdiskriminierung in der Bewerbungs- und Einstellungsphase sowie bei der Informationserlangung

1. Diskriminierung in der Einstellungsphase

Auch wenn das Alter eines Bewerbers für die Entscheidungsfindung des Arbeitsgebers keine ausschlaggebende Rolle spielen sollte, so gibt es wissenschaftliche Studien, die das genaue Gegenteil belegen.[325] Denn zumindest beeinflusst das Alter des jeweiligen

---

319 *Walker*, Age and Employment (1997) 17 Australasian Journal on Ageing 99; Attorney Generals Department of New South Wales, Age Discrimination – Options for New South Wales, A Discussion Paper (2000) 9; *Kurland*, The Impact of Legal Age Discrimination on Women in Professional Occupation (2001) 11 Business Ethic Quarterly 33.

320 *Bennington*, Prime Age Recruitment: The Challenges For Age Discrimination Legislation (2004) Elder Law Review 8.

321 *Patrickson/Harmann*, Managing An Ageing Workforce (1998), 56.

322 *Patrickson/Harmann*, Managing An Ageing Workforce (1998), 56.

323 *Patrickson/Harmann*, Managing An Ageing Workforce (1998), 56.

324 *Bennington*, Prime Age Recruitment: The Challenges For Age Discrimination Legislation (2004) Elder Law Review 8; vgl. auch *Drury*, Older Workers in the European Community: Pervasive Discrimination, Little Awarness (1993) 20 Ageing International 12; Australian Employers Convention, The Human Resource Costs and Benefits of Maintaining an Age-Balanced Workforce (2001), 4.

325 *Lawrence*, Organizational Age Norms: Why Is It So Hard To Know One When You See One? (1996) 36 The Gerontologgist 209; *Bennington/Wein*, Anti-Discrimination Legislation in Australia: Fair, Effective, Efficient or Irrelevant? (2000) 21 International Journal of Manpower 21; *Bennington*, Age Discrimination: Converging Evidence From Four Australian Studies (2001) 13 Employee Responsibilities and Rights Journal 125; *dies.*, Aiding and Abetting Employer Dis-

Kandidaten die Phase der Bewerbung und Einstellung indirekt und wird nicht selten bei informellen Entscheidungen berücksichtigt.[326] Darüber hinaus werden vor allem in Stellenanzeigen Begriffe verwendet, welche die Nennung eines bestimmten Alters des gewünschten Stellenbewerbers überflüssig werden lassen, aber dennoch einen erkennbaren Bezug zur gewünschten Altersgruppe herstellen.[327] So nehmen Begriffe und Beschreibungen von Anforderungsmerkmalen wie *„high-flyer"*, *„recent graduate"*, *„go-getter"* oder *„fast-paced"* vornehmlich Bezug zur Altersgruppe der 30iger und Verweise auf langjährige Berufserfahrung mit der Bezeichnung *„senior level"* werden nicht selten mit der Altersgruppe der 50jährigen in Zusammenhang gebracht.[328] Aufgrund dessen sind sie immer wieder Gegenstand kritischer Betrachtungen im Antidiskriminierungsrecht.[329]

Daher ist die gesetzliche Regelung des § 18 ADA im Rahmen von Arbeits- und Beschäftigungsverhältnissen besonders bedeutsam und entsprechend hervorzuheben. So ist es gemäß § 18 Abs. 1 ADA für einen Arbeitgeber oder eine andere Person, die wie ein Arbeitgeber handelt oder dazu befugt ist, rechtswidrig, jemanden aufgrund seines Alters bereits innerhalb der Vorbereitungen über die Festlegung oder bei der Bestimmung selbst, wem eine bestimmte Beschäftigung angeboten werden soll oder aber durch die Festlegung von bestimmten mit dem Angebot verbundenen Bedingungen und Anforderungen, zu diskriminieren.[330] Weiterhin ist es einem Arbeitgeber oder einer anderen Person, die wie ein Arbeitgeber handelt oder dazu befugt ist, gemäß § 18 Abs. 2 ADA verboten, jemanden aufgrund seines Alters durch bestimmte Beschäftigungsbedingungen und –anforderungen, durch die Weigerung dem Arbeitnehmer den Zugang zu Ausbildungs- und Weiterbildungsmöglichkeiten und anderen mit der Beschäftigung in Verbindung stehenden Unterstützungen zu gewähren, durch eine Entlassung des Arbeitnehmers oder durch jegliche andere Nachteilszufügung zu diskriminieren.

In diesem Zusammenhang gilt es zu beachten, dass die Weigerung im Sinne von § 18 Abs. 2 lit. d) ADA dem Arbeitnehmer den Zugang zu Ausbildungs- und Weiterbildungsmöglichkeiten und anderen mit der Beschäftigung in Verbindung stehenden Unterstützungen zu

crimination: the Job Applicant's (2002) 14 Employee Responsibilities and Rights Journal 3; *dies.*, Does the Secretarial Resume Open The Door to Age Discrimination? (2003) 22 Australasian Journal on Ageing 70.

326 *Arrowsmith/McGoldrick*, Bridging The Theory And Practice Divide Through Collaborative Research – The Case of Ageism in Employment (1996); vgl. auch *Hallier*, Greenfield Recruitment and Selection: Implications for the Older Worker (2001) 30 Personnel Review 331.

327 *Paddison*, The Targeted Approach to Recruitment (1990) 22 Personnel Management 54; *Bennington*, Prime Age Recruitment: The Challenges For Age Discrimination Legislation (2004) Elder Law Review 8 m.w.N..

328 *Bennington*, Age Discrimination: Converging Evidence From Four Australian Studies (2001) 13 Employee Responsibilities and Rights Journal 125.

329 *Redman/Matthews*, Advertising for Effective Managerial Recruitment (1992) 18 Journal of General Management 29; *dies.*, Getting Personal in Personnel Recruitment (1996) 18 Employee Relations 68.

330 Vgl. u.a. *Burnett v MLA Holdings and Gavin Coulthard* [1999] VCAT; *Bloomfield v Westco Jeans Pty Limited* (2001) EOC 93-161.

gewähren, sich nach Auffassung der Rechtsprechung nur auf vertragliche Ansprüche beziehen kann.[331]

Bei der Suche nach geeigneten Angestellten und Mitarbeitern besteht die Gefahr, zu verkennen, dass die Personalentscheidung nicht auf dem Alter des Bewerbers basieren, sondern vielmehr die persönlichen Fähigkeiten und Fachkenntnisse, Berufserfahrung sowie Gesundheit und soziale Kompetenz die Entscheidung prägen sollte.[332] Zwar ist das Lebensalter bei der Personalentscheidung ein einfach handhabbares Merkmal und es herrscht in der Praxis das weit verbreitete Vorurteil, dass sich das Maß an Produktivität und Leistungsfähigkeit eines einzelnen Arbeitnehmers anhand seines Alters bestimmen lässt. Gerade aber eine solche Negativselektion – ohne zusätzliche rechtfertigende Gründe – führt aufgrund des personenbezogenen Charakters des Einstellungsprozesses zu Diskriminierungen wegen Alters. Daher sind Arbeitgeber verpflichtet, für den Auswahlprozess nachvollziehbare Selektionskriterien aufzustellen, die sich insbesondere auf die vorgenannten beruflichen sowie auch außerberuflichen Maßstäbe beziehen.[333]

2. Diskriminierung bei der Informationserlangung

Darüber hinaus verdient auch der § 32 ADA besondere Erwähnung. Dieses, besonders im Bereich des Arbeitsrechts relevante, Diskriminierungsverbot ist aus den Regelungen der § 30 des Disability Discrimination Act 1992 (Cth) und § 27 Abs. 1 des Sex Discrimination Act 1984 (Cth) entwickelt worden.[334]

Danach ist es rechtswidrig, wenn eine Person („*the first person*") eine andere Person („*the second person*") auffordert oder veranlasst, Informationen durch Vervollständigung eines Formulars oder aber auch in jeglicher anderer Form herauszugeben, sofern dadurch eine bestimmte Handlung und somit eine Altersdiskriminierung erreicht werden soll und Personen eines anderen Alters unter den gleichen Umständen nicht zur Informationsverschaffung aufgefordert oder veranlasst worden wären.

3. Diskriminierung durch Fragen beim Vorstellungsgespräch

Oftmals werden beim Vorstellungsgespräch vom potentiellen Arbeitgeber unzulässige Fragen an den Bewerber gestellt, die diesen auch aufgrund seines Alters zu diskriminieren geeignet sind.[335] Deshalb sollte sich der Arbeitgeber vor dem Hintergrund der

331 *State of Victoria v Shou* (2001) 3 VR 655; *Kelly v TPG Internet* [2003] FMCA.

332 Anti-Discrimination Board of New South Wales, Age Old Dilemmas (2004) 60 Equal Times 1 mit Verweis auf Beispiele aus der Rechtsprechung.

333 Vgl. aus der Rechtsprechung des EuGH zu Altersgrenzen für die Einstellung in den feuerwehrtechnischen Dienst und zu deren Rechtfertigung im Sinne von Art. 4 Abs. 1 der RL 2000/78/EG das EuGH Urteil vom 12.01.2010 – C-229/08 = EuZW 2010, 142 = NJW 2010, 2193.

334 Explanatory Memorandum of the Age Discrimination Bill 2003 (Cth), Annexure C, Clause 32, Requests for information.

335 *Bloomfield v Westco Jeans Pty Limited* (2001) EOC 93-161; *Catanzariti*, (1999) 4 Employment Law Bulletin 92; vgl. die Empfehlung an Arbeitgeber zur Vorgehensweise bei Fragen an einen

Diskriminierungsproblematik genauestens überlegen, welche Fragen er dem jeweiligen Bewerber stellt:

> „The general rule of thumb is that if age is irrelevant to the position, then questions about age should not be asked."[336]

Erfordert die zu besetzende Stelle nicht ausnahmsweise Informationen über das konkrete Alter des Kandidaten – etwa um Kinderarbeit auszuschließen und die Mindestaltersgrenze nicht zu unterschreiten –, so vermeidet der Arbeitgeber den Vorwurf altersdiskriminierenden Verhaltens, wenn er erst gar nicht nach dem Alter des Bewerbers fragt.[337]

4. Diskriminierungsfreie Organisation

Die Regelungen der §§ 18 und 32 ADA haben folglich das Potential, dem Arbeitgeber zu veranschaulichen, dass insbesondere durch die Aufforderung an einen Bewerber bestimmte Informationen vor, während oder nach der Bewerbungsphase preiszugeben, durch die Verwendung bestimmter Auswahlkriterien für den (potentiellen) Arbeitnehmer sowie durch das Aufstellen bestimmter Bedingungen und Anforderungen nach der erfolgreichen Bewerbung ein Klagebegehren wegen einer Altersdiskriminierung begründet werden kann, wenn der Arbeitgeber primär aufgrund des Alters des (potentiellen) Arbeitnehmers zu seinem Verhalten motiviert ist. Wegen der vielfältigen Gefahrenquellen sollte der Arbeitgeber darum bemüht sein, eine diskriminierungsfreie Organisation des Arbeitsbereichs zu schaffen und sehr sorgfältig prüfen, welche geschriebenen und ungeschriebenen Auswahlkriterien er bei der Rekrutierung neuer Mitarbeiter benutzt. Ebenso sollte auf die ausdrückliche Verwendung von bestimmten Begriffen, wie etwa der direkten Nachfrage nach einem Absolventen oder einem erfahrenen Arbeitnehmer, sowie auf die Beschreibung bestimmter Personenmerkmale, wie etwa energisch, lebhaft oder dynamisch, und der damit möglicherweise verbundenen Diskriminierung wegen Alters Acht gegeben werden. Zwar existiert noch keine Rechtsprechung zum Age Discrimination Act 2004 (Cth) zu diesem Problembereich, aber dennoch kann hierzu vergleichsweise die zu anderen Antidiskriminierungsgesetzen ergangene Rechtsprechung zur Problemverdeutlichung und zur Lösung dieser in entsprechender Anwendung herangezogen werden.[338]

a. Der Fall North v City of Sydney Council

So verdeutlicht die Entscheidung in Sachen *North v City of Sydney Council* das Erfordernis, dass der Arbeitgeber vor dem Bewerbungsverfahren klar verständliche Aus-

---

Bewerber im Rahmen eines Vorstellungsgesprächs Bourke/Ronalds, Discrimination Laws - Striving Towards Equality, in Macken, The Law of Employment, 624.

336 *Catanzariti*, Age and employment (1999) 4 Employment Law Bulletin 92.

337 *Catanzariti*, Age and employment (1999) 4 Employment Law Bulletin 92.

338 *Rochas v The University of Sydney* [2004] NSWADT 14 (21 January 2004).

wahlkriterien aufstellen und diese dann beibehalten muss, um eine Diskriminierung wegen Alters zu verhindern. Denn im genannten Fall machte der Bewerber und Kläger geltend, dass der Arbeitgeber die Bewerbungskriterien hinsichtlich des Alters potentieller Arbeitnehmer nach Eingang seiner Bewerbung geändert habe und er diese mit seiner Bewerbung somit nicht (mehr) erfüllen konnte. Deshalb und weil er als 42-jähriger Arbeitnehmer der älteste Bewerber gewesen sei sowie weil der Arbeitgeber einen jüngeren Bewerber mit der Begründung eingestellt habe, dass dieser für Weiterbildungsmaßnahmen aufgrund seines jungen Alters zugänglicher sei, liege nach Ansicht des Klägers und der ihm sodann zustimmenden Entscheidung eine Altersdiskriminierung vor.[339]

b. Der Fall Dewan v Main Roads WA

Durch die Rechtsprechung des Equal Opportunity Tribunal of Western Australia zum Fall *Dewan v Main Roads WA* zeigt sich das besondere Bedürfnis des Arbeitgebers an einer Verdeutlichung und Rechtfertigung der verwendeten Auswahlkriterien und der für sie maßgebenden Gründe, um einer möglichen Diskriminierung von Bewerbern vorzubeugen.[340]

Im vorliegenden Fall hatte sich ein 45-jähriger Arbeitnehmer auf eine Stellenausschreibung, in der ausdrücklich die Bewerbung von Absolventen verlangt wurde, die erst kürzlich ihren Ausbildungs- bzw. Studienabschluss erreicht haben, beworben und war abgelehnt worden. Er machte mit seiner Klage eine indirekte Altersdiskriminierung geltend, weil mit dieser Stellenausschreibung ausschließlich Bewerber, die zum Bewerbungszeitpunkt jünger als 25 Jahre waren, berücksichtigt werden konnten.[341] Allerdings hatte er mit seiner Klage aber ebenso wenig Erfolg wie mit seiner Bewerbung. Denn der Beklagte führte zur Überzeugung des Gerichts aus, dass er die Eingrenzung einerseits deshalb vorgenommen habe, da – seiner Auffassung nach – einerseits nur vor kurzer Zeit mit ihrer Ausbildung bzw. mit ihrem Studium fertig gewordene Absolventen in der Lage wären, die neuesten Technologien und Ideen in die Unternehmensorganisation einzubringen und er andererseits zugleich Stellen anbiete, die ausschließlich für erfahrene Arbeitnehmer gedacht sind und bei denen demnach der Zugang für junge Absolventen vergleichsweise schwieriger sein dürfte.[342] Diese Begründung legte die Rechtsprechung hier als ausreichende Rechtfertigung für die vorgenommene Eingrenzung des Bewerberbereichs und verursachte Altersdiskriminierung des Klägers aus und ließ in diesem Einzelfall das Fehlen einer ausgewogenen Altersstruktur („*age diversity*“) zu.

---

339 *North v City of Sydney Council* (2001) EOC 93-149.
340 *Dewan v Main Roads WA* (2005) EOC 93-362.
341 *Dewan v Main Roads WA* (2005) EOC 93, 74, 164.
342 *Dewan v Main Roads WA* (2005) EOC 93, 74, 164.

c. Der Fall Bloomfield v Westco Jeans Pty Limited

Im Fall *Bloomfield v Westco Jeans Pty Limited* hatte sich das Australian Capital Territory (ACT) Discrimination Tribunal mit den zusätzlichen Risiken und Gefahren von formlosen Stellenangeboten und Bewerbungen auf solche zu befassen. In diesem Fall hatte sich die 46-jährige Klägerin direkt in einem Geschäft gegenüber einem Mitarbeiter im Beisein ihrer 16-jährigen Tochter beworben. Frau Bloomfield wurde zuerst von dem Mitarbeiter gefragt, ob sie eine Stelle für sich suche, während er deutlich die Tochter der Klägerin anschaute und erhielt zusätzlich die ablehnende Aussage, dass man nach Bewerbern im Alter von 17 bis 21 Jahren suche.[343] Die Rechtsprechung erkannte in dem Verhalten des Mitarbeiters des Geschäfts, obwohl dieser seine Äußerung umfassend bestritt, eine Diskriminierung der Klägerin wegen deren Alters an.

d. Die Fälle Director-General of Education v Atkins & Ors und Rochas v The University of Sydney

Klagen wegen Altersdiskriminierungen in der Bewerbungs- und Einstellungsphase können deshalb überaus schwierig sein, weil es zur hinreichenden Substantiierung grundsätzlich einer direkten Verbindung zwischen dem diskriminierenden Verhalten und einer diskriminierenden Motivation des Arbeitgebers (Ursachenzusammenhang) bedarf.

In den Fällen *Director-General of Education v Atkins & Ors* und *Rochas v The University of Sydney* hat die Rechtsprechung die Anforderungen an die Beweislast unter Berücksichtigung der Schutzbedürftigkeit der diskriminierten Bewerber jedoch erheblich abgesenkt. So soll es nach Ansicht der Rechtsprechung in der Regel ausreichen, dass der Kläger mangels Kenntnis der Beweggründe des Arbeitgebers einfach auf Verknüpfung mehrerer Umstände des Falles vertrauen und somit aus ihnen den Rückschluss ziehen könne, dass eine unrechtmäßige Altersdiskriminierung gegeben sei.[344] Der Umstand, dass dem Kläger ein ausreichender Beweis der Verbindung zwischen dem diskriminierenden Verhalten und der diskriminierenden Absicht des Arbeitgebers in der Regel nicht gelingen werde, schließt eine gerichtliche Überprüfung des Einzelfalles nicht automatisch aus, weil sich das Beweismaterial nicht selten in der Hand des Beklagten befinde und der Kläger somit keinen Zugriff darauf haben könne.[345]

---

343 *Bloomfield v Westco Jeans Pty Limited* (2001) EOC 93-161.

344 *Director-General of Education v Atkins & Ors* (1989) EOC 92-263; *Rochas v The University of Sydney* [2004] NSWADT 14 (21 January 2004).

345 *Rochas v The University of Sydney* [2004] NSWADT 14 (21 January 2004).

e. Die Fälle Shaikh v Commissioner, NSW Fire Brigades, Lavery v Commissioner of Fire Brigades und Sivananthan v Commissioner of Police

Besondere Bedeutung erlangt darüber hinaus die Rechtsprechung zu den Fällen *Shaikh v Commissioner, NSW Fire Brigades* und *Sivananthan v Commissioner of Police*, da sie auf die Frage eingeht, ob ein Nachteil, den ein Arbeitnehmer erfahren hat, als eine Diskriminierung im Sinne von § 18 Abs. 2 lit. d) ADA wegen der Weigerung dem Arbeitnehmer den Zugang zu Ausbildungs- und Weiterbildungsmöglichkeiten und anderen mit der Beschäftigung in Verbindung stehenden Unterstützungen zu gewähren, angesehen werden kann.[346]

In Sachen *Shaikh v Commissioner, NSW Fire Brigades* wurde hervorgehoben, dass für einen Nachteil im Sinne von § 18 Abs. 2 lit. d) ADA die herkömmliche Bedeutung heranzuziehen sei und folglich immer dann ein Nachteil vorliege, wenn ein Verlust, eine Beschädigung oder eine Verletzung eingetreten sei.[347] In Sachen *Sivananthan v Commissioner of Police* führte die Rechtsprechung erweiternd aus, dass tatsächlich ein nicht unerheblicher Nachteil eingetreten sein müsse und die Bewertung nicht subjektiv, sondern vielmehr aus der Sicht eines objektiven Beobachters vorzunehmen sei.[348]

Die Entscheidung *Lavery v Commissioner of Fire Brigades* beschäftigte sich mit der Klage eines Feuerwehrmannes, der aufgrund eines Einsatzes ein Auge verloren hatte, deshalb nicht mehr in seiner alten Position beschäftigt wurde und folglich aufgrund der Weigerung seines Arbeitgebers auch nicht mehr an für den Einsatz als Feuerwehrmann zwingend erforderlichen Weiterbildungen und Übungen teilnehmen durfte.[349] Entgegen der Ansicht der Beklagten sah die Rechtsprechung in diesem Fall einen Nachteil als für den Kläger gegeben an, da er nicht mehr zu den Weiterbildungen und Übungen zugelassen worden war und er somit im Vergleich zu seiner vorherigen Tätigkeit eine Einbuße erlitten habe. Aufgrund der Weigerung des Arbeitgebers und mangels der Teilnahme an den Weiterbildungen und Übungen sei der Feuerwehrmann – auch wenn er aufgrund seiner Behinderung grundsätzlich nicht mehr als solcher eingesetzt werden könne – der theoretischen Möglichkeit des Einsatzes entzogen worden. Hierin liege ein erheblicher Nachteil im Sinne des § 18 Abs. 2 lit. d) ADA.[350]

---

346 *Shaikh v Commissioner, NSW Fire Brigades* (1996) EOC 92-808; *Sivananthan v Commissioner of Police* [2004] NSWADT 44.

347 *Shaikh v Commissioner, NSW Fire Brigades* (1996) EOC 92-808.

348 *Sivananthan v Commissioner of Police* [2004] NSWADT 44.

349 *Lavery v Commissioner of Fire Brigades* (2003) EOC 93-274.

350 *Lavery v Commissioner of Fire Brigades* (2003) EOC 93-274.

II. Altersdiskriminierung in der Phase der Beendigung und der unbilligen Kündigung des Arbeits- und Beschäftigungsverhältnisses durch den Arbeitgeber

1. Das besondere Konfliktpotential der Beendigung eine Arbeits- und Beschäftigungsverhältnis

Rechtsschutz wegen einer Altersdiskriminierung im Rahmen der Beendigung des Arbeits- und Beschäftigungsverhältnisses ist insbesondere aufgrund der Regelung des § 18 Abs. 2 lit. c) ADA und darüber hinaus auch auf der Basis von bundesstaatlichen bzw. territorialen Recht denkbar. Da die Beendigung eines Arbeits- und Beschäftigungsverhältnisses in der Regel bereits grundsätzlich Probleme aufwerfen kann und diese durch Fragen der Diskriminierung wegen Alters zusätzlich verschärft werden, kommt diesem Problembereich eine enorme Bedeutung zu. Deshalb existieren hierzu zahlreiche Gerichtsentscheidungen.[351]

2. Der Fall Lightning Bolt Co Pty Limited v Skinner & Anor

Im bereits erwähnten Verfahren *Lightning Bolt Co Pty Limited v Skinner & Anor* vor dem Supreme Court of Queensland stellte dieser in seiner Rechtsprechung fest, dass ein Beschäftigungsverhältnis mit einem älteren Arbeitnehmer nicht deshalb beendet werden dürfe, weil der Arbeitgeber der Auffassung sei, dass jüngere Arbeitnehmer in der Regel leistungsstärker sind und somit besser jüngere Mitarbeiter eingestellt werden sollen.[352] Die Rechtsprechung sah in diesem Verfahren in der Beendigung von zwei Arbeitsverhältnissen aus den genannten Gründen und den damit zeitnah verbundenen Neueinstellungen von jüngeren, aber zugleich auch wesentlich unerfahrenen, Mitarbeitern eine direkte Diskriminierung als begründet an. Gleichzeitig wurde in dieser Entscheidung auch betont, dass selbst für den Fall, dass das Alter nicht im Vordergrund der unternehmerischen Entscheidung gestanden und der Arbeitnehmer allein auf eine vermeintlich bessere körperliche Verfassung von jüngeren Mitarbeitern abgestellt hätte, noch immer eine indirekte Altersdiskriminierung zu bejahen gewesen wäre.[353]

3. Der Fall Richards v Webforge Australia Pty Limited

So werden vor allem durch die Rechtsprechung der Western Australian Industrial Relations Commission in Sachen *Richards v Webforge Australia Pty Limited* die Um-

---

351 Vgl. etwa nur *Peacock v Human Rights and Equal Opportunity Commission* [2005] FCAFC 45; *Lightning Bolt Co Pty Limited v Skinner & Anor* [2002] QSC 062.

352 *Lightning Bolt Co Pty Limited v Skinner & Anor* [2002] QSC 062; vgl. auch aus deutscher Sicht zur Frage der Verbesserung der Beschäftigungschancen und der damit einhergehenden Vorurteile gegenüber älteren Arbeitnehmern, Kohte AuR 2008, 281ff..

353 *Lightning Bolt Co Pty Limited v Skinner & Anor* [2002] QSC 062.

stände deutlich, die bei der Beendigung des Arbeits- und Beschäftigungsverhältnisses und bei einer unbilligen Arbeitgeberkündigung zu einer Altersdiskriminierung führen können.[354] Denn dort wandte sich ein 60-jähriger Arbeitnehmer, der seit 23 Jahren im selben Unternehmen gearbeitet hatte dagegen, dass seine Stelle mit einem jüngeren Arbeitnehmer besetzt werden sollte, weil dieser besser für die neuen unternehmerischen Anforderungen zu schulen sei. Der Kläger behauptet, dass eine derartige Beendigung des Arbeits- und Beschäftigungsverhältnisses eine sittenwidrige, unterdrückende und unbillige Kündigung darstelle, was sodann auch die Western Australian Industrial Relations Commission in diesem Fall bestätigte.[355]

III. Altersdiskriminierung durch altersbedingte Kündigung wegen Erreichen eines bestimmten Alters – compulsory retirement

Der Age Discrimination Act 2004 (Cth) enthält entgegen der praktischen Bedeutung keine spezifischen Regelungen über das Problem der Altersdiskriminierung durch eine altersbedingte Kündigung aufgrund des Erreichens eines bestimmten Alters bzw. zum Problem der altersbedingten Kündigung (*„compulsory retirement“*) und somit erscheint es fraglich, welche wesentlichen Anforderungen an ein substantiiertes Vorgehen gegen eine solche Altersdiskriminierung zu stellen sind und ob diese überhaupt zulässig ist.[356]

Allerdings statuiert § 18 Abs. 2 lit. c) ADA ein Diskriminierungsverbot, welches ausdrücklich eine Kündigung als unrechtmäßig qualifiziert, sofern diese mit dem Alter des Arbeitnehmers begründet wird. Da sich der Arbeitgeber bei einer altersbedingten

---

354 *Richards v Webforge Australia Pty Limited* (2005) EOC 93-360.

355 *Richards v Webforge Australia Pty Limited* (2005) EOC 93-360.

356 Trotz Aufhebung der Zulässigkeit von altersbedingten Kündigungen erwarten in der Praxis die Arbeitgeber oftmals, dass ihre Arbeitnehmer und Beschäftigten nicht wesentlich später als mit Erreichen des Alters von 65 Jahren – vorzugsweise früher – in den Ruhestand gehen. Denn jüngere Arbeitnehmer sind nicht zuletzt zu günstigeren Vergütungen zu beschäftigen; vgl. hierzu Equal Opportunity Commission of Victoria, Age Limits: Report by the Equal Opportunity Commission of Victoria, South Australia and Western Australia (2001), 14; ebenso *Fredman*, Discrimination Law, 61; *Goulding*, The Law Handbook, 517 mit Verweis auf die Ausnahmen vor Erlass des Age Discrimination Act 2004 (Cth); vgl. zur Rechtfertigung der Beendigung eines Arbeitsverhältnisses aufgrund Erreichen einer Altersgrenze nach europäischem Recht auch *Colneric*, Antidiskriminierung – quo vadis? – Europäisches Recht, NZA-Beilage 2008, Heft 2, 71f. mit Verweis auf die Rechtsprechung des EuGH zur Rechtssache *Palacios de la Villa*, EuGH Urteil vom 15.02.2007 – C-411/05 = BB 2007, 2629; vgl. zur Zulässigkeit der altersbedingten Kündigung durch Erreichen eines bestimmten Alters und der Entwicklung der Rechtsprechung des EuGH die Urteile in Sachen *Age Concern*, EuGH Urteil vom 05.03.2009 – C-388/07 = NZA 2009, 305 sowie *Petersen* EuGH Urteil vom 12.01.2010 – C-341/08 = NZA 2010, 155 = NJW 2010, 587 und *Rosenbladt* EuGH Urteil vom 12.10.2010 – C-45/09 = NZA 2010, 1167 = NJW 2010, 3767 sowie *Georgiev* EuGH Urteil vom 18.11.2010 – C-250/09 und C-268/09 = NZA 2011, 29 = NJW 2011, 42 = Urteilsbesprechung von Kohte, jurisPR-ArbR2/2011, Anm. 7.

Kündigung immer auf das Erreichen einer bestimmten – zuvor festgelegten – Altersgrenze und somit auf das individuelle Alter des jeweiligen Beschäftigten berufen wird, erfolgt diese altersbedingte Kündigung ausschließlich aufgrund des Alters einer Person. Folglich muss gerade die altersbedingte Kündigung von § 18 Abs. 2 lit. c) ADA erfasst werden. Die fehlende Stellungnahme des australischen Gesetzgebers zu diesem Umstand kann dabei konsequenterweise nur als Bestätigung dieser Ansicht verstanden werden, da er sich ansonsten in Widerspruch zu seinen mit § 3 ADA weitgesteckten Zielen setzen würde.[357]

Zwar sind altersbedingte Kündigungen somit per se durch das Diskriminierungsverbot des § 18 Abs. 2 lit. c) ADA untersagt. Allerdings soll es – wie bereits zuvor dargestellt – in Einzelfällen die Möglichkeit der Rechtfertigung einer derartigen altersbedingten Kündigung geben, § 18 Abs. 4 und Abs. 5 ADA. Denn insbesondere für das Diskriminierungsverbot des § 18 Abs. 2 lit. c) ADA kann sich aufgrund der besonderen Anforderungen der jeweiligen Beschäftigung die Notwendigkeit einer Rechtfertigung gemäß § 18. Abs. 4 ADA ergeben (*„inherent requirements"*). Bei der Frage, ob die betreffende Person die speziellen Anforderungen tatsächlich gerade aufgrund ihres Alters nicht erfüllen kann, ist eine Interessenabwägung anhand der in § 18 Abs. 5 ADA allgemein umschriebenen Faktoren vorzunehmen, so dass sich mithin eine zweistufige Rechtfertigungsprüfung ergibt. Zuerst gilt es zu untersuchen, ob *„inherent requirements"* vorliegen und sodann ist genau zu prüfen, ob es dem Arbeitnehmer tatsächlich nicht möglich ist, diese (ordnungsgemäß) zu erfüllen.

Beispielhaft für die Problematik der altersbedingte Kündigungen und der Rechtfertigung dieser stehen die beiden Entscheidungen der Rechtsprechung in den Fällen *Christie v Qantas Airways Limited* und *Peacock v Human Rights and Equal Opportunity Commission*. Obwohl vor allem im staatlichen Beschäftigungssektor in Australien die Vorgehensweise der *„compulsory retirement"* offiziell beseitigt werden konnte, gibt es dennoch weiterhin zahlreiche Beschwerden zur Human Rights and Equal Opportunity Commission zu dieser Form der Altersdiskriminierung.[358] Zur Verschärfung der Altersdiskriminierung kommt hinzu, dass altersbedingte Kündigungen vor dem Inkrafttreten des Age Discrimination Act 2004 (Cth) ein probates Mittel zur Regulierung der Altersstruktur auf dem Beschäftigungsmarkt gewesen sind.[359]

---

357 Vgl. die lediglich allgemeinen Ausführungen im Explanatory Memorandum of the Age Discrimination Bill 2003 (Cth), Annexure C, Clause 18 - Discrimination in employment.

358 Human Rights and Equal Opportunity Commission, Report of inquiry into complaints of discrimination in employment and occupation, 1997, 2.

359 Vor Inkrafttreten des Age Discrimination Act 2004 (Cth) gab es auf der Grundlage des Human Rights and Equal Opportunity Commission Act 1986 (Cth) im Zeitraum 2003/2004 insgesamt 18 Beschwerden zur Human Rights and Equal Opportunity Commission (vgl. Human Rights and Equal Opportunity Commission, Annual Report 2003-2004, 85). Bereits im Berichtszeitraum 2004/2005, also nach Inkrafttreten des Age Discrimination Act 2004 (Cth) wurden insgesamt 404 Anfragen wegen Altersdiskriminierungen und dabei allein 13 wegen altersbedingten Kündigungen sowie zusätzlich 78 Beschwerden aus diesen Gründen gestellt (Human Rights and Equal Opportunity Commission, Annual Report 2004-2005, 62, 64).; im Berichtszeitraum 2007/2008 nahm die Anzahl der eingegangenen und bearbeiteten Anfragen und Beschwerden nochmals zu. So wurden insgesamt 768 Anfragen wegen Altersdiskrimierungen und davon al-

1. Die altersbedingte Kündigung von Piloten der Australian Airlines

So hatte sich die Human Rights and Equal Opportunity Commission bereits im Vorfeld zu den vorgenannten Gerichtsentscheidungen im Jahr 1992 mit einer Beschwerde der Piloten Bill Bone, Bill Craig, Peter Ivanoff und Kingsley Love zu befassen, die aufgrund des erreichten Alters von 60 Jahren durch ihren Arbeitsgeber die frühere Australian Airlines – heutzutage Unternehmensteil der Qantas Airways Limited – im Zeitraum von 1990 – 1992 altersbedingt gekündigt und somit zwangsweise pensioniert worden sind.

Dieses Verfahren wird in der australischen Rechtspraxis als der Grundstein der gerichtlichen Diskussion um die Zulässigkeit und Rechtfertigung von altersbedingten Kündigungen angesehen.[360]

a. Die Auffassung der Piloten und der Human Rights and Equal Opportunity Commission

Nach Auffassung der Piloten und der Human Rights and Equal Opportunity Commission begründete das Vorgehen des Arbeitgebers eine nicht durch die *„inherent requirements"* gerechtfertigte direkte Diskriminierung wegen Alters. Denn die Beendigung des Beschäftigungsverhältnisses hatte ihre Ursache allein im Erreichen des Alters von 60 Jahren und stellt eine Ausgrenzung älterer Arbeitskräfte dar, so dass eine Gleichbehandlung ohne Unterscheidung nach dem Alter nicht mehr gewährleistet gewesen ist.[361] Darüber hinaus sei ein Zusammenhang zwischen dem Alter der Piloten und der Fähigkeit zur Erfüllung von vorgegebenen Sicherheitsstandards nicht ersichtlich. Es sei auch keine vertragliche Vereinbarung getroffen worden, nach welcher bei Erreichen des Alters von 60 Jahren die Beschäftigung als Pilot automatisch enden solle.

Weiterhin sollte auch ein Bezug auf die Regel 2.1.10.1 des Convention of International Civil Aviation, wonach auf internationalen Flügen eine Pilotenlizenz nicht für Piloten erteilt werden dürfe, die älter als 60 Jahre sind, nicht zulässig sein. Denn die Piloten waren ausschließlich auf nationalen Flugrouten innerhalb Australien eingesetzt.

---

lein 14 wegen altersbedingten Kündigungen gestellt. (Human Rights and Equal Opportunity Commission, Annual Report 2007-2008, 60, 74).

360 Die vorzeitige Beendigung von Arbeitsverhältnissen von Piloten ist auch in Deutschland und im Rahmen eines aktuellen Vorlageverfahrens durch das BAG an den EuGH bekannt und wird ausührlich diskutiert; vgl. inbsesondere BAG NZA 2009, 1355 sowie die Schlussanträge des Generalanwalts am Europäischen Gerichtshof vom 19.05.2011 (C-447/09), nach denen eine im Tarifvertrag vereinbarte Altersgrenze für Piloten von 60 Jahren gegen europäisches Recht verstosse und auch nicht durch die Gewährung der öffentlichen Sicherheit oder zum Schutz der Gesundheit gerechtfertigt werden könne.

361 Human Rights and Equal Opportunity Commission, Report of inquiry into complaints of discrimination in employment and occupation, 1997, 6.

b. Die Ansicht der Australian Airlines

Diese Ansicht wurde von der Gegenseite jedoch abgelehnt, da sie die speziellen Anforderungen im Beruf eines Piloten und die im Interesse der Öffentlichkeit überwiegende Sicherheit des Luftverkehrs als rechtfertigende Gründe („*inherent requirements*“) für ihr Verhalten ansahen. Die „*inherent requirements*“ konkretisierte die Australian Airlines dabei folgendermaßen: Die Piloten müssen im Besitz einer Airline Transport Pilot Licence sein sowie den vom Chefpilot festgelegten Grundsätzen und Methoden entsprechen, um einen bestmöglichen Standard an Sicherheit und ein möglichst niedriges Sicherheitsrisiko darzustellen. Ebenso soll ein hohes Maß an physiologischer und psychologischer Gesundheit und Fitness vorhanden sein, um den fehlerfreien Betrieb eines Flugzeugs im Normal- und Notfall sicherstellen zu können.[362] Daher habe es im Ergebnis auch keiner gesonderten arbeitsvertraglichen Regelung bedurft.

Weiterhin hat die Australian Airlines in ihrer Stellungnahme darauf hingewiesen, dass sie grundsätzlich keine spezielle Politik der altersbedingten Kündigung betreibe, die sich ausschließlich am Alter eines Beschäftigten orientiere, so dass schon aus diesem Grund eine entsprechende Regelung im Arbeitsvertrag fehle. Einzig gebe es vereinzelte Ausnahmen, wenn ersichtlich wird, dass ältere Piloten die Anforderungen ihrer beruflichen Tätigkeit aufgrund ihres Alters nicht mehr im erforderlichen Maße erfüllen können.[363] Denn ebenso gut wie ein Pilot, der älter ist als 59 Jahre, die beruflichen Anforderungen (weiterhin) fehlerfrei erfüllen könne, besteht die Möglichkeit eines erhöhten Sicherheitsrisikos durch Piloten über 60 Jahre, die aufgrund ihrer körperlichen und geistigen Verfassung nicht mehr in vollem Umfang in der Lage sind, den nicht unerheblichen Anforderungen gerecht werden zu können. Somit sollte nach Ansicht der Australian Airlines ein Zusammenhang zwischen dem Alter des Piloten und der Erfüllung von Sicherheitsstandards bestehen.

c. Das Ergebnis der Verhandlung vor der Human Rights and Equal Opportunity Commission

Die Human Rights and Equal Opportunity Commission hat versucht, eine vermittelnde Lösung zu finden und hat demnach keinen eindeutig für die Antragsteller bzw. für die Antragsgegner sprechenden Kurs eingeschlagen. Unverkennbar ist jedoch, dass nach Auffassung der Human Rights and Equal Opportunity Commission eine Altersdiskriminierung durch die altersbedingte Kündigungen vorliegt, sie aber dennoch davon überzeugt ist, dass das Alter des Piloten sich in Verbindung mit seinem körperlichen und gesundheitlichen Zustand auf die Erfüllung der Sicherheitsstandards auswirken könne. Daher hat die Human Rights and Equal Opportunity Commission der Australian Airlines empfohlen, ihre Entlassungspolitik und Praxis der altersbedingten Kündi-

---

362 Human Rights and Equal Opportunity Commission, Report of inquiry into complaints of discrimination in employment and occupation, 1997, 10f..

363 Human Rights and Equal Opportunity Commission, Report of inquiry into complaints of discrimination in employment and occupation, 1997, 6.

gungen aufzugeben, die betroffenen Piloten – sofern sie alle erforderlichen gesundheitlichen Tests erfolgreich absolvieren – wieder einzustellen und sie für den erlittenen Verdienstausfall zu entschädigen.[364]

Obwohl diese vermittelnde Ansicht der Human Rights and Equal Opportunity Commission alle Interessen ausreichend zu berücksichtigen scheint und die Einzelfallbetrachtung unter Einbeziehung des konkreten physiologischen und psychischen Zustands des betroffenen Piloten eine generelle altersbedingte Kündigung nach einem abstrakten Schema bevorzugt, konnte eine einvernehmliche Lösung nicht erzielt werden.

Aus dem dargelegten Fall gingen deshalb die sich anschließenden gerichtlichen Verfahren *Allman v Australian Airlines Limited* und *Christie v Qantas Airlines Limited* vor dem Industrial Relation Court of Australia hervor, die im Mai 1995 verhandelt worden.[365]

Insbesondere das Verfahren *Christie v Qantas Airlines Limited* (sowie das Berufungsverfahren *Qantas Airways Limited v Christie*) erregte dabei – nicht zuletzt aufgrund der Argumentation des Arbeitgebers und der Rechtsprechung – das Interesse der Öffentlichkeit.[366]

2. Der Fall Christie v Qantas Airways Limited

In diesem Gerichtsverfahren war demnach eine Altersdiskriminierung Gegenstand der Klage des Flugkapitäns Christie. Mit ihm war die Frage verbunden, ob die automatische altersbedingte Kündigung („*compulsory retirement*“) eines Piloten, der bei der australischen Fluggesellschaft Qantas auf internationalen Flugrouten beschäftigt ist, sobald er 60 Jahre alt wird, einen Verstoß gegen ein Diskriminierungsverbot des Age Discrimination Act 2004 (Cth) darstellt oder ob diese Personalpolitik von Qantas unter Diskriminierungsgesichtspunkten rechtmäßig ist. Im Rahmen dieser gerichtlichen Auseinandersetzung wurde geltend gemacht, dass die altersbedingte Kündigung allein aufgrund des Alters erfolgt und der Kläger somit auch ausschließlich aufgrund seines Alters diskriminiert worden sei.[367]

Der Industrial Relations Court of Australia hat die Klage abgewiesen, wurde in seiner Entscheidung jedoch vom Full Court of the Industrial Relation Court aufgehoben. Im durch dann von Qantas angestrengtem Berufungsverfahren gegen John Baillie Christie hat der High Court abschließend zwar eine Diskriminierung der Piloten wegen Alters bejaht, aber gleichzeitig die altersbedingte Kündigung beim Erreichen eines bestimmten Alters als gerechtfertigt anerkannt. In seiner wichtigen Entscheidung teilte

364 Human Rights and Equal Opportunity Commission, Report of inquiry into complaints of discrimination in employment and occupation, 1997, 20.

365 *Allman v Australian Airlines Limited* (1995) 60 IR 17; *Christie v Qatnas Airways Limited* [1995] EOC 92-705; (1996) 60 IR 17.

366 *Mac* Dermott, Age Discrimination and Employment Law: The Sky's the Limit, (1998) 11 AJLL 144 mit Verweis auf *Christie v Qatnas Airways Limited* [1995] EOC 92-705; (1995) 60 IR 17; (1996) 138 ALR 19; *Qantas Airways Limited v Christie* (1998) 193 CLR 280.

367 *Qantas Airways Limited v Christie* (1998) 193 CLR 280.

der High Court darüber hinaus die grundsätzliche Ansicht des Gesetzgebers, dass es einer allgemeingültigen Regelung zur Rechtfertigung von Diskriminierung wegen Alters bedürfe, nicht in vollem Umfang und schränkte den Anwendungsbereich des Age Discrimination Act dahingehend ein, als dass er gerade auch eine Einzelfallbetrachtung zuließ.[368] Denn das Alter eines Piloten sei nach seiner Auffassung eine innerhalb dieses speziellen Berufs wurzelnde Anforderung und habe nicht unbedeutende internationale Auswirkungen, die den persönlichen Interessen und Rechten des Klägers vorgehen müssten.[369] In der Entscheidung zu *Qantas Airways Limited v Christie* hat sich die Rechtsprechung demnach ausführlich mit dem Begriff des *„particular employment"* und dessen Abgrenzung zur *„particular position"* auseinandergesetzt.[370]

a. Die Auffassung von Qantas Airways Limited

Qantas hat sich zur Rechtfertigung der von ihr ausgesprochenen altersbedingten Kündigung und der dadurch herbeigeführten altersbedingten Kündigung auf gesetzliche Bestimmungen, denen das Unternehmen als Fluggesellschaft durch internationale Luftverkehrsabkommen unterworfen sei, berufen. Durch die Convention of International Civil Aviation sei es gerechtfertigt, einen Piloten dann nicht mehr fliegen zu lassen, wenn er das Alter von 60 Jahren erreicht hat und die altersbedingte Kündigung somit durch diese besonderen mit dem Beruf des Piloten verbundenen Anforderungen gerechtfertigt sei.[371] Diese Regelung war jedoch zum streitgegenständlichen Zeitpunkt mangels Umsetzung in australisches Bundesrecht im australischen Commonwealth gerade nicht anwendbar. Qantas berief sich deshalb darauf, dass dieses Abkommen aber von zahlreichen Staaten angewendet werde, deren Luftraum Qantas bei internationalen Flügen durchqueren müsse.[372] So seien insbesondere Neuseeland, Denpasar auf Bali (Indonesien) sowie die Fiji-Inseln nicht als Flugrouten in den Dienstplan von Christie zu integrieren. Dadurch müsse er vermehrt auf kürzeren Flugstrecken eingesetzt werden, was jedoch für Qantas ein organisatorisches Problem darstelle und aufgrund der Verteilung der Langstreckenflüge auf andere Piloten für diese zu einer unangemessenen Benachteiligung und Belastung führen würde. Folglich stellte für Qantas gerade die Einbindung in den Flugplan ein *„inherent requirement"* dar, welche eine altersbedingte Kündigung des Piloten Christie erlauben solle.

---

368 *Qantas Airways Limited v Christie* (1998) 193 CLR 280; vgl. auch *MacDermott*, Age Discrimination and Employment Law: The Sky's the Limit (1998) Australian Journal of Labour Law 144.

369 Ursprünglich wurde auf das Diskriminierungsverbot des § 170DF Abs. 1 lit. f) des Industrial Relations Act 1988 (Cth) Bezug genommen.

370 *Qantas Airways Limited v Christie* (1998) 193 CLR 280; *MacDermott*, Age Discrimination and Employment Law: The Sky's the Limit (1998) Australian Journal of Labour Law 144.

371 *Qantas Airways Limited v Christie* (1998) 193 CLR 280.

372 *Qantas Airways Limited v Christie* (1998) 193 CLR 280.

b. Die Ansicht des High Court

Die Rechtsprechung hatte demnach zu beurteilen, ob die altersbedingte Kündigung des Flugkapitäns im Hinblick auf die aus der konkreten Beschäftigung („*particular employment*“) resultierenden Anforderungen gerechtfertigt gewesen ist, wobei der High Court zur Beantwortung dieser Frage vor allem auch auf die spezielle Tätigkeit („*the particular position*“) abstellte.

Der High Court stellte zu Beginn fest, dass das Arbeitsverhältnis nicht automatisch mit Erreichen des Alters von 60 Jahren beendet worden ist, sondern vielmehr Qantas das Beschäftigungsverhältnis gekündigt habe. Sodann kommt der High Court zur Frage, ob eine Rechtfertigung der altersbedingten Kündigung und der damit verbundenen altersbedingten Kündigung aufgrund von „*inherent requirements*“ vorliegt und vertrat die Auffassung, dass sich die mit einer bestimmten Beschäftigung verbundenen Anforderungen hauptsächlich anhand der konkreten Anstellung und des jeweiligen Anforderungsniveaus der Arbeit beurteilen lassen. Denn die mit einer bestimmten Beschäftigung zusammenhängenden Anforderungen lassen sich in der Regel nicht abstrakt für alle Arbeitsverhältnisse, sondern nur im Rahmen einer genauen Untersuchung der jeweiligen einzelfallbezogenen Aufgabe feststellen.[373] Folglich war die konkrete Tätigkeit des Piloten Christie als Kapitän einer Boing 747-400 und nicht allgemein die eines Piloten Gegenstand der Betrachtung des High Court.

In seinem Urteil schlussfolgerte der High Court deshalb, dass die Fähigkeit den Anforderungen des Dienst- und Flugplans und somit der Personaleinsatzplanung („*rostering system*“) der Fluggesellschaft zu entsprechen und die aufgestellten Verpflichtungen zu befolgen, die aus der allgemeinen Beschäftigung als Flugkapitän auf internationalen Flügen resultierenden Anforderungen darstellen und der Kläger die Erfüllung dieser Anforderung mit einem Alter von 60 Jahren nicht mehr sicherstellen könne. Folglich sah der High Court in der Personalpolitik kein Diskriminierungsverbot des Age Discrimination Act 2004 (Cth) verwirklicht, so dass die Klage keinen Erfolg haben konnte.[374] Dabei ist der High Court jedoch nicht auf die Frage eingegangen, ob es anstelle der altersbedingten Kündigung ein milderes Mittel gegeben habe, welches den Kläger weniger belastet hätte. Eine typisierende Betrachtung auch für Inlandsflüge oder aber ein etwaiger Vorrang von der Anpassung organisatorischer Gegebenheiten im Unternehmen hat das Gericht nicht angesprochen und ihren Einfluss auf das Ergebnis somit offen gelassen.

c. Eigene Stellungnahme

Mit dieser Entscheidung hat die Rechtsprechung gezeigt, dass die Fähigkeit die Anforderungen einer bestimmten Beschäftigung zu erfüllen, nicht allein auf die Erfüllung von allgemeinen physischen Voraussetzungen begrenzt ist. Denn im vorliegenden Fall stand für die Parteien außer Frage, dass der Flugkapitän in hinreichendem Umfang in

373 *Qantas Airways Limited v Christie* (1998) 193 CLR 280, 304.

374 *MacDermott*, Age Discrimination and Employment Law: The Sky's the Limit, (1998) 11 AJLL 144.

der Lage war, die körperlichen und auch technischen Anforderungen, die allgemein an einen Flugkapitän gestellt werden, zu erfüllen.

Die Rechtsprechung bestätigte aber darüber hinaus, dass zusätzlich auch der konkrete Arbeitsplatz und die daraus resultierenden bzw. vom Arbeitgeber aufgestellten speziellen Anforderungen im jeweiligen Einzelfall berücksichtigt werden dürfen und müssen.[375] So sollen selbst solche Anforderungen zulässig sein, die der Arbeitgeber im Einzelfall aufgestellt hat, die aber nicht zwingend verallgemeinerungswürdig sind.

Zutreffend hebt der High Court hervor, dass als Bewertungsmaßstab die allgemeine Beurteilungsebene verlassen werden und eine konkrete Einzelfallbetrachtung vorgenommen werden müsse, da oftmals kein praktikabler Unterscheidungsmaßstab zwischen den *„inherent requirements of a job“* und den *„inherent requirements of a position“* existiert.[376] Der umfassenden und effektiven Verhinderung und Beseitigung von Altersdiskriminierungen ist diese Rechtsprechung jedoch nicht zuträglich. Denn durch dieses Urteil wird dem Arbeitgeber die Möglichkeit eröffnet, einzelfallbezogene Anforderungen aufzustellen, die bereits mit einer auf den ersten Blick plausiblen Begründung eine Diskriminierung wegen Alters zu rechtfertigen vermögen. Darüber hinaus hat die Rechtsprechung die Beantwortung der Frage offengelassen, ob das von der Qantas Airways Limited in Bezug genommene internationale Luftverkehrsabkommen ein *„other relevant factor“* im Sinne von § 18 Abs. 5 ADA darstellt, welcher zulässiger Weise in die Interessenabwägung einbezogen werden darf oder ob eine solche Einbeziehung zu weit geht.

Dadurch werden vor allem die vom Gesetzgeber schon zahlreich aufgestellten Befreiungen von den Diskriminierungsverboten des Age Discrimination Act 2004 (Cth) nochmals erheblich erweitert, ohne zugleich konkrete und für den Einzelnen erkennbare und nachvollziehbare Grenzen aufzuzeigen. Gesteigerte Rechtssicherheit dürfte somit im Bereich der Diskriminierung wegen Alters nicht geschaffen worden sein.

3. Der Fall Peacock v Human Rights and Equal Opportunity Commission

Vergleichbar schwierig stellte sich auch im Fall *Peacock v Human Rights and Equal Opportunity Commission* die erfolgreiche Geltendmachung einer Altersdiskriminierung wegen einer altersbedingten Kündigung des Offiziers Mortimer John Peacock durch das Verteidigungsministerium des Commonwealth aufgrund des Erreichens der Altersgrenze von 65 Jahren dar.[377]

So hatte das Commonwealth das Beschäftigungsverhältnis mit dem Offizier des Australian Public Service unter Berufung auf die gesetzliche Regelung des § 76V des damaligen Public Service Act 1922 (Cth) durch eine altersbedingte Kündigung am 19.07.1996 beendet. Er wandte sich nach Ankündigung der beabsichtigten Kündigung zur Prüfung dieser Entscheidung an seinen Arbeitgeber, welcher jedoch an der alters-

375 *Qantas Airways Limited v Christie* (1998) 193 CLR 280.

376 *MacDermott*, Age Discrimination and Employment Law: The Sky's the Limit, (1998) 11 AJLL 144.

377 *Peacock v Human Rights and Equal Opportunity Commission* [2005] FCAFC 45.

bedingten Kündigung unter der Begründung festhielt, dass die altersbedingte Kündigung ein gewöhnlicher Vorgang sei.[378] Da der Offizier Peacock die Entscheidung sowie auch deren Begründung nicht akzeptieren konnte und zwischenzeitlich der Zeitpunkt der altersbedingten Kündigung und somit des Ausscheidens aus dem Beschäftigungsverhältnis kurz bevorstand, reichte er bei der Human Rights and Equal Opportunity Commission eine entsprechende Beschwerde ein, die jedoch die altersbedingte Kündigung tatsächlich nicht zu verhindern vermochte.[379]

a. Die Ansicht der Human Rights and Equal Opportunity Commission und deren gerichtliche Überprüfung

Die Human Rights and Equal Opportunity Commission sah in der altersbedingten Kündigung und der damit ebenfalls verbundenen altersbedingten Kündigung des Offiziers mit Erreichen eines bestimmten Alters (vorerst) eine nicht gerechtfertigte Diskriminierung wegen Alters als gegeben an. Dem Antragsgegner – dem Commonwealth – wurde allerdings vom Federal Court vorgeschlagen, den Antragssteller zu entschädigen und eine Ausgleichszahlung in Höhe von 20.000 AUD als aufgrund des durch die diskriminierende altersbedingte Kündigung erlittenen Verdienstausfalles zu zahlen. Der Antragssteller vertrat jedoch die Auffassung, dass der angebotene Zahlbetrag nicht adäquat im Verhältnis zur erlittenen Diskriminierung sei und das Commonwealth lehnte jegliche Zahlung und sonstige Leistung zur Wiedergutmachung ab, weil keine Diskriminierung wegen Alters vorgelegen habe.[380]

Im Rahmen des nachfolgenden gerichtlichen Verfahrens wurde der Lösungsvorschlag der Human Rights and Equal Opportunity Commission dann auch als nicht geeignet angesehen, da hier die Bejahung einer ungerechtfertigten Altersdiskriminierung überaus fraglich sei. Das Gericht wies in seiner Entscheidung vom 17.08.2000 darauf hin, dass die Human Rights and Equal Opportunity Commission zwar zutreffend eine Altersdiskriminierung bejaht, sich jedoch bei der Beurteilung einer etwaigen Rechtfertigung nicht mit der Frage auseinandergesetzt habe, ob und wie durch die altersbedingte Kündigung möglicherweise ein Ausgleichs der Altersstruktur zwischen jungen und älteren Beschäftigten erfolgen könne, und sei daher zu einem unzutreffenden Ergebnis gelangt.[381]

> „It follows from these factual findings that the decision ... was materially affected by a distinction made by him on the basis of age: the need to provide a balanced age profile and to provide career opportunities for younger officers. But how did that distinction affect equality of opportunity or treatment in employment? As between Mr Peacock and younger officers, at material times there was never relevant quality... He [Mr Peacock] was not in

378 Vgl. das zuvor anhängige Verfahren von 3 ebenfalls zwangspensionierten Arbeitnehmern des Verteidigungsministeriums *Secretary, Department of Defence v Human Rights and Equal Opportunity Commission* (1997) 78 FCR 208.

379 *Peacock v Human Rights and Equal Opportunity Commission* [2005] FCAFC 45.

380 Vgl. auch *Commonwealth of Australia v Peacock* (2000) 104 FCR 464.

381 *Peacock v Human Rights and Equal Opportunity Commission* [2005] FCAFC 45; *Commonwealth of Australia v Peacock* (2000) 104 FCR 464.

> competition with any other officers who might have been approaching the age of 65 years and seeking extensions..."[382]

Daher wurde an die Human Rights and Equal Opportunity Commission zurück verwiesen, um nunmehr eine umfassende Interessenabwägung vorzunehmen und das Vorliegen einer ungerechtfertigten Altersdiskriminierung in Folge der altersbedingten Kündigung erneut zu beurteilen. Allerdings blieb eine solche Interessenabwägung gänzlich aus. Vielmehr schloss sich die Human Rights and Equal Opportunity Commission in ihrer erneuten Entscheidung vom 11. Januar 2002 nunmehr der durch die Rechtsprechung vertretenen Interpretation an und verneinte eine Altersdiskriminierung, indem es diese als gerechtfertigt beurteilte.[383]

b. Die Auffassung des Federal Court

Nachdem auch gegen dieses Verfahrensergebnis der Human Rights and Equal Opportunity Commission Rechtsmittel eingelegt wurde und eine weitere Gerichtsentscheidung in der altersbedingten Kündigung keine ungerechtfertigte Diskriminierung wegen Alters aus den vorgenannten Gründen erkennen konnte, hatte sich schließlich der (Full) Federal Court mit dieser Rechtsfrage zu befassen.[384]

Der Federal Court vermochte ebenfalls keine ungerechtfertigte Diskriminierung wegen Alters und auch keine ungleiche Behandlung mit anderen Offizieren, die sich gerade der Altersgrenze von 65 Jahren nähern und eine Verlängerung ihrer Arbeitsverträge begehren, zu erkennen und verwies den Fall deshalb an die Human Rights and Equal Opportunity Commission zurück.[385] Auf der Grundlage der Entscheidung und der Argumentation des Federal Court wurde eine Altersdiskriminierung zwar dem Grunde nach bejaht, im Ergebnis aber aufgrund einer hinreichenden Rechtfertigung abgelehnt.

c. Eigene Stellungnahme

Auch wenn die Entscheidung des Federal Court in Sachen *Peacock v Human Rights and Equal Opportunity Commission* eine Streitigkeit wegen einer Altersdiskriminierung betrifft, die ihren Ursprung im Zeitraum vor der Geltung des Age Discrimination Act 2004 (Cth) hatte und daher auch nicht anhand des gesetzlich in § 18 Abs. 2 ADA verankerten Diskriminierungsverbots sowie der Rechtfertigungsmöglichkeit gemäß § 18 Abs. 4 und Abs. 5 ADA beurteilt wurde, so erscheint das gefundene Ergebnis dennoch fraglich. Denn die als Rechtfertigung der altersbedingten Kündigung angeführte

---

382 *Peacock v Human Rights and Equal Opportunity Commission* [2005] FCAFC 45; *Commonwealth of Australia v Peacock* (2000) 104 FCR 464.

383 *Peacock v Human Rights and Equal Opportunity Commission* [2005] FCAFC 45; *Commonwealth of Australia v Peacock* (2000) 104 FCR 464.

384 Vgl. zum weiteren Verfahrensgang auch *Peacock v Human Rights and Equal Opportunity Commission* (2003) 73 ALD 34; *Commonwealth of Australia v Peacock* (2000) 104 FCR 464; *Peacock v Human Rights and Equal Opportunity Commission* [2005] FCAFC 45.

385 *Peacock v Human Rights and Equal Opportunity Commission* [2005] FCAFC 45.

Gewährleistung einer ausgewogenen Altersstruktur (*"age diversity"*) kann zwar ein *"inherent requirement"* der Tätigkeit des Offiziers Peacock darstellen. Ob diese Anforderungen jedoch einer Interessenabwägung (im Sinne der Grundgedanken des § 18 Abs. 5 ADA) standhalten, wurde nicht geklärt.[386]

4. Verbot einer altersbedingten Kündigung eines Arbeitnehmers wegen Erreichen eines bestimmten Alters in den Gesetzen der einzelnen Bundesstaaten

In den gesetzlichen Regelungen der einzelnen australischen Bundesstaaten existieren zahlreiche Vorschriften zur Rechtfertigung von altersbedingten Kündigungen wegen des Erreichens eines bestimmten Alters.

So erklärt § 15 Abs. 1 und 3 des Anti-Discrimination Act 1991 (Qld) die Entlassung eines Arbeiters als rechtswidrig, wenn sie infolge einer entsprechenden altersbedingten Kündigung erfolgt. Ebenfalls sind gemäß § 268 Abs. 1, 3 und 4 des Anti-Discrimination Act 1991 (Qld) auch Bestimmungen in Form von früheren betrieblichen Weisungen, Vereinbarungen oder Richtlinien unwirksam, sofern sie zur altersbedingten Kündigung eines Arbeiters aufgrund oder infolge des Erreichens eines bestimmten Alters berechtigen. Auch der Anti-Discrimination Act 1977 (NSW) statuiert in § 49ZV, dass die altersbedingte Kündigung wegen Erreichens eines bestimmten Lebensalters rechtswidrig ist.[387] Vergleichbar mit diesen Vorschriften ist auch die Regelung der §§ 14 und 15 des Equal Opportunity Act 1995 (Vic), der die Beendigung von Arbeits- und Beschäftigungsverhältnissen oder ein Arbeitsverbot sowie jeden vergleichbaren Nachteil als rechtswidrige Diskriminierung wegen Alters einordnet.

Da es neben den vorgenannten Vorschriften aber kein ausdrückliches Verbot einer Altersdiskriminierung durch eine altersbedingte Kündigung wegen Erreichens eines bestimmten Alters gegeben hat und gibt, existierten insbesondere im Equal Opportunity Act 1984 (SA) – § 85f Abs. 6 EOA – und im Discrimination Act 1991 (ACT) – § 57D DAA – über mehrere Jahre unbeachtet Ausnahmen von einem solchen Verbot. Inzwischen hat der Gesetzgeber reagiert und diese Ausnahmevorschriften aber aufgehoben. Auch für die Beschäftigung im öffentlichen Sektor hat der australische Gesetzgeber mit dem Abolition of Compulsory Retirement (Statutory Officeholders) Act

---

386 In der aktuellen Entscheidung des Federal Court *Carr v Blade Repairs Australia Pty Ltd* (No 2) [2010] FCA 688 konnte aber ausdrücklich festgestellt werden, dass eine Kündigung gerade aufgrund eines jungen Alters und auf der Basis des Mottos „last hired, first fired" bereits deshalb eine ungerechtfertigte Diskriminierung wegen Alters darstellt, weil keinerlei Abwägung im Rahmen einer Verhältnismäßigkeitsprüfung unter Berücksichtigung der Arbeitsleistung, Qualifikation und Berufserfahrung des Arbeitnehmers erfolgt ist.

387 Zu dieser gesetzlichen Regelung existieren im Vergleich mit den anderen Gesetzen der einzelnen Bundesstaaten eine erhebliche Anzahl an Gerichtsurteilen. Vgl. etwa *Christley v University of Newcastle* (1992) EOC 92-474; *Upton v The Benevolent Society of New South Wales* (1994) EOC 92-600; *Kinley v East Sydney Area Health Service & Anor* (1994) EOC 92-559; *Lorang v Mater Misericordiae Hospital & Anor* (1994) EOC 92-602; *Goodworth v Marsden Motors Pty Limited* (1996) EOC 92-837.

2001 reagiert und verstärkt somit die Diskriminierungsverbote des Age Discrimination Act 2004 (Cth) im Hinblick auf altersbedingten Kündigungen.

5. Schlussfolgerung zu den inherent requirements

Wie zuvor bereits angedeutet, stellt die Rechtsprechung zur Bestimmung und Auslegung der *„inherent requirements of the particular employment"* überwiegend einen sehr weiten Beurteilungsmaßstab für die *„essential elements"* und für die Beantwortung der Frage, ob der jeweilige Arbeitnehmer die aufgestellten Anforderungen erfüllen kann, auf. Dies resultiert vor allem aus den gesetzlichen Vorgaben gemäß § 18 Abs. 5 ADA. Durch sie wird eine grobe Orientierung vorgegeben, nach der gemäß § 18 Abs. 5 lit. a) ADA die berufliche Ausbildung, die Qualifikation und die Erfahrungen, gemäß § 18 Abs. 5 lit. b) ADA das Verhalten und die Leistung als Arbeitnehmer und gemäß § 18 Abs. 5 lit. c) ADA alle sonstigen vernünftigerweise maßgeblichen Faktoren in die Beurteilung einfließen sollen.[388] Zusätzlich zeichnet sich dadurch eine konsequente Fortführung der Rechtsprechung aus dem Verfahren *Commonwealth v Human Rights and Equal Opportunity Commission* ab.[389] Denn bereits in diesem Fall hatte die Rechtsprechung einen weiten Auslegungsmaßstab für die Beurteilung der *„inherent requirements"* angenommen und somit zahlreiche Faktoren – wie etwa die Beziehung zu anderen Arbeitnehmern, das Beschäftigungsumfeld, Aspekte des Arbeitsschutzes und der Gesundheit sowie die Auswirkungen auf den Arbeitgeber und Dritte – einbezogen.

> „...So understood, the inherent requirements of the particular employment will have functional requirements and requirements as to the satisfaction of any externally imposed personal characteristics or qualifications."[390]

Unter Berücksichtigung der vorgenannten Rechtsprechung sollte sich ein Arbeitgeber nur dann auf die Rechtfertigung stützen, dass sein Verhalten durch die *„inherent requirements"* gedeckt ist und somit keine Alterdiskriminierung darstellt, wenn der Arbeitnehmer unter physischen Gesichtspunkten aufgrund seines Alters nicht zur Erfüllung der Arbeit in der Lage ist, das Alter des Arbeitnehmers nicht mit den vom Arbeitgeber zusätzlich erwarteten Anforderungen konform ist und wenn die Beschäftigung gerade ein bestimmtes Alter verlangt.[391] Allerdings können sich weder der Arbeitgeber noch der Arbeitnehmer sicher sein, dass ihre Beurteilung zu einer Rechtfertigung führt, da die Befreiung von den Diskriminierungsverboten des Age Discrimination Act 2004 (Cth) in Bezug auf die der Beschäftigung anhaftenden Anforderungen (*„inherent requirements"*) nicht eindeutig ist. Darüber hinaus obliegt es dem Arbeitgeber zu

---

388 *Eastman*, Exemptions and exceptions, in: Baker & McKenzie, Age Discrimination: Mitigating Risk in the Workplace, S. 76.

389 *Commonwealth v Human Rights and Equal Opportunity Commission* (1998) 152 ALR 182.

390 *Commonwealth v Human Rights and Equal Opportunity Commission* (1998) 152 ALR 182.

391 *Eastman*, Exemptions and exceptions, in: Baker & McKenzie, Age Discrimination: Mitigating Risk in the Workplace, S. 77.

überprüfen, ob er durch Modifizierungen der Anforderungen zu einem anderen Ergebnis gelangen könnte. Lässt er diese Möglichkeit unberücksichtigt, so muss er für die daraus resultierenden Rechtsfolgen die alleinige Verantwortung tragen.

IV. Das Verhältnis des Age Discrimination Act 2004 (Cth) zum Arbeitsrecht

Die Einbeziehung der Bereiche von Arbeit und Beschäftigung in das Anti-Diskriminierungsrecht wird aufgrund der zuvor aufgezeigten praktischen Bedeutung bestätigt. Die Abstimmung der gesetzlichen Regelungen zur Diskriminierung wegen Alters mit arbeitsrechtlichen Schutzgesetzen gegen Diskriminierungen ist aber dennoch erst eine recht junge Erscheinung. Zu Beginn der 1990iger Jahre konnten die Schnittstellen dieser beiden Rechtsgebiete verbindlich miteinander vereinbart und somit ein nahtloser Übergang geschaffen werden. Der Vollständigkeit halber ist aber zu berücksichtigen, dass keine absolute Überdeckung gegeben ist und es sich bei den arbeitsrechtlichen Vorschriften vielmehr um eine Ergänzung des Anti-Diskriminierungsrechts – auch des Age Discrimination Act 2004 – handelt.[392]

So beinhalten insbesondere die arbeitsrechtlichen Vorschriften im Workplace Relations Amendment (Work Choices) Act 2005 (Cth) etwa in § 3 lit. m) altersdiskriminierungsrechtliche Bezüge.[393]

> „The principal objects of this Act is to provide a framework for cooperative workplace relations which promotes the economic prosperity and welfare of the people of Australia by:...
>
> (m) respecting and valuing the diversity of the work force by helping to prevent and eliminate discrimination on the basis of race, colour, sex, sexual preference, age, physical or mental disability, marital status, family responsibilities, pregnancy, religion, political opinion, national extraction or social origin.“[394]

Durch die gesetzlichen Regelung des Workplace Relations Amendment (Work Choices) Act 2005 (Cth) soll eine Arbeits- und Beschäftigungsvielfalt geschaffen werden, welche frei ist von Diskriminierungen, wie auch aufgrund des Alters. Durch die gegenüber dem Age Discrimination Act 2004 (Cth) spezialgesetzlichen Arbeitsrechtsvorschriften des Workplace Relations Amendment (Work Choices) Act 2005 (Cth) bestehen verbindliche Regelungen, wie etwa in der Regelung des § 659 Abs. 2 lit. f) – zuvor § 170CK Abs. 2 lit. f) – welche arbeitsvertragliche Regelungen untersagen, die altersdiskriminierend sein können.[395] Zugleich wird im Rahmen dieser spezialgesetzli-

---

392 *Bourke/Ronalds*, Discrimination Laws – Striving For Equality, in: *Macken*, The Law of Employment, 2002, 605.

393 Vgl. auch die ursprüngliche Regelung in § 3 lit. j) des Workplace Relations Act 1996 (Cth); vgl auch *Hemingway*, Roadmap to ADA: The Age Discrimination Act 2004, 5 abrufbar unter http://www.hreoc.gov.au/age/roadmap_ADA.html.

394 Vgl. auch § 3 lit. f) des Industrial Relations Act 1996 (NSW), § 3 lit. c) des Industrial Relations Act 1999 (Qld) sowie § 3 lit. m) Industrial and Employees Relations Act 1994 (SA).

395 *Riley/Peterson*, Work Choices, A Guide to the 2005 Changes, 493.

chen Regelung Rückgriff auf die Rechtfertigungsmöglichkeiten der „*inherent requirements*" aus dem Age Discrimination Act 2004 (Cth) genommen und eine Diskriminierung aufgrund Alters im Ausnahmefall zugelassen.[396]

Darüber hinaus werden durch § 44B des Workplace Relations Amendment (Work Choices) Act 2005 (Cth) die für arbeitsrechtliche Fragen zuständigen Stellen – etwa die Industrial Relations Commission – ermächtigt, diskriminierungsrechtliche Aspekte im Lichte der spezialgesetzlichen Regelungen mit zu klären.

„In the perfomance of its functions, the Commission must take into account the following:
(a) the need to apply the principles of equal pay for work of equal value;
(b) the need to prevent and eliminate discrimination on the basis of race, colour, sex, sexual preference, age, physical or mental disability, marital status, family responsibilities, pregnancy, religion, political opinion, national extraction or social origin."[397]

Auch gemäß § 46PW des Human Rights and Equal Opportunity Commission Act 1986 (Cth) soll der Human Rights Commissioner eine arbeitsvertragliche Vereinbarung an die Australian Industrial Relation Commission weiterleiten, wenn hierzu eine entsprechende Beschwerde aufgrund einer behaupteten Diskriminierung eingegangen ist.

Allein durch die gesetzliche Berücksichtigung einer Verzahnung des Anti-Diskriminierungsrechts mit Vorschriften aus dem Arbeitsrecht und der damit verbundenen Ermächtigung zum gleichzeitigen Rückgriff auf den Age Discrimination Act 2004 (Cth) ist der Schutz von Arbeitnehmern und Beschäftigten gestärkt worden. Denn über das Arbeitsrecht werden insbesondere auch Schutzmechanismen für gewerkschaftlich organisierte Arbeitnehmer in das Anti-Diskriminierungsrecht eingebracht und ermöglichen somit einen gleichzeitigen Rechtschutz für mehrere Beschäftigte. Diese sind somit nicht zwingend auf individualrechtliches Vorgehen gegen diskriminierende Verhaltensweise beschränkt.[398] Demzufolge besteht beispielsweise auch die Möglichkeit, dass sich gewerkschaftlich organisierte Arbeitnehmer durch ihre Gewerkschaft bei einer Beschwerde an die Human Rights and Equal Opportunity Commission vertreten lassen.[399] Denn ohne Einbeziehung allgemeiner arbeitsrechtlicher Regelungen wäre eine solche Bevollmächtigung einer Gewerkschaft nicht möglich.

396 *Riley/Peterson*, Work Choices, A Guide to the 2005 Changes, 493.

397 Vgl. auch § 169 Industrial Relations Act 1996 (NSW).

398 *Borke/Ronalds*, Discrimination Laws – Striving For Equality, in: *Macken*, The Law of Employment, 2002, 608 m.w.N.; vgl. auch *Catanzariti*, WorkChoices – a rise in discrimination claims? (2006) 12 Employment Law Bulletin 25.

399 *Hunter*, Indirect discrimination in the workplace (1992), 254 m.w.N..

F. Rechtsfolgen eines Verstoßes gegen den Age Discrimination Act 2004 (Cth)

Zwar wird durch die Anwendung des Age Discrimination Act 2004 (Cth) deutlich, wann eine unrechtmäßige Altersdiskriminierung vorliegt. Mangels einer ausdrücklichen gesetzlichen Regelung wird jedoch nicht ersichtlich, welche genauen Rechtsfolgen ein Verstoß gegen ein gesetzliches Diskriminierungsverbot nach sich zieht.[400] Erst durch einen Rückgriff auf § 46PO Abs. 4 HREOC können die gerichtlich – durch den Federal Court bzw. den Federal Magistrates Court – festzulegenden Rechtsfolgen für eine erfolgreiche Klage wegen einer Altersdiskriminierung klassifiziert werden.[401] Nach der mündlichen Verhandlung – dem *„hearing“* – verfassen die Gerichte eine Entscheidung und treffen Anordnungen.

Zu diesen gehören Schadensersatz- und Entschädigungszahlungen, die Abgabe von Unterlassungsverpflichtungen, die Anstellung oder Wiederanstellung des Diskriminierungsopfers, die Modifizierung von getroffenen Vereinbarungen im Einzelfall sowie die Verpflichtung zur Vornahme von bestimmten Handlungs- bzw. Verhaltensweisen zur Beseitigung der Altersdiskriminierung:

> „If the court concerned is satisfied that there has been unlawful discrimination by any respondent, the court may make such orders (including a declaration of right) as it thinks fit, including any of the following orders or any order to a similar effect:
>
> (a) an order declaring that the respondent has committed unlawful discrimination and directing the respondent not to repeat or continue such unlawful discrimination;
>
> (b) an order requiring a respondent to perform any reasonable act or course of conduct to redress any loss or damage suffered by an applicant;
>
> (c) an order requiring a respondent to employ or reemploy an applicant;
>
> (d) an order requiring a respondent to pay to an applicant damages by way of compensation for any loss or damage suffered because of the conduct of the respondent;
>
> (e) an order requiring a respondent to vary the termination of a contract or agreement to redress any loss or damage suffered by an applicant;
>
> (f) an order declaring that it would be inappropriate for any further action to be taken in the matter.“

I. Die Verpflichtung zur Zahlung von Schadensersatz

Die in der Praxis bei Altersdiskriminierung bedeutendste und am häufigsten begehrteste Rechtsfolge ist die Verpflichtung zur Leistung von Schadensersatz gemäß § 46PO

400 Anders nur bei den Straftatbeständen des ADA, die mit einer konkreten Strafdrohung versehen sind.

401 § 46 PO Abs. 4 HREOC Act ist ebenso auch bei Diskriminierungen wegen der Rasse, des Geschlechts und/oder einer Behinderung anwendbar.

lit. d) HREOC Act.[402] Dem Schadensersatz kommt dabei eine ausschließlich auf dem Wiedergutmachungs- und Entschädigungsgedanken basierende Funktion zu.[403] Selbst der Bezug zum Age Discrimination Act 2004 (Cth) verleiht der durch die Rechtsprechung festzulegenden Schadensersatzverpflichtung keinen strafenden Charakter.[404]

Die Verpflichtung zur Zahlung von Schadensersatz kann in einigen Bundesstaaten der Höhe nach begrenzt sowie mehreren Schädigern als Gesamtschuld auferlegt werden.[405] Denn nicht selten tritt nicht nur eine Person auf, sondern oftmals handeln mehrere gemeinschaftlich diskriminierend. Grundsätzlich aber ist eine Schadensersatzzahlung spätestens ab Rechtshängigkeit zu verzinsen.[406]

1. Der Rückgriff auf die Grundsätze des Deliktsrechts

Zur Berechnung der jeweiligen Schadensersatzleistung berufen sich die Gerichte oftmals auf eine aus dem Recht der unerlaubten Handlungen („*law of torts*“) stammende Methode.[407] Nach dieser wird grundsätzlich zwischen den „*special damages*“ und den „*general damages*“, also zwischen materiellem Schaden/Vermögensschaden („*economic loss*“) und immateriellem Schaden/Nichtvermögensschaden („*non-economic loss*“) unterschieden.[408] Demnach erfassen die „*special damages*“ jeglichen – durch die Altersdiskriminierung verursachten – finanziellen Aufwand, wie etwa der Verlust von Arbeitseinkommen. Dagegen wird durch die „*general damages*“ vor allem ein Ersatz in Geld für erlittene Schmerzen, Leiden, Erniedrigungen etc. geleistet.[409]

Allerdings soll eine starre und unflexible Anwendung dieser Unterscheidung nicht das (Haupt-)Ziel der Schadensersatzrechtsprechung in Fällen von Altersdiskriminierung sein.[410] Vielmehr kann und soll – sofern es der Einzelfall erfordert – eine entsprechende Modifizierung in der konkreten Schadensberechnung vorgenommen werden, um so einen umfassenderen und gerechten Ausgleich für das Diskriminierungsopfer erlangen zu können und um nicht Gefahr zu laufen, eine Analogie herzustellen, ob-

402 *Eastman,* Procedures, in: Baker & McKenzie, Age Discrimination: Mitigating Risk in the Workplace, 103.

403 Vgl. u.a. *Font v Paspaley Pearls* [2002] FMCA 142.

404 *Eastman,* Procedures, in: Baker & McKenzie, Age Discrimination: Mitigating Risk in the Workplace, 102; vgl. auch *Hall v A & A Sheiban Pty Ltd* (1989) 20 FCR 217.

405 *Elliot v Nanda & Commonwealth* [2001] FCA 550.

406 *Gilroy v Angelov* (2000) 181 ALR 57; *Wattle v Kirkland (No 2)* [2002] FMCA 135.

407 Vgl. u.a. *Australian Postal Commission v Dao* (1985) 3 NSWLR 565; *Allders International Pty Limited v Anstee* (1986) EOC 92-157; *Alexander v Home Office* (1988) 1 WLR 968; *Bennett v Everitt* (1988) EOC 92-157; *Hall v Sheiban* (1989) 20 FCR 217; *Gilroy v Angelov* (2000) 181 ALR 57; *Shiels v Lipman* [2000] FMC 2; *Leslie v Graham* [2002] FCA 32.

408 Human Rights and Equal Opportunity Commission, Federal Discrimination Law 2005, 270; *Ronalds/Pepper*, Discrimination Law and Practice, 216.

409 Human Rights and Equal Opportunity Commission, Federal Discrimination Law 2005, 270; vgl. ErfK/*Schlachter*, § 15 Rn. 2ff. zum verschuldensabhängigen Anspruch gegen den Arbeitgeber auf Ersatz des materiellen Schadens sowie zum verschuldensunabhängigen Entschädigungsanspruch bei immateriellen Schäden im deutschen Recht.

410 *Ardeshirian v Robe River Iron Associates* (1993) 43 FCR 475; *Stephenson v Human Rights and Equal Opportunity Commission* (1995) 61 FCR 134.

wohl dazu kein hinreichendes Bedürfnis besteht.[411] Denn im Ergebnis ist es das vorrangige Ziel der Gesetzgebung und der Rechtsprechung, dass das Opfer von Diskriminierungshandlungen im Ergebnis so gestellt wird, als wenn die Altersdiskriminierung nicht stattgefunden hätte.[412] Dieses Ziel kann grundsätzlich mit den Grundsätzen des Rechts der unerlaubten Handlung erreicht werden, wobei eine Modifizierung nicht per se ausgeschlossen werden darf. Denn eine angemessene und verhältnismäßige Abänderung kann eine umfassendere Einzelfallgerechtigkeit erzeugen, als es die pauschale Anwendung der Rechtsgrundsätze des Deliktsrechts zu gewährleisten vermag.

> „As anti-discrimination ... legislation and case law with respect to it is still at an early stage of development in Australia, it is difficult and would be unwise to prescribe an inflexible measure of damage in cases of this kind and, in particular, to do so exclusively by reference to common law tests in branches of the law that are not the same, though analogous in varying degress, with anti-discrimination law. Although in my view it cannot be stated that in all claims for loss or damage under the Act the measure of damages is the same as the genereal principles respecting measure of damages in tort, it is closest analogy that I can find and one that would in most foreseeable cases be a sensible and sound test. I would not, however, shut the door to some case arising which calls for a different approach.“[413]

a. Special damages

Die *„special damages“* werden von den Gerichten immer dann zugesprochen, wenn ein Schadensersatzanspruch ohne weiteres dem Umfang nach und daher quantitativ bestimmbar ist. Dabei ist etwa an solche Fälle zu denken, in denen aufgrund der Altersdiskriminierung ein Arbeitnehmer seinen Arbeitsplatz verloren hat und ihm dadurch ein wirtschaftlicher Schaden entstanden ist. Dies kann etwa der Fall sein, wenn er für einen bestimmten Zeitraum arbeitslos ist, weil er keine Anstellung findet.[414] Hier kann zur Berechnung der Höhe des zuzusprechenden Schadensersatzes auf den sonst tatsächlich erreichten Verdienst – genauer auf den Bruttoverdienst einschließlich der Lohnsteuern – abgestellt werden.[415]

Zugleich muss bei der Schadensberechnung das durch das Diskriminierungsopfer von einem Dritten, wie etwa von einem Sozialleistungsträger, Erlangte berücksichtigt

---

411 *Ronalds/Pepper*, Discrimination Law and Practice, 215; vgl. auch das konkrete Verfahren samt Berechnung in Human Rights and Equal Opportunity Commission, Report of an Inquiry into a Complaint of Discrimination in Employment and Occupation, Discrimination on the Ground of Age, HRC Report No. 11.

412 *Haines v Bendall* (1991) 172 CLR 60; *Hall v Sheiban* (1989) 20 FCR 217; vgl. auch *Cooke v Plauen Holdings Pty Ltd* [2001] FMCA 91; *Johanson v Blackledge* (2001) 163 FLR 58; *Borg v Commissioner, Department of Corrective Services* (2002) EOC 93-198; *Escobar v Rainbow Printing Pty Ltd* [2002] FMCA 122; *Darlington v CASCO Australia Pty Ltd* [2002] FMCA 176; *McAlister v SEQ Aboriginal Corporation* [2002] FMCA 109; *Wattle v Kirkland (No 2)* [2002] FMCA 135; *Evans v National Crime Authority* [2003] FMCA 375; *Carr v Boree Aboriginal Corporation* [2003] FMCA 408; *Bassanelli v QBE Insurance* [2003] FMCA 412; *McBride v Victoria (No 1)* [2003] FMCA 285; *Rispoli v Merck Sharpe & Dohme (Australia) Pty Ltd* [2003] FMCA 160.

413 *Hall v Sheiban* (1989) 20 FCR 217.

414 *Ronalds/Pepper*, Discrimination Law and Practice, 217.

415 *Lawrence v Clark* (1993) EOC 92-539; *Fetherston v Peninsula Health* [2004] FCA 485.

und folglich von der zugesprochenen Schadensersatzsumme in Abzug gebracht werden.[416] Ebenfalls ist die Pflicht zur Schadensminderung angemessen in der Schadensberechnung zu erfassen. So hat das Diskriminierungsopfer aktiv dazu beizutragen, dass sich der Schaden minimiert bzw. zumindest nicht weiter erhöht.[417] Ersatzfähig sind ebenso auch in der Zukunft eintretende Folgeschäden, wobei sich die Rechtsprechung mit der Gewährung von Schadensersatz für *„future loss"* streng zurückhält. So gibt es nur sehr wenige Fälle, in denen mehr als 100.000 AUD zugesprochen worden sind.[418]

Da aber nicht immer der Arbeitslohn als Bezugsgröße zur Schadensberechnung herangezogen werden kann, werden daher oftmals die dem Diskriminierungsopfer durch die Verletzungshandlung tatsächlich entstandenen Kosten für die im jeweiligen Einzelfall erforderliche Inanspruchnahme besonderer Dienst- und Serviceleistungen, Aus- und Weiterbildungen, Unterkünfte etc. als Maßstab zu Grunde gelegt. Allgemein gesprochen, ist die Richtgröße der durch die Altersdiskriminierung konkret erlittene finanzielle Verlust.

b. General damages

Schwieriger wird die Schadenserfassung im Zusammenhang mit den *„general damages"*. Denn hier geht es weniger um einen rechnerisch und quantitativ erfassbaren Schaden, als vielmehr um immaterielle Schäden, wie eine Verletzung des Ansehens, der Würde und von Emotionen oder auch um die Beeinträchtigung von Beziehungen des Diskriminierungsopfers zu anderen Personen.[419]

Nicht selten fallen hier die zugesprochenen Schadensersatzleistungen erheblich geringer aus, als bei den *„special damages"*. Oftmals werden nicht mehr als 5.000 – 15.000 AUD als Entschädigung zugesprochen.[420] Daran vermag selbst das aus dem Deliktsrecht übernommene und in seiner Konsequenz sehr weitreichende *„egg shell skull"*-Prinzip nichts zu ändern. Denn danach wird die Zurechnung eines Schadens nicht dadurch gehindert, dass der Schadenseintritt oder das Schadensausmaß durch eine Eigenschaft des Opfers begünstigt wurde und somit nicht vorhersehbar gewesen ist.[421] Folglich ist grundsätzlich jeder durch die Altersdiskriminierung hervorgerufene Schaden ersatzfähig.

Dennoch wurde etwa im Zusammenhang mit einer erzwungenen Pensionierung im Alter von 53 Jahren und der damit verbundenen Altersdiskriminierung eine Entschädigung in Höhe von lediglich 4.000,00 AUD zugesprochen oder aber auch nur ein Schadensersatz in Höhe von 250,00 AUD gewährt, weil ein Bewerber offensichtlich nicht

---

416 *Dobrovsak v AR Jamieson Investments Pty Ltd & Anor* [1995] HREOCA 32.
417 *Daghlian v Australian Postal Corporation* [2003] FCA 759.
418 *Dunn-Dyer v ANZ Banking Group Ltd* (1997) EOC 92-897; *Hickie v Hunt and Hunt* (1998) EOC 92-910; *Victoria v McKenna* (2000) EOC 93-080.
419 *Hall v A & A Sheiban Pty Ltd* (1989) 20 FCR 217.
420 *Ronalds/Pepper*, Disrimination Law and Practice, 218.
421 *Smith v Leech Brain & Co.* (1962) 2 QB 405.

in die gewünschten Altersstruktur von 17 bis 21 Jahren passte.[422] Deshalb sah sich bereits die Rechtsprechung dazu veranlasst, in ihren Entscheidungen durch die deutliche Erhöhung der zugesprochenen Zahlbeträge darauf hinzuweisen, dass eine Gegensteuerung zu veranlassen ist.[423] Denn ansonsten würde die Gefahr einer Verharmlosung und Trivialisierung der *„general damages"* in der Öffentlichkeit verstärkt werden.[424] Weiterhin würde dem Opfer keinerlei Genugtuung und Entschädigung für die erlittene Diskriminierung wegen Alters zukommen, wenn die zugesprochenen Schadensersatzleistungen im Umfang nicht über die Verfahrenskosten hinausgehen.[425] So werden mittlerweile Schadensersatzleistungen zwischen 5.000,00 – 15.000,00 AUD zugesprochen, aber teilweise sprechen die Gerichte auch größere Summen zu, um den emotionalen Schaden zumindest ansatzweise lindern zu können.[426]

Im Ergebnis aber können die *„general damages"* nicht berechnet werden, sondern oftmals nur anhand der Erfahrungen und des Rechtsempfindens des jeweiligen Richters festgelegt werden.[427]

2. Der Schadensersatz in der konkreten Einzelfallbeurteilung

In der konkreten Einzelfallbetrachtung ist es oftmals notwendig von den allgemeinen Regeln abzuweichen und entweder eine Ausweitung oder aber eine Begrenzung des zuzusprechenden Schadensersatzes vorzunehmen. In der Gerichtspraxis wird eine Ausweitung der Schadensersatzleistung allerdings recht restriktiv gehandhabt und nur in den begrenzten Fällen der *„aggravated damages"* und der *„exemplary damages"* zugelassen.

---

422 *Goodworth v Marsden (No 2)* (1996) EOC 92-846; *Bloomfield v Westco Jeans Pty Ltd* [2001] ACTDT 4; vgl. auch *Ivory v Griffith University* [1997] QADT 4; *Gardener v Norcott* [2004] QADT 39.

423 *Morrison v Gallipoli Legion Club Newcastle Limited* (1986) EOC 92-144; *Burke v Tralaggan* (1986) EOC 92-161; *Fares v Box Hill College of TAFE* (1992) EOC 92-931; *Beu v PR Exhibitions Pty Ltd* (1998) EOC 92-939; *McKenna v State of Victoria* (1998) EOC 92-927; *Cooke v Plauen Holdings Pty Ltd* [2001] FMCA 91; *Fetherston v Peninsula Health* [2004] FCA 485.

424 *Horne v Press Clough Joint Venture* (1994) EOC 92-591; *Hall v Sheiban* (1989) 20 FCR 217; *Gilroy v Angelov* (2000) 181 ALR 57; *Johanson v Blackledge* (2001) 163 FLR 58; *Wattle v Kirkland (No 2)* [2002] FMCA 135.

425 *Clarke v Catholic Education Office* (2003) 202 ALR 340.

426 Human Rights and Equal Opportunity Commission, Federal Discrimination Law 2005, 272; vgl. auch *Shiels v James* [2000] FMCA 2; *Clarke v Catholic Education Office* (2003) 202 ALR 340; *Commonwealth v Evans* [2004] FCA 654; vgl. auch die Übersichten bei Human Rights and Equal Opportunity Commission, Federal Discrimination Law 2005, 276ff..

427 Human Rights and Equal Opportunity Commission, Federal Discrimination 2005, 271.

a. Ausweitung des Schadensersatzes

aa. Aggravated damages

Sollte das Verhalten des Beklagten durch seinen willkürlichen, böswilligen, beleidigenden oder schikanösen Charakter einen ganz erheblichen Schaden herbeigeführt haben, so kann das Gericht dies selbstverständlich in der Festsetzung des Schadensersatzes berücksichtigen und dem Kläger grundsätzlich eine angemessen hohe Entschädigung zusprechen, die sogar über den Umfang des tatsächlich entstandenen Schaden hinausgeht und damit verschärfend wirkt (*„aggravated damages"*).[428]

Allerdings wird eine zusätzliche Entschädigung nur sehr selten gewährt, da einerseits nicht geklärt ist, wann im Einzelfall ein besonders erheblicher Schaden gegeben ist und das Diskriminierungsopfer andererseits im vollen Umfang beweispflichtig ist, dass die erlittene Diskriminierung aufgrund ihrer Erheblichkeit und Schwere eine zusätzliche Kompensation erfordert.[429] Zusätzlich fordert die Rechtsprechung oftmals, dass der Kläger beweisen müsse, dass sein Fall besonders ungehörig, unvertretbar und gegen jegliche Regeln von Treu und Glauben verstößt.[430]

Die zusätzliche und damit über die eigentliche Entschädigung für die erlittene Altersdiskriminierung hinausgehende Zahlung von Schadensersatz kann nach Ansicht der australischen Rechtsprechung auch mit besonderen Umständen im Diskriminierungsprozess gerechtfertigt werden. So soll es vor allem dann zulässig sein, *„aggravated damages"* zuzusprechen, wenn der Beklagte durch die Art und Weise seiner Beweisführung beabsichtigt, das Diskriminierungsopfer anzuschwärzen und in der öffentlichen Wahrnehmung zu verunglimpfen.[431]

bb. Exemplary damages

Nach Ansicht eines Teils der Rechtsprechung sollte bei zusätzlich erlittenen Schäden während des Verfahrens begrifflich jedoch nicht von *„aggravated damages"* gesprochen werden, sondern vielmehr müsse die Abschreckungs- und Strafwirkung im Vordergrund der Betrachtung stehen.[432] Denn letztendlich liegt in derartigen Fällen eine verwerfliche Handlungs- und Verhaltensweise des Beklagten vor, die es rechtfertige, eine Bestrafung auszusprechen, ohne zugleich vom grundsätzlichen Wiedergutmachungszweck der Anti-Diskriminierungsrechtsprechung abzuweichen.[433] Denn die bloße – zusätzliche – Feststellung von weiteren während des Prozesses zugefügten Ehrverletzungen, Kränkungen und Demütigungen würde gerade diesem Zweck zuwider laufen. Aus diesem Grund sei die Gewährung eines Schadensersatzes mit strafendem und abschreckendem Charakter, welcher nicht mehr dem Ziel dient, den eingetre-

---

428 Vgl. zu den *„aggravated damages" Dreyer*, Race Relations Act 1976 und Rassendiskriminierung in Großbritannien, 223.

429 *Spencer v Dowling* [1997] 2 VR 127; *Elliot v Nanda & Commonwealth* [2001] FCA 418.

430 *Elliot v Nanda & Commonwealth* [2001] FCA 418; *Oberoi v Human Rights and Equal Opportunity Commission* [2001] FMCA 34.

431 *Hughes v Car Buyers Pty Ltd* (2004) 210 ALR 645.

432 *Font v Paspaley Pearls* [2002] FMCA 142.

433 *Font v Paspaley Pearls* [2002] FMCA 142.

tenen Schaden in zivilrechtlicher Art und Weise zu regulieren, die für das Diskriminierungsopfer interessengerechteste Lösung (*„exemplary damages"*).[434]

cc. Eigene Stellungnahme

Die in der Entscheidung *Font v Paspaley Pearls* verfolgte Ansicht ist unter dem Gesichtspunkt eines umfassenden Entschädigungsgedankens zu begrüßen. Allerdings werden im Prozess zusätzlich dem Diskriminierungsopfer zugefügte Ehrverletzungen und weitere Schädigungen im Rahmen der *„aggravated damages"* erfasst und nicht lediglich im Urteil festgestellt. Vielmehr wird eine zusätzliche Schadensersatzzahlung gewährt.

Weiterhin steht dem Gericht gemäß § 46PO Abs. 4 HREOC Act keine Befugnis zur Gewährung von *„exemplary damages"* zu.[435] Denn der Gesetzgeber hat ausdrücklich festgelegt, dass dem Diskriminierungsopfer allein aufgrund des verwerflichen Verhaltens des Beklagten eine zusätzliche Kompensation zur Wiedergutmachung des erlittenen Leids und des zugefügten Schadens gewährt werden solle. Eine Bestrafung für das diskriminierende Verhalten ist nicht vorgesehen und daher auch nicht gewollt. Mit der gesetzlichen Regelung des § 46PO Abs. 4 HREOC kann darüber hinaus ebenso eine umfassende Entschädigung des Opfers erzielt werden. Denn im Ergebnis dürfte es für das Diskriminierungsopfer unerheblich sein, ob die an ihn fließende Zahlung von Schadensersatz aufgrund einer Wiedergutmachung oder einer Sanktion erfolgt.

Zusätzlich darf der begriffliche Unterschied zwischen den *„aggravated damages"* und den *„exemplary damages"* nicht verwischt werden. Denn die *„aggravated damages"* werden immer dann zugesprochen, wenn das unrechtmäßige Verhalten gerade durch seine Art und Weise eine besondere Erheblichkeit und Verschlimmerung des Schadens herbeigeführt hat. Die *„exemplary damages"* dagegen sollen den Beklagten bestrafen und zur Durchsetzung der Strafziele – Vergeltung und Abschreckung – erfolgen.[436] Daraus resultiert auch der unterschiedliche Blickwinkel. Bei den *„aggravated damages"* steht das Diskriminierungsopfer im Mittelpunkt und bildet den Schwerpunkt der Ermittlungen, wohingegen bei den *„exemplary damages"* es gerade nicht die diskriminierte Person, sondern der Diskriminierende und sein Verhalten ist.

b. Begrenzung des Schadensersatzes

Da den Gerichten aber grundsätzlich zur Berechnung des Schadensersatzes ein nicht unerhebliches Ermessen zusteht, können sie den Umfang nicht nur entsprechend ausweiten, sondern ihn anderenfalls auch entsprechend absenken und begrenzen. Allerdings wird in der Rechtspraxis gerade bei den *„general damages"* nur höchst selten eine Begrenzung ausgesprochen.[437] In seltenen Ausnahmefällen aber hat die Recht-

434 *Font v Paspaley Pearls* [2002] FMCA 142; vgl. zum pönalisierenden Schadensersatz der *„exemplary damages"* auch *Dreyer*, Race Relations Act 1976 und Rassendiskriminierung in Großbritannien, 224.

435 Vgl. auch *Hughes v Car Buyers Pty Ltd* (2004) 210 ALR 645.

436 *Hughes v Car Buyers Pty Ltd* (2004) 210 ALR 645.

437 *Eastman*, Procedures, in: Baker & McKenzie, Age Discrimination: Mitigating Risk in the Workplace, 106.

sprechung dennoch den angemessen Schadensersatz der Höhe nach reduziert, weil z.B. eine umfassende und freiwillige Entschuldigung erfolgt ist. So hat der Federal Magistrates Court die Schadenssumme von 6.000,00 AUD um ein Drittel gekürzt, weil nach Ansicht des Gerichts die Entschuldigung beim Diskriminierungsopfer – auch wenn sie erst sehr spät während des Verfahrens erfolgt ist – bereits eine hinreichende Genugtuungs- und Wiedergutmachungswirkung erzielen konnte.[438] Bemerkenswert bei dieser Entscheidung ist, dass keinerlei Beweis für die behaupteten Folgen der Entschuldigung vorgelegen hat und das Gericht hier allein aufgrund einer Verallgemeinerung zur Entscheidungsbegründung gefunden hat.

c. Zinsen im Rahmen des Schadensersatzes

Zu den Schadensersatzleistungen können ebenfalls Zinsen für den Zeitraum vom Zeitpunkt der diskriminierenden Behandlung bis zum Tag der Entscheidung des Gerichts zugesprochen werden, r 26.01 *FM Rules*.[439]

II. Weitere Rechtsfolgen

Da oftmals die Zahlung eines bestimmten Geldbetrages die erlittene Diskriminierung und die mit dieser verbundenen Ehrverletzungen und Demütigungen nicht gänzlich zu beseitigen vermögen, verweisen die Gerichte oftmals auch auf andere Rechtsfolgen. Sofern diese im Verhältnis zum erlittenen Schaden angemessen sind, stehen der Kreativität der Rechtsprechung keine Bedenken gegenüber.[440]

Als weitere Rechtsfolgen eines Verstoßes gegen ein Diskriminierungsverbot des Age Discrimination Act 2004 (Cth) kommen neben dem Anspruch auf Schadensersatz deshalb auch die Verpflichtung zur Unterlassung („*injunctive relief*“) sowie zur Vornahme einer bestimmten Handlung in Betracht.

1. Verpflichtung zum Unterlassen des diskriminierenden Verhaltens

In zahlreichen Fällen spricht das Gericht die Verpflichtung aus, das diskriminierende Verhalten zu unterlassen und zukünftig nicht mehr zu wiederholen, § 46PO lit. a) HREOC Act.[441] Dies geschieht unabhängig davon, ob die erlittene Diskriminierung zeitnah durch einen Dritten wiederholt werden kann. Denn vorrangig sollen die Verhinderung von (erneuten) diskriminierenden Handlungen sowie die grundsätzliche Vorbeugung gegen öffentliche Denunziationen und Diskriminierungen sein.

---

438 *Johanson v Michael Blackledge Meats* [2001] FMCA 66.

439 *Gilroy v Angelov* (2000) 181 ALR 57; *Mayer v ANSTO* [2003] FMCA 209.

440 *Eastman,* Procedures, in: Baker & McKenzie, Age Discrimination: Mitigating Risk in the Workplace, 109.

441 *Jones v Scully* (2002) 120 FCR 243; *Jones v Toben* [2002] FCA 1150.

Um im Diskriminierungsprozess aber erfolgreich eine Verpflichtung zum Unterlassen des diskriminierenden Verhaltens als Rechtsfolge herbeiführen zu können, muss der Kläger sich absichern, dass sein Verlangen adäquat und erforderlich ist und sich nur an den Beklagten und nicht an Dritte richtet. Von der Rechtsprechung wird zudem auch verlangt, dass der Antrag auf die begehrte Rechtsfolge soweit bestimmt und konkret auf ein bestimmtes Verhalten bezogen ist, dass der Adressat – der Diskriminierende – genau weiß, worauf sich das Unterlassen bezieht.[442] Denn ein abstrakter Ausspruch, jegliches diskriminierendes Verhalten und sämtliche diskriminierende Handlungsweisen zu unterlassen, wird grundsätzlich als zu weit und unbestimmt angesehen, da er keinen direkten Bezug zum streitgegenständlichen Sachverhalt aufweist.[443]

Oftmals besteht das diskriminierende Verhalten aus einer dauerhaften Handlung. Um ausreichenden Rechtsschutz zu erhalten, wird deshalb auch in diesen Fällen im Rahmen eines Unterlassungsausspruchs dem Beklagten auferlegt, die Altersdiskriminierung nicht fortzusetzen und zukünftig nicht zu wiederholen.[444]

Die Verpflichtung zum Unterlassen des diskriminierenden Verhaltens wurde durch die Rechtsprechung zum Rechtsstreit *Najdovska v Australian Iron & Steel Pty Ltd.* bekräftigt.[445] Die Klage richtet sich gegen die Australian Iron & Steel Pty Ltd., die in ihren Stahlwerken in Kembla im Bundesstaat New South Wales ausschließlich Männer beschäftigte und weibliche Bewerber auf eine betriebsinterne Warteliste setze. Die Frauen blieben über Jahre hinweg auf dieser Liste stehen, ohne eingestellt zu werden, während männliche Bewerber binnen kurzer Zeit nach Ihrer Bewerbung einen Arbeitsplatz im Stahlwerk erhalten haben. Sofern dennoch Frauen beschäftigt wurden, haben diese oftmals nach dem Grundsatz *„last hired, first fired“* ihren Arbeitsplatz im Gegensatz zu den männlichen Beschäftigten zuerst wieder verloren. Denn die Australian Iron & Steel Pty Ltd. meinte, dass die Männer ihre Anstellung behalten können und von Personaleinsparungen nicht erfasst werden dürfen, da sie bereits eine ausreichend lange Dienstzeit im Unternehmen verbracht haben.[446]

Resultiert die Diskriminierung (wegen Alters) demnach aus einer besonderen Methode im Betrieb des Arbeitgebers, dann kann die Aufrechterhaltung und Anwendung dieser, vor allem in den Bereichen der Personalbeschaffung, -auswahl und -förderung gerichtlich beendet werden.[447]

---

442 *Eastman,* Procedures, in: Baker & McKenzie, Age Discrimination: Mitigating Risk in the Workplace, 106.

443 *Series Cricket v Parish* (1977) 16 ALR 181; *Tobacco Institute of Australia Ltd v Australian Federation of Consumer Organisations Inc* (1992) 38 FCR 1.

444 *Ronalds/Pepper*, Discrimination Law and Practice, 220; Commonwealth *of Australia v Evans* [2004] FCA 654.

445 *Najdovska v Australian Iron & Steel Pty Ltd* (1986) EOC 92-176.

446 *Najdovska v Australian Iron & Steel Pty Ltd* (1986) EOC 92-176.

447 *Blatchford v Qantas Airways Ltd* (1997) EOC 92-888.

2. Aktive Handlungen

a. Entschuldigung beim Diskriminierungsopfer

Weiterhin kann das Gericht dem Beklagten gemäß § 46PO lit. b) HREOC Act aufgeben, sich beim Diskriminierungsopfer in aller Form und – je nach Ausmaß der Altersdiskriminierung – (öffentlich) zu entschuldigen.[448] Allerdings gehen die Auffassungen in der Rechtsprechung auseinander, ob die Verpflichtung zur Entschuldigung beim Diskriminierungsopfer eine geeignete Wiedergutmachung darstellt. Zwar ist ein großer Teil der Rechtsprechung der Auffassung, dass der Ausspruch zur Verpflichtung einer Entschuldigung ein geeignetes Mittel zur Entschädigung sei, da vor allem materielle Schäden schwerlich mit einem Geldbetrag aufzuwiegen seien und entschuldigende Worte oftmals mehr bewirken können, als eine Schadensersatzzahlung.[449]

Gegen diese Ansicht wendet sich ein anderer Teil der Rechtsprechung mit dem Argument, dass eine Entschuldigung nur dann zur Wiedergutmachung und Entschädigung geeignet sein könne, wenn sie aus autonomen Beweggründen erfolge.[450] Sofern das Gericht im Sinne des § 46PO lit. b) HREOC Act jedoch eine Verpflichtung zur Entschuldigung ausspricht und somit die Entschuldigung nicht freiwillig erfolge und nicht von Herzen kommt bzw. ernst gemeint ist, könne der gesetzliche Zweck nicht erreicht werden.[451] Darüber hinaus sei die durch das Gericht auferlegte Verpflichtung, sich beim Diskriminierungsopfer zu entschuldigen, ein Widerspruch in sich, so dass es grundsätzlich nicht erforderlich sei,

> „...to seek to compel the respondent to articulate a sentiment that he plainly enough does not feel.“[452]

Darüber hinaus kommt diese Form der Wiedergutmachung aber nur bei natürlichen Personen in Frage. Bei juristischen Personen scheidet sie nach Ansicht der Rechtsprechung aus, obwohl sie ebenso durch bzw. dem gesetzlichen Vertretungsorgan erfolgen könnte.[453]

---

448 *Burrows v Coomonwealth of Police* (1995) EOC 92-676; *Coleman v Commission of Police* [2001] NSWADT 32.

449 *Oberoi v Human Rights and Equal Opportunity Commission* [2001] FMCA 34; *Cooke v Plauen Holdings* [2001] FMCA 91; *Escobar v Rainbow Printing Pty Ltd (No 2)* [2002] FMCA 122; *Forbes v Commonwealth of Australia* [2003] FMCA 140; *Rispoli v Merck Sharpe & Dohme (Australia) Pty Ltd* [2003] FMCA 160; vgl. zu Beispielen von gerichtlich angeordneten Entschuldigungen *Ronalds/Pepper*, Discrimination Law and Practice, 220.

450 *Travers v New South Wales* (2001 163 FLR 99; *Jones v Toben* [2002] FCA 1150; *Jones v Scully* (2002) 120 FCR 243; *Evans v National Crime Authority* [2003] FMCA 375..

451 *Evans v National Crime Authority* [2003] FMCA 375.

452 *Jones v Toben* [2002] FCA 1150; ähnlich *Travers v New South Wales* (2001) 163 FLR 99.

453 *Grulke v KC Canvas* [2000] FCA 1415.

b. Feststellung des diskriminierenden Verhaltens

Aufgrund des zuvor aufgezeigten Problems der Effektivität einer durch das Gericht angeordneten Entschuldigung beim Opfer, erlangt eine weitere Rechtsfolge nicht unerheblich an Bedeutung. So genügt es oftmals, dass zugunsten des Diskriminierungsopfers gerichtlich festgestellt wird, dass das angegriffene Verhalten bzw. die betreffenden Handlungsweise unrechtmäßig gewesen ist. Denn wird einem solchen Begehren stattgegeben, so wird durch den Feststellungsausspruch in brauchbarer und angemessener Art und Weise die Öffentlichkeit über das Diskriminierungsverhalten in Kenntnis gesetzt und somit auch das Ansehen des Beklagten im Gegenzug beeinträchtigt.[454] Eine solche Beeinträchtigung ist jedoch nur dann gerechtfertigt und rechtmäßig, wenn die Feststellung der Altersdiskriminierung bewiesen werden konnte.[455]

Neben der möglichen Herabsetzung des Ansehens des Beklagten und sodann verurteilten Diskriminierenden erscheint zudem die gesetzliche Regelung des § 46PO Abs. 4 lit. a HREOC als nicht verhältnismäßig. Denn sie räumt der Rechtsprechung eine allgemeine Befugnis zur Feststellung ein, dass der Beklagte eine unrechtmäßige Diskriminierung begangen hat:

> „... an order declaring that the respondent has committed unlawful discrimination..."

Diese Befugnis wird von der Rechtsprechung als zu weit angesehen und deshalb kritisiert, weil die getroffene Feststellung die diskriminierende Handlung bzw. Verhaltensweise nicht konkret beschreiben muss und somit die Gefahr einer willkürlichen Entscheidung drohe.[456]

c. Sonstige Rechtsfolgen

Weiterhin besteht auch die Möglichkeit, zugunsten eines wegen Alters diskriminierten Arbeitnehmers den bestehenden Arbeitsvertrag und somit die aktuellen Beschäftigungsmodalitäten zu ändern, § 46PO lit. e) HREOC Act. Im Zusammenhang mit der Altersdiskriminierung im Bereich der Arbeit und Beschäftigung wird nicht selten eine Wiedereinstellung oder Weiterbeschäftigung als Rechtsfolge ausgesprochen, § 46PO lit. c) HREOC Act.[457] Vor allem zum Problem der Zwangspensionierung beim Erreichen eines bestimmten Alters gibt es zahlreiche Entscheidungen, in denen die Gerichte dem Diskriminierenden aufgeben, die betroffene Person, entgegen der unternehmensinternen Personalpolitik, über eine bestimmte Altersgrenze hinaus zu beschäftigen.[458]

---

454 *McGlade v Lightfoot* (2002) 124 FCR 106.

455 *Rural Press v Australian Competition and Consumer Commission* (2003) 203 ALR 217; *Commonwealth v Evans* [2004] FCA 654.

456 *Warramunda Village Inc v Pryde* (2001) 105 FCR 437; [2004] FCA 654.

457 *Vgl. etwa Song v Ainsworth Game Technology Pty Ltd* [2002] FMCA 31.

G. Die Reaktionsmöglichkeiten der Human Rights and Equal Opportunity Commission und das *conciliation*-Verfahren bei Altersdiskriminierungen

I. Die grundlegenden Befugnisse der Human Rights and Equal Opportunity Commission im Bereich der Diskriminierung wegen Alters

1. Die Ermächtigung zur Untersuchung und Nachforschung im Bereich der Altersdiskriminierung

Die Gesetzesbegründung zum Age Discrimination Act 2004 (Cth) verdeutlicht die primäre Zielsetzung des Gesetzes unter gleichzeitiger Berücksichtigung der internationalen Verpflichtungen Australiens:

> „Dieser Abschnitt stellt dar, was die Gesetzgebung beabsichtigt zu erreichen. Dieser Abschnitt ist geschaffen worden, um das Bewusstsein der Gesellschaft zu stärken, dass Menschen jeden Alters dieselben Rechte haben. Dieser Abschnitt zeigt auf, dass der Gesetzesentwurf geschaffen wurde, um Diskriminierungen wegen Alters ... so weit wie möglich aus dem Bereich des öffentlichen Lebens zu beseitigen. Das Gesetz reagiert ebenso auf den demografischen Wandel und auf die Alterung der Bevölkerung, indem es beabsichtigt, Vorurteile gegenüber älteren Menschen zu ändern und Hindernisse zur Beteiligung älterer Menschen am Arbeitsmarkt zu entfernen.“[459]

Diese Zielsetzung resultiert im Ergebnis insbesondere aus den zahlreichen internationalen Verpflichtungen Australiens, auf die in der Gesetzesbegründung zum Age Discrimination Act 2004 (Cth) Bezug genommen wird. Maßgeblich ist sie aus den in der Allgemeinen Erklärung der Menschenrechte (*Universal Declaration of Human Rights*) aufgestellten Grundsätzen zum Schutz der Menschenrechte abgeleitet.[460]

---

458 Vgl. etwa *Holdaway v Qantas Airways Limited* (1992) EOC 92-430; *Kinley v East Sydney Area Health Service* (1994) EOC 92-559.

459 Explanatory Memorandum of the Age Discrimination Bill 2003 (Cth), Annexure C, Clause 3, Objects.

460 *Bourke/Ronalds*, Discrimination Laws – Striving For Equality, in: *Macken*, The Law of Employment, 2002, 596; Der gesamte Text der Allgemeinen Erklärung der Menschenrechte (*Universal Declaration of Human Rights*) – Resolution 217 A (III) der Generalversammlung vom

Art. 2

(1) Jeder Mensch hat Anspruch auf die in dieser Erklärung verkündeten Rechte und Freiheiten, ohne irgendeine Unterscheidung, wie etwa nach Rasse, Farbe, Geschlecht, Sprache, Religion, politischer und sonstiger Überzeugung, nationaler oder sozialer Herkunft, nach Eigentum, Geburt oder sonstigen Umständen.

(2) Weiter darf keine Unterscheidung gemacht werden aufgrund der politischen, rechtlichen oder internationalen Stellung des Landes oder Gebietes, dem eine Person angehört, ohne Rücksicht darauf, ob es unabhängig ist, unter Treuhandschaft steht, keine Selbstregierung besitzt oder irgendeiner anderen Beschränkung seiner Souveränität unterworfen ist.

Art. 7

Alle Menschen sind vor dem Gesetze gleich und haben ohne Unterschied Anspruch auf gleichen Schutz durch das Gesetz. Alle haben Anspruch auf den gleichen Schutz gegen jede unterschiedliche Behandlung, welche die vorliegende Erklärung verletzen würde, und gegen jede Aufreizung zu einer derartigen unterschiedlichen Behandlung.

Die internationalen Verpflichtungen Australiens im Bereich des Antidiskriminierungsrechts leiten sich daneben auch aus den weiteren internationalen Instrumenten der International Labour Organisation (ILO 111),[461] des International Covenant on Civil and Political Rights (ICCPR),[462] der UN Declaration of the Rights of the Child[463] und der Convention on the Rights of the Child (CROC)[464] ab.[465] Die in den vorgenannten internationalen Abkommen zum Schutz der Menschenrechte enthaltenen Grundprinzipien sowie deren Konkretisierung in den zuvor zusätzlich aufgezeigten internationalen Instrumenten soll die Human Rights and Equal Opportunity Commission durch ihre Tätigkeit zur bestmöglichen innerstaatlichen Durchsetzung verhelfen und somit den internationalen Verpflichtungen des Commonwealth of Australia dienen.[466]

Die Human Rights and Equal Opportunity Commission wurde gesetzlich gemäß §§ 11 Abs. 1 lit. f) und 31 lit. b) HREOC Act und Reg. 4 der HREOC Regulations ermächtigt, Erkundigungen und Nachforschungen zur Beseitigung von Verstößen gegen

---

10. Dezember 1948 – der Vereinten Nationen ist unter http://www.unhchr.ch/udhr/lang/ger.htm abrufbar.

461 Vgl. Schedule 1 des HREOC Act.

462 Vgl. Schedule 2 des HREOC Act.

463 Vgl. Schedule 3 des HREOC Act.

464 Vgl. § 47 Abs. 1 HREOC Act.

465 *Bourke/Ronalds*, Discrimination Laws – Striving For Equality, in: *Macken*, The Law of Employment, 2002, 596.

466 *Mason*, The role of the Judiciary in developing Human Rights in Australian Law, in: Kinley, Human Rights in Australian Law, 1998, 26; vgl. auch *Kinley*, Textbook on International Human Rights Law, 2006.

die internationalen Verpflichtungen anzustellen. Durch diese – gegenüber der Anwendung des Age Discrimination Act 2004 (Cth) Vorrang genießenden – Ermächtigungen begehrt die Gesetzgebung des Commonwealth darüber hinaus aber zugleich auch, auf die durch die internationalen Instrumente aufgestellten Verpflichtungen Australiens einzuwirken.[467]

Im Hinblick auf die Altersdiskriminierung bestehen demnach im Grundsatz zwei verschiedene Handlungsmöglichkeiten, zu denen die Human Rights and Equal Opportunity Commission innerhalb des ihr zugewiesenen Verantwortungsbereichs ermächtigt ist. Einerseits ist die Human Rights and Equal Opportunity Commission gemäß § 31 lit. b) HREOC Act und Reg. 4 der HREOC Regulations berechtigt, jegliche Handlung oder Praxis, die eine Diskriminierung wegen Alters in der Beschäftigung und im Beruf begründen oder darstellen könnte, zu untersuchen. Zugleich steht ihr gemäß § 11 Abs. 1 lit. f) HREOC Act das Recht zu, jede Handlung oder Praxis zu untersuchen, die im Widerspruch zu den Menschenrechten steht oder mit diesen unvereinbar ist.

2. Der Geltungsbereich der Ermächtigung zur Untersuchung und Nachforschung im Bereich der Altersdiskriminierung

Der Human Rights and Equal Opportunity Commission stehen aufgrund der gesetzlichen Regelungen des Human Rights and Equal Opportunity Act 1986 (Cth) nicht nur zahlreiche Befugnisse zu. Sie sind zusätzlich in ihrem örtlichen Geltungsbereich sehr umfassend zu verstehen.

a. Der örtliche Geltungsbereich

Aufgrund der gesetzlichen Klarstellung in § 30 Abs. 1 HREOC werden die Begriffe der (diskriminierenden) Handlungen und Praktiken sehr weit verstanden, so dass darunter nicht nur die eines Staates oder seiner Behörden (§ 30 Abs. 1 lit. a) HREOC Act) zu erfassen sind, sondern auch all solche, die entweder aufgrund des Rechts eines Bundesstaates (§ 30 Abs. 1 lit. b) HREOC Act) oder aber ausschließlich (§ 30 Abs. 1 lit. c) HREOC Act) bzw. teilweise (§ 30 Abs. 1 lit. d) HREOC Act) aufgrund eines innerhalb eines bestimmten Bundesstaates geltenden Rechts vorgenommen worden sind. Demnach kann die Human Rights and Equal Opportunity Commission, im Rahmen ihr durch den Human Rights and Equal Opportunity Commission Act 1986 (Cth) wegen Verstößen gegen die vorgenannten internationalen Verpflichtungen eingeräumten Befugnisse, nur gegen den Bundesstaat als Beschwerdegegner selbst vorgehen.

---

467 *Thew*, Age discriminationn and the Human Rights and Equal Opportunity Commission Act 1986 (Cth), in: Baker & McKenzie, Age Discrimination: Mitigating Risk in the Workplace, S.31.

b. Der sachliche Geltungsbereich

Der Begriff der Diskriminierung und folglich auch der sachliche Geltungsbereich der Befugnisse der Human Rights and Equal Opportunity Commission wird durch die Definition in § 3 Abs. 1 HREOC Act begrenzt. Danach beinhaltet eine Diskriminierung wegen Alters im Sinne des Human Rights and Equal Opportunity Act 1986 (Cth) lediglich solche Unterscheidungen, Ausschlüsse oder Bevorzugungen auf der Grundlage des Alters, die eine Gleichstellung oder gleichartige Behandlung im Bereich der Beschäftigung und des Berufes aufheben oder beeinträchtigen. Aufgrund des eindeutigen Wortlauts besteht, entgegen dem praktischen Bedürfnis, Einigkeit darüber, dass keine weiteren Bereiche von den Befugnissen der Human Rights and Equal Opportunity Commission erfasst werden und sie folglich nur zu einem Einschreiten bei einer im Zusammenhang mit der im ILO-Abkommen Nr. 111 aufgelisteten Benachteiligungen innerhalb eines Arbeitsverhältnisses, also insbesondere bei der im Zusammenhang mit einer Beschäftigung und dem Beruf behaupteten Diskriminierung wegen Alters ermächtigt ist.[468]

II. Verletzung von Menschenrechten im Geltungsbereich des Human Rights and Equal Opportunity Commission Act 1986 (Cth)

1. Die Befugnisse bei Menschenrechtsverletzungen

Neben der Ermächtigung zu Untersuchungen über behauptete Handlungen und Praktiken, die eine Diskriminierung im Bereich der Beschäftigung und des Berufs darstellen können, kommen der Human Rights and Equal Opportunity Commission aber gemäß § 11 Abs. 1 lit. f) HREOC Act dieselben Rechte in Hinsicht auf eine mögliche Verletzung von Menschenrechten zu.[469]

2. Die Einschränkung der Ermächtigung der Human Rights and Equal Opportunity Commission

Allerdings besteht auch hier einerseits die Einschränkung, dass nur gegen solche Menschenrechtsverletzungen vorgegangen werden kann, die von bzw. durch das Commonwealth oder eine seiner Behörden, durch eine Verfügung oder Anordnung des Commonwealth oder eines Territoriums oder die ganz oder teilweise innerhalb eines Territoriums vorgenommen worden sind, § 3 Abs. 1 HREOC Act. Folglich können

---

468 *Thew*, Age discriminationn and the Human Rights and Equal Opportunity Commission Act 1986 (Cth), in: Baker & McKenzie, Age Discrimination: Mitigating Risk in the Workplace, S.32.

469 Human Rights and Equal Opportunity Commission, Federal Discrimination Law 2005, 7.

Verletzungen von Menschenrechten, die in oder von einem Bundesstaat oder seinen Behörden begangen worden sind oder in den privaten Bereich einzuordnen sind, nicht von der Ermächtigung des § 11 Abs. 1 lit. f) HREOC Act erfasst werden.[470]

Andererseits wird der Rahmen des § 11 Abs. 1 lit. f) HREOC Act zusätzlich durch die Definition der Menschenrechte begrenzt. Die Menschenrechte werden durch die Verpflichtungen und Erklärungen („*Covenants and Declarations*") zum Human Rights and Equal Opportunity Commission Act 1986 (Cth) als Rechte und Freiheiten beschrieben, § 3 Abs. 1 HREOC Act.

3. Verhinderung eines effektiven Vorgehens gegen Verletzungen der Menschenrechte

Durch die genannten Beschränkungen wird jedoch ein effektives Vorgehen gegen mögliche Verletzungen von Menschenrechten in der Praxis erschwert. So sollte im Fall *Peacock v Human Rights and Equal Opportunity Commission* gegen eine behauptete Altersdiskriminierung und Verletzung der Menschenrechte vorgegangen werden. Statt aber insbesondere eine Verletzung der Menschenrechte im Ergebnis festzustellen, wurde sie von der Rechtsprechung mit der Begründung abgelehnt, dass die vorliegende zwangsweise Pensionierung bei Erreichen des Alters von 65 Jahren aufgrund von § 76V des Public Service Act 1922 (Cth) nicht als einer der unter § 3 Abs. 1 HREOC Act zu subsumierenden Handlungen oder Praktiken („*act or practice*") angesehen werden könne.[471]

III. Das Nebeneinander von Age Discrimination Act 2004 (Cth) und Human Rights and Equal Opportunity Commission Act 1986 (Cth)

Während die vorgenannten Ermächtigungen mit denen des Age Discrimination Act 2004 (Cth) konkurrieren, verbessert der Age Discrimination Act 2004 (Cth) die Regelung des § 11 Abs. 1 lit. a) HREOC Act, indem er die Funktionen der Human Rights and Equal Opportunity Commission ganz grundsätzlich durch die Einbeziehung und Übertragung derjenigen des Age Discrimination Act 2004 (Cth) erweitert. So erlaubt etwa § 46P HREOC Act das Vorgehen der Human Rights and Equal Opportunity Commission gegen Verstöße im Sinne des Age Discrimination Act, während § 46H HREOC Act dagegen die Befugnis zur Beendigung der Verfolgung eines derartigen Verstoßes einräumt.

---

470 *Thew*, Age discriminationn and the Human Rights and Equal Opportunity Commission Act 1986 (Cth), in: Baker & McKenzie, Age Discrimination: Mitigating Risk in the Workplace, S.33.

471 *Peacock v Human Rights and Equal Opportunity Commission* [2005] FCAFC 45; vgl. auch *Secretary, Department of Defence v Human Rights and Equal Opportunity Commission* (1997) 78 FCR 208.

IV. Die konkreten Reaktionsmöglichkeiten der Human Rights and Equal Opportunity Commission bei Altersdiskriminierungen und das conciliation-Verfahren nach dem Human Rights and Equal Opportunity Commission Act 1986 (Cth)

1. Die Untersuchungen und das Schlichtungsverfahren

Sobald wegen eines Verstoßes gegen das Verbot der Altersdiskriminierung im Bereich der Beschäftigung und des Berufes vorgegangen wird, ist die Human Rights and Equal Opportunity Commission gemäß § 31 lit. b) HREOC Act befugt, Untersuchungen und Nachforschungen über den behaupteten Fall einer Diskriminierung wegen Alters anzustellen und soweit sie es für erforderlich hält, sich im Rahmen eines – im Detail noch näher darzustellenden – Schlichtungsverfahrens („*conciliation*") zu bemühen, eine Einigung und Klärung des aufgeworfenen Diskriminierungssachverhalts zu erwirken und den Parteien einen geeigneten Lösungsvorschlag zu unterbreiten, §§ 31 lit. b) (i), 35 Abs. 2 HREOC Act.

2. Der Report an den Bundesjustizminister

a. Unterrichtung des Bundesjustizministers gemäß § 31 lit. b) (ii) HREOC Act

Sofern die Human Rights and Equal Opportunity Commission darüber hinaus der Auffassung ist, dass tatsächlich eine altersdiskriminierende Behandlung vorliegt und sie es als ungeeignet erachtet, im Rahmen eines Schlichtungsverfahrens eine einvernehmliche Lösung herbeizuführen oder ein solches gescheitert ist, dann ist die Human Rights and Equal Opportunity Commission berechtigt, den zuständigen Bundesjustizminister über ihre Untersuchungen mit einem gesonderten Bericht zur Vorlage an das Parlament zu unterrichten, § 31 lit. b) (ii) HREOC Act.[472] Den Bundesjustizminister trifft sodann gemäß § 46 HREOC Act eine Aushangpflicht im House of Parliament binnen der auf den Report folgenden 15 Sitzungstagen.

b. Report No 1 - Compulsory Age Retirement 1996

Eine Vielzahl von Altersdiskriminierungen – immerhin circa fünf bis zehn Prozent aller jährlich erhobenen Beschwerden betreffen den Bereich der Diskriminierung we-

---

472 *Bourke/Ronalds*, Discrimination Laws - Striving Towards Equality, in: *Macken/O'Grady/Sappideen/Warburton*, The Law of Employment, 2002, 600, Human Rights and Equal Opportunity Commission, Annual Report 2007 – 2008, 44; Human Rights and Equal Opportunity Commission, Federal Discrimination Law 2005, 8.

gen Alters[473] – sind infolge der Unterrichtungsmöglichkeit des § 31 lit. b) (ii) HREOC Act an den Bundesjustizminister erfolgt und nachfolgend gemäß § 35 Abs. 2 HREOC Act als solche festgestellt und bestätigt worden.[474] In diesem Zusammenhang besonders erwähnenswert ist der erste Report der Human Rights and Equal Opportunity Commission, dem der Fall *Bone, Craig, Ivanoff Love v QANTAS* zu Grunde lag.[475] Dort war der Leiter der Human Rights and Equal Opportunity Commission der Auffassung, dass die verpflichtetende Pensionierung der betroffenen Piloten eine Diskriminierung wegen Alters darstellen würde und dass die Anforderung, nach der die Piloten zur Ausübung ihres Berufes eine bestimmte Altersgrenze nicht überschreiten dürfen, keine diesem Beruf automatisch innewohnende Voraussetzung sei.[476]

3. Klagemöglichkeit der Human Rights and Equal Opportunity Commission

Die Human Rights and Equal Opportunity Commission ist aber nicht nur berechtigt, im dargestellten Rahmen umfassende Nachforschungen und Untersuchungen anzustellen. Vielmehr kann sie auch Klagen wegen Altersdiskriminierungen im Bereich der Beschäftigung und des Berufs oder wegen Verletzungen der Menschenrechte erheben und somit in Konkurrenz zu den Rechtsschutzmöglichkeiten des Age Discrimination Act 2004 (Cth) tätig werden.

---

473 Vgl. Human Rights and Equal Opportunity Commission, Annual Report 2006 – 2007, 71 – Table 11: Complaints received and finalised by Act (Age Discrimination Act (ADA) 106 received, 115 finalised; Total 1779 received, 1656 finalised); vgl. ebenso Human Rights and Equal Opportunity Commission, Annual Report 2007 – 2008, 63 – Table 11: Complaints received and finalised by Act (Age Discrimination Act (ADA) 126 received, 114 finalised; Total 2077 received, 1883 finalised); im Vergleich hierzu betreffen nur ca. 2 bis 3% aller arbeitsrechtlichen Streitigkeiten in Deutschland Diskriminierungssachverhalte im Sinne des AGG, vgl. Statistisches Bundesamt, Justizgeschäftsstatistik, Geschäftsentwicklung bei Gerichten und Staatsanwaltschaften seit 1995., Stand 01.01.2010; gemäß dem Landesarbeitsgericht Baden-Württemberg gingen im Zeitraum vom 18. August 2006 bis zum 18. April 2007 insgesamt 109 Verfahren bei den Arbeitsgerichten in Baden-Württemberg ein, bei denen Normen aus dem AGG zur Anwendung kamen – im Ergebnis entspricht dies 0,3% der erstinstanzlichen Verfahren, vgl. Pressemitteilung des LAG Baden-Württemberg vom 27. Juni 2007 abrufbar unter http://www.lag-baden-wuerttemberg.de/servlet/PB/show/1208853/Pressemitteilung27.06.07.pdf.

474 Vgl. beispielhaft No 1 Compulsory Age Retirement 1996, No 2 Redundancy Arrangements and Age Discrimination 1997, No 4 Age Discrimination in Trade Union Membership 1997, No 8 Age Discrimination in the Australian Defence Force 2000, No 11 Discrimination on the Ground of Age 2000, No 14 Age Discrimination in the Australian Defence Force 2002, No 26 Age Discrimination in the Australian Defence Force 2004, No 30 Report of an Inquiry into a complaint by Mr William Mayne of age discrimination in the Australian Defence Force, dargestellt unter http://www.humanrights.gov.au/legal/reports_hreoca.html

475 No 1 Compulsory Age Retirement 1996.

476 Vgl. dagegen die spätere Entscheidung des High Court of Australia im Fall *Qantas v Christie* (1998) 193 CLR 280, in welcher von der Rechtsprechung eine Altersdiskriminierung bejaht, aber im Ergebnis als rechtmäßig bewertet wurde, da das Alter eines Piloten eine diesem Beruf innewohnende Anforderung darstellen würde.

4. Grenzen der Befugnisse der Human Rights and Equal Opportunity Commission

Die Human Rights and Equal Opportunity Commission ist aber trotz der ihr übertragenen Ermächtigungen nicht zur Durchsetzung und Vollstreckung eines wirksamen Rechtsschutzes gegen Altersdiskriminierungen imstande. Trotz langjähriger Diskussionen innerhalb der australischen Gesetzgebung und zahlreichen Reformbemühungen, ist es nicht gelungen der Human Rights and Equal Opportunity Commission eine richterliche Gewalt zu verleihen.[477]

a. Die Entwicklung der Entscheidungskompetenzen der Human Rights and Equal Opportunity Commission

aa. Das public hearing-Verfahren

In Australien bestand über Jahre hinweg – und besteht auch noch heute – das grundsätzliche Bedürfnis danach, eine Chancengleichheit vor allem durch die Aushandlung einer Einigung zwischen den Parteien eines Diskriminierungsfalles herzustellen und eine solche Angelegenheit möglichst nicht auf dem Rechtsweg einer Lösung zuzuführen. Weiterhin sollte bestimmten Gruppen der Gesellschaft, die nach Ansicht des Gesetzgebers vorwiegend Diskriminierungen ausgesetzt sind, mit dieser alternativen Streitbeilegung durch ein außergerichtliches Verfahren ein äußerst kostengünstiger, zeitsparender und unformalistischer Weg zur Verwirklichung der Chancengleichheit eingeräumt werden.[478]

Andererseits sollte eine Konfliktlösung selbst gegen den Willen der freiwillig nicht zur Herstellung von Chancengleichheit und zur Beseitigung von geschehenen Diskriminierungen bereiten Partei durch eine autoritäre Beendigung im Wege der Entscheidung im Anhörungsverfahrens (*„conciliation“*) ermöglicht werden.

Deshalb wurde der Human Rights and Equal Opportunity Commission die – ausdrücklich nicht formulierte – Kompetenz eingeräumt, ein sog. *public hearing*-Verfahren durchzuführen. Dieses Verfahren sollte mit einer abschließenden Entscheidung des vorgebrachten Diskriminierungsfalles enden und auch gegen den Willen des Beschwerdegegners durchgeführt werden können. Auch sollte es in zahlreichen Fällen als notwendige Prozessvoraussetzung für eine später zu erhebende Klage gelten.

Der zu behandelnde Diskriminierungsfall war dabei mit den Ergebnissen der Untersuchungsphase insbesondere dann in das, prozessualen Grundsätzen folgende, *public hearing*-Verfahren zu verweisen, wenn eine Einigung zwischen den Parteien im Vorfeld nicht erreicht werden konnte oder wenn der die Untersuchung leitende Mitarbeiter der Human Rights and Equal Opportunity Commission die vorliegende Angele-

---

477 *Smith*, Australian Anti-Discrimination Laws – Framework, Developments and Issues, New Developments in Employment Discrimination Law – The 9 JILPT Comparative Labour Law Seminar (2008) 8.

478 *Ronalds*, Discrimination – Law and Practice, 2004, 176.

genheit als nicht vermittelbar oder als besonders schwierig einstufte.[479] Dem das öffentliche Verfahren leitenden *Hearing Commissioner* oblag es, die Parteien aufzufordern, ihre Beweise vorzubringen und gegebenenfalls. Zwangsmittel zur Durchsetzung von Mitwirkungshandlungen einzusetzen. Die Entscheidung des Verfahrens unterschied sich kaum von einer gerichtlichen Entscheidung, da die unterliegende Partei zu einem Tun oder Unterlassen verpflichtet, die Zahlung eines Schmerzensgeld festgelegt sowie die Einstellung oder Wiedereinstellung verfügt werden konnte.[480]

Da die letztlich gefundene Entscheidung in ihrer Vollstreckung und Beachtung grundsätzlich aber von der Freiwilligkeit der Parteien abhing, wurde diese Kompetenzerweiterung der Durchführung des *public hearing*-Verfahrens als nur wenig effektiv und als im Ergebnis unbefriedigend beurteilt.[481] Denn nur ausnahmsweise, d.h. wenn gegen das Commonwealth of Australia oder gegen eine bundeseigene Behörde oder gegen eine bundeseigene Einrichtung eine Entscheidung erging, sollte das Ergebnis des *public hearing*-Verfahrens Rechtsbindung entfalten.

Darüber hinaus galt diese Zweiteilung der Vorgehensweise – Aufklärung und Vermittlung durch die Human Rights and Equal Opportunity Commission und Rechtsdurchsetzung und Vollstreckung durch die Gerichte – als für Missbrauch anfällig.[482]

bb. Die Befugnis zum Erlass vollstreckungsfähiger Entscheidungen

Um gegen Missbrauch in ausreichendem Maße geschützt zu sein und Opfern von Diskriminierungen den mit der verfahrensrechtlichen Zerteilung verbundenen erheblichen Zeit- und Kostenaufwand zu ersparen, wurden die Kompetenzen der Human Rights and Equal Opportunity Commission erweitert.[483] Sie wurde im Jahre 1993 durch den Sex Discrimination and other Legislation Amendment Act (1992) deshalb zum Erlass vollstreckungsfähiger Entscheidungen in der Form befugt, als dass die von ihr im Anhörungsverfahren getroffenen Entscheidungen beim Federal Court angemeldet und registriert werden mussten und infolge dessen als sog. Quasi-Gerichtsentscheidung galten und in vollem Umfang vollstreckbar waren.[484]

Die Entscheidungen der Human Rights and Equal Opportunity Commission mussten dazu an den Federal Court übersandt werden. Dort wurden sie registriert und ab der Bekanntgabe der Registrierung beim Gericht hatte der Antragsgegner insgesamt 28 Tage Zeit, die gerichtliche Überprüfung der Entscheidung aus dem *public hearing*-Verfahren zu beantragen. Ließ er diese Frist aber erfolglos verstreichen, dann wurde die Entscheidung der Human Rights and Equal Opportunity Commission – ebenso wie ein Urteil des Federal Court – durchsetzbar und somit vollstreckbar.

---

479 *Bailey/Devereux*, The operation of Antidiscrimination Laws in Australia, in: Kinley, Human Rights in Australian Law, 1998, 292.

480 *Thornton*, Antidiscrimination Remedies (1993) 9, The Adelaide Law Review, 235.

481 *Hunter*, Indirect Discrimination in the Workplace, 1992, 287.

482 Vgl. dazu die Entscheidung *Aldrige v Booth* (1988) 80 ALR 1 und den Report of the Senate Standing Committee on Legal and Constitutional Affairs, Review of Determinations of the HREOC and the Privacy Commissioner, November 1992, 8.

483 Zur Kostenbelastung vgl. *Neilson v Maynard* (1988) EOC 92-226 = (1988) 15 ALD 364.

484 *Gaze*, The costs of Equal Opportunity (2000) 25, Alternative Law Journal, 125.

Neben der Gefahr einer Verletzung des Grundsatzes der Gewaltenteilung bestand neben der Übernahme des grundsätzlichen Prozessrisikos vor allem das für die Parteien praktisch nachvollziehbarere Risiko, dass sie den Prozess verlieren könnten und im Nachgang somit zur Erstattung der Kosten der Gegenseite verpflichtet wären.

Trotz dieser Gefahren bedürfen aber auch die nicht abzustreitenden Vorteile des *public hearing*-Verfahrens einer genaueren Betrachtung. Denn die Durchführung dieses Verfahrens beinhaltete ein gewisses Drohpotential für den Diskriminierenden, da er damit rechnen musste, dass er bei einem fehlgeschlagenen Einigungsversuch diesem weiteren Verfahrensabschnitt nicht entgehen könne. Auch galt das Verfahren als Probelauf eines vermeintlichen Gerichtsprozess, ohne dass zunächst Verfahrenskosten angefallen wären. Weiterhin war es stellenweise möglich, die Parteien doch zu einer gütlichen Einigung zu bewegen, indem vor der Durchführung des *public hearing*-Verfahrens die Beteiligten und der jeweilige Verfahrensgegenstand von der Human Rights and Equal Opportunity Commission zur Information der Öffentlichkeit in der Tagespresse veröffentlicht wurde. Dadurch stieg nicht zuletzt die Bereitschaft der Parteien, vor der Veröffentlichung des Verfahrens, die Auseinandersetzung durch eine Einigung zu beenden und somit in der Öffentlichkeit nicht genannt zu werden.[485]

cc. Der Fall Brandy v Human Rights and Equal Opportunity Commission und die Verletzung des Gewaltenteilungsgrundsatzes

(1) Die Verfassungswidrigkeit des *public hearing*-Verfahrens

Trotz dieser Vorteile überwogen aber die Nachteile des *public hearing*-Verfahrens, so dass durch die Entscheidung des High Courts aus dem Jahr 1995 im Fall *Brandy v Human Rights and Equal Opportunity Commission* diese Verfahrenslösung kurze Zeit nach ihrer Einführung wieder aufgehoben wurde.[486] Zugleich wurde die bereits im Vorfeld laut gewordene Kritik, nach welcher durch die Ausübung von richterlicher Gewalt durch eine Verwaltungsbehörde wie der Human Rights and Equal Opportunity Commission ein Verstoß gegen den Gewaltenteilungsgrundsatz in der Verfassung des australischen Commonwealth vorgelegen haben sollte, höchstrichterlich bestätigt.[487] Der High Court sah es als erwiesen an, dass der Human Rights and Equal Opportunity Commission – unabhängig davon, wie der Begriff der rechtsprechenden Gewalt im Detail auszulegen ist – ohne Zweifel richterliche Gewalt zugewiesen wurde und diese Befugnis als verfassungswidrig aufzuheben sei.[488]

485 Vgl. Human Rights and Equal Opportunity Commission, Annual Report 1999 – 2000, 42.

486 *Brandy v Human Rights and Equal Opportunity Commission* (1995) EOC 2-662 = (1995) 183 Commonwealth Law Reports 245 = (1995) 127 Australian Law Report 1.

487 *Mason*, The role of the Judiciary in developing Human Rights in Australian Law, in: Kinley, Human Rights in Australian Law, 1998, 26; *Mac Dermott*, The Implications for Employment Law (1995) 8, Australian Journal of Labour Law, 276.

488 *Brandy v Human Rights and Equal Opportunity Commission* (1995) EOC 2-662; 183 Commonwealth Law Reports 245.

(2) Die Argumentation des High Court of Australia

(a) Die richterliche Gewalt und ihre Tatbestandsmerkmale

In Art. 71 des Commonwealth of Australia Constitution Act 1901 wird statuiert, dass nur der High Court oder aber andere, ausdrücklich vom Parlament des Commonwealth geschaffene Bundesgerichte befugt sind, richterliche Gewalt auszuüben:[489]

> "The judicial power of the Commonwealth shall be vested in a Federal Supreme Court, to be called the High Court of Australia, and in such other federal courts as the Parliament creates, and in such other courts as it invests with federal jurisdiction. The High Court shall consist of a Chief Justice, and so many other Justices, not less than two, as the Parliament prescribes."

Der Begriff der richterlichen Gewalt wird dabei mangels einer in der Verfassung des Commonwealth oder in einer anderen Rechtsnorm enthaltenen Definition von der Rechtsprechung als eine Entscheidung über Rechte und Pflichten der streitenden Parteien sowie als die Durchsetzbarkeit dieser Entscheidung beschrieben.[490]

(b) Entscheidung über Rechte und Pflichte der streitenden Parteien

Das erste tatbestandsbegründende Element – eine Entscheidung über Rechte und Pflichten streitender Parteien – konnte der High Court nach umfassender Prüfung ohne nennenswerte Probleme und Schwierigkeiten bejahen. Denn die Human Rights and Equal Opportunity Commission überprüfte, ob der Beschwerdegegner gegen ein Diskriminierungsverbot verstoßen hatte und stellte gleichzeitig die gebotene Ausgleichsmaßnahme fest, so dass sie über Rechte und Pflichten einer Partei entschied.[491]

(c) Durchsetzbarkeit der Entscheidung

Beim Merkmal der Durchsetzbarkeit dieser Entscheidung sah es jedoch weit problematischer aus. So trug der Beschwerdegegner nicht ohne Grund vor, dass die Human Rights and Equal Opportunity Commission selbst nicht die Befugnis besitzen würde, ihre Entscheidung für vollstreckbar zu erklären, denn nicht umsonst hatte der Gesetzgeber die Möglichkeit der Registrierung beim Federal Court eingeführt. Denn dadurch

---

489 *Crawford*, Australian Courts of Law, 2004, 26.

490 *Precision Data Holdings Ltd. v Wills* (1991) 173 Commonwealth Law Reports 167; *Dixon J./Tiernan J./Reg v Davison* (1954) 90, Commonwealth Law Reports, 353; *Huddart, Parker & Co. Proprietary Ltd. v Morrehead* (1908) 8, Commonwealth Law Reports, 330; *Waterside Workers' Federation of Australia v J. W. Alexander Ltd.* (1918) 25, Commonwealth Law Reports, 434; *Nand*, Judicial Power and Administrative Tribunals: The Decision in Brandy v HREOC (1997) 14, Australian Institute of Administrative Law Forum, 15; *Crawford*, Australian Courts of Law, 2004, 30.

491 Im vorliegenden Fall wurden Harry Brandy und sein Arbeitgeber zu einer Entschuldigung beim und zu einer Entschädigung des Beschwerdeführers John Bell verurteilt, da Harry Brandy diesen nachweislich wegen seiner Herkunft mittels Beschimpfungen und Drohungen diskriminiert hatte und sein Arbeitgeber nicht gegen dieses Vorgehen eingeschritten ist; vgl. *Brandy v Human Rights and Equal Opportunity Commission* (1995) EOC 2-662; 183 Commonwealth Law Reports 245.

müsse gerade der Federal Court innerhalb des Registrierungsverfahrens die Entscheidung der Human Rights and Equal Opportunity Commission in tatsächlich und rechtlich vollständiger Weise überprüfen, um diese entweder zu bestätigen oder gegebenenfalls von ihr teilweise oder in vollem Umfang abzuweichen, so dass ausschließlich das Registrierungsverfahren dazu führen könne, ein neues Verfahren vor dem Federal Court in Gang zu setzen. Folglich sollte nach Ansicht des Beschwerdegegners allein die Entscheidung des Federal Court durchsetzbar sein.[492]

Diese Argumentation ging jedoch fehl, so dass sich der High Court ihr im Ergebnis nicht anzuschließen vermochte. Denn sie hätte nur dann Platz greifen können, wenn der Beschwerdegegner fristgerecht gegen die Entscheidung der Human Rights and Equal Opportunity Commission vorgehen würde. Unterlässt er dies aber und wendet sich nicht gegen die Entscheidung, so erlangte diese die Wirkung eines Gerichtsurteils des Federal Court, ohne dass dieser in irgendeiner Art und Weise hätte beteiligt werden müssen.[493] Folglich konnte einerseits, entgegen der Ansicht des Beschwerdegegners, die Registrierung der Entscheidung der Human Rights and Equal Opportunity Commission nicht nur als bloße Einleitung eines neuen Verfahrens angesehen werden. Andererseits war der Federal Court selbst bei der Durchführung eines Verfahrens nicht verpflichtet, sondern allenfalls berechtigt, neue Beweismittel zuzulassen. In der Regel wurden also die Beweismittel herangezogen, die bereits innerhalb des *public hearing*-Verfahrens erlangt worden waren.[494] Als zusätzliches Argument nahm der High Court vor allem auf den Zweck des Registrierungsverfahrens Bezug. Denn dieses Verfahren war insbesondere deshalb eingeführt worden, weil die zur früheren Rechtslage vorgetragenen Kritikpunkte beseitigt werden sollten, nach denen eine Verdoppelung der Verfahrensschritte zu erheblichen Mehrkosten führen würden.[495] Weiterhin sollten die Beschwerdegegner zu einem möglichst vollständigen Vortrag innerhalb des Verfahrens vor der Human Rights and Equal Opportunity Commission veranlasst werden.[496] All diese Argumente veranlassten den High Court im Ergebnis dazu, den Antrag an den Federal Court nicht als ein erstinstanzliches Verfahren anzusehen, sondern es vielmehr als eine Art Entscheidungsüberprüfung zu beurteilen und somit als Resultat eine nicht unerhebliche Kontrollmöglichkeit der Human Rights and Equal Opportunity Commission festzustellen.[497]

(d) Zwischenergebnis

Folglich hatte der High Court im Ergebnis eindeutig feststellen können, dass die Entscheidungen der Human Rights and Equal Opportunity Commission beide Tatbe-

492 *Brandy v Human Rights and Equal Opportunity Commission* (1995) EOC 2-662; 183 Commonwealth Law Reports 245.

493 *Mac Dermott*, The Implications for Employment Law (1995) 8, Australian Journal of Labour Law, 276.

494 *Brandy v Human Rights and Equal Opportunity Commission* (1995) EOC 2-662; 183 Commonwealth Law Reports 245.

495 *Wilcox, J., Maynard v Neilson* (1988) EOC 92-226.

496 *Wilcox, J., Maynard v Neilson* (1988) EOC 92-226.

497 *Brandy v Human Rights and Equal Opportunity Commission* (1995) EOC 2-662; 183 Commonwealth Law Reports 245.

standsvoraussetzungen für die Ausübung richterlicher Gewalt erfüllten und deshalb mit der vom High Court entwickelten Auslegung des Gewaltenteilungsgrundsatzes unvereinbar waren.[498]

(3) Kritik an der Entscheidung des High Court

Die Entscheidung in Sachen *Brandy v Human Rights and Equal Opportunity Commission* veranlasste vor allem die Literatur zu erheblicher Kritik. So gab es Stimmen, dass die Anwendung des Gewaltenteilungsgrundsatzes als zu formalistisch und begriffsjuristisch strapaziert worden sei und der High Court auf der Grundlage der Zielsetzung des Gesetzgebers besser einen Weg hätte erarbeiten sollen, der eine Arbeitsteilung zwischen der Human Rights and Equal Opportunity Commission und dem Federal Court ermöglichen würde.[499] So wurde insbesondere vorgeschlagen, das Verfahren der Human Rights and Equal Opportunity Commission selbst anstatt als Akt der Exekutive als Ausübung rechtsprechender Gewalt anzuerkennen, um dann die Antidiskriminierungsgesetze als Grundlage für eine Arbeitsteilung zwischen der Human Rights and Equal Opportunity Commission und dem Federal Court zu verstehen und diese zugleich unter die Aufsicht des Federal Court zu stellen.[500]

dd. Rückkehr zur alten Rechtslage

Aufgrund dieser einschneidenden Entscheidung des High Court im Fall *Brandy v Human Rights and Equal Opportunity Commission* wurde die im Jahre 1993 eingeführte Neuerung wieder aufgehoben und es wurde wieder zur davor geltenden Gesetzeslage zurückgekehrt.[501] Nach dieser war es der Human Rights and Equal Opportunity Commission nur erlaubt, Untersuchungen zur Sachverhaltsermittlung anzustellen, zu versuchen zu einer außergerichtlichen und einvernehmlichen Lösung zu finden und für den Fall des Scheiterns, die Angelegenheit in einem förmlichen, im Ergebnis aber unverbindlichen, Anhörungsverfahren zu klären.

Zur Vollstreckung aber bedurfte es nun der Anrufung des Federal Courts, vor dem ein Rechtsstreit durchgeführt werden musste. Problematisch und überaus zeitaufwändig war dabei die erneute vollständige Sachverhaltsermittlung durch das Gericht. Denn weil die Human Rights and Equal Opportunity Commission ihr Verfahren nicht nach den prozessualen Regeln eines Rechtsstreits durchzuführen verpflichtet war, konnte das Gericht nicht einmal die Akten der Human Rights and Equal Opportunity Commission beiziehen und bereits erbrachte Beweise verwerten.[502]

---

498 *Brandy v Human Rights and Equal Opportunity Commission* (1995) EOC 2-662; 183 Commonwealth Law Reports 245; vgl. auch *Cantanzariti*; Federal discrimination claims after Brandy (1995) 33, (4) Law Society Journal, 16.

499 *Omar*, Darkness on the edge of town: the High Court and Human Rights in the Brandy case (1995) 2, (1) Australian Journal of Human Rights.

500 *Omar*, Darkness on the edge of town: the High Court and Human Rights in the Brandy case (1995) 2, (1) Australian Journal of Human Rights.

501 *Mac Dermott*, The Implications for Employment Law (1995) 8, Australian Journal of Labour Law, 276.

502 *Schlachter*, Außergerichtliche Konfliktlösung im Arbeitsverhältnis, Verwirklichung von Chancengleichheit auf dem Verhandlungswege in Australien und Deutschland, 2002, 23.

ee. *Der erneute Regelungsbedarf des Gesetzgebers*

Kurz nach dieser Änderung wurden die vorgenannten Kritikpunkte der Ineffektivität und des hohen Zeitaufwandes gegen den nun geltenden Verfahrensablauf erneut aufgegriffen. War etwa eine Entscheidung nicht durchsetzbar, dann konnte sich die unterlegene Partei gefahrlos darüber hinwegsetzen und ohne weiteres darauf vertrauen, dass es die Gegenseite nicht auf einen Rechtsstreit ankommen lassen würde.[503]

Somit sah sich der Gesetzgeber erneut zur Handlung gezwungen.[504] Nach einer Überprüfung im Rechts- und Verfassungsausschuss des Senats gelang es dem Gesetzgeber, zu einer Neuregelung der Kompetenzen der Human Rights and Equal Opportunity Commission zu finden.[505]

b. Die unverbindliche Entscheidung der Human Rights and Equal Opportunity Commission und ihre Vollstreckung

Aufgrund dieser am 14.4.2000 in Kraft getretenen Änderung ist die Human Rights and Equal Commission auf die Sachverhaltsermittlung und –untersuchung sowie auf das Herbeiführen einer einvernehmlichen, aber für die Parteien unverbindlichen, Lösung beschränkt. Ihr obliegt es im Ergebnis folglich nur noch, innerhalb einer Schlichtung zu versuchen, zu vertragsmäßigen Absprachen zwischen den betreffenden Parteien hinzuführen und eine gütliche Einigung zu finden.[506] Kann eine Einigung aber nicht erzielt werden, dann hat die Human Rights and Equal Opportunity Commission dem Beschwerdeführer eine Bescheinigung über die Beendigung des Verfahrens auszustellen. Weitere Befugnisse stehen ihr nicht (mehr) zu.

Eine Weiterverfolgung des Konflikts zur Erzielung einer durchsetzbaren und der Vollstreckung gegen den Beschwerdegegner zugänglichen Entscheidung kann dann nur noch dadurch erreicht werden, dass innerhalb von 28 Tagen nach Zugang der über die Beendigung des Verfahrens auszustellenden Bescheinigung direkt ein Rechtsstreit angestrengt wird.[507] In diesem Rechtsstreit dürfen die bereits vorliegenden Ermitt-

---

503 *Roberts/Redmann*, Full service handling of Human Rights complaints (2000), Law Institute Journal, 57; *Allen*, Equal opportunity (1996) 5, Res Publica, 16.

504 *Mac Dermott*, The Implications for Employment Law (1995) 8, 276.

505 Vgl. Human Rights Legislation Amendment Act No. 1; *Offenberger/Banks*, Wind out of the sails – new federal structure for the administration of human rights legislation (2000) 6, Australian Journal of Human Rights, 239; *Boniface* (1997) 4, Australian Journal of Human Rights, 188.

506 *Smith*, Australian Anti-Discrimination Laws – Framework, Developments and Issues, New Developments in Employment Discrimination Law – The 9 JILPT Comparative Labour Law Seminar (2008) 8; vgl. auch *Baker*, Access vs Process in Employment Discrimination: Why ADR suits the US but not the UK (2002) 31 Industrial Law Journal 113; Sternlight, In Search of the Best Procedure for Enforcing Employment Discrimination Laws: A Comparative Analysis (2004) 78 Tulane Law Review 1401.

507 *Offenberger/Banks*, Wind out of the sails – new federal structure for the administration of human rights legislation (2000) 6, Australian Journal of Human Rights, 239.

lungsergebnisse der Human Rights and Equal Opportunity Commission jedoch nicht verwendet werden.[508]

Im Ergebnis kann es aufgrund dieser Regelung der Kompetenz der Human Rights and Equal Opportunity Commission keine Probleme mit der verfassungsrechtlich sensiblen Frage der Ausübung richterlicher Gewalt geben, weil der Human Rights and Equal Opportunity Commission keine Befugnis zu einer inhaltlichen Entscheidung mehr zukommt. Denn einigen sich die Parteien gütlich, dann besteht eine Vereinbarung zwischen diesen. Einigen sich die Parteien dagegen nicht, dann kommt allenfalls eine Entscheidung durch das zuständige und verfassungsmäßig legitimierte Gericht zustande.

c. Die Kritik der Literatur an den Reformen zur Entscheidungskompetenz der Human Rights and Equal Opportunity Commission und ihre Rechtsfolgen

aa. Einzelne Kritikpunkte

Die Literatur lehnte die vorgenommenen Reformen weitgehend ab, da sie nicht nur die Effektivität der Arbeit der Human Rights and Equal Opportunity Commission als bedroht angesehen hat, sondern es zugleich auch als erheblichen Schwachpunkt einschätzte, dass die bloße Verweigerung einer Partei zu einer einvernehmlichen Lösung zu finden, genügen sollte jedwede Alternative zur gerichtlichen Rechtsdurchsetzung zu beseitigen.[509]

Das Hauptargument der Literatur war jedoch, dass ein Rechtsstreit vor dem Federal Court wegen der anfallenden Anwalts- und Gerichtskosten sowie aufgrund des zusätzlichen Risikos mit den Kosten der gegnerischen Seite belastet zu werden und aufgrund der komplizierten förmlichen Beweislastverteilung das Diskriminierungsopfer am Ende von der Durchsetzung und Vollstreckung seiner Rechte abschrecken und ihm somit ein effektiver Rechtsschutz faktisch entzogen werde.[510] Das Potential, mit den anfallenden Kosten zu drohen ist nicht unbeachtlich. Denn in der Regel stehen sich oftmals finanziell schlecht gestellte Diskriminierungsopfer und auf der Gegenseite finanzstarke Unternehmen mit einer hochqualifizierten rechtlichen Vertretung gegenüber.[511]

Zwar sind die Gerichtskosten in Australien in einer in etwa mit der deutschen Rechtslage vergleichbaren Weise geregelt, aber insbesondere die anfallenden Kosten für einen Rechtsanwalt, die mitunter im Ergebnis nicht selten höher liegen als der eigentliche Streitwert, und für benötigte Sachverständige sind oftmals im Vorfeld für die Partei kaum überschaubar. In Australien rechnen die Rechtsanwälte in der Regel ihre Kosten auf einen vereinbarten Stundensatz ab. Sie sind aber in der Festsetzung des diesem Stundensatz zu Grunde gelegten Gebührensatzes völlig frei, da sie mangels gesetzlicher Regelung nicht an existierende Empfehlungen über Berechnungsgrundla-

508 *Ronalds*, Discrimination – Law and Practice, 2004, 180.
509 *Ronalds*, Discrimination – Law and Practice, 2004, 182.
510 *Ronalds*, Discrimination – Law and Practice, 2004, 182.
511 *Gaze*, The costs of Equal Opportunity (2000) 25, Alternative Law Journal, 125.

gen für Stundensätze und Auslagenpauschalen gebunden sind. Zusätzlich ist es für einen Mandanten nur schwer einschätzbar, wie viel Zeit der Rechtsanwalt allein für die Vorbereitung des, ebenfalls in seiner Dauer kaum voraussehbaren, Prozesses aufzuwenden benötigt.[512] Erschwerend kommt bei diesem Gesichtspunkt vor allem hinzu, dass die Vorbereitungsphase der Verantwortung des Gerichts entzogen ist. Allein den Parteien und ihren Rechtsanwälten ist im Rahmen eines sog. *discovery*-Verfahrens die Vorbereitung des Prozesses und somit die Informations-, Urkunden- und Beweisbeschaffung sowie die Aus- und Bearbeitung der streitrelevanten Fragen überlassen.[513]

Auch die Möglichkeit sich bei nachgewiesener Bedürftigkeit mit der Beantragung von Prozesskostenhilfe („*legal aid*") zu helfen, vermag die Kostengefahren nicht vollumfänglich zu beseitigen. Denn in Australien umfasst die Prozesskostenhilfe die Kosten des Gegners nicht.[514]

bb. Lösungsmöglichkeiten

(1) Die Errichtung des Federal Magistrates Court

Im Nachgang zu dieser erheblichen Kritik aus der Literatur hat der australische Gesetzgeber den Federal Magistrates Court als neuen Gerichtszweig mit der Federal Magistrates Bill im Jahr 1999 eingerichtet. Denn gemäß Art. 77 Abs. iii des Commonwealth of Australia Constitution Act 1901 kann Gerichten, die von einzelnen Bundesstaaten eingerichtet worden sind, in besonderen Gesetzen vom Parlament des Commonwealth die Zuständigkeit in Angelegenheiten aus Bundesgesetzen übertragen werden. Somit konnte insbesondere die bundesrechtliche Zuständigkeit im Antidiskriminierungsrecht auf diese erstinstanzlichen Gerichte übertragen werden.

Gleichfalls mit der Einrichtung des Federal Magistrates Courts wurde sowohl den betreffenden Parteien als auch dem Richter des Federal Court die Möglichkeit eingeräumt, in autonomer Weise zu beantragen bzw. zu entscheiden, dass der wegen einer Verletzung eines Diskriminierungsverbotes geführte Rechtsstreit, gerichtlich nicht überprüfbar und anfechtbar, an den Federal Magistrates Court abgegeben wird.

Durch die Einführung des Federal Magistrates Court und der Abgabemöglichkeit sollten die Parteien insbesondere von der kürzeren Verfahrensdauer des dort geltenden sog. *summary jurisdiction*-Verfahrens profitieren. Vor allem aber sollte das enorme Kostenrisiko gemildert werden, indem die Kosten der obsiegenden Partei dem Gegner auferlegt werden können.[515] Da das Gericht aber nicht gezwungen ist, eine solche Entscheidung tatsächlich zu treffen, kann die Effektivität dieser Regelung zu Recht angezweifelt und im Ergebnis weiterhin an den aufgezeigten Kritikpunkten festgehalten werden.

---

512 *Schlachter*, Außergerichtliche Konfliktlösung im Arbeitsverhältnis, Verwirklichung von Chancengleichheit auf dem Verhandlungswege in Australien und Deutschland, 2002, 13.

513 *Cairns*, Australian Civil Procedure, 2004, 358; *Resnik*, Failing Faith, Adjudicatory Procedure in Decline (1986) 53, The University of Chicago Law Review, 494.

514 *Offenberger/Banks*, Wind out of the sails – new federal structure for the administration of human rights legislation (2000) 6, Australian Journal of Human Rights, 239.

515 *Ronalds*, Discrimination – Law and Practice, 2004, 182.

Ein möglicher Konflikt mit dem Gewaltenteilungsgrundsatz kann durch die Einführung des Federal Magistrates Court verneint werden. Denn nach überzeugender Ansicht der Rechtsprechung des High Court of Australia kann die rechtsprechende Gewalt in wirksamer Weise selbst auf Gerichtsbedienstete („*registrars*") delegiert werden, die selbst keine verfassungsrechtlich geforderte Unabhängigkeit besitzen.[516] Dagegen wurde der Federal Magistrates Court nicht nur als förmliches Bundesgericht errichtet, sondern die Richter wurden dagegen sogar verfassungsmäßig bestellt und mit der Gesamtverantwortung für die Entscheidung betraut.[517] Darüber hinaus wurde ihnen zugleich die den Vorgaben der Verfassung des Commonwealth genügende richterliche Unabhängigkeit verliehen.

(2) Kritik an der Errichtung des Federal Magistrates Court

Aber auch gegen den Versuch, die vorgenannten Probleme zu lösen, indem der Federal Magistrates Court errichtet wurde, gab es zahlreiche Kritiker. Sie schätzten den neuen Rechtsweg für eine effektive Durchsetzung von Ansprüchen auf Gleichbehandlung grundsätzlich als ungeeignet ein und sprachen von einer Monopolisierung der Entscheidungsbefugnisse der Gerichtsbarkeit.[518] Diese bedeute nicht nur eine Beschneidung der Befugnisse der Human Rights and Equal Opportunity Commission, sondern zugleich auch eine Verringerung ihres Ansehens und ihrer Funktionsfähigkeit, da der Human Rights Legislation Amendment Act No. 1 nur eine Rechtsdurchsetzung mit Hilfe des Gerichts ermögliche, obwohl die Human Rights and Equal Opportunity Commission gerade als Alternative zum Rechtsstreit eingerichtet worden war. Nichtsdestotrotz vermochte diese Kritik keine abermalige Änderung der Kompetenzen der Human Rights and Equal Opportunity Commission. Es blieb bei der zuvor erläuterten Abschaffung des *public hearing*-Verfahrens.

5. Das Problem der Effektivität der Herstellung von Chancengleichheit im Wege eines Rechtsstreits und die Entscheidungskompetenz der Human Rights and Equal Opportunity Commission in nicht einigungsgeeigneten Fällen

Unabhängig von den zuvor dargestellten Lösungsmöglichkeiten muss der australische Gesetzgeber aber dafür sorgen, dass insbesondere die aus internationalen Abkommen übernommenen Verpflichtungen durch effektive gesetzliche Regelungen eingehalten und ihnen zu voller Wirkkraft und Durchsetzbarkeit verholfen werden. Die ausschließ-

---

516 *Harris v Caladine* (1991) 99 ALR 193, Commonwealth Law Reports, 84; *Shell Company of Australia Ltd. v Federal Commissioner of Taxation* (1930) 44, Commonwealth Law Reports, 530.

517 Federal Magistrates Bill 1999; *Crawford*, Australian Courts of Law 2004, 31.

518 *Boniface*, Does anyone really know where we're going? Changes to the HREOC (1998) 4, (1) Australian Journal of Human Rights m.w.N.; *Offenberger/Banks*, Wind out of the sails – new federal structure for the administration of human rights legislation (2000) 6, Australian Journal of Human Rights, 239.

liche gerichtliche Durchsetzung wegen der Verletzung von auf internationalen Abkommen beruhenden Diskriminierungsverboten erzielt dabei nach verbreiteter Ansicht nur wenig Effekt.[519] Das hat der australische Gesetzgeber erkannt und sich somit frühzeitig von der Möglichkeit verabschiedet, Diskriminierungsverbote ausschließlich von den Betroffenen im Gerichtsprozess durchsetzen zu lassen. Vielmehr wurde und wird gerade die Schlichtung und Einigung im Rahmen des *conciliation*-Verfahrens durch die Human Rights and Equal Opportunity Commission zur Herstellung von Chancengleichheit bevorzugt und so versucht den Rechtsweg – trotz des Rechtsschutzes durch den Federal Court bzw. Federal Magistrates Court – entbehrlich werden zu lassen.

Fraglich erscheint aber, ob der Human Rights and Equal Opportunity Commission zur effektiven Schaffung bzw. Wiederherstellung von Chancengleichheit darüber hinaus auch die Kompetenz zukommen soll, in nicht einigungsgeeigneten Fällen zu entscheiden und ob sich der Rechtsweg zur Behandlung von Diskriminierungsverboten im Ergebnis wirklich als ungeeignet erweist. Diese Frage ist in ihrer Betrachtung streng von der durch die Entscheidung des High Court in Sachen *Brandy v Human Rights and Equal Opportunity Commission* abschließend geklärten Problematik der Zulässigkeit der Durchsetzung und Vollstreckung einer Entscheidung zu trennen.

a. Die mit dem Rechtsweg verbundenen Risiken

aa. Der Kostenaufwand für optimale Interessenvertretung im Rechtsstreit

In zahlreichen Fällen werden überwiegend Personen von Diskriminierungen (wegen Alters) betroffen, die aufgrund ihrer niedrigen Bildung oder ihres geringen Einkommens nur eine schwache Position in der Gesellschaft bekleiden und die oftmals nur wenig Zutrauen in das Rechtssystem haben. Solche Menschen entwickeln nur sehr selten das notwendige Vertrauen, dass sie sich durch gerichtliche Inanspruchnahme gegen Benachteiligungen effektiv schützen können.[520] Vielmehr sehen sie das Rechtssystem und dessen Funktionsweise im schlimmsten Fall sogar als unzugänglichen Fremdkörper an.[521] Bereits dieser Umstand erschwert eine erfolgreiche Rechtsdurchsetzung enorm. Hinzu kommt aber auch, dass eine Prozessführung ohne Rechtsvertretung nicht angeraten werden kann und die Erfolgsaussichten nur dann als optimal angesehen werden können, wenn ein erfahrener Rechtsvertreter zur Seite steht, der sich aufgrund seiner notwendigen Kenntnisse und Fähigkeiten der Sache annimmt. So wird in der Literatur deshalb ausdrücklich die Meinung vertreten *„unaided litigation has always been a risky and expensive business“*.[522] Wie aber sollen finanzschwache Men-

519 *Thornton*, Antidiscrimination Remedies (1983) 9, The Adelaide Law Review, 235; *Lustgarten*, Racial Inequality and the Limits of the Law (1986) 49, Modern Law Review, 68; *Hunter*, Indirect Discrimination in the Workplace, 1992, 287; *Stubbs*, Feminism and Legal Positivism, in: Weisberg, Feminist Legal Theory: Foundations, 1993, 454; vgl. auch Weisberg, Application of Feminist Legal Theory to Women's Live, 1996..

520 *Gaze*, The costs of Equal Opportunity (2000) 25, Alternative Law Journal, 125.

521 *Thorton*, Equivocations of Conciliation: The Resolution of Discrimination Complaints in Australia (1989) 52, The Modern Law Review, 733.

522 *Crawford*, Australian Courts of Law, 2004, 70.

schen einen teuren Beistand für Ihre Interessenvertretung gewinnen und wie sollen sie vor allem die erforderliche Qualifikation dessen in hinreichendem Maße beurteilen?

bb. Das Prozess- und Kostenrisiko

Grundsätzlich besteht weiterhin das allgemeine Prozessrisiko und die Gefahr von enormen – durch einen möglichen Prozessverlust anfallenden – Kosten der Gegenseite.[523]

Oftmals stehen auf der Gegenseite finanzstarke Wirtschaftsunternehmen oder Einrichtungen des Staates, für die sich die finanzielle Belastung durch einen Gerichtsprozess grundlegend anders darstellt. Das Diskriminierungsopfer kann im Gegensatz zu einem Unternehmen die Gerichts- und Prozesskosten nicht als Betriebsausgaben steuerlich geltend machen.[524] Durch die steuerliche Absetzungsmöglichkeit wird ein Prozess für ein Unternehmen, selbst bei gleichem Kostenumfang wie für den Kläger, im Ergebnis billiger sein.[525] Darüber hinaus steht die steuerliche Abzugsfähigkeit in keinerlei Zusammenhang mit den Erfolgsaussichten des Verfahrens, so dass die Subventionierung von Gerichtsprozessen von Unternehmen und Privatpersonen nach grundlegend verschiedenen Kriterien erfolgt. Auch ist die Gewährung von Prozesskostenhilfe mangels finanzieller Möglichkeiten nur sehr eingeschränkt erreichbar und in Diskriminierungsprozessen nicht allein nur von den Erfolgsaussichten abhängig. Vielmehr wird zusätzlich das Vorliegen eines besonderen öffentlichen Interesses am Gegenstand des Rechtsstreits gefordert, ohne das Prozesskostenhilfe nicht in Anspruch genommen werden darf.[526]

Hinzu kommt die Ungleichgewichtslage hinsichtlich des Prozessrisikos. Ein Wirtschaftsunternehmen bzw. dessen Rechtsabteilung oder aber auch die staatliche Verwaltung sind in der Regel mit (Diskriminierungs-)Klagen erfahren und dadurch sicherer im Umgang mit der Rechtsmaterie und dem Gericht, während die benachteiligte Person nur selten oder aber zum ersten Mal mit einer derartigen Situation konfrontiert wird.[527] Auch können es sich finanzstarke Beklagte eher leisten, Entscheidungen, die sie verlieren würden zu vermeiden, indem sie attraktive Vergleichszahlungen unterbreiten oder diesen zustimmen. Ebenso ist es für sie einfacher, Fälle, die voraussichtlich mit ihrer Rechtsauffassung im Einklang stehen, auch um den Preis hoher Verfahrenskosten einer Entscheidung zuzuführen.[528]

---

523 *Offenberger/Banks*, Wind out of the sails – new federal structure for the administration of human rights legislation (2000) 6, Australian Journal of Human Rights, 239.

524 *Offenberger/Banks*, Wind out of the sails – new federal structure for the administration of human rights legislation (2000) 6, Australian Journal of Human Rights, 239.

525 *Gaze*, The costs of Equal Opportunity (2000) 25, Alternative Law Journal, 125; *Korac-Kakabadse/Reeves-Knyght/Konzmin*, Inequality of Discourse and the Problem of Access to Justice, in: Social Justice Social Judgment, 1995.

526 *Offenberger/Banks*, Wind out of the sails – new federal structure for the administration of human rights legislation (2000) 6, Australian Journal of Human Rights, 239.

527 *Bryson*, "And the leopard shall lie down with the kid": A Conciliation Model for Workplace Disputes (1998) 8, Australian Dispute Resolution Journal, 245.

528 *Scutt*, The Privatisation of Justice: Power Differentials, Inequality and the Palliative of Counselling and Mediation, in: Mugford, Alternative Dispute Resolution, 1986, 185; *Thorton*, Equivo-

cc. *Die Gestaltung des Gerichtsverfahrens für Diskriminierungsklagen*

Wird durch die Human Rights and Equal Opportunity Commission versucht, eine gütliche Einigung zwischen den Parteien herbeizuführen, so ist es ihr grundsätzlich erlaubt, eine im Vergleich zum Gerichtsprozess weniger formelle und leichter handhabbare Verfahrensweise durchzuführen, um auch einer nicht anwaltlich vertretenen Partei eine hinreichende Chance zu geben, dass ihre Rechte angemessen berücksichtigt werden können.[529] Auch ist die Human Rights and Equal Opportunity Commission nicht an das strikte und im Einzelnen komplizierte Beweisverfahren der *„rule of evidence"* gebunden und sie ist vor allem ausschließlich auf das Diskriminierungsrecht spezialisiert.[530]

Diese nicht unerheblichen Vorteile können nicht zur Anwendung gelangen, wenn in das technisch besonders ausgestaltete Gerichtsverfahren zur Rechtsverfolgung eingetreten wird. Denn dort können einerseits weder ausschließlich auf Diskriminierungsrecht spezialisierte Personen zur Entscheidung herangezogen werden noch kann andererseits von den bestehenden Verfahrensregeln abgewichen werden.

dd. *Die Stellung des Richters im Prozess*

Im *common law*-System kommt dem Richter im Prozess darüber hinaus die Rolle eines bloßen Schiedsrichters zu, was als weitere Hürde eines Prozesses angesehen werden kann. Denn er ist gezwungen, die Prozessführung weitestgehend dem Geschick und der Fähigkeit der Parteien bzw. deren Vertretern zu überlassen.[531] Im australischen Prozessrecht wird davon ausgegangen, dass beide Parteien die gleichen Voraussetzungen zur Durchsetzung ihrer Rechte haben und sie somit ihre Belange in vergleichbarer Weise verfolgen können. Da es aber Aufgabe der Parteien ist, das maßgebliche Beweismaterial herbeizuschaffen, zu bezeichnen und Sachverständige zu beauftragen, wirken sich insbesondere eine taktisch durchdachte Vorbereitung und Aufbereitung des Prozess- und Beweismaterials sowie aber auch die Gewandtheit und die Ressourcen der Vertretung deutlich auf die Chancen der Prozesspartei aus. Da sich gerade in Diskriminierungsprozessen die Parteien jedoch meistens in unterschiedlichen Ausgangslagen befinden und sie, nicht zuletzt aufgrund der ihnen zur Rechtsverfolgung zur Verfügung stehenden Geldmittel, deutlich unterschiedliche Chancen zur Durchsetzung ihrer Rechte besitzen, besteht nur sehr selten eine Chancengleichheit. Diese

---

cations of Conciliation: The Resolution of Discrimination Complaints in Australia (1989) 52, The Modern Law Review, 733.

529 *Bailey*, Human Rights – Australia in an International Context, 1990, 215.

530 *Mac Dermott*, The Implications for Employment Law (1995) 8, Australian Journal of Labour Law, 276; *Roberts/Redman*, Full service handling of Human Rights complaints (2000), Law Institute Journal, 57.

531 Australian Law Reform Commission, Report No. 89, 2000, Managing justice: continuity and change in the federal civil justice system.

Mangel vermag der Richter aufgrund seiner passiven Schiedsrichterrolle in der Regel jedoch nicht zu beseitigen.[532]

ee. Der Umfang der zugesprochenen Ersatzleistungen

Überaus fraglich ist der Anreiz für den verfahrensrechtlichen Übergang in das Gerichtsverfahren, da die vom Gericht zugesprochenen Entschädigungs- und Ersatzleistungen für erlittene Diskriminierungen erheblich geringer ausfallen, als etwa in Fällen von Verletzungen des Körpers und der Schädigung der Gesundheit und die von der Human Rights and Equal Opportunity Commission zugesprochenen Schmerzensgeldbeträge nicht mehr als 10.000 AUD betragen.[533] Demgegenüber steht aber das enorme Kostenrisiko eines Prozesses, so dass die möglicherweise erreichbaren Ersatzleistungen für eine benachteiligte Person in der Regel keinen effektiven Anreiz darstellt, einen Gerichtsprozess anzustrengen, um zu erreichen, dass sie zukünftig besser behandelt wird.[534]

Allerdings könnte das Interesse der Anwaltschaft an nicht unerheblichen Gebühreneinnahmen zu einer Steigerung der Zahlen von Diskriminierungsprozessen gesehen werden. Denn würden die Prozesskosten auch in derartigen Fällen in vollem Umfang auf die unterliegende Partei abgewälzt werden können, dann könnte die Vertretung wenig zahlungskräftiger aber rechtlich aussichtsreicher Mandate für Rechtsanwälte interessant werden.[535] Da aber in Australien die für die rechtliche Vertretung in Diskriminierungsprozessen zu erwartenden Einnahmen für Rechtsanwälte insbesondere im Vergleich zu den in den Vereinigten Staaten verbreiteten Gruppenklagen („*class action*“) nicht sehr hoch ausfallen, wird das Interesse der Anwaltschaft an der Vertretung einer finanzschwachen Mandantschaft und an der Bearbeitung von häufig mit rechtlichen Schwierigkeiten verbundenen Diskriminierungsfällen die Prozesszahlen im Ergebnis nicht erhöhen können.[536]

ff. Bewertung der mit einem Gerichtsprozess verbundenen Nachteile und Gedanken zur Problemlösung

Die vorgebrachten Gründe, die gegen eine gerichtliche Durchsetzung zu sprechen versuchen, scheinen im Ergebnis immer Ausprägungen der Einwände zu sein, die im Allgemeinen gegen die Kosten- und Verfahrensregeln des *common law*-Systems vorge-

532 *Gaze*, The costs of Equal Opportunity (2000) 25, Alternative Law Journal, 125; *Boniface*, Does anyone really know where we're going? Changes to the HREOC (1998) 4, (1) Australian Journal of Human Rights.

533 *Ronalds*, Discrimination – Law and Practice, 2004, 198.

534 *Thornton*, Antidiscrimination Remedies (1983) 9, The Adelaide Law Review, 235.

535 *Offenberger/Banks*, Wind out of the sails – new federal structure for the administration of human rights legislation (2000) 6, Australian Journal of Human Rights, 239; Australian Law Reform Commission: Practice, procedure and case management in the Federal Court of Australia.

536 *Offenberger/Banks*, Wind out of the sails – new federal structure for the administration of human rights legislation (2000) 6, Australian Journal of Human Rights, 239; *Ronalds*, Discrimination – Law and Practice, 2004, 164; *Gaze*, The costs of Equal Opportunity (2000) 25, Alternative Law Journal, 125.

bracht werden. Sie stellen demnach keine speziell nur für Diskriminierungsklagen geltenden Nachteile dar.

Darüber hinaus darf nicht außer Acht gelassen werden, dass sich die gegenüber der Schlichtungskompetenz der Human Rights and Equal Opportunity Commission überwiegende Leistungsfähigkeit eines Gerichtsprozesses vor allem aufgrund der Möglichkeit zur repressiven Rechtsdurchsetzung im Wege staatlicher Zwangsmittel kennzeichnet.

Weiterhin hat der australische Gesetzgeber ausdrücklich die schiedsgerichtliche Funktion der Human Rights and Equal Opportunity Commission beseitigt, indem er das *public hearing*-Verfahren abgeschafft hat, weil er neben den vorgenannten Gründen nicht zuletzt auch von der Leistungsfähigkeit eines Gerichtsprozesses überzeugt war. Allein aus diesem Grund sollte nicht versucht werden, die Kompetenzen der Human Rights and Equal Opportunity Commission erneut – stillschweigend – zu erweitern.

Im Ergebnis sind deshalb keine besonderen – allein für Diskriminierungsfälle Geltung entfachenden – Gründe ersichtlich, die eine gerichtliche Rechtsverfolgung und somit prozessuale Durchsetzung von Diskriminierungsverboten als im Grundsatz ungeeignet erscheinen lassen würde. Es ist folglich nur konsequent, dass eine Erweiterung der Kompetenzen der Human Rights and Equal Opportunity Commission zur effektiven Schaffung bzw. Wiederherstellung von Chancengleichheit durch eine Entscheidungsbefugnis in nicht einigungsgeeigneten Fällen nicht bejaht werden kann.

b. Milderung der mit einem Gerichtsprozess für das Diskriminierungsopfer verbundenen Härten durch die Kompetenz der Human Rights and Equal Opportunity Commission zur Verhandlung mit den Partei en

Die vorangestellte Diskussionsdarstellung zeigt zugleich, dass grundsätzlich in Australien die Bewältigung von Diskriminierungskonflikten im Wege einer Verhandlung nicht angezweifelt wird.

Bei allen Argumenten, die gegen die Kritik an der Rechtsdurchsetzung in einem Gerichtsprozess vorgebracht werden, können aber die dennoch bestehenden Schwierigkeiten eines Prozesses nicht gänzlich unberücksichtig bleiben. Denn gerade die den Parteien zugewiesene aktive Rolle und die Eigenschaft des Richters als passiver Beobachter sowie das damit verbundene ungleichartige Kräfteverhältnis der Parteien können sich im Ergebnis nicht unerheblich auf den Ausgang des Gerichtsverfahrens auswirken. Somit kann es nicht von der Hand gewiesen werden, dass dennoch die Gefahr besteht, die Parteien nicht ausreichend gleich zu behandeln und somit nicht wirksam genug gegen Diskriminierungen vorzugehen. Aber gerade die Einrichtung der Kompetenz der Human Rights and Equal Opportunity Commission im Rahmen einer Verhandlung mit den Parteien zu einer gütlichen und außergerichtlichen Einigung zu finden, scheint vielfach die offensichtlichen Härten zu mildern und teilweise auszugleichen.

aa. Die Effektivität der conciliation und die Durchsetzung des access to justice

So bietet das Verfahren vor der Human Rights and Equal Opportunity Commission nicht nur einen im Gegensatz zu einem Gerichtsprozess schnelleren, billigeren und für das Diskriminierungsopfer weniger abschreckenderen Weg zur Herstellung eines fairen Interessenausgleichs, sondern sorgt zugleich dafür, jedem Bürger den Zugang zum Recht (*„access to justice“*) dergestalt zu eröffnen, dass er seine aufgrund zahlreicher Diskriminierungsverbote bestehenden Rechte tatsächlich in Anspruch nehmen kann. Das dies auch tatsächlich geschieht, belegt die Verfahrensstatistik der Human Rights and Equal Opportunity Commission aus den Jahren 2005 – 2006, nach der insgesamt 1.397 Beschwerden eingegangen und davon 1.205 abschließend bearbeitet werden konnten.[537] Ganz deutlich wird dies darüber hinaus bei einem Blick auf die Zahl der eingegangenen Beschwerden und der bearbeiteten Beschwerden im Berichtszeitraum 2006 – 2007. In diesem Zeitraum sind 1.779 Beschwerden bei der Human Rights and Equal Opportunity Commission erhoben worden, wovon insgesamt 1.656 abschließend bearbeitet werden konnten.[538]

bb. Die psychologische und verfahrensrechtliche Stellung der Verfahrensbeteiligten

Für das Opfer einer (Alters-)Diskriminierung kommt als wesentlicher Vorteil des außergerichtlichen Verfahrens hinzu, dass ihm im jeweiligen Fall die Fortsetzung der sozialen Beziehung zur Gegenpartei versucht wird zu ermöglichen und ein nicht zu verachtender psychologischer Vorteil an Bedeutung gewinnt:[539] Es gibt weder einen Gewinner noch einen Verlierer des Falles.[540]

Auch der Ablauf und die Besonderheiten des *conciliation*-Verfahrens sprechen für sich, da grundsätzlich der Verhandlungsstoff von den Parteien und nicht von einem Gericht oder von den Rechtsanwälten kontrolliert wird und somit ein gewisses Gleichgewicht gewährleistet werden kann. Als wichtiger Bestandteil des Verfahrens ist ebenfalls hervorzuheben, dass zwar die rechtlichen Aspekte des betreffenden Diskriminierungsfalles ermittelt werden, der Gegenstand der Verhandlung aber umfassend verstanden und folglich keinesfalls auf die Rechtslage begrenzt wird.[541] Denn auch die

537 Human Rights and Equal Opportunity Commission, Annual Report 2005 – 2006, 50; dem Age Discrimination Act (2004) Cth unterfielen dabei 106 Beschwerden, wobei insgesamt 80 von ihnen innerhalb des Berichtszeitraumes abschließend bearbeitet werden konnten und insgesamt 74 Prozent davon den Bereich der Beschäftigung betrafen.

538 Human Rights and Equal Opportunity Commission, Annual Report 2006 – 2007, 70; dem Age Discrimination Act (2004) Cth unterfielen dabei 106 Beschwerden, wobei allerdings insgesamt 115 Beschwerden innerhalb des Berichtszeitraumes abschließend bearbeitet werden konnten; vgl. zur weiteren Entwicklung auch Human Rights and Equal Opportunity Commission, Annual Report 2007 – 2008, 74.

539 *Bailey*, Human Rights – Australia in an International Context, 1990, 218; *Devereux*, Human Rights by Agreement? (1996) 7, Australian Dispute Resolution Journal, 280; *Montoya*, Let's Mediate – a whole new ballgame at EEOC (1999) 24, Employee Relations Law Journal, 53.

540 *Alexander*, Family Mediation under the Microscope (1999) 10, Australasian Dispute Resolution Journal, 18.

541 *Thornton*, Equivocations of Conciliation: The Resolution of Discrimination Complaints in Australia (1989) 52, The Modern Law Review, 733.

Wiederherstellung des Ansehens und der Würde der diskriminierten Person kann zugleich den Gegenstand der Verhandlung ausmachen und somit zu einer Einigung führen, die nicht nur an gesetzlich vorgesehenen Ersatz- und Entschädigungszahlungen orientiert wird, sondern vor allem die Interessen der Parteien in ausreichendem Maße zu berücksichtigen vermag.

cc. Der Vertraulichkeitsfaktor

Nicht nur diese Umstände, sondern auch die Nichtöffentlichkeit des Verfahrens vor der Human Rights and Equal Opportunity Commission verbessern die Bereitschaft der Verfahrensbeteiligten zu einer gütlichen Einigung zu finden und ihnen die erforderliche Vertraulichkeit ihrer Angelegenheit zu gewährleisten.[542] Nicht nur die Öffentlichkeit und die Presse sind vom jeweiligen Verfahren ausgeschlossen, auch die Verfahrensunterlagen der Human Rights and Equal Opportunity Commission und somit all das, was im Rahmen des Verfahrens gesagt oder bereits zugestanden wurde, dürfen nicht in einem sich möglicherweise anschließenden Gerichtsverfahren beigezogen und verwendet werden[543] So kann es insbesondere für Wirtschaftsunternehmen als Verfahrensgegner sehr interessant sein, in diesem vertraulichen Rahmen das Diskriminierungsopfer im Rahmen einer für dieses vorteilhaften Einigung zu befriedigen und zu entschädigen, ohne das in der Öffentlichkeit Aufsehen erregt wird.

dd. Die Durchsetzung der Einigung

Die vielfach geäußerte Kritik an der fehlenden Möglichkeit der Human Rights and Equal Opportunity Commission zur Durchsetzung der getroffenen Einigungen läuft bereits deshalb ins Leere, weil in der Praxis die Durchsetzung der von den Verfahrensbeteiligten getroffenen Vereinbarungen meistens unproblematisch ist. Denn das Verhandlungsergebnis ist Ausfluss und Ausdruck ihrer eigenen Bemühungen und Anstrengungen, so dass oftmals das Zugesagte ohne weiteres auch eingehalten wird.[544]

---

542 *Landau*, Conciliation as a mode of settlement of discrimination complaints (1988) 11, Adelaide Law Review, 273; *Ronalds*, Discrimination – Law and Practice, 2004, 198.

543 *Thornton*, Equivocations of Conciliation: The Resolution of Discrimination Complaints in Australia (1989) 52, The Modern Law Review, 733.

544 So sind im Zeitraum 2005 – 2006 93 Prozent aller Verfahrensbeteiligten mit der Arbeit und dem erzielten Ergebnis zufrieden gewesen; vgl. Human Rights and Equal Opportunity Commission, Annual Report 2005 – 2006, 7; im Berichtszeitraum 2006 – 2007 waren es wiederum 92 Prozent; vgl. Human Rights and Equal Opportunity Commission, Annual Report 2006 – 2007, 51; diese Zahlen bestätigten sich im Berichtszeitraum 2007 – 2008; vgl. Human Rights and Equal Opportunity Commission, Annual Report 2007 – 2008, 45.

ee. *Bedenken gegen das conciliation-Verfahren vor der Human Rights and Equal Opportunity Commission*

Zwar scheint grundsätzlich das einem Gerichtsprozess gemäß § 46 PO HREOC Act zwingend vorgeschaltete *conciliation*-Verfahren vor der Human Rights and Equal Opportunity Commission aufgrund der zahlreichen Vorzüge dazu geeignet zu sein, die mit der gerichtlichen Rechtsverfolgung verbundenen Härten und Risiken zu mildern bzw. teilweise sogar gänzlich zu beseitigen. Dennoch bestehen aber gegen die positiven Merkmale des Schlichtungsverfahrens zahlreiche Bedenken, die letztendlich die Abschaffung des *public hearing*-Verfahrens durch den Gesetzgeber und die aufeinander aufbauenden Verfahren vor der Human Rights and Equal Opportunity Commission und des Federal Court bzw. Federal Magistrates Court als richtige Lösung bestätigen könnten.

(1) Das *conciliation*-Verfahren als Privatverfahren

Ein grundsätzlicher und sehr allgemeiner Kritikpunkt, dem sich das Vermittlungsverfahren vor der Human Rights and Equal Opportunity Commission ausgesetzt sieht, entspringt der Eigenschaft des Verfahrens als Privatverfahren.[545] Denn die nichtöffentliche Verfahrensweise sei gleichbedeutend mit fehlender Kontrolle und mit einer fehlenden institutionellen Willkürabsicherung, wodurch die Verfahrensbeteiligten nicht hinreichend durch demokratische Verfahrensgarantien geschützt würden.[546] Hinzu komme ein erhebliches Maß an Intransparenz, welches vor allem dadurch entstehe, indem eine nicht unerhebliche Anzahl von Diskriminierungsfällen nicht in einem Gerichtsverfahren gelöst werde. Somit bliebe die entscheidende Aufgabe eines Gerichts, die Auslegung eines Gesetzes und die Rechtsfortbildung handhabbar werden zu lassen, unerfüllt und zugleich wird eine Orientierung an veröffentlichten Gerichtsentscheidungen für die Herausbildung von Beurteilungsmaßstäben für mögliche Diskriminierungsfälle in der Praxis versagt.[547] Des Weiteren wird von Kritikern vorgetragen, dass die Vertraulichkeit des Verfahrens dazu führen könnte, dass die Verbreitung positiver Kenntnisse über Diskriminierungsfälle beschränkt werde und somit dem Beschwerdeführer die Bildung eines auf seinen Fall anzulegenden Maßstabes nicht möglich wäre.[548] Dadurch bestünde die Gefahr, dass er mangels gesetzlicher Vorgaben eine Einigung trifft, die dem Inhalt eines Gerichtsurteils nicht annähernd entsprechen würde.

---

545 *Astor/Chinkin*, Dispute Resolution in Australia 1992, 274; *Chapman*, Sexuality and Workplace Oppression (1995) 20, Melbourne University Law Review, 311; *Regan*, Dilemmas of Dispute Resolution Policy (1997) 8, Australian Dispute Resolution Journal 5.

546 *Hunter*, Indirect Discrimination in the Workplace, 1992, 262.

547 *Scutt*, The Privatisation of Justice, in: Mugford, Alternative Dispute Resolution, Australian Institute of Criminology, 1986, 185; *Astor/Chinkin*, Dispute Resolution in Australia (1992) 262; *Thornton*, Equivocation of Conciliation: The Resolution of Discrimination Complaints in Australia (1989) 52, The Modern Law Review, 733; *ders.*, The Liberal Promise: Anti-Discrimination Legislation in Australia, 1990, 153.

548 *Scutt*, The Privatisation of Justice: Power Differentials, Inequality and the Palliative of Counseling and Mediation, in: Australian Institute of Criminology, Conference on Alternative Dispute Resolution, Canberra, 1986, 195; *Hunter*, Indirect Discrimination in the Workplace, 1992, 260;

Dass im Vermittlungsverfahren von einer durch ein Gesetz angeordneten Rechtsfolge im Ergebnis abgewichen wird, ist jedoch dem *conciliation*-Verfahren geradezu immanent und kann deshalb vielmehr als wichtigster Vorteil der Verhandlungslösung und als Chance anstatt als Gefahr angesehen werden.[549] Denn nur so können alternative, rechtstechnisch mit der geschehenen Diskriminierung nicht verknüpfte Bereiche, in eine Entschädigung eingebunden und ebenso auch flexible Wege zur Entschädigung beschritten werden. Ebenso können deshalb die Entschädigungszahlungen weitaus höher liegen, als es irgendein Gesetz vorschreibt.

Darüber hinaus vermögen aber nicht nur die bereits zuvor aufgezeigten Vorzüge eines vertraulichen Verfahrens, sondern auch die Vertraulichkeit als wichtiger und mittlerweile in der Rechtspraxis in Diskriminierungsfällen unverzichtbarer Bestandteil des *conciliation*-Verfahrens die vorgebrachten Einwände zu beseitigen. Denn ohne eine gewisse Vertraulichkeit würde sich bereits die Wahrscheinlichkeit einer gütlichen Einigung erheblich verringern, da eine große Anzahl von Verfahrensbeteiligten in einem privaten Rahmen eher gewillt sind, ihre hinter den Rechtsansichten stehenden Interessen und Ziele in das Verfahren einzubinden und dem Gegner gegenüber preiszugeben.[550] Im Übrigen bemüht sich die Human Rights and Equal Opportunity Commission zur Gewährleistung einer umfassenden Transparenz des Verfahrens. So können nicht nur die Beteiligten des *conciliation*-Verfahrens, sondern auch nichtbeteiligte Dritte sowie die Öffentlichkeit Ergebnisse vergleichbarer Fälle sowie von Präjudizentscheidungen zur Kenntnis nehmen, indem sie von der Human Rights and Equal Opportunity Commission informiert werden. Dies geschieht gegenüber den Verfahrensbeteiligten automatisch während des Verfahrens, bei nichtbeteiligten Dritten auf Nachfrage und bei der Öffentlichkeit durch Herausgabe von Jahresberichten, in denen in der Regel typische Diskriminierungsfälle sowie konkrete Fallbeispiele und erzielte Einigungen eines jeden Kalenderjahres veröffentlicht werden.[551]

Nicht zuletzt kommt der Human Rights and Equal Opportunity Commission die Befugnis zu, die Annahme von Diskriminierungsverfahren, die für die Fortentwicklung der Rechtsprechung besonders geeignet erscheinen oder die aufgrund ihrer besonderen Bedeutung für die Öffentlichkeit den vertraulichen privaten Verfahrensablauf ausschließen, zu verweigern und derartige Fälle ausdrücklich zur Durchführung eines Prozesses an das Gericht zu verweisen.[552]

Chapmann, Sexuality and Workplace Oppression (1995) 20, Melbourne University Law Review, 311.

549 *Landau*, Conciliation as a mode of settlement of discrimination complaints (1988) 11, Adelaide Law Review, 258; *Bailey*, Human Rights – Australia in an International Context, 1990, 217.

550 *Thornton*, Equivocations of Conciliation: The Resolution of Discrimination Complaints in Australia (1999) 52, The Modern Law Review, 733.

551 Vgl. zuletzt Human Rights and Equal Opportunity Commission, Annual Report 2007 – 2008; im Internet abrufbar unter http://www.humanrights.gov.au/about/publications/annual_reports/2007_2008/AR_2007_2008_complete.pdf; die Tätigkeitsberichte aus den Vorjahren sind abrufbar unter http://www.hreoc.gov.au/about/publications/annual_reports/index.html.

(2) Ungleichgewicht zwischen der Stellung der Verfahrensbeteiligten

Grundsätzlich können Indizien für ein Ungleichgewicht zwischen den Parteien in einer unterschiedlichen Bildung, in einem voneinander abweichenden beruflichen Status, Reichtum oder auch in einer bestimmten Stellung in der Gesellschaft wurzeln. Ob jedoch der generelle Einwand gegen die Verhandlungslösung aufgrund eines fehlenden Gleichgewichts zwischen den Verfahrensbeteiligten begründet ist, erscheint fraglich.[553]

Dafür spricht, dass einerseits eine (Alters-)Diskriminierung im Beschäftigungs- und Arbeitsverhältnis in der Regel dann geschieht, wenn sich die Beteiligten nicht auf Augenhöhe begegnen können und deshalb signifikante Unterschiede zwischen ihnen bestehen. So wird eine starke Partei allein aufgrund ihrer Position ernster genommen und respektvoller behandelt sowie nicht etwa wegen sachfremder Merkmale oder anderweitiger Umstände diskriminiert.[554] Dieses Machtungleichgewicht wird jedoch nicht automatisch mit Betreiben eines Schlichtungsverfahrens und der Durchführung eines Vermittlungsgespräches beendet und ausgeglichen werden können.

Jedoch ist zu bedenken, dass ein Ungleichgewicht keine charakteristische Ausformung des Verfahrens vor der Human Rights and Equal Opportunity Commission darstellt und genauso auch im Gerichtsverfahren vorzufinden sein kann.[555] Folglich kann eine möglicherweise ungleich starke Stellung der Beteiligten im *conciliation*-Verfahren nicht per se als Einwand gegen die Verhandlungslösung gewertet werden. Hinzu kommt, dass der Streitschlichter („*conciliator*") gegenüber dem passiven Richter im Gerichtsprozess sogar die Möglichkeit zusteht, das *conciliation*-Verfahren bei sich aus dem Machtungleichgewicht ergebenden Benachteiligungen als gescheitert zu erklären und somit die Gefahr eines Rechtsstreits zu verstärken.

(3) Entzug des verfassungsmäßigen Rechts auf ein faires Gerichtsverfahren

Weiterhin mehren sich die Stimmen, die an der verfassungsrechtlichen Qualität des Verfahrens vor der Human Rights and Equal Opportunity Commission Zweifel hegen. Denn es bestünde die Gefahr, dass eine „*second class justice*" gezüchtet wird, die zu einer Verkürzung des verfassungsmäßig garantierten Rechts der Diskriminierungsopfer auf ein faires Gerichtsverfahren führen könnte.[556] Zwar würde versucht werden,

---

552 Response by the HREOC to the National Alternative Dispute Resolution Advisory Council's, "Issues of fairness and justice in ADR", Discussion Paper (1997) 55.

553 *Thornton*, Equivocation of Conciliation: The Resolution of Discrimination Complaints in Australia (1989) 52, The Modern Law Review, 733; *Bailey*, Human Rights – Australia in an International Context, 1990, 215; *Alexander*, Family Mediation under the Microscope (1999) 10, Australasian Dispute Resolution Journal, 18.

554 *Scutt*, The Privatisation of Justice, in: Mugford, Alternative Dispute Resolution, Australian Institute of Criminology, 1985, 185.

555 *Resnik*, Failing Faith: Adjudicatory Procedure in Decline (1986) 53, The University of Chicago Law Review, 494; *Scholz*, Lohngleichheit durch Verfahren, 2000, 20.

556 *Garth*, The Movement toward Procedural Informalism in North American and Western Europe: A Critical Survey, in: Richard L. Abel, The Politics of Informal Justice, 1982, 184; *Fiss*, Against Settlement (1984) 93, The Yale Law Yournal, 1073; *Christian*, Community Dispute Resolution: First Class-Process or Second-Class Justice? (1986) 14, NYU Review of Law &

eine schnellere und weniger kostenintensivere Lösung des betreffenden Diskriminierungsfalles herbeizuführen, aber zugleich würde der erleichterte Zugang zu einem außergerichtlichen Schlichtungsverfahren dazu führen, nicht vor einem juristisch gebildeten Richter unter den Regeln des Prozessrechts verhandeln und somit sein subjektives Recht auf rechtliches Gehör nicht in hinreichendem Maße zur Geltend bringen zu können.[557] Durch das keinen prozessualen Verfahrensregeln unterworfene *conciliation*-Verfahren würde es den Verfahrensbeteiligten zusätzlich verwehrt, Rechtsfehler durch eine übergeordnete Instanz kontrollieren zu lassen, so dass sich diese auch auf das Ergebnis der gütlichen Einigung negativ für das Diskriminierungsopfer auswirken könnten.[558]

Damit aber genau diese Befürchtungen nicht eintreten, ist der Vermittler (*„conciliator"*) im *conciliation*-Verfahren verpflichtet, zur Sicherung prozessualer Fairness beizutragen und seine Ausgleichsfunktion besonders zu beachten.[559] Um darüber hinaus zu Ergebnissen finden zu können, die den tatsächlichen Bedürfnissen der Verfahrensbeteiligten am besten entsprechen, soll die Human Rights and Equal Opportunity Commission nach ihren prozessualen Richtlinien nicht die verstärkt ergebnisoffene Vermittlungstechnik der Mediation (*„mediation"*), sondern vielmehr das vorwiegend von gesetzlichen Bestimmungen geleitete *conciliation*-Verfahren einsetzen.[560] So unterscheiden sich das Mediationsverfahren und das *conciliation*-Verfahren vor allem wie folgt:

> „Mediation is a progress in which the parties to a dispute, with the assistance of a neutral third party, identify the disputed issues, develop options, consider alternatives and endeavour to reach an agreement. The mediator has no advisory or determinative role in regard to the content of the dispute or the outcome of its resolution, but may advise on or determine the process of mediation."[561]

Social Change, 771; *Thornton*, Equivocations of Conciliation: The Resolution of Discrimination Complaints in Australia (1989) 52, The Modern Law Review, 733.

557 *Scutt*, The Privatisation of Justice, in: Mugford, Alternative Dispute Resolution, Australian Institute of Criminology, 1986, 185.

558 *Kinley*, Human Rights in Australian Law, 1998, 303; *Alexander*, Family Mediation under the Microscope (1999) 10, Australasian Dispute Resolution Journal, 18.

559 *Ury/Brett*/Goldberg, Getting disputes resolved – designing systems to cut the cost of conflict, 1989, 3; Bailey/*Devereux*, The Operation in Antidiscrimination Laws in Australia, in: Kinley, Human Rights in Australian Law, 1998, 292.

560 *Nelson*, The use of conciliation in Australia to resolve complaints of discrimination made under federal and state legislation, in: Mugford, Alternative Dispute Resolution, Australian Institute of Criminology, 1986, 129. *Thornton*, Equivocations of Conciliation: The Resolution of Discrimination Complaints in Australia (1989) 52, The Modern Law Review, 733; zum Unterschied von *mediation* und *conciliation* vgl. insbesondere *Pentony*, Conciliation under the Racial Discrimination Act 1975, in: Human Rights Commission Occasional Paper No. 15 (1986), 10; *Bryson*, Mediator and Advocate: Conciliating Human Rights Complaints (1990) 1, Australian Dispute Resolution Journal, 136; *Alexander*, Wirtschaftsmediation in Theorie und Praxis, 1999, 20.

561 *Foenander*, Industrial Conciliation and Arbitration in Australia, 1959, 89; *Boland*, The Prospects for Mediation Having a Formal Role in Australia's Industrial Relations System, Alternative Dispute Resolution Bulletin, 1998, 219; *Creigthon/Stewart*, Australian Labour Law, 2005, 67; Definitionen des National Alternative Dispute Resolution Advisory Council unter http://law.gov.au/aghome/advisory/nadrac/adrdefinitions.html.

> "Conciliation is a progress in which the parties to a dispute, with the assistance of a neutral third party, identify the disputed issues, develop options, consider alternatives and endeavour to reach an agreement. The conciliator may have an advisory role on the content of the dispute or the outcome of its resolution, but not a determinative role. The conciliator may advise on or determine the process of conciliation whereby resolution is attempted, and may make suggestions for terms of settlement, give expert advice on likely settlement terms, and may actively encourage the participants to reach an agreement." [562]

Demnach kann das *conciliation*-Verfahren zusammengefasst als das Zusammentreffen von Parteien zur Diskussion von Konfliktfragen und zur gütlichen Klärung dieser unter Einbeziehung eines aktiv mitwirkenden, Vorschläge unterbreitenden, die Parteien beratenden und unterstützenden Dritten beschrieben werden.[563]

Die Definitionen verdeutlichen darüber hinaus die Rolle des Streitschlichters. Im *conciliation*-Verfahren kommt dem *„conciliator"* folglich eine überaus aktivere Rolle als dem *„mediator"* im Mediationsverfahren zu. Er hat demnach vor allem solche Einigungen zu verhindern, die aufgrund ihrer Gesetzes- oder Sittenwidrigkeit nichtig wären sowie aktiv darauf hinzuwirken, dass die einzelnen von den Diskriminierungsverboten verfolgten Normzwecke eingehalten und nicht verfehlt werden. Nicht zuletzt wird gerade auch durch die aktive Einflussnahme des *„conciliators"* in das Schlichtungsverfahren die verfahrensrechtliche Fairness in ausreichendem Maße gewährleistet, so dass ein Verstoß gegen das Recht auf ein faires Verfahren nicht automatisch näher liegt als im vom Prozessrecht geprägten Gerichtsverfahren. Allerdings reicht seine Mitwirkung nicht so weit, als dass ihm verbindliche Entscheidungsbefugnisse zustehen würden.[564]

Auch werden einer Kritik an der Qualität des Vermittlungsverfahrens und dem Einwand der Begründung einer *„second class justice"* dadurch der Boden entzogen, indem auf die besonders gute und beständige Ausbildung der *„conciliators"* innerhalb der Human Rights and Equal Opportunity Commission verwiesen wird.[565] So müssen die Mitarbeiter der Human Rights and Equal Opportunity Commission allein drei verschieden Kurse aus den zwei insgesamt bestehenden und sehr speziellen Aus- und Weiterbildungsprogrammen zur Beschwerdebearbeitung und Konfliktlösung belegen.[566] Ebenfalls ist im Laufe der durchgeführten Verfahren die Zufriedenheit der Beteiligten mit dem Verfahrensablauf sehr hoch, was sich nicht zuletzt mit der vor allem

562 *Foenander*, Industrial Conciliation and Arbitration in Australia, 1959, 89; *Boland*, The Prospects for Mediation Having a Formal Role in Australia's Industrial Relations System, Alternative Dispute Resolution Bulletin, 1998, 219; *Creigthon/Stewart*, Australian Labour Law, 2005, 67; Definitionen des National Alternative Dispute Resolution Advisory Council unter http://law.gov.au/aghome/advisory/nadrac/adrdefinitions.html.

563 *Wheelwright*, Butterworths Casebook Companions, Labour Law, 2002/2003, 164; vgl. auch die Entscheidung des High Court *Australian Railways Union v Victorian Railways Commissioners* (1930) 44 CLR 319 – *"... the coming together of the parties for the discussion of questions with a view to amicable settlement."*.

564 *Gunningham*, Industrial Law and the Constitution, 1988, 132

565 Human Rights and Equal Opportunity Commission, Annual Report 2005 – 2006, 54 und Annual Report 2006 – 2007, 53 sowie Annual Report 2007 – 2008, 47.

566 Human Rights and Equal Opportunity Commission, Annual Report 2005 – 2006, 54 und Annual Report 2006 – 2007, 53 sowie Annual Report 2007 – 2008, 45.

in Wirtschaftsangelegenheiten vermehrten Inanspruchnahme des *conciliation*-Verfahrens belegen lässt.[567]

(4) Die Human Rights and Equal Opportunity Commission als staatliche Behörde

Schwierigkeiten im *conciliation*-Verfahren könnten sich vor allem aber dadurch ergeben, dass die Human Rights and Equal Opportunity Commission eine als staatliche Behörde organisierte Einrichtung ist.[568] Denn die Einrichtung, Organisation und der Betrieb einer solchen Behörde hängt unmittelbar von der personellen Ausstattung und der Zuweisung ausreichender finanzieller Mittel ab, weshalb sich Mängel in einem dieser Bereiche schnell als Hindernis für eine effektive Rechtsverfolgung bei Diskriminierungsverboten auswirken könnten und der Einfluss der Politik auf die Effizienz der Arbeit der Human Rights and Equal Opportunity Commission nicht unerheblich sein dürfte.[569]

So müssen sich die Human Rights and Equal Opportunity Commission und vor allem ihre Mitarbeiter in der Öffentlichkeit präsentieren, um ausreichend über das Vorgehen gegen Diskriminierung zu informieren, die Auswirkungen ausstehender politischer und finanzpolitischer Entscheidungen auf ihre Arbeit zu verdeutlichen und nicht zuletzt ihre Arbeitskraft auch für begründete Gegenvorschläge einsetzen. Durch diesen internen aus der Organisation als Behörde resultierenden Konflikt muss Arbeitskraft und Geld aufgewendet werden, welches besser in die Arbeit gegen Diskriminierungen investiert werden sollte. Entscheidend aber ist, dass sich die Human Rights and Equal Opportunity Commission durch derartige öffentliche Aktionen nicht selten in Gegensatz zu den Entscheidungen der Regierung positioniert und sich damit gegen den Geldgeber stellt.

567 *Sordo*, The Lawyer's Role in Mediation (1996) 7, Australian Dispute Resolution Journal, 20; *Caroll/Mackie*, International Mediation – The Art of Business Diplomacy (2000), 27.

568 Vgl. die Übersicht zur Organisation der Human Rights and Equal Opportunity Commission in: Human Rights and Equal Opportunity Commission, Annual Report 2007 – 2008, XV:

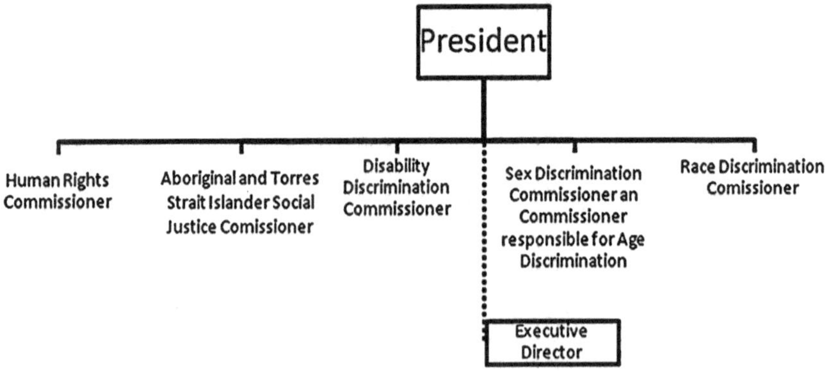

569 Vgl. zu den vergleichbaren Erfahrungen der US-amerikanischen Equal Employment Opportunity Commission: *Montoya*, Let's Mediate – a whole new ballgame at EEOC (1999) 24, Employee Relations Law Journal, 53; *Bailey*, Human Rights – Australia in an International Context, 1990, 222.

Aber nicht allein die Finanzierung – auch im Berichtszeitraum 2005 – 2006 lagen die Ausgaben der Human Rights and Equal Opportunity Commission über ihren Budgetzuweisungen – an sich stellt ein erhebliches Problem- und Konfliktpotential dar.[570] Allein die behördentechnische Strukturierung, welche die Human Rights and Equal Opportunity Commission den Maßstäben des Verwaltungshandelns unterstellt, beinhaltet gesondertes Konfliktpotential und damit wiederum eine Gefahr für die Effektivität der Arbeit. Denn so muss die Arbeit nach dem Prinzip der sparsamen Mittelverwendung erfolgen, so dass bei möglichst geringen Kosten versucht werden soll, möglichst hohe Erledigungszahlen vorweisen zu können.[571] Hinzukommt der für eine staatliche Behörde bekannte Personalmangel und ständige Abbau des Personals.[572]

Dazu im Widerspruch steht jedoch der Umstand, dass eine außergerichtliche Konfliktlösung und Einigung nicht automatisch einfacher ist als die Vorbereitung und Durchführung eines Gerichtsverfahrens und teilweise ein enormer Zeitdruck für die Mitarbeiter der Human Rights and Equal Opportunity Commission aufgebaut wird.[573] Um jedoch die hohen Anforderungen an die vorzuweisenden Erledigungszahlen erreichen zu können, scheint sich ein gewisser Anreiz zur Beeinflussung der Verfahrensbeteiligten in Richtung einer gütlichen Einigung zu ergeben. Auch erscheint ein gewisses Beeinflussungspotential in einem der Öffentlichkeit nicht zugänglichen Verfahren, in dem der *„conciliator"* nicht den strengen Regeln des Prozessrechts unterliegt, eröffnet.

Zwar sind dies lediglich grundsätzliche Überlegungen, die keinerlei Anspruch darauf erheben, dass sich die praktische Arbeit der Human Rights and Equal Opportunity Commission tatsächlich von Beeinflussungen ihrer Vermittler lenken lässt. Aber dennoch wird deutlich, dass die Übertragung der Aufgabe zur Durchführung des *conciliation*-Verfahrens auf eine staatliche Behörde nicht nur mit Vorteilen verbunden ist. Nicht vernachlässigt werden soll deshalb der Hinweis auf die mit einer solchen Organisation verbundenen Risiken, durch die eine effiziente Aufgabenwahrnehmung zur Beseitigung bestehender Diskriminierungen beeinträchtigt werden kann. Noch dazu ließe sich eine außergerichtliche Streitbeilegung auch durch innerbetriebliche Vermittlungsorgane oder durch eine vom Gericht zu bestimmende private Vermittlungspersonen bestimmt auch in effektiver Weise erreichen, ohne das die zuvor dargestellten Verwaltungsprobleme zur Geltung gelangen könnten. Für eine außergerichtliche Eini-

---

570 Vgl. zur Budgetausstattung der Human Rights and Equal Opportunity Commission im Berichtszeitraum 2005 – 2006 die Übersicht in: Human Rights and Equal Opportunity Commission, Annual Report 2005 – 2006, 22; für den Berichtszeitraum 2006 – 2007 die Übersicht im Annual Report 2006 – 2007, 22; für den Berichtszeitraum 2007 – 2008 die Übersicht im Annual Report 2007 – 2008, 12.

571 *Hofrichter*, Neighbourhood Justice and the Social Control Problems of American Capitalism, in: Abel: The Politics of Informal Justice, Vol. 1, 1982, 241; *Thorton*, Equivocations of Conciliation: The Resolution of Discrimination Complaints in Australia (1989) 52, The Modern Law Review, 733.

572 Vgl. zur rückläufigen Entwicklung der Personalzahlen die Übersicht in: Human Rights and Equal Opportunity Commission, Annual Report 2005 – 2006, 22 ;Annual Report 2006 – 2007, 22; Annual Report 2007 – 2008, 12.

573 *Bailey*, Human Rights – Australia in an International Context, 1990, 218.

gung ist die Errichtung einer staatlichen Behörde jedenfalls keine zwingende Voraussetzung.

c. Ergebnis zur Frage der Effektivität der Durchführung eines Gerichtsprozesses zur Herstellung von Chancengleichheit und eigene Stellungnahme

Zwar bestehen im Ergebnis zahlreiche Bedenken gegen die und diverse Risiken bei der Durchführung eines gerichtlichen Prozesses zur Wiedergutmachung einer erlittenen Altersdiskriminierung. Gleiches gilt jedoch grundsätzlich auch für das Schlichtungsverfahren vor der Human Rights and Equal Opportunity Commission, dessen größtes Manko sicherlich die fehlende Befugnis der Human Rights and Equal Opportunity Commission zur Durchsetzung der getroffenen Vereinbarungen ist. Mindestens genauso schwer wiegen auch die Bedenken verursachenden Umstände, dass das *conciliation*-Verfahren als obligatorisches Verfahren vor die Eröffnung des Rechtsweges gegen Diskriminierungen tritt und vor einer staatlichen Behörde mit der daraus resultierenden Abhängigkeit von staatlicher Finanzierung und politischem Einfluss durchgeführt wird.

Aber gerade aufgrund der mit dem Schlichtungsverfahren verbundenen zahlreichen Vorteile, ist in Verbindung mit der sich anschließenden gerichtlichen Durchsetzung eine effektive Möglichkeit zur Rechtsverfolgung geschaffen worden. So führt die Vertraulichkeit des Verfahrens vor der Human Rights and Equal Opportunity Commission zur Sicherstellung, dass sämtliche Interessen der Verfahrensbeteiligten berücksichtigt werden können, ohne aufgrund prozesstaktischer Überlegungen auf die Darstellung einzelner Gesichtspunkte verzichten zu müssen. Weiterhin bietet der kooperative Verfahrensstil einen nicht unerheblichen psychologischen Vorteil gegenüber dem antagonistisch geführten Prozess und trägt vermehrt dazu bei, dass die Beteiligten von der Wahrnehmung abrücken, als Gewinner dastehen zu wollen, sondern dass sie sich vielmehr gemeinsam der Konfliktlösung annehmen und somit bereits frühzeitig die Durchsetzung der getroffenen Vereinbarung sichern. Die aktive Verfahrensleitung durch einen neutralen Dritten und die Flexibilität des Schlichtungsverfahrens können den Bedürfnissen der Beteiligten im konkreten Einzelfall darüber hinaus eine flexible Lösung ermöglichen, ohne an gesetzlich vorgeschriebene Entschädigungs- und Konfliktlösungsmuster gebunden zu sein.

So hat es der australische Gesetzgeber durch das Zusammenspiel des vorprozessualen Schlichtungsverfahrens und des sich anschließenden Gerichtsprozesses geschafft, eine unter mehreren Gesichtspunkten effektive Konfliktlösungsmöglichkeit für das arbeitsrechtliche Antidiskriminierungsrecht zu schaffen, die als Vorbild auch für andere Rechtsbereiche stehen kann.

6. Der Ablauf des conciliaton-Verfahrens vor der Human Rights and Equal Opportunity Commission

a. Allgemeiner Überblick

Das Verfahren vor der Human Rights and Equal Opportunity Commission konzentriert sich auf das *conciliation*-Verfahren, das sich übersichtsartig wie folgt gliedert:[574]

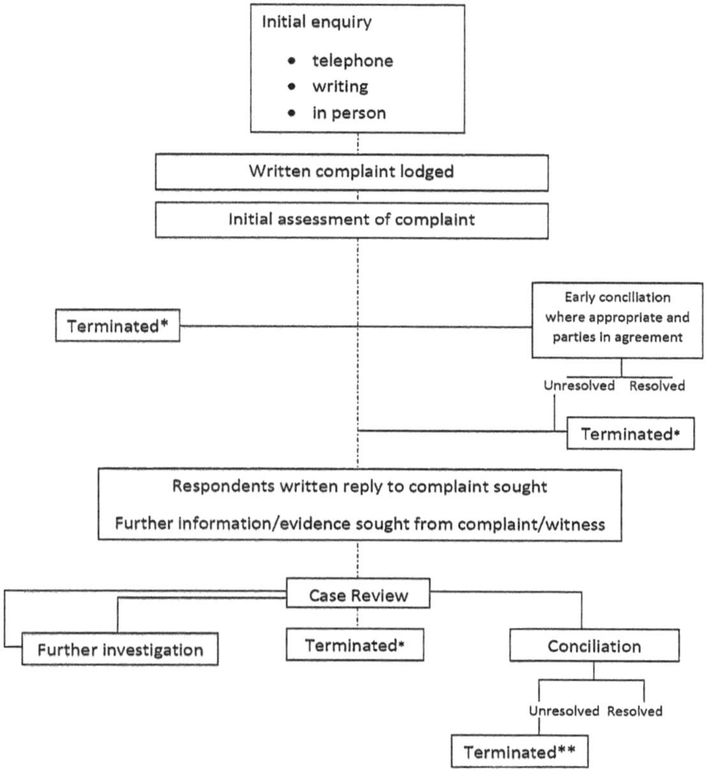

* When complaints under the Age, Racial, Sex and Disability Discrimination Acts are terminated, the complainant may apply to have the allegations heard and determined by the Federal Court of Australia or the Federal Magistrates Court.

** Complaints under the Human Rights and Equal Opportunity Commission Act concerning discrimination in employment or a breach of human rights, which cannot be conciliated, cannot be taken court. If the President is satisfied that the subject matter of the compliant constitutes discrimination or a breach of human rights these findings are reported to the Attorney-General for tabling in Parliament.

574 *Bailey*, Human Rights – Australia in an International Context, 1990, 214; *Bryson*, Mediator and Advocate: Conciliating Human Rights Complaints (1990) 1, Australian Dispute Resolution Journal, 136; Human Rights and Equal Opportunity Commission, Annual Report 2007 – 2008, Appendix 4, 165.

Tätig werden der Präsident der Human Rights and Equal Opportunity Commission sowie deren Mitarbeiter, genauer die *Investigation/Conciliation Officers* der *Complaint Handling Section (CHS).*[575]

b. Die Einleitung des *conciliation*-Verfahrens durch Einreichen einer schriftlichen Beschwerde

aa. Die Schriftform

Ausdrückliche Voraussetzung für die Einleitung des *conciliation*-Verfahrens vor der Human Rights and Equal Opportunity Commission ist das Einreichen einer schriftlichen Beschwerde im Sinne von § 46P Abs. 1 HREOC Act.[576]

Zwar können sich vermeintliche Diskriminierungsopfer auch telefonisch oder persönlich an die Human Rights and Equal Opportunity Commission wenden. Allerdings ist die Human Rights and Equal Opportunity Commission verpflichtet, derartiges Vorbringen zurückzuweisen und auf die schriftliche Beschwerde hinzuwirken. Gleichzeitig trifft sie die Verpflichtung, von sich aus darauf hinzuweisen, dass gemäß § 46P Abs. 4 HREOC Act eine Unterstützung bei der Abfassung der Beschwerde möglich ist. Folglich darf auch nur eine solche Unterstützung und nicht zugleich eine rechtliche Beratung vorgenommen werden.

Zweck der Schriftform ist es, sicherzustellen, dass die betroffene Person für ihr Vorbringen einsteht und für die Human Rights and Equal Opportunity Commission somit hinreichend identifizierbar ist.

bb. Der Beschwerdeführer

Beschwerdeführer kann gemäß § 46P Abs. 2 lit. a) HREOC Act entweder die von einer Diskriminierung betroffene Person selbst sein. Jedoch ist es nicht zwingend vorgeschrieben, dass das Verfahren von jeder betroffenen Person selbst eingeleitet wird. Denn sind mehrere, aber mindestens zwei Personen von demselben, einem Diskriminierungsverbot unterliegendem, Verhalten eines Dritten betroffen, dann können sie außer im eigenen Namen aufzutreten, zugleich auch die Verletzung von subjektiven Rechten der anderen Person bzw. Personen geltend machen, § 46P Abs. 2 lit. b) HREOC Act. Ebenso ist es aber auch zulässig durch einen bestimmten Repräsentanten eine Gruppenbeschwerde zu erheben, so dass auch Gewerkschaften das *conciliation*-Verfahren einleiten können, § 46 P Abs. 2 lit. c) HREOC Act (*„representative complaints“*). Hierzu ist es nicht erforderlich, dass der Repräsentant alle *„class members“* benennt oder zu erkennen gibt, wie viele Personen tatsächlich in das Verfahren involviert sind.[577] Ebenso sind nach Abschluss des Verfahrens vor der Human Rights and Equal Opportunity Commission nicht alle *„class members“* zur Beteiligung am

---

575 Human Rights and Equal Opportunity Commission, Annual Report 2007 – 2008, 43.

576 *Ronalds*, Discrimination – Law and Practice, 2004, 162; vgl. das aktuelle Beschwerdeformular der Human Rights and Equal Opportunity Commission am Ende der Arbeit in K. Anhang – auch abrufbar unter http://www.hreoc.gov.au/complaints_information/index.html.

577 Human Rights and Equal Opportunity Commission, Federal Discrimination Law 2005, 225.

gerichtlichen Verfahren vor dem Federal Magistrates Court oder Federal Court verpflichtet.[578]

cc. Die Beschwerdebefugnis

Als Voraussetzung zur Einleitung des *conciliation*-Verfahren genügt jedoch das Einreichen einer schriftlichen Beschwerde allein nicht. Vielmehr muss der Beschwerdeführer die Befugnis zur Beschwerde haben und in eigenen subjektiven Rechten betroffen sein. Er muss eine solche Rechtsverletzung zumindest behaupten können und demnach ist es Voraussetzung der Beschwerdebefugnis, dass dem Beschwerdeführer an dem Ausgang des *conciliation*-Verfahrens ein materielles Eigeninteresse zukommt.[579]

Zwar würde die Darlegung eines solchen Eigeninteresses eine nicht unerhebliche rechtliche Argumentation erfordern. Damit jedoch der Normzweck durch zu strenge Rechtsverfolgungsvoraussetzungen nicht unterlaufen wird, sind die praktischen Anforderungen nicht sehr hoch angesetzt.[580] Aus diesem Grund bedarf es der bloßen Behauptung des Vorliegens eines rechtswidrigen diskriminierenden Verhaltens eines Dritten und einer dadurch hervorgerufenen Rechtsverletzung, um die Beschwerdebefugnis in ausreichendem Umfang nachzuweisen. In der Verfahrenspraxis hat sich eine recht großzügige Prüfung der Beschwerdebefugnis durch die Human Rights and Equal Opportunity Commission herausgebildet und eine Beschwerde wird nur sehr selten aufgrund fehlender Beschwerdebefugnis verworfen. Dies geschieht aber vor allem dann, wenn das diskriminierende Verhalten nicht eindeutig in den Geltungsbereich eines Gesetzes fällt, für dessen Durchsetzung die Human Rights and Equal Opportunity Commission zuständig ist.[581]

Der eine Gruppe von Beschwerdeführern nach § 46P Abs. 2 lit. c) HREOC Act Repräsentierende braucht dagegen aber selbst nicht die Verletzung eigener Rechte geltend zu machen. In einem solchen Fall kommt es ebenfalls auf die Beschwerdebefugnis der eigentlichen Beschwerdeführer und nicht auf die des Repräsentanten an.

dd. Die Registrierung der Beschwerde

Die schriftlich eingereichten Beschwerden, die die Hürde der Beschwerdebefugnis erfolgreich übersprungen haben, werden von der Human Rights and Equal Opportunity Commission sodann registriert.[582] Zusätzlich werden zur internen Verwendung Vorschläge zur weiteren Behandlung hinzugefügt, so dass in jedem Stadium des Verfahrens ein anderer Mitarbeiter der Human Rights and Equal Opportunity Commission zur Übernahme der Bearbeitung ohne nennenswerte Schwierigkeiten in der Lage wäre.

---

578 *Jones v Scully* [2001] FCA 879.

579 *Bailey/Devereux*, The Operation of Antidiscrimination Laws in Australia, in: Kinley, Human Rights in Australian Law, 1998, 301.

580 *Ronalds*, Discrimination – Law and Practice, 2004, 165.

581 *Bailey/Devereux*, The Operation of Antidiscrimination Laws in Australia, in: Kinley, Human Rights in Australian Law, 1998, 302.

582 *Eastman*, Procedures, in: Baker & McKenzie, Age Discrimination: Mitigating Risk in the Workplace, S. 94.

ee. Die Versendung eines Standardfragebogens

Im Anschluss an die Registrierung der eingegangenen Beschwerde wird ein nach einem Standardverfahren erstellter Fragebogen an den Beschwerdeführer versandt, um die für den vorliegenden Einzelfall relevanten Informationen so genau wie möglich erhalten zu können.

c. Die frühzeitige Verwerfung der Beschwerde

Bevor in das Verfahrensstadium der Tatsachenfeststellung und –untersuchung eingetreten wird, besteht bereits die grundsätzliche Möglichkeit, die Beschwerde aus den in § 46PH Abs. 1 HREOC Act zahlreich aufgeführten Gründen zu verwerfen.[583]

aa. Die frühzeitige Verwerfung wegen fehlender Rechtswidrigkeit

Das wird vor allem dann der Fall sein, wenn der Präsident der Human Rights and Equal Opportunity Commission – ihm allein ist die Verwerfung vorbehalten – zu der Auffassung gelangt, dass das behauptete Verhalten keinen diskriminierenden Charakter hat und somit nicht gegen ein Diskriminierungsverbot verstößt, § 46PH Abs. 1 lit. a) HREOC Act. Nach Ansicht der Rechtsprechung liegt die Voraussetzung für eine frühzeitige Verwerfung aufgrund von § 46PH Abs. 1 lit. a) HREOC Act erst dann vor, wenn sie auf der Grundlage des vorhandenen Beweismaterials für jeden vernünftigen Menschen ohne weiteres einsichtig erscheint.[584] Im Ergebnis bedarf es also eines rechtlich eindeutigen Falles, um zu einer Verwerfung nach § 46PH Abs. 1 lit. a) HREOC Act kommen zu können.

bb. Die frühzeitige Verwerfung wegen Zeitablaufs

Ebenfalls kann die bereits erhobene Beschwerde dann frühzeitig verworfen werden, wenn zwischen der Erhebung der Beschwerde und der beanstandeten Diskriminierungshandlung ein Zeitraum von mehr als zwölf Monaten verstrichen ist, § 46PH Abs. 1 lit. b) HREOC Act. Allerdings handelt es sich hierbei nicht um einen zwingenden Verwerfungsgrund. Vielmehr kommt der Human Rights and Equal Opportunity Commission ein Entscheidungsermessen zu, wonach die Gründe für die zeitliche Verzögerung sowie die Erfolgsaussicht der Beschwerde in angemessenem Umfang zu bewerten sind. Anhand dieser Ermessenseinschätzung und -abwägung beurteilt sich die Zulässigkeit, von der Möglichkeit der frühzeitigen Verwerfung wegen Zeitablaufs Gebrauch zu machen.

cc. Die frühzeitige Verwerfung mangels hinreichend substantiierter Beschwerde

Weiter ist der Präsident der Human Rights and Equal Opportunity Conmission zur frühzeitigen Verwerfung der erhobenen Beschwerde berechtigt, wenn er zu der Überzeugung gelangen sollte, dass das durch die Beschwerde angegriffene Verhalten be-

---

583 *Ronalds*, Discrimination – Law and Practice, 2004, 173; *Eastman*, Procedures, in: Baker & McKenzie, Age Discrimination: Mitigating Risk in the Workplace, S. 95.

584 *Briginshaw v Briginshaw* (1938) 60, Commonwealth Law Review, 336.

langlos ist und die Beschwerde somit leichtfertig erhoben wurde, sie schikanös ist, auf einem Missverständnis beruht oder sich als völlig unsubstantiiert darstellt, § 46PH Abs. 1 lit. c) HREOC Act. Entgegen des praktisch weiten Verständnisses, das bei der Prüfung der Beschwerdebefugnis überwiegt, macht die Human Rights and Equal Opportunity Commission vom vorgenannten Verwerfungsgrund nur sehr zurückhaltend Gebrauch. Denn es ist ihr erklärtes Ziel, die sich typischerweise nur zwischen den Beteiligten vorfallenden und somit der Öffentlichkeit in der Regel nicht erkennbaren Diskriminierungen bestmöglich aufzuklären, anstatt die für den Beschwerdeführer wichtige Beschwerde voreilig mangels tatsächlicher Erkennbarkeit der sie begründenden Anhaltspunkte als unsubstantiiert zu verwerfen.

dd. Die frühzeitige Verwerfung mangels ausreichender Geeignetheit des conciliation-Verfahrens

Des weiteren kann die Verfügbarkeit besser geeigneter oder schnelleren und größeren Erfolg versprechenderer Rechtsmittel auf der Grundlage eines anderen, außerhalb des Zuständigkeitsbereichs der Human Rights and Equal Opportunity Commission liegenden, Gesetzes als des Human Rights and Equal Opportunity Commission Act 1986 (Cth) einen Grund für eine frühzeitige Verwerfung der Beschwerde darstellen, § 46PH Abs. 1 lit. d) bis g) HREOC. Unabhängig davon, ob die Beschwerde verworfen wird, ist die Human Rights and Equal Opportunity Commission verpflichtet, den Beschwerdeführer auf das für ihn günstigere Verfahren ausdrücklich hinzuweisen.

ee. Die frühzeitige Verwerfung wegen besonderem öffentlichen Interesse

Darüber hinaus kann der Präsident der Human Rights and Equal Opportunity Commission die Beschwerde frühzeitig verwerfen, wenn er der betreffenden Angelegenheit ein derart hohes öffentliches Interesse beimisst, dass er der Auffassung ist, dass sich besser der Federal Court bzw. der Federal Magistrates Court dem Verfahren annehmen und zu einer Entscheidung finden sollte, § 46PH Abs. 1 lit. h) HREOC Act.

ff. Die frühzeitige Verwerfung mangels hinreichender Aussicht auf eine gütliche Einigung

Letztlich kann auch das Fehlen einer hinreichenden Aussicht auf eine im *conciliation*-Verfahren zu findende gütliche Einigung den Präsidenten der Human Rights and Equal Opportunity Commission dazu berechtigen die Beschwerde ebenfalls frühzeitig zu verwerfen, § 46PH Abs. 1 lit. i) HREOC Act. Ebenfalls – wie bei einer frühzeitigen Verwerfung der Beschwerde im Sinne von § 46PH Abs. 1 lit. c) HREOC Act – sollte die Human Rights and Equal Opportunity Commission sehr sorgfältig prüfen, ob das *conciliation*-Verfahren nicht tatsächlich zu einer gütlichen Einigung zwischen dem Beschwerdeführer und dem Beschwerdegegner führen kann. Denn nur so kann – unabhängig von der prozessualen Einordnung des *conciliation*-Verfahrens – in ausreichendem Maß der Rechtsschutz für den Beschwerdeführer gesichert werden.

gg. *Rechtsschutz gegen die frühzeitige Verwerfung der Beschwerde*

Dem Beschwerdeführer ist nach einer frühzeitigen Verwerfung seiner Beschwerde die schriftliche und mit Gründen versehene Verwerfungsentscheidung zuzustellen, § 46PH Abs. 2 HREOC Act. Dieser kann dann binnen 28 Tagen nach Zustellung der Verwerfungsentscheidung einen Antrag auf gerichtliche Überprüfung dieser Entscheidung beim Federal Court oder beim Federal Magistrates Court stellen, § 46PO Abs. 1 und Abs. 2 HREOC Act, und somit die Verfahrensdauer unter Umständen verkürzen, da das Gericht die Rechtsfrage selbst entscheiden wird, ohne wieder an die Human Rights and Equal Opportunity Commission zurückzuverweisen. Folglich ist der Präsident der Human Rights and Equal Opportunity Commission auch nur bis zur Einlegung des Rechtsmittels zur Aufhebung seiner Verwerfungsentscheidung befugt, § 46PH Abs. 4 HREOC Act.

d. Die Ermittlung und Untersuchung der verfahrensrelevanten Tatsa chen

aa. *Die Tatsachenermittlung*

(1) Einzelfallorientierte Ermittlung

Nach der erfolgreichen Einleitung des *conciliation*-Verfahrens durch Einreichen der Beschwerde müssen, bevor überhaupt versucht werden kann, eine einvernehmliche Lösung des Diskriminierungsfalles herbeizuführen, die verfahrensrelevanten Tatsachen ermittelt werden. Um eine einheitliche Vorgehensweise bei der Tatsachenermittlung gewährleisten zu können, hat die Human Rights and Equal Opportunity Commission in ihrem Arbeitshandbuch die einzelnen Arbeitsschritte aufgezeigt. Dabei stellt sie aber zugleich ausdrücklich klar, dass wegen des Fehlens einer gesetzlichen Regelung der mit der jeweiligen Beschwerde befasste Mitarbeiter sich vorwiegend an den konkreten Umständen des Einzelfalls orientieren solle und wenn nötig vom vorgezeichneten Arbeitsablauf abweichen solle, um eine möglichst sachgerechte Bearbeitung gewährleisten zu können.[585]

(2) Tatsachenbeibringung durch den Beschwerdeführer

Zwar kommt der Human Rights and Equal Opportunity Commission gemäß § 46PI Abs. 1 HREOC die weitreichende Befugnis zu, die fallrelevanten Informationen bei jeder für sie in Betracht kommenden Person mittels eines förmlichen Bescheids im Sinne von § 46PI Abs. 2 HREOC („*notice to produce*“) etwa durch Vorlage von Dokumenten einzuholen.[586]

---

585 *Thornton*, Equivocations of Conciliation: The Resolution of Discrimination Complaints in Australia (1989) 52, The Modern Law Review, 733; *Bryson*, Mediator and Advocate: Conciliating Human Rights Complaints (1990) 1, Australian Dispute Resolution Journal, 136; *Charlton/Dewdney*, The Mediator's Handbook: Skills and Strategies for Practicioners, 2004, 7.

In der Regel wird die Human Rights and Equal Opportunity Commission aber gesteigerten Wert auf eine möglichst umfassende Tatsachenbeibringung durch den Beschwerdeführer sowie zugleich auf die Vorlage der möglichen Beweismittel legen. Durch diese Vorgehensweise wird an den Beschwerdegegner erst dann herangetreten, wenn hinreichende Klarheit über das diskriminierende Verhalten gegeben ist, die ersten Beweise dafür vorliegen und somit die Gefahr, ein förmliches Verfahren nur aufgrund von Behauptungen zu eröffnen, nahezu ausgeräumt wird.

(3) Informelle Kontaktaufnahme und Gespräche

Aufgrund der nicht gesetzlich geregelten und nur internen Vorgaben ist in Diskriminierungsfällen, in denen die Beurteilung des bereits vorliegenden Tatsachenmaterials zu eindeutigen Ergebnissen führt, aber auch eine Kontaktaufnahme zum Beschwerdegegner in informeller Art möglich, um so zu einer raschen und abschließenden Klärung des jeweiligen Sachverhalts zu gelangen.[587] Gleichfalls kann die Herstellung derartiger Kontakte zum Beschwerdegegner dazu dienen, eine zeitnahe Einigungsmöglichkeit zu eröffnen und den sich normalerweise an die Tatsachenermittlung anschließenden Arbeitsschritt der Untersuchung der Tatsachengrundlagen auszulassen. Solche Abläufe sind praktisch vor allem dann denkbar, wenn das angestrebte Ziel des Verfahrens für den Beschwerdeführer nur von untergeordnetem wirtschaftlichen Wert ist, die Diskriminierung auf einem Missverständnis beruht oder ganz allgemein die Tatsachen nicht bestritten werden.[588] Besteht in diesem Stadium zur Überzeugung der Human Rights and Equal Opportunity Commission schon die Ansicht, dass die Verfahrensbeteiligten die wesentlichen Fragen bereits geklärt haben und zu einer Einigung bereit sind, dann kann die Human Rights and Equal Opportunity ihre Unterstützung bei einem informellen Gespräch anbieten. Kommt ein solches Gespräch zwischen den Parteien aber nicht zustande, dann gilt es den förmlichen Verfahrensablauf fortzusetzen.

bb. Die Tatsachenuntersuchung

Im Rahmen der anschließenden Tatsachenuntersuchung eröffnen sich für die weitere Verfahrensweise zwei alternative Fortsetzungsmöglichkeiten. Entweder gelingt es bereits in diesem frühzeitigen Stadium – infolge der informellen Gespräche – einen Erfolg versprechenden Einigungsversuch herbeizuführen oder aber es zeigt sich, dass die Beschwerde nicht hinreichend substantiiert eingelegt wurde und es somit gilt, die Tatsachenuntersuchung abzubrechen. Bestehen jedoch weiterhin Zweifel – egal in welche Richtung –, dann bedarf es einer dritten Lösungsmöglichkeit, bei welcher der Beschwerdegegner informiert und um die Abgabe einer Stellungnahme gebeten wird.[589] Dazu müssen ihm alle bereits vorliegenden Beweise einschließlich einer Kopie der Beschwerde übersandt werden.

---

586 Die Nichtbefolgung dieser rechtsstaatlichen Auskunftspflicht führt zu strafrechtlichen Konsequenzen, vgl. §§ 46PM und 46PN HREOC.

587 *Ronalds*, Discrimination – Law and Practice, 2004, 162.

588 *Thornton*, Equivocations of Conciliation: The Resolution of Discrimination Complaints in Australia (1989) 52, The Modern Law Review, 733.

589 *Ronalds*, Discrimination – Law and Practice, 2004, 162.

Dem Beschwerdegegner steht für seine Stellungnahme im Grundsatz eine Argumentation der formellen Art oder auf der inhaltlichen Verfahrensstufe zu. Er kann folglich einwenden, dass z.B. eine Untersuchung nicht hätte stattfinden dürfen, weil die Beschwerde aus formellen Gründen bereits zu verwerfen gewesen wäre. Über einen solchen Einwand gegen die Rechtmäßigkeit des Verfahrens muss die Human Rights and Equal Opportunity Commission vorab entscheiden. Dabei gilt es zu verdeutlichen, dass und mit welchem Ergebnis das Ermessen, über die Verwerfung der Beschwerde zu entscheiden, ordnungsgemäß ausgeübt worden ist. Ebenso kann der Beschwerdegegner aber auch inhaltlich Stellung beziehen und das behauptete Diskriminierungsverhalten bestreiten oder sogar inhaltliche Gegenvorstellungen vornehmen. Die Human Rights and Equal Opportunity Commission ist dabei im konkreten Einzelfall befugt, präzise Nachfragen an den Beschwerdegegner zu stellen und auf die gesetzliche Möglichkeit der zwangsweisen Informationsbeschaffung im Sinne von § 46PM HREOC hinzuweisen.

Bei der Tatsachenuntersuchung und Beurteilung ist die Human Rights and Equal Opportunity Commission nicht an Beweisregeln gebunden, sondern kann den Sachverhalt durch Beiziehung aller ihrer Meinung nach geeigneten Beweismittel versuchen aufzuklären.[590] Zwar muss der Beschwerdeführer das Vorliegen einer Benachteiligung beweisen, aber für einen solchen Beweis soll innerhalb des nur wenig technischen *conciliation*-Verfahrens das Beweismaß der überwiegenden Wahrscheinlichkeit genügen.[591]

e. Die Vermittlungsverhandlung und die Einigung

Zwar besteht die wesentliche Aufgabe der Human Rights and Equal Opportunity Commission darin, Diskriminierungsfälle außergerichtlich einer Einigung zuzuführen. Ein Einigungsversuch soll aber dennoch nur dann vorgenommen werden, wenn der jeweilige Sachverhalt nach Einschätzung der Human Rights and Equal Opportunity Commission dafür geeignet erscheint.[592] Alle anderen Fälle sind zu von der Human Rights and Equal Opportunity Commission zu verwerfen, so dass dann nur noch eine gerichtliche Lösungsmöglichkeit verbleibt, § 46PH Abs. 1 HREOC.

aa. Die Rolle des conciliators im Verfahren und die damit zusammenhängenden Verfahrensgrundsätze

Zum Verständnis des konkreten Verfahrensablaufs und der Beurteilung der Erfolgsaussichten für eine Einigung ist es unablässlich die Rolle des *„conciliators"* sowie die einzelnen Verfahrensgrundsätze zu betrachten. Denn das *conciliation*-Verfahren ist gerade kein förmliches Verfahren und unterliegt folglich nicht der Bindung an das Prozessrecht. Allerdings sollen und müssen dennoch die Rechte der Verfahrensbeteiligten geschützt werden. Gleichfalls gilt es, eine zeit- und kostenintensive

590 *O'Neill/Handley*, Retreat from Injustice, Human Rights in Australian Law, 1994, 344.

591 *O'Neill/Handley*, Retreat from Injustice, Human Rights in Australian Law, 1994, 344; *Campbell v. FH Productions* (1984) EOC 92 - 104.

592 *Hunter*, Indirect Discrimination in the Workplace, 1992, 260.

Durchführung eines Rechtsstreits zur Konfliktlösung zu vermeiden und den Diskriminierungsfall vorgerichtlich zu lösen.

(1) Die Rolle des conciliators

Der *„conciliator"* ist für die Herbeiführung einer umfassenden Konfliktlösung die ausschlaggebende Person, denn von seinen Fähigkeiten hängt es ab, ob die Verfahrensbeteiligten zu einer einvernehmlichen Lösung finden und ihre Meinungsverschiedenheiten in interessengerechter Art und Weise ausräumen können.[593]

Allerdings darf der *„conciliator"* einerseits tatsächlich lediglich neutraler Vermittler und nicht etwa Richter oder Schiedsrichter sein.[594] Andererseits muss er aber darauf achten und dafür Sorge tragen, dass die wesentlichen Verfahrensgrundsätze eingehalten werden, die Einigung zwischen den Parteien gefördert und vor allem aber ein hinreichender Schutz vor Diskriminierung praktiziert wird, § 28 HREOC.

(2) Der Verfahrensgrundsatz der Neutralität

Der Verfahrensgrundsatz der Neutralität wird weit ausgelegt, so dass bereits der Anschein der Unparteilichkeit vermieden werden soll. Beurteilungsmaßstab hierfür ist, ob nach der Sichtweise eines vernünftigen Dritten durch das fragliche Verhalten des *„conciliators"* Zweifel an seiner Neutralität entstehen können. Besonders problematisch stellen sich deshalb Eingriffe des *„conciliators"* in das Verhandlungsverfahren dar, wobei jedoch der Grundsatz gilt, dass ein Verweis auf Ergebnisse in anderen ähnlich gelagerten Fällen zulässig ist, um den Verfahrensbeteiligten an konkreten Beispielen hinreichend zu verdeutlichen, ob ihre Erwartungen realistisch oder aber überzogen sind.

(3) Der Verfahrensgrundsatz der vollständigen Vertraulichkeit

Um den Parteien die Möglichkeit einzuräumen, die ihrem Konflikt zu Grunde liegenden Interessen, ohne Sorge vor einer Veröffentlichung oder einer etwaigen Verwendung gegen sie, vorzutragen und somit durch einen selbstbestimmten Einigungsversuch zu einer schnellen Einigung zu finden, ist der *„conciliator"* zu absoluter Vertraulichkeit verpflichtet.[595] Vor allem aber sollen die Verfahrensbeteiligten von der Gefahr befreit werden, dass ihr Entgegenkommen im Laufe eines sich möglicherweise anschließenden Prozesses als Schuldanerkenntnis bewertet wird.

(4) Weitere Verfahrensgrundsätze

Weiterhin wird das *conciliation*-Verfahren aber auch vom Grundsatz der jederzeitigen Gewähr des rechtlichen Gehörs sowie vom Prinzip der Freiwilligkeit geprägt. Demnach besteht keinerlei Zwang, in Anwesenheit aller Verfahrensbeteiligten zu verhan-

593 *Thornton*, Equivocations of Conciliation: The Resolution of Discrimination Complaints in Australia (1989) 52, The Modern Law Review, 733.

594 *Eastman*, Procedures, in: Baker & McKenzie, Age Discrimination: Mitigating Risk in the Workplace, S. 96.

595 *Ronalds*, Discrimination – Law and Practice, 2004, 172.

deln, so dass je nach konkretem Erfordernis auch eine Verhandlung mal mit der einen, mal mit der anderen Seite vorgenommen werden kann, um etwa negative Emotionen aus dem Verfahren auszuschließen und mögliche Benachteiligungen der schwächeren Partei zu verhindern.[596]

bb. Die Vorbereitung der Einigung und die Verfahrenseröffnung

Es versteht sich nahezu von selbst, dass die Vermittlungsverhandlung nicht nur von Seiten der Human Rights and Equal Opportunity Commission, sondern auch den Verfahrensbeteiligten gewissenhaft vorbereitet werden muss. Insbesondere aber soll darauf geachtet werden, dass der Ablauf so geplant wird, dass keinerlei Anzeichen für ein etwaiges Machtungleichgewicht zwischen dem Beschwerdeführer und dem Beschwerdegegner entstehen. Deshalb muss der anderen Partei mitgeteilt werden, wenn ihr Gegenüber sich eines Rechtsvertreters oder Beistands bedient. Auch ist es Aufgabe des *„conciliators"* darauf zu achten, dass die Verfahrensbeteiligten respektvoll miteinander umgehen und ausgeglichen zu Wort kommen.[597]

Direkt bei der Eröffnung des Vermittlungsverfahrens ist der *„conciliator"* als Vermittler verpflichtet, den Verfahrensbeteiligten nicht nur die Regeln und Grundsätze des Verfahrens (wie etwa den Grundsatz der Vertraulichkeit) zu verdeutlichen, sondern er muss auch die Identität aller Anwesenden und ihre Funktion im Verfahren den Beteiligten erklären. Vor allem aber hat er weiterhin für eine ausgewogene Stellung der Verfahrensbeteiligten zueinander zu sorgen und für den Fall der Befürchtung einer Unausgeglichenheit der Machtverhältnisse für die (Wieder-)Herstellung der Waffengleichheit zu sorgen. So kann der *„conciliator"* vorschlagen, dass Rechtsanwälte oder sonstige unterstützende Personen den Raum verlassen und nicht aktiv am Vermittlungsprozess mitwirken, um somit die Verhandlungsmöglichkeit der schwächeren Seite nicht einzuschränken.[598] Denn es ist gerade der Hauptzweck des *conciliation*-Verfahrens, dass die Verfahrensbeteiligten die Verhandlung mehr oder weniger selbst führen und nur im Notfall auf ihre Rechtsberater zurückgreifen sollen, um dadurch die wirklichen Interessen der Parteien zu erfahren und ausgleichen zu können.[599] Allerdings kann der *„conciliator"* den Ausschluss der Rechtsanwälte nicht erzwingen. Denn wenn die am Verfahren Beteiligten ausdrücklich auf eine Verhandlungsführung durch ihre Rechtsanwälte bestehen, dann ist dieser Wunsch zu akzeptieren, wobei jedoch weiterhin berücksichtigt werden muss, dass keine Bindung an das förmliche Pro-

---

596 *Bryson*, Mediator and Advocate: Conciliating Human Rights Complaints (1990) 1, Australian Dispute Resolution Journal 136; *Bailey/Devereux*, The Operation of Antidiscrimination Laws in Australia, in: Kinley, Human Rights in Australian Law, 1998, 292.

597 *Bryson*, Mediator and Advocate: Conciliating Human Rights Complaints (1990) 1, Australian Dispute Resolution Journal 136; *Sordo*, The Lawyer's Role in Mediation (1996) 7, Dispute Resolution Journal 20.

598 *Sordo*, The Lawyer's Role in Mediation (1996) 7, Dispute Resolution Journal 20.

599 *Bryson*, Mediator and Advocate: Conciliating Human Rights Complaints (1990) 1, Australian Dispute Resolution Journal 136; *Bailey/Devereux*, The Operation of Antidiscrimination Laws in Australia, in: Kinley, Human Rights in Australian Law, 1998, 292; *Ronalds*, Discrimination – Law and Practice, 2004, 163.

zessrecht besteht.[600] Darüber hinaus sind der Verlauf der Verhandlung zu skizzieren und der voraussichtliche Zeitumfang zu beraten.

cc. Der Sachvortrag und die Stellungnahme der Verfahrensbeteiligten

Im Anschluss daran hat der Beschwerdeführer das Wort und trägt eine zusammenhängende und von keinem Anwesenden zu unterbrechende Einführung in den Verfahrensstand vor, wobei er aus subjektiver Sicht die Diskriminierung, den Umfang und die Bedeutung für seine Person schildert.[601] Anschließend erhält der Beschwerdegegner ebenfalls das Recht zur Äußerung, wobei ihm ein gleichlanger Zeitraum zur Erwiderung eingeräumt wird.

Durch die Vorträge der Beteiligten kann sich der *„conciliator"* versichern, ob er den vorliegenden Fall in seiner Bewertung zutreffend eingeschätzt hat und zugleich werden die Bewertungsunterschiede zwischen den Verfahrensbeteiligten direkt verdeutlicht. Somit können relativ schnell die klärungsbedürftigen Punkte eingegrenzt werden.

dd. Die eigentliche Verhandlungsphase

Vor allem die sich aus den Vorträgen der Verfahrensbeteiligten ergebenden Differenzen gilt es anschließend zu klären. Dazu bedarf es in der Regel zuerst der Festlegung in welcher Reihenfolge die aufgeworfenen Problemfelder abgearbeitet werden sollen und anschließend einer weiteren Sachverhaltsaufklärung und Klärung der nunmehr relevanten Tatsachen. Dazu muss der *„conciliator"* den Beteiligten ermöglichen, ihre Sichtweise zu jedem einzelnen Problempunkt darzulegen und erneut Stellung zu beziehen.

Die eigentliche Verhandlungs- und Einigungsphase muss mangels einer Bindung an das Prozessrecht nicht in Gegenwart aller Verfahrensbeteiligten geführt werden. Denn gerade in emotional stark beeinflussten Fragen empfiehlt es sich, das Verfahren in Einzelgesprächen fortzusetzen (*„shuttle conciliation"*).[602] Denn nicht selten gelingt es dann, dass die Verfahrensbeteiligten in umfassender Offenheit Stellung beziehen und einzelne Hintergründe und Zusammenhänge zur Entstehung des Konfliktes offenbaren, die im Beisein der Gegenseite nicht vorgetragen worden wären. Der *„conciliator"* muss jedoch absolute Vertraulichkeit zusichern und darf erst nach Absprache mit der jeweiligen Partei die so erhaltenen Informationen in der sich anschließenden gemeinsamen Verhandlung verwerten.[603] Gleichzeitig ist er verpflichtet, jeder Seite den gleichen Zeitumfang für ein Einzelgespräch zur Verfügung zu stellen, um so seine neutrale Stellung im Verfahren zu verdeutlichen und zu erfüllen. Auch sollte der *„conciliator"* aus diesem Grund weder Wertungen zum vorliegenden Fall noch zu den

600 *Sordo*, The Lawyer's Role in Mediation (1996) 7, Dispute Resolution Journal 20.

601 *Bryson*, Mediator and Advocate: Conciliating Human Rights Complaints (1990) 1, Australian Dispute Resolution Journal 136.

602 *Bryson*, Mediator and Advocate: Conciliating Human Rights Complaints (1990) 1, Australian Dispute Resolution Journal 136; *Charlton/Dewdney*, The Mediator's Handbook: Skills and Strategies for Practicioners, 2004, 88.

603 *Alexander*, Wirtschaftsmediation in Theorie und Praxis (1999), 84.

Erfolgsaussichten der Beschwerde gegenüber den Verfahrensbeteiligten vornehmen. Keine Beeinflussung seiner Neutralität stellt dagegen jedoch der Hinweis auf die Lösung von ähnlich gelagerten Fällen dar.

In Bezug auf das Einigungsergebnis bedarf es auf Seiten des Vermittlers ebenfalls strenger Zurückhaltung, da die Verfahrensbeteiligten selbst für sie akzeptable Lösungen vorschlagen, besprechen und modifizieren sollen. Nur wenn sie keine eigenen Vorschläge unterbreiten oder diese auf unrealistischen Vorstellungen basieren, ist es dem *„conciliator"* erlaubt einzugreifen und einen eigenen Vorschlag zur Lösung des Konflikts einzubringen.[604] Dabei ist aber darauf zu achten, dass den Verfahrensbeteiligten verdeutlicht wird, dass es sich tatsächlich nur um einen unverbindlichen Vorschlag und keinerlei Stellungnahme zur Rechtslage und zu den Erfolgsaussichten handelt.

Der *conciliator* muss jedoch nicht sehenden Auges jeden Einigungsvorschlag der Parteien unwidersprochen lassen. Denn wenn die Einigung der Verfahrensbeteiligten inhaltlich nicht mit den Prinzipien der Antidiskriminierungsgesetzgebung und -rechtsprechung vereinbar ist, dann muss er ausdrücklich darauf hinweisen und klarstellen, dass die Human Rights and Equal Opportunity Commission eine derartige Einigung nicht unterstützen wird.

Haben die Beteiligten zu einer Einigung gefunden, so ist eine förmliche Niederschrift der gefundenen Konfliktlösung vorzunehmen und von beiden Seiten zu unterschreiben. Ist die Einigung dagegen in einem Termin noch nicht erreichbar, zeichnet sich aber die Bereitschaft der Beteiligten zu einer Einigung bereits ab, so ist ein Folgetermin zu bestimmen.

f. Schlussbetrachtung zum *conciliation*-Verfahren

Die Konzentration auf das *conciliation*-Verfahren und die Durchführung an sich lassen die wesentliche Vorzüge und Qualitäten dieses Vermittlungsverfahrens für die Lösung von Diskriminierungsfällen deutlich werden. Denn in derartigen Fällen werden in der Regel persönliche Konfliktbereiche berührt und somit eine nicht unerheblich emotionale Beziehung zu der jeweiligen Angelegenheit gefördert. Damit vor allem die Diskriminierungsopfer nicht nur ein Gefühl der Gleichwertigkeit erfahren, sondern sie tatsächlich mit ihrem Anliegen ernst genommen werden und die Gegenseite ihre Interessen ebenfalls ausreichend berücksichtigt sieht, muss es vermieden werden, dass der Konflikt in der Öffentlichkeit ausgebreitet wird. Dies lässt sich im Verfahren vor der Human Rights and Equal Opportunity Commission aber aufgrund des Vertraulichkeitsgrundsatzes besser erreichen als in einem öffentlichen Gerichtsverfahren.

Neben diesem in der Praxis überaus wichtigen Aspekt tritt hinzu, dass durch das *conciliation*-Verfahren der Zugang zum Recht erleichtert ist, indem es nicht nur nicht öffentlich, sondern auch weniger formell als das Gerichtsverfahren ausgestaltet ist. Dadurch können insbesondere aber alle für die Verfahrensbeteiligten wichtigen Bereiche des Konflikts einbezogen werden. Eine Begrenzung durch eine gesetzlich vorgegebene prozessuale Rahmenvorschrift existiert nicht. Ebenfalls wirkt sich die geringe

604 *Hunter*, Indirect Discrimination in the Workplace, 1992, 262.

Zeit- und Kostenlast für eine aktive Beteiligung am Verfahren ebenso förderlich aus, wie die Aussicht, eine pragmatische und an den tatsächlichen Interessen der Verfahrensbeteiligten orientierte Einigung zu formulieren. Denn diese kann vor allem im Arbeitsverhältnis dazu beitragen, dass auch zukünftig friedvolle Beziehungen zwischen den Parteien ermöglicht werden.

H. Die prozessualen Reaktionsmöglichkeiten gegen eine Altersdiskriminierung unter Einbeziehung der Vortrags- und Beweislastproblematik im gerichtlichen Verfahren

Wie bereits dargelegt, bietet vor allem der Human Rights and Equal Opportunity Commission Act 1986 (Cth) ein breites Programm für Untersuchungen, für das *conciliation*-Verfahren und für die Entscheidung von Diskriminierungsklagen, um so dem Interesse der Parteien an einer schnellen und effektiven Lösung von vor allem aufgrund des Alters aufgetretenen Diskriminierungskonflikten gerecht zu werden.

I. Bundesrecht und bundesstaatliches bzw. territoriales Recht als Grundlage für eine Klage wegen Altersdiskriminierung

Sofern ein Fall von Altersdiskriminierung und somit ein Verstoß gegen ein Diskriminierungsverbot vorliegt, muss sich das Diskriminierungsopfer entscheiden, ob es mit einer Klage auf der Grundlage des Age Discrimination Act 2004 (Cth) oder aufgrund des jeweiligen Rechts des Bundesstaates oder eines Territoriums vorgehen möchte. Denn sobald eine Klage nach bundesstaatlichen Regeln erhoben worden ist, kann der Verstoß gegen das Diskriminierungsverbot nicht zugleich auch im Geltungsbereich des Age Discrimination Act 2004 (Cth) mit einer Klage verfolgt werden.[605] Der Kläger muss also vorab zwischen dem Bundesrecht und dem des jeweiligen Bundesstaates oder Territoriums wählen.[606]

Daneben muss das Diskriminierungsopfer aber vor allem bei Diskriminierungsfällen im Bereich der Beschäftigung nicht nur zwischen der Klagemöglichkeit aufgrund des Age Discrimination Act 2004 (Cth) und dem jeweiligen Recht des Bundesstaates oder Territoriums, sondern auch zwischen der Klageerhebung im Geltungsbereich des Age Discrimination Act 2004 (Cth) und von möglicherweise anwendbaren speziellen Arbeitsrechtsregelungen wählen. So statuiert § 659 Abs. 2 lit. f) WR Act – zuvor § 170CK Abs. 2 lit. f) WR Act – ein selbständiges Verbot der unrechtmäßigen Kündigung eines Arbeitnehmers wegen Alters, welches das Diskriminierungsopfer als Rechtsgrundlage für sein Klagebegehren heranziehen kann. Allerdings verbietet § 672 WR Act – zuvor § 170HB WR Act – die Erhebung mehrerer Klagen, so dass sich das Diskriminierungsopfer hinsichtlich der Rechtsgrundlage seiner Klage entscheiden muss und nicht etwa alternativ aufgrund des Age Discrimination Act 2004 (Cth) sowie

605 *Elekwachi v Human Rights and Equal Opportunity Commission* (1997) 79 FCR 271.

606 Explanatory Memorandum of the Age Discrimination Bill 2003 (Cth), Annexure C, Clause 12, Operation of State and Territory laws.

gleichzeitig auf der Grundlage des Workplace Relation Acts 1996 (Cth) gegen das diskriminierende Verhalten seines Arbeitgebers vorgehen kann.[607]

Für die Wahl der Grundlage der zu erhebenden Klage sollten dabei insbesondere Überlegungen über Fristen und besondere (Prozess-)Voraussetzungen zur Klageerhebung und zur rechtlichen Vertretung, die jeweilige(n) Verfahrensdauer und -kosten, aber auch über nachfolgende Rechtsmittel ausschlaggebend sein.

II. Die Beschwerde- und Klageerhebung auf der Grundlage des Age Discrimination Act 2004 (Cth)

1. Die Beschwerde zur Human Rights and Equal Opportunity Commission

Wie bereits dargelegt, ist grundsätzlich das – kostenfreie – Beschwerdeverfahren zur Human Rights and Equal Opportunity Commission einer etwaigen gerichtlichen Klärung der jeweiligen Diskriminierung wegen Alters vorgeschalten.[608] Die Gerichte nehmen daher Klagen nicht an, solange nicht zuvor eine Beschwerde zur Human Rights and Equal Opportunity Commission erhoben wurde.[609]

a. Die Anforderungen an eine zulässige Beschwerde

aa. Schriftform

Für die Einreichung der Beschwerde zur Human Rights and Equal Opportunity Commission legt der Human Rights and Equal Opportunity Act 1986 (Cth) zwar grundsätzlich den Rahmen für den Ablauf und die Verfahrensvoraussetzungen vor der Erhebung einer Klage wegen Altersdiskriminierung und die sich anschließende Vorgehensweise nach der Klageerhebung dar. Außer aber gemäß § 46P Abs. 1 HREOC Act die Schriftform für die Beschwerde vorzuschreiben, stellt der Human Rights and Equal Opportunity Commission Act 1986 (Cth) keine weiteren Voraussetzungen in Bezug auf die Form und den Inhalt für eine Klage wegen Altersdiskriminierung auf. Vielmehr ist die Human Rights and Equal Opportunity Commission gemäß § 46 Abs. 4 HREOC Act dazu angehalten, bei der Einreichung einer Klage behilflich zu sein. So hält die Human Rights and Equal Opportunity Commission sogar ein Formular für eine Beschwerde

---

607 *Eastman*, Procedures, in: Baker & McKenzie, Age Discrimination: Mitigating Risk in the Workplace, S. 90.

608 *Eastman*, Procedures, in: Baker & McKenzie, Age Discrimination: Mitigating Risk in the Workplace, S. 90; vgl. auch Human Rights and Equal Opportunity Commission, Report into complaints of discrimination in employment and occupation: compulsory age retirement, HRC Report No. 1.

609 Human Rights and Equal Opportunity Commission, Federal Discrimination Law 2005, 222; vgl. auch *Gerhardy v Brown* (1985) 159 CLR 70; *Re East; Ex parte Nguyen* (1998) 196 CLR 354; *Bropho v Western Australia* [2004] FCA 1209.

vor, welches direkt als online-Formular ausgefüllt oder aber auch heruntergeladen werden kann.[610]

bb. *Inhalt der Beschwerde*

Eine solche Beschwerde ist jedoch nicht zu vergleichen mit einer Strafanzeige oder einem Schriftsatz in einem Zivilrechtsstreit.[611] Denn die Anforderungen an eine Beschwerde zur Human Rights and Equal Opportunity Commission sind weitaus geringer.[612] So ist es erforderlich, dass die schriftliche Beschwerde zumindest den Namen des Beschwerdeführers und falls erforderlich weitere Angaben zur hinreichenden Indentifizierung des Beschwerdegegners sowie weiterer Personen, denen vorgeworfen wird, dass sie gegen eine Bestimmung des Age Discrimination Act 2004 (Cth) verstoßen haben, enthält. Auch eine Beschreibung oder Zusammenfassung der wichtigsten Details, welche die Behauptung des Beschwerdeführers über das diskriminierende Verhaltens stützen, wie etwa wann und wo die Altersdiskriminierung stattgefunden hat, welche Zeugen oder Beweisdokumente es gibt, welchen Schaden der Beschwerdeführer erlitten hat und ob bereits im Vorfeld Gespräche oder ein Kontakt zum Beschwerdegegner zur Lösung des jeweiligen Falles stattgefunden haben, sollten in der Beschwerde enthalten sein. Denn nur eine detaillierte und umfassend zu dem diskriminierenden Verhalten Stellung beziehende Beschwerde vermag die Chance zu erhöhen, dass der jeweilige Fall bereits im Verfahren vor der Human Rights and Equal Opportunity Commission gelöst werden kann. Sollte dieses aber nicht zu einer Lösung des Konflikts führen, so wird der Beschwerdeinhalt gemäß § 46PO Abs. 3 HREOC Act zur Grundlage des gerichtlichen Verfahrens gemacht.

Darüber hinaus ist es auch wichtig, dass der Beschwerdeführer jegliches Vorbringen auf die tatsächlich geschehene bzw. zumindest behauptete diskriminierende Behandlung bezieht. Denn nur hypothetische Angelegenheiten in Bezug auf eine Diskriminierung wegen Alters werden nicht zur Zulässigkeit und zum Erfolg der eingereichten Beschwerde führen.

cc. *Zäsurwirkung der erhobenen Beschwerde*

Ist die Beschwerde erfolgreich eingereicht, so können weitere, nach diesem Zeitpunkt geschehene, Altersdiskriminierungen jedoch nicht automatisch im Rahmen der bereits erhobenen Beschwerde und behaupteten Verstöße gegen Diskriminierungsverbote untersucht und bearbeitet werden.[613] Vielmehr tritt eine Zäsurwirkung ein, die es erforderlich werden lässt, eine zusätzliche Beschwerde einzureichen oder aber die bereits erhobene Beschwerde nachträglich zu ändern bzw. zu erweitern.

---

610 Formular abrufbar unter http://www.hreoc.gov.au/complaints_information/lodge/lodging.html; abgedruckt am Ende der Arbeit in K. Anhang..

611 *Langley v Niland* [1981] 2 NSWLR 104.

612 *Commonwealth of Australia v Sex Discrimination Commissioner* (1998) 90 FCR 179.

613 *Charles v Fuji Xerox Australia Pty Ltd* (2000) 105 FCR 573.

dd. Inhaltliche Änderung und Erweiterung der bereits erhobenen Beschwerde

Eine Möglichkeit der inhaltlichen Änderung der Beschwerde besteht nämlich auch noch nach Einreichung bei der Human Rights and Equal Opportunity Commission. Denn nur so können die Rechte des Diskriminierungsopfers und Beschwerdeführers umfassend gewahrt werden. Aber nicht nur der Beschwerdeführer kann ein erhebliches Interesse an der Änderung oder aber Erweiterung seiner Ausführungen haben. Auch der Beschwerdegegner kann mitunter daran interessiert sein, einen weiteren Beschwerdegegner in das Verfahren einzubinden und somit die Beschwerde abzuändern. Die Änderung ist jedoch gemäß §§ 46PA, 46PF HREOC Act nur nach vorheriger Erlaubnis des Präsidenten der Human Rights and Equal Opportunity Commission zulässig.

ee. Anforderungen an den Beschwerdeführer als „aggrieved person"

(1) „Aggrieved Person"

Grundsätzlich muss dem Beschwerdeführer die Beschwerde(führungs)befugnis gemäß § 46P Abs. 2 HREOC zukommen. Er muss folglich von dem geltend gemachten Verstoß gegen ein Diskriminierungsverbot des Age Discrimination Act 2004 (Cth) betroffen sein (*„aggrieved person"*). Eine gesetzliche Definition der *„aggrieved person"* findet sich jedoch weder im Age Discrimination Act 2004 (Cth) noch im Human Rights and Equal Opportunity Commission Act 1986 (Cth).[614] Nach der in der Rechtsprechung gebildeten Definition wird der Begriff der *„aggrieved person"* grundsätzlich in der Form interpretiert und ausgelegt, als dass es sich hierbei um eine Person handeln müsse, die entweder direkt von dem diskriminierenden Verhalten betroffen sei oder aber zumindest einen Schaden oder sonstigen Nachteil erlitten habe.[615] Dabei kommt es folglich nicht auf das subjektive Empfinden, sondern vielmehr auf die objektiven Umstände an.[616] Einer Person kann danach die Beschwerdebefugnis nicht allein deshalb zukommen, weil sie sich als von einer diskriminierenden Behandlung betroffen fühlt.[617]

Fraglich ist, ob auch eine juristische Person (*„body corporate"*) als eine *„aggrieved person"* gilt und sie somit ebenfalls beschwerdebefugt sein kann. Die Rechtsprechung bejaht diese Frage, obwohl sie eindeutig herausstellt, dass der Schutz von natürlichen und nicht von juristischen Personen im Vordergrund stehen solle und müsse:[618]

> „The words "person aggrieved" have appeared in many statutes, English and Australian, and their meaning has been discussed in many cases. In the end of course the meaning of

614 Human Rights and Equal Opportunity Commission, Federal Discrimination Law 2005, 214.

615 *Cameron v Human Rights and Equal Opportunity Commission* (1993) 46 FCR 509; *Executive Council of Australian Jewry v Scully* (1998) 79 FCR 537.

616 Human Rights and Equal Opportunity Commission, Federal Discrimination Law 2005, 215, mit Verweis auf *Cameron v Human Rights and Equal Opportunity Commission* (1993) 46 FCR 509.

617 *Tooheys Ltd v Minister for Business and Consumer Affairs* (1981) 54 FLR 421; *Executive Council of Australian Jewry v Scully* (1998) 79 FCR 537.

618 *Koowarta v Bjelke-Petersen* (1982) 153 CLR 236.

> the words must depend on the context of the particular statute. It has often been said that the words connote a person with a legal grievance..."[619]

Denn es erscheint bereits fraglich, wie eine Altersdiskriminierung einer juristischen Person konkret aussehen solle. Um jedoch einen umfassenden Schutz gegen Diskriminierungen zu schaffen, bedarf es in der Praxis aber auch der Gewährung von Rechtsschutz für eine juristische Person.[620] Denn zumindest bei einer direkten oder indirekten Altersdiskriminierung der die juristische Person prägenden natürlichen Personen und Organen ist eine Auswirkung auf diese denkbar und bedarf ebenfalls des rechtlichen Schutzes. Dies gilt insbesondere in den Fällen, in welchen sich die Altersdiskriminierung im Bereich eines Arbeits- und Beschäftigungsverhältnisses realisiert. Denn innerhalb eines solchen Vertragsverhältnisses kann je nach Umfang und Intensität der diskriminierenden Verhaltensweise im Einzelfall auf eine Beeinträchtigung der hinter der juristischen Person stehenden natürlichen Person(en) geschlossen werden.[621]

(2) Minderjährige

Mangels einer ausdrücklichen Regelung im Human Rights and Equal Opportunity Commission Act 1986 (Cth) erscheint es fraglich, ob für die Position als Beschwerdeführer ein bestimmtes Alter vorausgesetzt wird oder ob sogar Kinder und Jugendliche ebenfalls Beschwerden erheben und somit beschwerdebefugt sein können. Grundsätzlich existieren – so auch im Common Law – Beschränkungen bezüglich der Rechtsverfolgungsbefugnis bei Kindern und Jugendlichen. Wird also das Recht zu klagen oder die Fähigkeit verklagt zu werden betroffen, so wird im Prozessrecht grundsätzlich die Beiordnung eines Vormundes („*guardian ad litem*") verlangt, der die Rechte und Interessen des Minderjährigen während des Verfahrens wahrnimmt.[622]

Dennoch ist eine solche Beschränkung für den Beschwerdeführer im Verfahren wegen einer Altersdiskriminierung nicht existent. Denn weder der Age Discrimination Act 2004 (Cth) stellt spezielle Anforderungen an das Alter des Beschwerdeführers oder an eine Vertretung durch einen Vormund auf. Auch die Rechtsprechung lehnt eine Beschränkung ab und bestätigt vielmehr, dass es für Minderjährige keinerlei Hin-

---

619 *Koowarta v Bjelke-Petersen* (1982) 153 CLR 236 m.w.N.; vgl. etwa die ständige Rechtsprechung *In re Sidebotham* (1880) 14 ChD 458; *Buxton v Minister of Housing and Local Government* (1961) 1 QB 278.

620 *Koowarta v Bjelke-Petersen* (1982) 153 CLR 236; *Simplot Australia Pty Ltd v Human Rights and Equal Opportunity Commission* (1996) 69 FCR 90.

621 *Simplot Australia Pty Ltd v Human Rights and Equal Opportunity Commission* (1996) 69 FCR 90.

622 „*Guardian ad litem*" (lat. *guardianus* = „Wächter, Hüter"), ein – insbesondere im angloamerikanischen Raum – einem Minderjährigen oder Unmündigen für die Dauer eines entsprechenden Prozesses zugeordneter Vormund und Rechtsbeistand. Im deutschen Recht ist dieser zum Teil mit einem Verfahrenspfleger, der in familiengerichtlichen Auseinandersetzungen um das Umgangs- und Sorgerecht von Kindern gemäß § 50 FGG bzw. in Unterbringungssachen gemäß § 70b FGG bestellt werden kann, vergleichbar.

dernisse geben dürfe, um sich auf der Grundlage des Age Discrimination Act 2004 (Cth) gegen eine Altersdiskriminierung verfahrensrechtlich zur Wehr zu setzen.[623]

Folglich besteht dem Grunde nach auch für Minderjährige die Möglichkeit, eine Beschwerde wegen einer erlittenen Altersdiskriminierung zu erheben und möglicherweise im Anschluss daran eine Klage einzureichen. Sollte es tatsächlich dazu kommen, so steht es außer Frage, dass das Kind oder der Jugendliche als Beschwerdeführer oder Kläger eines besonderen Schutzes bedarf. So werden Beschwerden von Minderjährigen von Seiten der Human Rights and Equal Opportunity Commission anonymisiert. Im Gerichtsverfahren vor dem Federal Court oder dem Federal Magistrates Court ist eine Vertretung des Minderjährigen teilweise vorgeschrieben.[624] In der Regel wird trotz fehlender Verfahrensvorschrift in der Gerichtspraxis die Klage der Eltern für den Minderjährigen akzeptiert und zugelassen.[625]

(3) Der Bevollmächtigte und die „representative complaint“

Einem Bevollmächtigten mehrerer Beschwerdeführer steht die Beschwerdebefugnis und damit auch das Recht zur Einreichung einer Beschwerde (*„representative complaint“*) bei der Human Rights and Equal Opportunity Commission zu, wenn unter Berücksichtigung der allgemeinen Verfahrensvorschriften des *„representative proceeding“* in Part IVA des Federal Court of Australia Act 1976 (Cth) gemäß § 46PB Abs. 1 lit. a) HREOC Act alle vom Bevollmächtigten vertretenen Mitglieder ihre Beschwerde gegen denselben Beschwerdegegner gerichtet werden würden, gemäß § 46PB Abs. 1 lit. b) HREOC Act alle Beschwerden in Bezug auf oder aufgrund der gleichen, ähnlichen oder verwandten Umstände erhoben werden würden und gemäß § 46PB Abs. 1 lit. c) HREOC Act alle Beschwerden zu einer gemeinsamen Rechts- oder Tatsachenfrage führen würden. Darüber hinaus besteht die Voraussetzung für eine *„representative complaint“*, dass gemäß § 46PB Abs. 2 lit. a) HREOC Act durch sie jeder einzelne der Beteiligten und Beschwerdeführer (*„class member“*) bezeichnet oder in irgendeiner Form identifiziert, dass gemäß § 46PB Abs. 2 lit. b) HREOC die Art der Beschwerde, die im Namen aller Beschwerdeführer erhoben wird, bestimmt und dass gemäß § 46PB Abs. 2 lit. c) HREOC Act das Klagebegehren spezifiziert wird.

Der von den Beschwerdeführern zur *„representative complaint“* Bevollmächtigte ist berechtigt, im Verfahren alle erforderlichen Anträge zu stellen, wobei dem einzelnen Beschwerdeführer die Berechtigung zur Vornahme von Verfahrenshandlungen nicht mehr zukommt und er auch keine selbständige Beschwerde erheben darf.[626] Allerdings kann er selbstverständlich weiterhin jederzeit autonom über die Beendigung

623 *Haines v Leves* [1987] 8 NSWLR 442; *Re NSW Corporal Punishment in School Case* (1986) EOC 92-160.

624 Vgl. Order 43 Federal Court Rules.

625 *A School v Human Rights and Equal Opportunity Commission (No 2)* [1998] FCA 145; *Hills Grammar School v Human Rights and Equal Opportunity Commission* (2000) 100 FCR 306; *Purvis v State of New South Wales* (2003) 217 CLR 92; *Catholic Education Office v Clarke* (2004) 138 FCR 12.

626 *Eastman*, Procedures, in: Baker & McKenzie, Age Discrimination: Mitigating Risk in the Workplace, S. 93.

seiner Verfahrensbeteiligung bestimmen, solange über die Beschwerde noch nicht entschieden worden ist.

Durch die *„representative complaint"* wird es vor allem gewerkschaftlich organisierten Beschäftigten ermöglicht, dass sie sich nach außen durch ihre Gewerkschaft vertreten lassen und somit die Initiative, eine Beschwerde an die Human Rights and Equal Opportunity Commission zu richten und gegen eine Altersdiskriminierung vorzugehen, auf die Gewerkschaft übertragen.[627] Dies bedeutet jedoch nicht, dass einer Gewerkschaft aus dem Age Discrimination Act 2004 (Cth) oder aus anderen Gründen ein eigener kollektiv-rechtlicher Unterlassungsanspruch zukommt. Vielmehr übt sie in einem solchen Fall die Rechte ihres Mitglieds im Rahmen einer Bevollmächtigung aus.[628]

(4) Verstorbener Beschwerdeführer

Verstirbt der Beschwerdeführer nachdem er die Beschwerde erfolgreich erhoben hat, so kann das Beschwerdeverfahren gleichwohl fortgesetzt werden.[629] Allerdings besteht keinerlei Befugnis zugunsten einer verstorbenen Person durch einen Dritten eine Beschwerde bei der Human Rights and Equal Opportunity Commission einzureichen.[630]

ff. Frist zur Beschwerdeerhebung

Eine gesetzliche Frist, die bei der Einreichung der Beschwerde zur Human Rights and Equal Opportunity Commission zu beachten wäre, existiert nicht. Allerdings wurde in § 46PH Abs. 1 lit. b) HREOC Act für den Präsidenten der Human Rights and Equal Opportunity Commission die Befugnis geschaffen eine Beschwerde abzuweisen, wenn das behauptete diskriminierende Verhalten länger als zwölf Monate zurückliegt. Dieser Zurückweisung kommt aber keine Rechtskraft zu, so dass das Diskriminierungsopfer im gerichtlichen Verfahren den Verstoß gegen ein Diskriminierungsverbot feststellen lassen kann.[631]

b. Das Scheitern des *conciliation*-Verfahrens

aa. Issue of Termination

Führt das *conciliation*-Verfahren nicht zu einer einvernehmlichen Lösung des Konflikts wegen der behaupteten Altersdiskriminierung, dann muss der Präsident der Human Rights and Equal Opportunity Commission die Beschwerde abweisen und das

627 Human Rights and Equal Opportunity Commission, An International Comparison of the Racial Discrimination Act 1975, Background Paper 1 (2008) 7; vgl. auch *Ierodiaconou,* Conciliation, Mediation and Federal Human Rights Complaints: Are Rights Compromised? (2005), 5, 17 m.w.N.; *Rees/Lindsay/Rice*, Australian Anti-Discrimination Law: Text, Cases and Materials (2008), 620.

628 *Rees/Lindsay/Rice*, Australian Anti-Discrimination Law: Text, Cases and Materials (2008), 620.

629 *Stephenson v Human Rights and Equal Opportunity Commission* (1996) 68 FCR 290.

630 *Cuna Mutual Group Ltd v Bryant* (2000) 102 FCR 270.

631 *Eastman*, Procedures, in: Baker & McKenzie, Age Discrimination: Mitigating Risk in the Workplace, S. 94.

Verfahren beenden und dem Beschwerdeführer diese Entscheidung („*Issue of Termination*") mit einer Begründung in schriftlicher Form mitteilen. In der Regel nimmt der Präsident in der Entscheidung auch Stellung zu den durch die Human Rights and Equal Opportunity Commission getätigten Untersuchungen während des Verfahrens und wie seiner Auffassung nach ein Bezug zu den Bestimmungen des Age Discrimination Act 2004 (Cth) zu bewerten ist.

Allerdings kann der Beschwerdeführer nach vorheriger Zustimmung des Präsidenten der Human Rights and Equal Opportunity Commission die Beschwerde auch in diesem Verfahrensstadium noch immer zurücknehmen, § 46PG HREOC Act.

bb. Frist zur Klageerhebung

Nach Zugang der „*Issue of Termination*" hat der Beschwerdeführer das Recht, ein Gerichtsverfahren vor dem Federal Court oder dem Federal Magistrates Court zu beantragen, um mit seinem Anliegen rechtlich gehört zu werden.

(1) Die 28-Tages-Frist und die Möglichkeit der Verlängerung

Die Frist zur Klageerhebung beträgt gemäß § 46 PO Abs. 2 HREOC Act ab Zugang der Entscheidung des Präsidenten der Human Rights and Equal Opportunity Commission 28 Tage, wobei das Gericht berechtigt ist, die Frist ermessensgerecht zu verlängern.[632] Das Gericht ist folglich bei der Entscheidung über das Ob und das Wie einer Fristverlängerung nicht an Vorschriften gebunden, wobei die Gewährung von allzu langen Fristen im Interesse einer effektiven Rechtsschutzmöglichkeit vermieden werden sollte.[633]

(2) Prinzipien für die Fristverlängerung

Im Laufe der Zeit haben sich – unter Billigung des Federal Courts – einige Prinzipien zur Beurteilung der Fristverlängerungsproblematik herausgebildet, so dass die Gerichte nicht völlig im rechtsleeren Raum entscheiden müssen und eine Grundlage für eine verhältnismäßige Entscheidung haben.[634]

So ist der Kläger etwa grundsätzlich nicht verpflichtet, das Vorliegen besonderer Umstände zu beweisen, die eine Fristverlängerung rechtfertigen würden.[635] Für die Entscheidung über die Gewährung einer Fristverlängerung ist aber insbesondere das Verhalten des Klägers ausschlaggebend, ob er etwa völlig untätig bleibt oder versucht auf anderem – nicht Erfolg versprechenden oder unzulässigen – Weg Rechtsschutz zu erlangen und ob die Fristversäumung in seinen Verantwortungsbereich fällt.[636] Das

632 *Low v Commonwealth of Australia* [2001] FCA 702.

633 *Phillips v Australian Girls' Choir Pty Ltd* [2001] FMCA 109; *Lawton v Lawson* [2002] FMCA 68.

634 Human Rights and Equal Opportunity Commission, Federal Discrimination Law 2005, 234; vgl. auch *Pham v Commonwealth of Australia* [2002] FCA 669.

635 *Ralkon v Aboriginal Development Commission* (1982) 43 ALR 535; *Corncare v A'Hearn* (1993) 45 FCR 441; *Dix v Crimes Compensation Tribunal* (1993) 1 VR 297.

636 *Doyle v Chief of General Staff* (1982) 42 ALR 283; *Horman v Distribution Group Limited* [2002] FCA 219; *Kennedy v ADI Ltd* [2002] FCA 1603.

Fehlen von Entscheidungen als Bewertungsgrundlage kann grundsätzlich nicht automatisch zu einer umfassenden Fristverlängerung führen. Weiterhin ist davon auszugehen, dass nach Ablauf der 28-Tage-Frist ein gerichtliches Verfahren trotz ordnungsgemäßer Klageerhebung nicht aufrechterhalten wird.[637] Ausnahmsweise kann auch ein völlig ungebührendes Verhalten oder ein sehr faires Verhalten in die Bewertung einfließen.[638] Im Ergebnis jedoch wird von der herrschenden Meinung davon ausgegangen, dass es der Verhältnismäßigkeit (*„balance of convenience"*) entspricht, dass eine Klage grundsätzlich innerhalb der gesetzlich vorgeschriebenen Frist zu erheben ist und es für eine Fristverlängerung einer nachvollziehbaren Erklärung seitens des Klägers bedarf.[639]

Auf der Basis der vorgenannten Prinzipien wurde von der Rechtsprechung ohne weiteres eine Fristverlängerung von acht Tagen gewährt, nachdem der Kläger eine nachvollziehbare Erklärung für die verspätete Klageerhebung vorgebracht hatte. Ebenfalls wurde eine Fristverlängerung gewährt, weil der Kläger in einer sehr abgelegenen Gegend wohnte oder er etwa in einem besonders jungen Alter war.[640] Hinzukommend war aber jedes Mal nach Ansicht des Gerichts eine hinreichende Erfolgsaussicht der Klage erforderlich und auch vorliegend.

Im Ergebnis ist folglich festzuhalten, dass eine kurze Fristverlängerung ohne eine erhebliche Beeinträchtigung der Rechte des Beklagten regelmäßig gewährt wird:

> „Where the delay is short and no injustice will be occasioned to the respondent, justice will usually be done if the extension of time is granted."[641]

2. Die Klageerhebung zum Federal Court und Federal Magistrates Court

a. Wahlmöglichkeit des Klägers

Nach dem zuvor dargestellten Abschluss des (gescheiterten) *conciliation*-Verfahrens, steht dem ehemaligen Beschwerdeführer die Wahl zu, ob er entweder am Federal Court oder am Federal Magistrates Court Klage erhebt.[642] Er kann aber auch nach Klageerhebung noch immer beantragen, dass das Verfahren an das jeweils anderen Gericht abgegeben wird, wobei eine Verweisung vom Federal Court an den Federal Ma-

---

637 *Lucic v Nolan* (1982) 45 ALR 411.

638 *Wedesweiler v Cole* (1983) 47 ALR 528.

639 *Gardner v National Netball League Pty Ltd* (2001) 182 ALR 408; *Low v Commonwealth of Australia* [2001] FCA 702; *Saddi v Active Employment* [2001] FMCA 73.

640 *Lawton v Lawson* [2002] FMCA 68; *Creek v Cairns Post Pty Ltd* [2001] FCA 293; *Philips v Australian Girls' Choir Pty Ltd* [2001] FMCA 109; *Rainsford v Victoria* [2002] FMCA 266.

641 *WAAD v Minister for Immigration and Multicultural Affairs* [2002] FCAFC 399.

642 *Smith*, Australian Anti-Discrimination Laws – Framework, Developments and Issues, New Developments in Employment Discrimination Law – The 9 JILPT Comparative Labour Law Seminar (2008) 4.

gistrates Court in der Praxis häufiger vorkommt, als eine solche vom Federal Magistrates Court zum Federal Court.[643]

Hierbei ist nochmals darauf hinzuweisen, dass eine Klageerhebung unter Bundesrecht aber nur dann möglich ist, wenn nicht bereits eine Klage in einem Bundesstaat oder einem Territorium erhoben wurde, § 12 Abs. 4 ADA.[644]

Beide Gerichte sind mit Bundesrichtern besetzt, die als Einzelrichter über die Klage entscheiden. Das kostenpflichtige Gerichtsverfahren unterliegt den *„Federal Court Rules"* bzw. den *„Federal Magistrates Court Rules"*, nach welchen sowohl für den Kläger als auch für den Beklagten Klage- und Replikformulare erhältlich sind.[645] Denn formale Schriftsätze sind zur Verfahrenseröffnung gesetzlich weder beim Federal Court noch beim Federal Magistrates Court erforderlich. Dennoch ist es üblich einen gesonderten Klageschriftsatz als Grundlage des Verfahrens zur Verdeutlichung des streitigen Diskriminierungssachverhaltes beim Gericht einzureichen.[646] Die Richter genießen – wie auch bei anderen Diskriminierungsfällen – im Bereich der Altersdiskriminierung volle Immunität, so dass sie nach dem Willen des Gesetzgebers aufgrund Ihrer Entscheidungen nicht in Anspruch genommen werden können.[647]

b. Klagebefugnis

Ferner muss der Kläger klagebefugt sein (*„an affected person"*), was aber aufgrund der früheren Beschwerdebefugnis im Verfahren bei der Human Rights and Equal Opportunity Commission regelmäßig der Fall sein wird.[648] Denn nach der Definition in § 3 Abs. 1 HREOC Act gilt als *„an affected person"* bereits jede Person, auf deren Veranlassung hin die Klage erhoben worden ist. Folglich steht vor allem die Identifizierung der hinter der Klage steckenden Person bzw. Personen im Vordergrund.[649]

aa. Representative proceedings

Die Klagebefugnis wird von der Rechtsprechung aber häufig auch dann verneint, wenn mehrere Beklagte existieren, aber nur gegen einen von diesen das Verfahren vor der Human Rights and Equal Opportunity Commission geführt wurde.[650] Ebenso fehlt dem Kläger im gerichtlichen Verfahren vor dem Federal Magistrates Court die Befugnis zur Erhebung einer Gruppenklage (*„representative proceeding"*). Sie können gemäß Part IVA des Federal Court of Australia Act 1976 (Cth) allein Gegenstand eines ge-

643 *Eastman*, Procedures, in: Baker & McKenzie, Age Discrimination: Mitigating Risk in the Workplace, S. 98.

644 Human Rights and Equal Opportunity Commission, Federal Discrimination Law 2005, 220.

645 Vgl. etwa form 167 and 168 auf der Grundlage von Order 81 of the Federal Court Rules; Human Rights and Equal Opportunity Commission, Federal Discrimination Law 2005, 212.

646 *Eastman*, Procedures, in: Baker & McKenzie, Age Discrimination: Mitigating Risk in the Workplace, S. 98.

647 *Re East; Ex parte Nguyen* (1998) 196 CLR 354.

648 *Oorloff v Lee* [2004] FMCA 893.

649 *Stokes v Royal Flying Doctor Service* [2003] FMCA 164.

650 *Jandruwanda v Regency Park College of TAFE* [2003] FCA 1455; *Jandruwanda v University of South Australia* [2003] FMCA 205.

richtlichen Verfahrens vor dem Federal Court sein, wenn gemäß § 33C Abs. 1 Federal Court Act 1976 (Cth) sieben oder mehr Personen gegen dieselbe Person klagen und derselbe Klagegegenstand betroffen ist. Voraussetzung hierfür ist aber, dass der Kläger ebenso vorerst als *„aggrieved person"* das Verfahren vor der Human Rights and Equal Opportunity Commission durchlaufen und demnach genügende eigene rechtliche Interessen an der *„representative proceeding"* hat.[651]

bb. Besondere Probleme in Bezug zum conciliation-Verfahren

Weiterhin muss die behauptete Diskriminierung (wegen Alters), wegen der das gerichtliche Verfahren angestrengt wird, den gleichen Lebenssachverhalt betreffen, wie die Beschwerde zur Human Rights and Equal Opportunity Commission, § 46PO Abs. 3 HREOC Act. Die Klagebefugnis darf jedoch nicht verneint werden, wenn der Kläger sich zwar auf den gleichen diskriminierenden Sachverhalt beruft, ihn in seiner Klage aber abweichend rechtlich würdigt. Denn die Vorschrift des § 46PO Abs. 3 HREOC Act erlaubt es nicht nur, die gleichen rechtlichen Wertungen wie im Beschwerdeverfahren zur Human Rights and Equal Opportunity Commission vorzunehmen. Vielmehr gibt sie dem Kläger auch das Recht, einen anderen rechtlichen Standpunkt einzunehmen.[652] Denn allein der Tatsachenvortrag zur Diskriminierungshandlung muss demjenigen des Beschwerdeverfahrens gleichen, so dass es dem Kläger auch versagt ist, sich in seinem Vortrag auf Umstände nach Einlegung der Beschwerde zur Human Rights and Equal Opportunity Commission zu beziehen.[653] Nur so kann der Vorrang des *conciliation*-Verfahrens vor dem gerichtlichen Verfahren nach Ansicht der Rechtsprechung hinreichend gewahrt werden.[654] Dabei wird jedoch nicht verkannt, dass es eines gewissen Maßes an Flexibilität zur Beurteilung bedarf, ob der Klagegegenstand dem Gegenstand des Beschwerdeverfahrens tatsächlich gleicht. Nicht selten verändert sich letzterer nach Einlegung der Beschwerde bis zum Verfahrensende in nicht unerheblichem Umfang. Deshalb stellt die Rechtsprechung konsequenterweise grundsätzlich auf den Zeitpunkt der Zurückweisung der Beschwerde durch die Human Rights and Equal Opportunity Commission und somit auf die Beendigung des Beschwerdeverfahrens ab.[655]

Als problematisch wird die Klagebefugnis häufig auch dann betrachtet, wenn die *„Issue of Termination"* nicht ordnungsgemäß in der Form ergangen ist, dass nicht alle Verfahrensbeteiligten genannt worden sind und es erst einer zweiten *„Issue of Termination"* bedurfte, um das Beschwerdeverfahren zu beenden. In einem solchen Fall soll nach Ansicht der Rechtsprechung die Klagebefugnis hinsichtlich der nicht genannten Personen fehlen, da die Human Rights and Equal Opportunity keinerlei Befugnis habe,

---

651 Human Rights and Equal Opportunity Commission, Federal Discrimination Law 2005, 226.

652 *Charles v Fuji Xerox Australia Pty Ltd* (2000) 105 FCR 573.

653 *Charles v Fuji Xerox Australia Pty Ltd* (2000) 105 FCR 573; *Travers v New South Wales* (2000) FCA 1565.

654 *Charles v Fuji Xerox Australia Pty Ltd* (2000) 105 FCR 573; *Travers v New South Wales* (2000) FCA 1565.

655 *Travers v New South Wales* (2000) FCA 1565; *Bender v Boris Lend Lease Pty Ltd* (2003) 175 FLR 446; *Ho v Regulator Australia Pty Ltd* [2004] FMCA 62; *Hollingdale v Northern Rivers Area Health Service* [2004] FMCA 721.

in ein und dem selben Fall mehrere Entscheidungen zur Verfahrensbeendigung zu erlassen.[656] Allerdings erscheint diese Auffassung einem umfassenden Rechtsschutz gegen Altersdiskriminierungen nicht sehr zuträglich. Denn bei offenkundigem Fehlen sollte es eine Möglichkeit zur Berichtigung der *„Issue of Termination"* geben, wobei der Rechtsprechung zuzustimmen ist, dass zwingende Voraussetzung sein müsse, dass das gerichtliche Verfahren noch nicht durch eine Klageerhebung eingeleitet worden ist.[657]

Die Rechtsprechung versucht aber andererseits die Klagebefugnis nicht unnötig einzugrenzen. So wird selbst dann die Klagemöglichkeit nicht verwehrt, wenn der Kläger das Beschwerdeverfahren bei der Human Rights and Equal Opportunity Commission bereits mehrfach wegen ein und derselben Diskriminierung erfolglos durchlaufen hat. Obwohl der Beklagte sich auf die Verwirkung des gerichtlichen Rechtsschutzes des Klägers berufen hat, sah die Rechtsprechung keine Veranlassung eine *„'repeat' complaint"* nicht zuzulassen. Denn ein besonderes Schutzbedürfnis des Beschwerdegegners und nunmehrigen Beklagten, welches gegen eine Überprüfung einer wiederholten Entscheidung der Human Rights and Equal Opportunity Commission sprechen würde, sei nicht ersichtlich.[658] Vielmehr helfen die entsprechenden Bestimmungen der Federal Court Rules schikanöse und missbräuchliche Klagen zu verhindern, wenn Anhaltspunkte nahe liegen, dass ein Kläger ständig, hartnäckig und vor allem ohne nachvollziehbaren Grund versucht, gerichtlichen Rechtsschutz zu erlangen.[659]

c. Prozessvertretung

Die Vertretung während des Prozesses findet ihre gesetzliche Grundlage in § 46PQ HREOC Act. Danach kann eine Partei gemäß § 46PQ Abs. 1 lit. a) HREOC entweder persönlich erscheinen, sich von einem Rechtsanwalt (*„barrister"* oder *„solicitor"*) gemäß § 46PQ Abs. 1 lit. b) HREOC oder aber auch gemäß § 46PQ Abs. 1 lit. c) HREOC von einer anderen Person vertreten lassen, sofern das Gericht der Überzeugung ist, dass ein persönliches Erscheinen der Partei nicht erforderlich ist. Allerdings ist bei einer Vertretung im Sinne von § 46PQ Abs. 1 lit. c) HREOC durch eine Person, die kein Rechtsanwalt ist, zu beachten, dass diese nicht berechtigt ist, ein Entgelt für die Prozessvertretung oder eine Entschädigung für ihre entstandenen Kosten zu verlangen oder zu vereinnahmen.

Erscheint eine Partei ohne einen rechtlichen Beistand vor Gericht und ist der Richter der Ansicht, dass sie eine rechtliche Beratung und Vertretung für das Verfahren benötigt, so kann es die Partei an einen Rechtsanwalt verweisen. In der Regel wird

---

656 *Speirs v Darling Range Brewing Co Pty Ltd* [2002] FMCA 126.

657 *Speirs v Darling Range Brewing Co Pty Ltd* [2002] FMCA 126.

658 *Yat Tung Investment Co Ltd v Doo Heng Bank* [1975] AC 581; *Port of Melbourne Authority v Anshun Pty* (1981) 147 CLR 589; *Midland Metals Overseas Ltd v Comptroller General of Customs* (1991) 30 FCR 87; *Stuart v Sanderson* (2000) 100 FCR 150; *McKenzie v Department of Urban Services & Canberra Hospital* (2001) 163 FLR 133.

659 Human Rights and Equal Opportunity Commission, Federal Discrimination Law 2005, 232.

dabei ein Verweis an einen Rechtsanwalt erfolgen, der die Vertretung übernimmt, ohne Gebühren zu verlangen („*pro bono*“).[660]

III. Die Grundzüge des Ablaufs des gerichtlichen Verfahrens beim Federal Court und Federal Magistrates Court auf der Grundlage des Age Discrimination Act 2004 (Cth)

1. Die mündliche Verhandlung

Die mündliche Verhandlung wird in der Regel durch gegenseitige Schriftsätze vorbereitet, in denen der jeweilige Standpunkt der Parteien zu Fragen bezüglich des Diskriminierungssachverhaltes sowie zur rechtlichen Beurteilung des diskriminierenden Verhaltens vorbereitet und präzisiert wird. Ein wichtiger Punkt ist dabei auch die Bezugnahme auf Beweise.

Der Richter entscheidet vorab je nach Umfang des Prozessstoffes, in welchem weiteren Verfahren die angebotenen Beweise gewürdigt werden sollen. Ihm obliegt die Auswahl zwischen dem schriftlichen und dem mündlichen Verfahren.

In der mündlichen Verhandlung selbst wird neben dem Hauptteil der Beweisaufnahme und der Vernehmung benannter Zeugen vor allem aber weiterhin durch den Richter versucht, die Parteien zu einer einvernehmlichen Streitbeilegung zu bewegen.[661] Dabei kann der Richter je nach Einzelfall unter Berücksichtigung der Interessen der Beteiligten die Bekanntgabe persönlicher Informationen einer Partei oder eines Zeugen, die Verwendung eines Beweismittels sowie den Zugang zu bestimmten Dokumenten verhindern.[662]

2. Klageabweisung

a. Vollständige Klageabweisung

Der Federal Court und der Federal Magistrates Court haben nicht die gleichen Befugnisse wie die Human Rights and Equal Opportunity Commission in § 46PH HREOC, um eine Klage abzuweisen. Um eine Klage in einem Fall wegen Altersdiskriminierung im vollen Umfang abzuweisen, muss das Gericht vielmehr davon überzeugt sein, dass zugunsten der Rechtsposition des Klägers kein weiteres Erfolg versprechendes Argument mehr existiert. Da eine solche Überzeugung nur schwer zu bilden ist, wird von

---

660 *Eastman*, Procedures, in: Baker & McKenzie, Age Discrimination: Mitigating Risk in the Workplace, S. 100.

661 *Eastman*, Procedures, in: Baker & McKenzie, Age Discrimination: Mitigating Risk in the Workplace, S. 98.

662 *Computer Interchange Pty Ltd v Microsoft Corporation* (1999) 88 FCR 438; *CC v Djerrkura* [2003] FMCA 372.

der vollständigen Klageabweisung in der Gerichtspraxis nur sehr selten Gebrauch gemacht und sie wird auch nicht empfohlen, solange der Klagegrund und der Anspruch des Klägers nicht vollumfänglich geklärt sind.[663]

b. Sofortige Klageabweisung

Anders verhält es sich dagegen mit einer Abweisung der Klage, wenn zur Überzeugung des Gerichts kein vernünftiger Klagegrund ersichtlich ist, ein Verfahren leichtfertig und querulatorisch erscheint oder ein Rechtsmissbrauch vorliegt.[664] Denn dann muss eine sofortige Klageabweisung („*summarily dismiss*") zwingende Folge sein. Ließe man derartige Klagen dagegen zu, so würde gegen den Grundsatz verstoßen werden, dass ein Verfahren nicht verfolgt werden solle, wenn es derart untragbar ist, dass offensichtlich keine hinreichende Aussicht auf Erfolg und keinerlei Bezug zu einer unrechtmäßigen Diskriminierung besteht.[665] Darüber hinaus kann weder bei den Parteien des Rechtsstreits noch bei der Öffentlichkeit ein Interesse daran bestehen, ein Verfahren durchzuführen, dem eine unsubstantiierte Klage zu Grunde liegt.[666]

Ausnahmsweise aber können die Gerichte von einer sofortigen Klageabweisung dann absehen, wenn es der Klärung einer wichtigen Tatsachen- oder Rechtsfrage bedarf und sich die Beantwortung dieser unmittelbar auf die Rechte der beteiligten Parteien auswirken könne.[667] Hier von einem leichtfertigen oder querulatorischen Verfahren zu sprechen, wäre nicht interessengerecht. Zur hinreichenden Wahrung der Interessen der Parteien und zur Gewährung eines umfassenden Rechtsschutzes erscheint es im Grundsatz darüber hinaus angebracht zu sein, von einer „*summarily dismiss*" nur sehr begrenzt Gebrauch zu machen und mit dieser Art der Verfahrensbeendigung sehr sorgsam umzugehen. Das gilt vor allem, wenn keine rechtliche Vertretung im Prozess erfolgt und deshalb die grundsätzliche Gefahr von Mängeln an und in der Klage besteht.[668]

Das Gericht muss zwar die Entscheidung treffen, ob es eine „*summarily dismiss*" vornimmt. Zur Beibringung der für eine sofortige Klageabweisung nötigen Tatsachen und Beweise ist jedoch der Beklagte verpflichtet. Er muss dafür sorgen, dass zur umfassenden Überzeugung des Gerichts eine Abweisung und somit Verfahrensbeendigung erforderlich ist.[669] Zu einer solchen Überzeugung sind der Federal Magistrates Court und der Federal Court zum Beispiel in Fällen gelangt, in denen zwischen der

---

663 *Chung v University of Sydney* [2001] FCMA 94; *Barnes v Northern Land Council & Ors* [2002] FMCA 54; vgl. zur Klagebweisung wegen Nichterscheinens vor Gericht auch *Pham v University of Queensland* [2002] FCAFC 40; *Ugur v Police Service of NSW* [2004] FCA 1032.

664 Human Rights and Equal Opportunity Commission, Federal Discrimination Law 2005, 243 mit Verweis auf die FMC Rules und die Federal Court Rules.

665 *Parker v Swan Hill Police* [2000] FCA 1688; *Paramasivam v Shier* [2001] FCA 545.

666 *Travers v New South Wales* [2000] FCA 1565.

667 *Stokes v Royal Flying Doctor Service (No 2)* [2003] FMCA 177; *Firew v Busway Trust (No 2)* [2003] FMCA 317.

668 *Paramasivam v Grant* [2001] FCA 882; *Chung v University of Sydney* [2001] FCMA 94; *Chung v University of Sydney* [2002] FCA 186; *Taylor v Morrison* [2003] FMCA 79; *Rana v University of South Australia* [2004] FCA 559.

669 *Paramasivam v Wheeler* [2000] FCA 1559.

behaupteten Diskriminierung und dem Verhalten des Beklagten keinerlei Zusammenhang erkennbar war, kein Bezug zu einem konkreten Fall bestand oder der Beklagte selbst nicht Beschwerdegegner des *conciliation*-Verfahrens bei der Human Rights and Equal Opportunity Commission gewesen ist.[670]

3. Vorläufiger Rechtsschutz

Der Federal Court und der Federal Magistrates Court sind gemäß § 46PP Abs. 1 HREOC Act ermächtigt, zur Sicherung des status quo in dringenden Fällen vorläufigen Rechtsschutz zu gewähren, indem sie auf Antrag einer Partei vor Klageerhebung eine einstweilige Verfügung erlassen.[671] So stellt die Rechtsprechung den Zweck der Gewährung vorläufigen Rechtsschutzes ausdrücklich klar:

> „...injunctions exist to prevent rights from being taken away from persons who have made a complaint to HREOC. They do not exist to create rights.“[672]

In der Regel wird zur Sicherung eines umfassenden Rechtsschutzes ein Antrag auf Gewährung vorläufigen Rechtsschutzes gleichzeitig mit der Klageschrift beim Gericht eingereicht.[673]

a. Der Zeitpunkt der Antragstellung

Allerdings sind der Federal Court und der Federal Magistrates Court nur dann zur Gewährung von vorläufigem Rechtsschutz befugt, wenn das Verfahren vor der Human Rights and Equal Opportunity Commission nicht bereits durch eine abschließende Entscheidung oder durch die Rücknahme der Beschwerde geendet hat, § 46PP Abs. 3 HREOC Act. Somit kann ein Antrag auf Gewährung vorläufigen Rechtsschutzes nach dem Gesetz nur im Verfahrensstadium zwischen Beschwerdeeinlegung und Beendigung des *conciliation*-Verfahrens zugelassen werden.[674]

Innerhalb der Rechtsprechung ist jedoch umstritten, ob es bei § 46PP Abs. 3 HREOC tatsächlich ausschließlich auf den Zeitpunkt der Antragsstellung ankommt oder ob nicht vielmehr auch die Entscheidung über den Antrag vor der Beendigung des *conciliation*-Verfahrens erfolgen müsse. So wird einerseits argumentiert, dass es allein auf den Zeitpunkt der Antragsstellung ankommen könne, da nur dieser vom Antragssteller beeinflusst werden könne.[675] Andererseits spricht für die letztgenannte Auffassung, dass eine einstweilige Verfügung immer Geltung bis zum Hauptsachever-

670 *Chung v University of Sydney* [2001] FMCA 94; *Rana v University of South Australia* [2003] FMCA 525; *Hassan v Hume* [2003] FMCA 476; *Croker v Sydney Institute of TAFE* [2003] FMCA 181; *Jandruwanda v University of South Australia (No 2)* [2003] FMCA 233: vgl. auch *Soreng v Victorian State Director of Public Housing* [2002] FMCA 124

671 Human Rights and Equal Opportunity Commission, Federal Discrimination Law 2005, 237.

672 *AB v New South Wales Minister for Education and Training* [2003] FMCA 16.

673 *Beck v Leichhardt Municipal Council* [2002] FCMA 331.

674 Human Rights and Equal Opportunity Commission, Federal Discrimination Law 2005, 239.

675 *McIntosh v Australian Postal Corporation* [2001] FCA 1012.

fahren und zur Entscheidung über die Hauptsacheklage habe und somit der Zeitpunkt der Entscheidung ausschlaggebend sein müsse.[676]

Allerdings erscheint die hinter diesem Streit stehende Problematik nicht konsequent bedacht und durchleuchtet zu sein. Zwar spricht vor allem für die erstgenannten Auffassung, dass sie den maßgeblichen Zeitpunkt in einer für den Antragsteller beeinflussbaren Art und Weise festlegt. Dennoch sollte, um eine bestmögliche Rechtsschutzmöglichkeit zu bieten, der Antrag auf Erlass einer einstweiligen Verfügung auch dann möglich sein, wenn das *conciliation*-Verfahren bereits geendet hat. Denn mitunter ergibt sich erst aus der Gesamtschau der abschließenden Entscheidung der Human Rights and Equal Opportunity Commission und mit dem diskriminierenden Verhalten des Beschwerdegegners das Bedürfnis nach einem zeitnahen und vorläufigem Rechtsschutz.[677]

Die Zuständigkeit ist unabhängig von dem aufgezeigten Streit aber auch dann gegeben, wenn es das Gericht als angemessen betrachtet, dass es aufgrund einer bevorstehenden Entscheidung der Human Rights and Equal Opportunity Commission entscheiden müsse, § 46PO Abs. 6 HREOC Act.[678] Dabei ist jedoch zu beachten, dass die Entscheidung der Human Rights and Equal Opportunity Commission nicht vorweggenommen werden und somit etwa keine Verpflichtung zur Zahlung von Schadensersatz erfolgen darf, § 46PO Abs. 8 HREOC Act.

b. Die Interessenabwägung

Wie in anderen Fällen auch, gestaltet sich eine Entscheidung über die Gewährung vorläufigen Rechtsschutzes in der Regel aufgrund der vorzunehmenden Abwägung zwischen den sich gegenüberstehenden Interessen und Rechten der Betroffen, der Würdigung von Beweismitteln und der Bewertung der Dringlichkeit einer solchen Entscheidung häufig als schwierig. Wie in der Rechtsprechung demnach festgestellt wird, ist sie

> „... not an easy one because clearly there is a duty to look at the background information, the evidence presented, to determine what the status quo is, whether it should be preserved by the granting of an interim injunction, and to also have regards to the rights of the respondent."[679]

Die zur Abwägung vorgegebenen Kriterien in § 46PP Abs. 1 lit. a) und b) HREOC Act sind jedoch nicht abschließend. Vielmehr ist das Gericht im Rahmen einer weiten Ermessensausübung befugt, neben dem aktuellen Stand der Sache und den Rechten des Anspruchsgegners zusätzliche Gesichtspunkte in die Bewertung einzustellen.[680] Denn auch im Common Law wird davon ausgegangen, dass für eine Entscheidung im vorläufigen Rechtsschutz nur dann ein Bedürfnis besteht, wenn zur Überzeugung des Ge-

---

676 *Rainsford v Group 4 Correctional Services* [2002] FMCA 36.

677 *Beck v Leichhardt Municipal Council* [2002] FMCA 331.

678 *Li v Minister for Immigration & Multicultural Affairs* [2001] FCA 1414.

679 *Gardner v National Netball League Pty Ltd* (2001) 182 ALR 408.

680 *Rainsford v Group 4 Correctional Services* [2002] FMCA 36.

richts feststeht, dass die Wahrscheinlichkeit einer Diskriminierung wegen Alters gegeben ist. Diese lässt sich aber nur für jeden Einzelfall konkret bewerten, so dass sich ein umfassender allgemeingültiger Beurteilungskatalog nicht als tragfähig erweisen kann.[681]

Einig ist sich die Rechtsprechung des Ferderal Magistrates Court und des Federal Court aber insbesondere dahingehend, dass in die Beurteilung zur Gewährung von vorläufigen Rechtsschutz insbesondere die Auswirkungen auf die Stellung des Antragstellers innerhalb des *conciliation*-Verfahrens und in Bezug auf den Antragsgegner einfließen müssen.[682]

Letztendlich sind jedoch im Ergebnis für die Entscheidung des Federal Magistrates Court und des Federal Court vorrangig die Prinzipien des Common Law maßgebend. Demnach bedarf es der Prüfung, ob ein vertretbarer und plausibler Fall vorliegt und der Grundsatz der Verhältnismäßigkeit hinreichend gewahrt wird.[683]

4. Die Beweislastproblematik im gerichtlichen Verfahren beim Federal Court und Federal Magistrates Court

a. Die Verteilung der Beweislast

Grundsätzlich trägt der Kläger im Prozess die Beweislast, welche nach dem Verfahrensrecht im *Case Law* und somit auch im Geltungsbereich des Age Discrimination Act 2004 (Cth) und des Human Rights and Equal Opportunity Commission Act 1986 (Cth) die sog. Abwägung der Wahrscheinlichkeiten (*„balance of probabilities"*) umfasst, § 140 Abs. 1 Evidence Act 1995 (Cth):[684]

> *„In a civil proceeding, the court must find the case of a party proved if it is satisfied that the case has been proved on the balance of probabilities."*

Die Methode der *„balance of probabilities"* in Antidiskriminierungsprozessen ist in zahlreichen Entscheidungen verdeutlicht.[685] Sie ist auch als *„beyound resonable doubt"* bekannt und besagt im Grunde, dass der Kläger im Zivilprozess den Beweis zu erbringen hat, dass die für die Begründetheit der Klage erforderlichen Tatsachen wahr sind, was immer dann der Fall ist, wenn ihr Vorliegen unter Berücksichtigung der vorgebrachten Beweise wahrscheinlicher ist, als ihr Fehlen.[686] Nicht ausreichend ist je-

---

681 Human Rights and Equal Opportunity Commission, Federal Discrimination Law 2005, 238.

682 *Rainsford v Group 4 Correctional Services* [2002] FMCA 36.

683 *Rainsford v Group 4 Correctional Services* [2002] FMCA 36; *De Alwis v Hair* [2002] FMCA 357.

684 *Bourke/Ronalds*, Discrimination Laws – Striving For Equality, in: *Macken*, The Law of Employment, 2002, 641.

685 Vgl. *Briginshaw v Briginshaw* (1938) 60 CLR 336; *Rejfek v McElroy* (1965) 112 CLR 517 = [1966] ALR 270.

686 Butterworths Australian Legal Dictionary, Sydney u.a., 1997, 108.

doch der bloße Vergleich der Wahrscheinlichkeiten, ohne einen Bezug zu den vorgebrachten Beweismitteln herzustellen.[687]

> „...when the law requires the proof of any fact, the tribunal must feel an actual persuasion of its occurrence or existence before it can be found. It cannot be found as a result of mere mechanical comparison of probabilities independently of any belief in its reality.“[688]

Daher muss das Gericht auf der Grundlage der *„balance of probabilities"* vor allem die Ernsthaftigkeit der klägerischen Behauptung und Beweise betrachten und zur Überzeugung gelangen, dass das diskriminierende Verhalten durch den Klägervortrag hinreichend begründet ist. Für diese Bewertung muss das Gericht gemäß § 140 Abs. 2 Evidence Act (Cth) insbesondere die Art und den Charakter des die Klage auslösenden Verhaltens, den konkreten Klagegegenstand sowie die Bedeutung der Angelegenheit betrachten, wobei die genannten Kriterien nicht als abschließend angesehen werden dürfen.[689] Folglich obliegt es dem Kläger, so substantiiert wie möglich vorzutragen und die erforderlichen Beweise für seinen Vortrag anzubringen, um die Überzeugung des Gerichts von seiner Ansicht zu erlangen.[690] Es ist jedoch für den Klägervortrag nicht erforderlich, die Absicht bzw. den Vorsatz für die Diskriminierung wegen Alters des Beklagten zu belegen.[691]

Die Beweislast kann sich nur durch eine gerichtliche Verfügung ändern, welche die Beweislast dem Beklagten aufbürdet. Ergeht eine derartige gerichtliche Verfügung über die Änderung der Beweislastverteilung, so ist dies ein Beleg dafür, dass der Klägervortrag nicht ausreichend gewesen ist, um das diskriminierende Verhalten des Beklagten zu begründen.[692] Allerdings scheint der Kläger dennoch bevorzugt zu werden, da die Übertragung der Beweislast auf den Beklagten für ihn eine Befreiung von dieser bedeutet.

Obwohl der Evidence Act 1995 (Cth) für Gerichtsverfahren vor dem Federal Court und dem Federal Magistrates Court die Beweisregeln aufstellt, wird durch § 46PQ HREOC Act geregelt, dass eine grundsätzliche Bindung des Gerichts an die Formalien für die Gerichtsverhandlung gerade nicht besteht. Somit steht es im Ermessen des Gerichts die *„rules of evidence"* nur begrenzt oder strikt anzuwenden, wobei aber dennoch der Grundsatz gilt, dass je wahrscheinlicher die klägerischen Behauptungen erscheinen, umso geringer müssen die Anforderungen an das Beweismaß sein, damit das Gericht von deren Richtigkeit überzeugt ist.[693]

---

687 *Briginshaw v Briginshaw* (1938) 60 CLR 336.

688 *Briginshaw v Briginshaw* (1938) 60 CLR 336.

689 *Neat Holdings Pty Ltd v Karajan Holdings Pty Ltd* (1992) 110 ALR 449.

690 *Collins*, Employment Law, Opportunity and Discrimination, 57 m.w.N..

691 *Human Rights and Equal Opportunity Commission v Mt Isa Mines Ltd* (1993) 46 FCR 301.

692 *Hill v University of New England* (1990) EOC 92-291; *Herring v Benevolent Society of New South Wales* (1992) EOC 92-408.

693 *Briginshaw v Briginshaw* (1938) 60 CLR 336; *Rejfek v McElroy* (1965) 112 CLR 517; *Victoria v Macedonien Teachers' Association* (1999) 91 FCR 47; *Sharma v Legal Aid Queensland* [2001] FCA 1699.

b. Der Beweis der Altersdiskriminierung

Allerdings schreibt § 16 ADA vor, dass der Kläger mit seiner Klage begründen muss, dass gerade das Alter das beherrschende Motiv für das Verhalten des Beklagten gewesen ist.[694]

> „If an act is done for 2 or more reasons, then, fort he purpose of this Act, the act is taken to be done for the reason of the age of a person only if:
> (a) one of the reasons is the age of the person; and
> (b) that reason is the dominant reason for doing the act."

Somit ist es also in jedem einzelnen Diskriminierungsfall von maßgeblichem Gewicht, ob die direkte oder indirekte Altersdiskriminierung aufgrund des bestimmten Alters einer Person vorgenommen wurde.[695] Dieser Beweis wird dem Kläger aber regelmäßig erhebliche Schwierigkeiten verursachen und die Gefahr einer Klageabweisung provozieren, da es nur sehr selten einen deutlichen Hinweis darauf gibt, dass gerade das Alter des Klägers den Beklagten zu seinem diskriminierenden Verhalten motiviert hat.[696] Meistens liegen die Umstände für diesen Beweis jedoch ausschließlich in der Hand des Beklagten oder sind für den Kläger schon gar nicht erkennbar, da sie sich nur im Kopf des Beklagten abspielen und es somit bereits schwierig ist, diese dem Beklagten überhaupt zu entlocken.[697] Darüber hinaus sind Verhaltensweisen denkbar, bei denen der Diskriminierende nicht in dem Bewusstsein bzw. nicht mit der Kenntnis handelt, eine Altersdiskriminierung vorzunehmen. Denn weder der Wille noch das Wissen um die diskriminierende Folge sind nach Ansicht der Rechtsprechung Voraussetzung für die Bejahung und den Nachweis einer Altersdiskriminierung.[698]

> „It would, in our view, significantly impede or hinder the attainment of the objects of the Act if [the definition of direct discrimination] were to be interpreted as requiring an intention or motive on the part of the alleged discriminator that is related to the status or private life of the person less favourably treated."[699]

---

694 Explanatory Memorandum of the Age Discrimination Bill 2003 (Cth), Annexure C, Clause 16, Act done because of age or other reason; Human Rights and Equal Opportunity Commission, Federal Discrimination Law 2005, 253; vgl. auch *Bourke/Ronalds*, Discrimination Laws – Striving For Equality, in: *Macken*, The Law of Employment, 2002, 613; Anti-Discrimination Board of New South Wales, Age Old Dilemmas (2004) 60 Equal Times 1; anders seit der Anpassung von § 16 ADA und der damit verbundenen Abschaffung des *"dominant reason test"* im Jahr 2010.

695 *Bourke/Ronalds*, Discrimination Laws – Striving For Equality, in: *Macken*, The Law of Employment, 2002, 614.

696 *Ellenbogen v Federated Municipal and Shire Council Employees Union of Australia & Ors* [1989] HREOCA 3; *Hill v University of New* England (1990) EOC 92-291, 77; Herring *v Benevolent Society of NSW* (1992) EOC 92-408, 78.

697 *Ellenbogen v Federated Municipal and Shire Council Employees Union of Australia & Ors* [1989] HREOCA 3.

698 *Waters v Public Transport Corporation* (1991) 173 CLR 359.

699 *Waters v Public Transport Corporation* (1991) 173 CLR 359.

Oftmals werden bestimmte Handlungen und Verhaltensweisen nicht mit einem Bezug zu einer diskriminierungsrelevanten Intention vorgenommen, sondern sind Resultat einer in bester Absicht vorgenommenen Aktion bzw. Reaktion.[700] Zwar mag es Fälle geben, in denen die Altersdiskriminierung aus dem bloßem Handlungsablauf und der Verhaltensweise des Beklagten geschlussfolgert werden kann, aber in den meisten Diskriminierungsfällen wird dies mangels eines direkten Beweises durch schriftliche oder mündlichen Äußerungen nicht möglich sein.[701]

So verbleibt dem Kläger zur Stütze des Beweises der Altersdiskriminierung in den meisten Fällen nur der Weg über Schlussfolgerungen aus den hauptsächlichen Gegebenheiten des jeweiligen Falles.[702] Das bedeutet für den Kläger, dass er den Beweis erbringen muss, der einen Schluss auf das diskriminierende Verhalten zulässt. Dabei soll es aber gerade nicht ausreichen, auf systematische oder historische Bezüge des Alters hinzuweisen und somit auf eine Altersdiskriminierung zu schließen. Denn die Tatsache, dass in der Arbeitswelt etwa eine generelle Bevorzugung von jüngeren Bewerbern stattfindet, rechtfertigt eine zwingende Schlussfolgerung, dass auch der Beklagte eine solche Diskriminierung begangen hat, nicht. Vielmehr kann dieser Umstand nur als einer von vielen Faktoren berücksichtigt werden.[703] Daher ist es im Ergebnis nicht verwunderlich, dass der Beweislast des Klägers eine maßgebliche Schlüsselrolle für das gerichtliche Verfahren zukommt. Trotz der zum Teil nicht unerheblichen Hürden für den Nachweis der diskriminierenden Verhaltensweise der beklagten Partei ist in Australien für Antidiskriminierungsfälle bis dato keine klare Beweislasterleichterung oder –umkehr erfolgt.[704]

Nicht als Beweismittel zugelassen sind Äußerungen der Human Rights and Equal Opportunity Commission, die während des *conciliation*-Verfahrens getätigt worden. Denn ein solches Beweismittel wäre unvereinbar mit und widersprüchlich zur gesetzgeberischen Absicht. Denn nicht nur, dass das *conciliation*-Verfahren nicht öffentlich durchgeführt werden soll, sondern auch die Weitergabe von Informationen seitens der Human Rights and Equal Opportunity Commission an das Gericht wird nicht erlaubt. So kann es zwangsläufig und konsequenterweise den Parteien nicht zugebilligt werden, auf Aussagen aus dem *conciliation*-Verfahren als gerichtliche Beweismittel zurückzugreifen und somit die Grundsätze und Prinzipien des *conciliation*-Verfahrens zu unterlaufen.[705]

---

700 *Bourke/Ronalds*, Discrimination Laws – Striving For Equality, in: *Macken*, The Law of Employment, 2002, 614 mit Verweis auf die unveröffentlichte Entscheidung *Prezzi v Discrimination Commissioner and Quest Group Pty Ltd.*

701 *Paramasivam v Wheeler & Ors* [2001] FCA 231.

702 *Fenwick v Beveridge Building Products Pty Ltd* (1986) EOC 92-147.

703 Vgl. zur Diskriminierung wegen des Geschlechts *Sharma v Legal Aid Queensland* [2001] FCA 1699.

704 Im europäischen Gemeinschaftsrech wird durch Art. 10 der RL 2000/78/EG und die nationale Vorschrift des § 22 AGG im deutschen Recht die besondere Bedeutung der Beweislasterleichterung zum Schutz des Diskriminierungsopfers und zur Gewährleistung der Rechtsdurchsetzung unterstrichen.

705 *Bender v Boris Lend Lease Pty Ltd* (2003) 175 FLR 446.

c. Verspätetes Vorbringen von Beweismitteln

Werden – neue – Beweismittel erst nach Ablauf der in den Federal Court Rules festgelegten Frist vorgebracht, so ist das Gericht zur Zurückweisung dieser berechtigt und braucht sie demnach nicht in seiner Entscheidung zu berücksichtigen.[706] Dies muss vor allem dann gelten, wenn nicht einmal ein Grund für das verspätete Vorbringen vorgetragen wurde und dieses Beweismittel die Entscheidung des Gerichts nicht zu ändern vermocht hätte.[707] Zwar sind der Federal Court und der Federal Magistrates Court gemäß § 46PR HREOC Act nicht an Formalien und an Formvorschriften gebunden, aber dennoch wird von der genannten Regel strikt Gebrauch gemacht, so das § 46PR HREOC insofern ohne Wirkung für den Beweisbelasteten bleibt.

5. Probleme bei der Vertretung vor Gericht

a. Vertretung vor Gericht

Unabhängig von den Fragen und Problemen, die sich im Zusammenhang mit einer anwaltlichen Vertretung gemäß § 46PQ Abs. 1 lit. b) HREOC Act vor Gericht stellen können, bieten oftmals auch Vertretungen durch Personen im Sinne von § 46PQ Abs. 1 lit. c) HREOC, die keine Anwälte („*barrister/solicitor*“) sind, ausreichend Konfliktpotential. Denn für deren Zulassung ist es erforderlich, dass das Gericht zur Überzeugung gelangt, dass ein Erscheinen der eigentlichen Partei nicht möglich ist, wobei zahlreiche Kriterien für die Beurteilung berücksichtigt werden müssen.[708]

So kann die Komplexität ausschlaggebend für die Zulassung einer Vertretung im Sinne von § 46PQ Abs. 1 lit. c) HREOC sein. Denn umso einfacher und überschaubarer ein Fall ist, um so eher kann ein Laie vor Gericht der Verhandlung folgen und eine Interessenvertretung wahrnehmen.[709] Weiterhin kann die beim Vertreter zu erwartende Objektivität von Bedeutung sein, da etwa ein Familienangehöriger aufgrund seines persönlichen Bezugs oftmals nicht zu einem ausgewogenen und informativen Vortrag in der Lage sein wird.[710] Darüber hinaus wird das Gericht eine Vertretung dieser Art untersagen, wenn die Gefahr einer erhöhten Kostenverursachung durch die nicht fachgerechte Interessenvertretung gegeben scheint.[711] Letztendlich wird in der Regel auch das Interesse an einer effektiven und effizienten Rechtspflege zu berücksichtigen sein, dass am besten bei einer Vertretung beider Parteien durch kompetente Rechtsanwälte sichergestellt werden kann.[712]

---

706 Order 36, r 6 Federal Court Rules.

707 Human Rights and Equal Opporunity Commission, Federal Discrimination Law 2005, 262.

708 *P & R (No 1)* [2002] FMCA 65.

709 *Groundwater v Territory Insurance Office* [2004] FMCA 381.

710 *Groundwater v Territory Insurance Office* [2004] FMCA 381.

711 *Groundwater v Territory Insurance Office* [2004] FMCA 381.

712 *Groundwater v Territory Insurance Office* [2004] FMCA 381.

b. Auftreten ohne Prozessbevollmächtigten

Oftmals verzichten die Kläger dagegen ganz auf eine Vertretung durch einen Prozessbevollmächtigten vor Gericht und bringen sich durch ihren eigenen rechtlich in der Regel unzureichenden Vortrag nicht selten in eine unvorteilhafte Prozesssituation. Allerdings ist sich die Rechtsprechung einig, dass zu einem umfassenden Schutz eines vermeintlichen Opfers einer Altersdiskriminierung das Auftreten ohne Prozessbevollmächtigten keine negativen Auswirkungen auf die Erfolgsaussichten der Klage haben dürfen:

> „This does not, however, mean that the appellant can have no chance of success in these proceedings."[713]

Vielmehr kann ein Richter verpflichtet sein, bei einem unrepräsentierten Kläger bei entsprechendem Bedarf handlungsleitend einzugreifen, um sicherzustellen, dass die Rechte des Klägers und vermeintlichen Diskriminierungsopfers hinreichend geschützt werden und das Gerichtsverfahren gerecht abläuft:

> „Whilst this Court has a duty not to intervene in matters involving unrepresented litigants to such an extent that the impartial function of the Judge is compromised, a judge may intervene to protect the rights of an unrepresented litigant and to ensure that the proceedings are fair and just."[714]

6. Wechselwirkungen zwischen dem Federal Magistrates Court und dem Federal Court

Der Federal Court ist berechtigt, auf Antrag einer Partei oder aufgrund eigener Überzeugung unter Berücksichtigung der in § 32AB Abs. 6 Federal Court Act 1976 (Cth) genannten Kriterien das Verfahren an den Federal Magistrates Court zu übertragen. Ausschlaggebend für eine Verweisungsentscheidung sollen dabei insbesondere die allgemeine Bedeutung des Rechtsstreits, die Kosten- und der Zeitaufwand sowie vergleichbare anhängige Verfahren beim Federal Magistrates Court und dessen Kapazitäten sein.[715] Somit kann aus Kostengründen und unter dem Gesichtspunkt der Prozesseffektivität eine beantragte Verweisung selbstverständlich auch abgelehnt werden.[716]

Aber auch in die andere Richtung kann auf Antrag eine Verweisung stattfinden. So ist gemäß des § 39 Abs. 3 FMA der Federal Magistrates Court ebenfalls zur Abgabe des Verfahrens an den Federal Court befugt, sofern das Verfahren allgemeine Bedeutung hat und deshalb vom Federal Court entschieden werden sollte, die Verfah-

713 *Barghouthi v Transfield Pty Ltd* (2002) 122 FCR 19.

714 *Barghouthi v Transfield Pty Ltd* (2002) 122 FCR 19; *Minogue v Human Rights and Equal Opportunity Commission* (1999) 84 FCR 438; *Awan v Minister for Immigration & Multicultural & Indigenous Affairs* [2002] FCA 594.

715 *Charles v Fuji Xerox Australia Pty Ltd* (2000) 105 FCR 573.

716 *Charles v Fuji Xerox Australia Pty Ltd* (2000) 105 FCR 573; vgl. auch *Travers v New South Wales* [2000] FCA 1565.

rensdauer und -kosten sowie auch die Interessen der Beteiligten ausreichend gewürdigt werden. Die Rechtsprechung stellt dabei ausdrücklich heraus, dass das bloße Behaupten von wichtigen Streit- und Rechtsfragen nicht automatisch und zwangsläufig zu einer Verweisung an den Federal Court führen muss.[717] Allerdings wird in der Regel das Verfahren ohne weiters an den Federal Court verwiesen, wenn der Federal Magistrates Court zu der Auffassung kommt, es liege ein Rechtsproblem von erheblicher und allgemeiner Bedeutung vor, der Prozess könne durch die Verweisung beschleunigt werden und es werden keine zusätzlichen Kosten verursacht.[718] Ebenso ist zu beachten, dass eine solche Verweisung nur bis zum ersten Prozesstag in Form eines ausdrücklichen Antrags erfolgen kann.[719]

Rechtsmittel gegen eine Entscheidung des Federal Magistrates Court werden entweder von einem Einzelrichter oder in voller Richterbesetzung beim Federal Court entschieden, §§ 14 Abs. 1, 24 Federal Court Act 1976 (Cth). Folglich können auch deshalb Verfahren des Federal Magistrates Court – allerdings erst nach ihrem Abschluss – zur weiteren Entscheidung an den Federal Court gehen. Wobei es sich hier nicht um ein Rechtsmittelverfahren im eigentlichen Sinne und nicht um einen sog. *„trial de novo"* handelt, sondern den Parteien vielmehr die Möglichkeit zur Verfahrensergänzung der ersten Instanz durch erneute Aufbereitung der Beweismittel gegeben wird.[720]

Der Federal Court und der Federal Magistrates Court sind sich aber trotz der Möglichkeiten, einen Diskriminierungsrechtsstreit an das jeweils andere Gericht zu verweisen, bewusst, dass der Schutz des Diskriminierungsopfers nicht unter dem Prozess leiden darf.[721] Daher ist einerseits die Rechtsprechung bei der Umsetzung der Anti-Diskriminierungsgesetze und somit auch des Age Discrimination Act 2004 (Cth) darauf bedacht, dass der Schutz vor diskriminierenden Behandlungen ausgeweitet anstatt eingeschränkt werden muss und dass sie verantwortungsvoll mit der Zulassung sowie Schaffung von Ausnahmen und Befreiungen von bestehenden Diskriminierungsverboten umgeht.[722]

IV. Die Kostenentscheidung

Mit der Entscheidung des Federal Court bzw. des Federal Magistrates Court über die Rechtsfolge für das diskriminierende Verhalten ist immer auch eine Entscheidung über die Kostentragung verbunden. Zwar gibt es für die Altersdiskriminierung keine spezialgesetzliche Kostenregelung. Den Gerichten steht aber aufgrund von § 43 des Federal

---

717 *Nizzari v Westpac Financial Services* [2003] FMCA 255.

718 *Nizzari v Westpac Financial Services* [2003] FMCA 255.

719 Human Rights and Equal Opportunity Commission, Federal Discrimination Law 2005, 249.

720 *Low v Commonwealth of Australia* [2001] FCA 702; *Chung v University of Sydney* [2002] FCA 186.

721 Human Rights and Equal Opportunity Commission, Federal Discrimination Law 2005, 251.

722 *Australian Iron and Steel v Banovic* (1989) 168 CLR 165; *Waters v Public Transport Corporation* (1991) 173 CLR 349; *IW v City of Perth* (1997) 191 CLR 1; *Qantas Airways Ltd v Christie* (1998) 193 CLR 280; *X v Commonwealth* (1999) 200 CLR 177;

Court Act 1976 (Cth) und § 79 des Federal Magistrates Act 1999 (Cth) die grundsätzliche Befugnis zu, über die Kosten des Verfahrens zu entscheiden.

1. Der Grundsatz der Kostenverteilung

a. The costs follow the event

Bei der Entscheidung über die Kosten gilt der Grundsatz, dass die Kosten dem Verfahren folgen („*costs follow the event*").[723] Deshalb werden der unterlegenen Partei die Gerichtskosten sowie die Kosten der Partei auferlegt, die den Prozess gewonnen hat.[724] Allerdings stehen der Erlass von „*costs orders*" und somit auch die Kostenverteilung im Ermessen des Gerichts.[725]

> „Ordinarily, a successful litigant has an exceptation that costs will follow the event; that is, that the unsuccessful litigant will be required to pay the costs of the successful litigant on a party/party basis."[726]

b. Ausnahmen

aa. Allgemeingültige Ausnahmen

Sofern es jedoch erforderlich erscheint, darf die Rechtsprechung von diesem Grundsatz abweichen und auch der obsiegenden Partei (einen Teil der) Kosten auferlegen. Die Kostenlast wird vor allem dann der obsiegenden Partei in einem bestimmten Umfang auferlegt, wenn sie den Prozess nur zum Teil gewonnen hat.[727] Ebenso soll die obsiegende Partei auch für den Kostenanteil einstehen, den sie durch nicht gerechtfertigte und somit erfolglose Anträge im Verfahren oder durch eine unnötige Verfahrensverzögerung bzw. -fortsetzung verursacht hat.[728]

> „One circumstance that might disentitle a successful litigant to an order for costs can be the behaviour of the litigant during the course of the proceedings, for example, by taking unnecessary technical points or otherwise inappropriately prolonging the proceeding..."[729]

---

723 *Hughes v Western Australian Cricket Association (Inc)* (1986) ATPR 40-748, 48-136; *Brenner v First Artists' Management Pty Ltd* [1993] 2 VR 221.

724 Die Verfahren unter den einzelnen bundesstaatlichen Diskriminierungsgeseten sind dabei oftmals kostenfrei („*no costs juristictions*"); vgl. *Ronalds/Pepper*, Discrimination Law and Practice, 223.

725 *Brenner v First Artists' Management Pty Ltd* [1993] 2 VR 221.

726 *Forbes v Commonwealth (No 2)* [2003] FMCA 262.

727 *Forster v Farquhar* (1893) 1 QB 564; *Hughes v Western Australian Cricket Association (Inc)* (1986) ATPR 40-748, 48-136.

728 *Ritter v Godfrey* (1920) 2 KB 47; *Cretazzo v Lombardi* (1975) 13 SASR 4; *Jamal v Secretary Department of Health* (1988) 13 NSWLR 252, 271; vgl. ebenso *Hughes v Western Australian Cricket Association (Inc)* (1986) ATPR 40-748, 48-136; *Xiros v Fortis Life Assurance Ltd* (2001) 162 FLR 433.

729 *Xiros v Fortis Life Assurance Ltd* (2001) 162 FLR 433.

So kommt es in zahlreichen Gerichtsverfahren wegen Altersdiskriminierung sogar vor, dass das Gericht tenoriert, jede Partei habe ihre eigenen Kosten zu tragen. Eine solche Entscheidung ist vor allem dann interessengerecht, wenn das Verfahren durch den Kläger unnötig verzögert wird und zudem den Zeugen der beklagten Partei eine nicht belegbare Absprache unterstellt.[730]

Sofern der Charakter und die Umstände des jeweiligen Diskriminierungsprozesses sich als besonders außergewöhnlich darstellen und es dadurch ausnahmsweise als ungeeignet erscheinen lassen, kann das Gericht davon absehen, der unterlegenen Partei die Kosten aufzuerlegen.[731] Dies wird jedoch nur sehr selten vorkommen, wenn sich etwa Fragen von grundsätzlicher Bedeutung in Bezug auf die Änderung einer Gesetzgebung o.ä. ergeben.

Häufiger und praktisch relevanter dürfte dagegen die Ausnahme vom Grundsatz *„costs follow the event"* sein, dass anteilig die Kosten des Verfahrens auch von der obsiegenden Partei zu bezahlen sind, wenn das Urteil ein Weniger als ein zuvor – im Verfahren oder bereits auf außergerichtlicher Ebene – von der Gegenseite angebotenen Vergleich enthält und dennoch ein obsiegendes Urteil darstellt.[732] Obwohl es sich hierbei bereits um Ausnahmeentscheidungen handelt, ist zu berücksichtigen, dass es auch Kostenentscheidungen in der Form geben kann, die der in Teilen obsiegenden Partei ihre ganzen Kosten auferlegt.[733]

Wie die angeführten Rechtsprechungsbeispiele zeigen, ist nahezu jedwede Art der Kostenverteilung – mit einer entsprechenden Argumentation – denkbar und vertretbar. Dies belegen diverse weitere Ausnahmen von Tenorierungen zur Kostentragung in zahlreichen weiteren Urteilen des Federal Court und des Federal Magistrates Court.[734] Dabei wird sogar so weit gegangen, dass der streitgegenständliche Fall in mehrere Abschnitte aufgeteilt werden soll, so dass für jeden dieser Abschnitte eine gesonderte Kostenentscheidung ergehen kann.[735]

bb. Ausnahmen durch zusätzliche Kostenbelastung

Als Gegenstück zur Ausweitung von Schadensersatzzahlungen in Form der *„aggravated damages"* steht dem Gericht grundsätzlich die Befugnis zu, sämtliche Kosten, die durch die Umstände entstanden sind, die bereits zu dem – neben der eigentlichen Diskriminierung – zusätzlichen Schaden geführt haben, entsprechend zu verteilen (*„indemnity costs"*). So können dem Diskriminierenden die gesamten entstandenen Kosten für das Verfahren vor der Human Rights and Equal Opportunity Commission sowie auch für den anschließenden Gerichtsprozess auferlegt werden, wenn der Antragsgegner bzw. Beklagte nicht erscheint und dem Kläger dadurch wiederum ein zusätzlicher

---

730 *Horman v Distribution Group Limited* [2001] FMCA 52.

731 *Ruddock v Vadarlis (No 2)* (2001) 115 FCR 229.

732 *Calderbank v Calderbank* [1975] 3 All ER 333; *Forbes v Commonwealth (No 2)* [2003] FMCA 262; *Rispoli v Merck Sharpe & Dohme (Australia) Pty Ltd (No 2)* [2003] FMCA 516.

733 *Howe v Qantas Airways Ltd (No 2)* [2004] FMCA 934.

734 Vgl. etwa *Tate v Rafin* [2000] FCA 1582; *Creek v Cairns Post Pty Ltd* [2001] FCA 1150; *Bruch v Commonwealth of Australia* [2002] FMCA 29; *Ho v Regulator Australia Pty Ltd (No 2)* [2004] FMCA 402.

735 *McBride v Victoria* [2003] FMCA 313.

Schaden entstanden ist.[736] Solche Entscheidungen werden oftmals – nicht nur von der betroffenen Partei – von der Rechtsprechung selbst stark kritisiert, da einerseits eine – neben den *„aggravated damages"* – zusätzliche Bestrafung stattfindet und die Grenzen nahezu fließend sind sowie oftmals nicht hinreichend bewiesen sei, dass das jeweilige Verhalten der kostenbelasteten Partei kausal war für die Prozessverzögerung.[737]

Grundsätzlich aber steht der Rechtsprechung diese Möglichkeit der Kostenverteilung immer dann offen, wenn eine Partei das Gericht missachtet (*„contempt of court"*), willkürlich ein Vergleichsangebot ablehnt, entgegen der tatsächlichen Sachkenntnis eine unnötige Verzögerung des Verfahrens verursacht oder sogar entgegen der Sachkenntnis bewusst wahrheitswidrig vorträgt und entsprechende Behauptungen aufstellt.[738] Sofern einer der genannten (aber nicht abschließenden) Umstände tatsächlich auftritt und ursächlich ist für eine Beeinträchtigung der anderen Partei, dann kann es im Sinne der Antidiskriminierungsgesetzgebung jedoch nur förderlich sein, konsequent zur Beseitigung und Unterbindung derartiger Verhaltensweisen beizutragen. Denn durch eine solche Verhaltensweise drückt der Diskriminierende seine Missachtung dem Opfer gegenüber ebenso aus und setzt die Diskriminierung fort, die eigentlich im Verfahren Streitgegenstand ist.[739]

> „...Applications of this nature, based upon untruthful evidence, are apt to bring anti-discrimination legislation into disrepute, and do a grave disservice to others wishing to pursue a genuine grievance. The respondents should not be out of pocket in having dealt with this application."[740]

cc. Ausnahmen im Verfahren beim Federal Magistrates Court

Der Grundsatz *„costs follow the event"* gilt im Verfahren beim Federal Magistrates Court nicht, denn dort steht es im Ermessen des Gerichts, eine Kostenentscheidung zu fällen, § 79 Federal Magistrates Act. Allerdings werden der unterlegenen Partei in der Regel – wie beim Verfahren am Federal Court – die Verfahrenskosten und die Kosten der obsiegenden Partei auferlegt.[741]

Daneben gibt es aber auch einige Entscheidungen, in denen auf eine Kostenentscheidung verzichtet worden ist.[742] In solchen Fällen muss durch den Federal Magistrates Court eine umfassende Abwägung erfolgen, ob eine Kostenentscheidung ergehen soll und wenn in welcher Form. Dabei ist insbesondere zu berücksichtigen, ob ein öffentliches Interesse daran besteht, nicht vom vorgenannten Grundsatz der Kostenver-

---

736 *Hughes v Car Buyers Pty Limited* (2004) 210 ALR 645; vgl auch *Hinchliffe v University of Sydney (No 2)* [2004] FMCA 640.

737 Human Rights and Equal Opportunity Commission, Federal Discrimination Law 2005, 270; *Ronalds/Pepper*, Discrimination Law and Practice, 324 m.w.N..

738 *Colgate-Palmolive v Cussons* (1993) 46 FCR 225.

739 Vgl. auch *Wong v Sue* [2001] FMCA 108.

740 *Wong v Sue* [2001] FMCA 108.

741 *Ball v Morgan* [2001] FMCA 127; *Minns v New South Wales (No 2)* [2002] FMCA 197; *Batzialas v Tony Davies Motors Pty Ltd* [2002] FMCA 243; *Murphy v Loper* [2002] FMCA 310.

742 *Tadawan v South Australia* [2001] FMCA 25; *Ryan v Presbytery of Wide Bay Sunshine Coast and Pesbyterian Church of Queensland* [2001] FMCA 15.

teilung abzuweichen und ob der Kläger durch einen Prozessbevollmächtigten im Verfahren vertreten wird.[743]

Darüber hinaus soll das Gericht grundsätzlich immer berücksichtigen, dass die obsiegende Partei nicht über Gebühr mit Kosten für die Rechtsverfolgung belastet wird, damit dies ihren Erfolg nicht schmälert. Zudem soll durch eine drohende Kostenlast, der Kläger mangels hinreichender Finanzkraft nicht davon abgehalten werden, eine (begründete) Klage zu erheben und seine Rechtsposition somit erfolgreich durchzusetzen.[744]

Aber nicht nur eine Kostenentscheidung, die entweder dem Kläger oder dem Beklagten die volle Kostenlast auferlegt oder der Verzicht auf eine Kostenentscheidung können die passenden Ergebnisse sein. So kann es beim Verfahren am Federal Magistrates Court – aus den oben genannten Gründen – ebenso erforderlich sein, die Kosten anteilig beiden Parteien aufzuerlegen.[745] Auch bietet es sich nicht selten an, die anfallenden Kosten nur durch eine Partei tragen zu lassen, aber zugleich den Umfang zu begrenzen, wenn die Kosten im Verhältnis zum Umfang des Prozesses und der verletzten Rechtsposition unverhältnismäßig hoch ausgefallen sind.[746]

dd. Ausnahmen bei Vergleichsangeboten

Daneben kann jedoch auch die für den Federal Court geltende Sonderregelung der r23 *FC Rules („offer of compromise")* Anwendung finden. Unterbreitet die eine Partei der anderen Partei einen Vergleichsvorschlag und lehnt die andere Partei diesen ab und erhält im Wege des Urteils weniger zugesprochen, als im Rahmen des Vergleichsangebots hätte geregelt werden können, so soll die eine Partei – sofern das Gericht nicht etwas anders anordnet – vom Zeitpunkt des Vergleichsvorschlag alle zusätzlichen Kosten (*„indemnity costs"*) geltend machen bzw. eine entsprechende Kostenverteilung beantragen können.[747]

Diese Ausnahmeregelung gilt allerdings auch im Verfahren vor dem Federal Magistrates Court, damit ein entsprechender Gleichlauf in den Verfahrensregeln sichergestellt ist.[748] Darüber hinaus gilt sie für beide Parteien – sowie den Widerkläger und Widerbeklagten – entsprechend und ist nicht auf den Kläger bzw. Beklagten beschränkt. Insofern wurde die zuvor bestehende Begrenzung aufgegeben, um einen um-

---

743 *Xiros v Fortis Life Assurance Ltd* [2001] FMCA 15; *Hassan v Smith Donaldson and Children's Hospital at Westmead* [2001] FMCA 58; *McLeod v Power* [2003] FMCA 2.

744 *Low v Australian Taxation Office* [2000] FMCA 6; *Saddi v Active Employment Break Thru Personnel Inc, Care Employment and Commonwealth* [2001] FMCA 73; *Xiros v Fortis Life Assurance Ltd* [2001] FMCA 15; *Hassan v Smith Donaldson and Children's Hospital at Westmead* [2001] FMCA 58; *Escobar v Rainbow Printing Pty Limited (No 3)* [2002] FMCA 160.

745 *McBride v Victoria (No 2)* [2003] FMCA 313.

746 *Barghouthi v Transfield Services* (2002) 122 FCR 19; *Kowalski v Domestic Violence Crisis Service Inc (No 2)* [2003] FMCA 210.

747 *Wills v Bigmac Pty Limited* [2004] FCA 949; *Port Kembla Coal Terminal Limited v Braverus Maritime Inc. (No 2)* [2004] FCA 1437.

748 *Part 2 of Schedule 3 FMC Rules*; *Batzialas v Tony Davis Motors Pty Limited* [2002] FMCA 243.

fassenden Interessenausgleich gewährleisten zu können und mögliche Benachteiligungen auszuschließen.[749]

Ein Vergleichsangebot („*notice of offer*"), welches nicht der r23 *FC Rules* – insbesondere den formalen Anforderungen – entspricht, braucht in der gerichtlichen Kostenentscheidung nicht berücksichtigt zu werden.[750] In der gerichtlichen Praxis spricht man insofern von „*Calderbank offers*", wobei hier im Gegensatz zu einem „*offer of compromise*" beurteilt werden soll, ob ein im Ganzen unangemessenes und unzumutbares Vergleichsangebot vorliegt und nicht etwa ein zumindest teilweise angemessener und vertretbarer Interessenausgleich.[751]

a. Abweichende Gerichtspraxis

Nicht selten jedoch gibt es Entscheidungen, die sich vom allgemeinen Grundsatz der Kostenverteilung abwenden und die Auffassung favorisieren, dass gerichtliche Verfahren in Diskriminierungsstreitigkeiten kostenfrei sein sollen.[752]

aa. „'No Costs' Jurisdiction"

Die „*'No Costs' Jurisdiction*" wird vor allem deshalb befürwortet, weil der obsiegenden Partei kein Nachteil durch anfallende bzw. bereits angefallene Kosten entstehen sollte und gerade im Recht der Altersdiskriminierung nicht ausschließlich private Interessen involviert sind, sondern oftmals auch Streitigkeiten von öffentlichem Interesse sein können.[753] Nach Ansicht der Rechtsprechung besteht zudem grundsätzlich die Gefahr, dass ein erfolgreiches gerichtliches Vorgehen gegen eine Altersdiskriminierung deshalb unterbleiben könnte, weil eine mögliche Kostenbelastung drohe.[754] Daher soll zumindest im frühen Verfahrensstadium von einer Kostenbelastung abgesehen werden, damit eine umfassende Aufklärung des Diskriminierungsfalles erreicht werden kann und das Diskriminierungsopfer nicht vor der Inanspruchnahme gerichtlichen Rechtsschutzes zurückschreckt.[755]

---

749 Human Rights and Equal Opportunity Commission, Federal Discrimination Law 2005, 327 mit Verweis auf die *Federal Court Amendment Rules 2004 (No 1)* vom 23.03.2004.

750 Human Rights and Equal Opportunity Commission, Federal Discrimination Law 2005, 327 mit Verweis auf *Black v Tomislav Lipovac BHNF Maria Lipovac & Ors* [1998] FCA 699; *Dr Martens Australia Pty Ltd v Figgins Holdings Pty Ltd (No 2)* [2000] FCA 602; *Fresh Express Australia Pty Ltd v Larridren Pty Ltd* [2002] FCA 1640; a.A. etwa *Rispoli v Merck Sharpe & Dohme & Ors (No 2)* [2003] FMCA 516 wonach selbst ein solches Angebot bei der Kostenverteilung nicht unberücksichtigt bleiben soll.

751 *Calderbank c Calderbank* (1975) 3 All ER 333; *Forbes v Commonwealth of Australia* [2003] FMCA 262; *Port Kembla Coal Terminal Limited v Braverus Maritime Inc. (No 2)* [2004] FCA 1437.

752 *McKenzie v Department of Urban Services and Canberra Hospital* (2001) 163 FLR 133; *Tadawan v South Australia* [2001] FMCA 25; *Ryan v Presbytery of Wide Bay Sunshine Coast* [2001] FMCA 12.

753 *Tadawan v South Australia* [2001] FMCA 25.

754 *Tadawan v South Australia* [2001] FMCA 25.

755 *Low v Australian Tax Office* [2000] FMCA 6; *Saddi v Active Employment* [2001] FMCA 73.

Die vorgebrachten Argumente führten in Teilen der Rechtsprechung dazu, dass in zahlreichen Entscheidungen die Kosten des Diskriminierungsprozesses der obsiegenden Partei erstattet werden und deshalb der unterlegenden Partei durch entsprechenden Urteilsausspruch die Kostenbelastung auferlegt wird.[756] So wird demnach oftmals der Grundsatz *„costs follow the event"* modifiziert in *„a wholly successful defendant should receive his or her costs unless good reason is shown in the contrary'"*.[757]

Eine beliebige Ausweitung der Abwendung vom Grundsatz *„costs follow the event"* soll aber nicht beabsichtigt sein. Denn eine willkürliche Abweichung und eigentümliche Kostenverteilung kann im Interesse der Parteien und im Interesse der Rechtssicherheit nicht gewollt sein. Es soll vielmehr berücksichtigt werden, dass gerade dann eine Kostenbelastung keinen Sinn macht, wenn die obsiegende Partei Recht bekommen hat oder besondere, eine abweichende Kostenlast, rechtfertigende Gründe vorliegen.[758]

(1) Rechtfertigung durch das öffentliche Interesse

Die abweichende Rechtsprechung nimmt bei der Entscheidung über die Verteilung der Kostenlast nicht selten Bezug auf das öffentliche Interesse der Allgemeinheit. Dabei ist grundsätzlich fraglich, was unter öffentlichem Interesse zu verstehen ist, wenn in Altersdiskriminierungsfällen doch vor allem subjektive Rechte betroffen werden.

Eine Definition des öffentlichen Interesses erfolgt durch die Rechtsprechung nicht, so dass in der Regel die besonderen Umstände des Einzelfalles betrachtet werden müssen und zu fragen ist, ob – bei der Entscheidung über die Kosten des Verfahrens und deren Verteilung – eine gewichtige Berührung mit Interessen der Allgemeinheit besteht.[759]

(2) Rechtfertigung durch Schutzbedürfnis der obsiegenden Partei

Oftmals werden in gerichtlichen Verfahren durch die enormen Gerichts- und Anwaltskosten zugesprochene Zahlungen aufgezehrt. Um die obsiegende Partei deshalb nicht um ihren Erfolg zu bringen, wird bei der Kostenentscheidung diese Problematik berücksichtigt und auch als angemessen angesehen.[760]

---

756 *Oshlack v Richmond River Council* (1998) 193 CLR 72; *De Silva v Ruddock* [1998] 311 FCA; *Physical Disability Council of NSW v Sydney City Council* [1999] FCA 815; *Ruddock v Vadarlis* (2001) 188 ALR 143; *Minns v New South Wales (No 2)* [2002] FMCA 197; *Sluggett v Human Rights and Equal Opportunity Commission* [2002] FCA 1060.

757 *Fetherston v Peninsula Health (No 2)* [2004] FCA 594.

758 *Donald v Campbell & Co v Pollack* [1927] AC 732; *Latoudis v Casey* (1990) 170 CLR 534; vgl. auch *Paramasivam v Wheeler* [2000] FCA 1559.

759 *Ferneley v The Boxing Authority of New South Wales* (2001) 115 FCR 306; *Xiros v Fortis Life Assurance Ltd* (2001) 162 FLR 433; *Jacomb v The Australian Municipal, Administrative, Clerical & Services Union* [2004] FCA 1600.

760 *Shiels v James* [2000] FMCA 2; *Travers v New South Wales* (2001) 163 FLR 99; *McKenzie v Department of Urban Services* (2001) 163 FLR 133; *Escobar v Rainbow Printing Pty Limited (No 3)* [2002] FMCA 160.

(3) Rechtfertigung durch Fehlen einer rechtlichen Vertretung

Darüber hinaus soll auch die fehlende Vertretung durch einen Rechtsanwalt im gerichtlichen Verfahren dazu führen, dass von der allgemeinen Regelung zur Kostenverteilung abgewichen wird. Allerdings soll dies vor allem bei verfahrensrechtlich schwierigen Prozessen die Folge sein.[761]

bb. Festhalten am Grundsatz „costs follow the event"

Andererseits hält der überwiegende Teil der Rechtsprechung aber konsequent am Grundsatz *„costs follow the event"* fest, da keine Veranlassung zu einer Ausweitung bestehe. Denn durch diese Regelung wird ebenso wie bei der *„'No Costs' Jurisdiction"* erreicht, dass die erfolgreiche Prozesspartei nicht mit Kosten belastet wird.[762] Zusätzlich könne durch die vorgenannten Ausnahmen und Modifikationen angemessener und vor allem interessengerecht auf Sonderfälle im Verfahren reagiert werden.

761 *Xiros v Fortis Life Assurance Ltd* (2001) 162 FLR 433.

762 *Tate v Rafin* [2000] FCA 1582; *Ball v Morgan* [2001] FMCA 127; *Creek v Cairns Post Pty Ltd* [2001] FCA 1150; *Li v Minister for Immigration & Multicultural Affairs* [2001] FCA 1414; *Paramasivam v Wheeler* [2001] FCA 231; *Rispoli v Merck Sharpe & Dohme (Australia) Pty Ltd (No 2)* [2003] FMCA 516; *Jacomb v Australian Municipal, Administrative, Clerical and Services Union* [2004] FCA 1600.

I. Überlegungen und Strategien zur Vermeidung von Altersdiskriminierung in der arbeitsrechtlichen Praxis und zur Verbesserung der Personalpolitik

Lediglich eine für das Problem der Altersdiskriminierung sensibilisierte und verantwortungsbewusste Personalpolitik kann im Bereich von Arbeit und Beschäftigung sicherstellen, dass Arbeitgeber eine Unternehmenskultur schaffen und erhalten können, in welcher sich die verschiedenen Altersgruppen optimal integrieren, ergänzen und somit hinreichend voneinander profitieren können. Denn nicht selten sieht die Praxis in der australischen Arbeits- und Beschäftigungswelt im Detail wie nachfolgend skizziert aus und wirkt zu Lasten älter Menschen.[763]

In Einzelfällen diskriminieren Arbeitgeber trotz der gesetzlichen Regelung im Age Discrimination Act 2004 (Cth) vorwiegend ältere Arbeitnehmer und Beschäftigte, obwohl diese in der Regel besonders erfahren, verlässlich und beständig sind.[764] Auch wenn versucht wird, direkte Diskriminierungen etwa durch bestimmte Verhaltensweisen, Formulierungen und Fragestellungen auszublenden, treten vor allem indirekte Diskriminierungen wegen Alters vermehrt auf. Hierzu gehören insbesondere die gezielte Sprachwahl im Einzelfall, die Ausgestaltung von Stellenannoncen und Bewerbungsgesprächen sowie auch die Auswahlphase bei Bewerbern.[765] So kann die Frage im Bewerbungsgespräch, wann der Bewerber die Schule/Hochschule abgeschlossen hat, indirekt diskriminierend sein, wenn aufgrund des höheren Alters der Person kein Bezug zur zu besetzenden Stelle hergestellt werden kann.[766] Weiter hält sich hartnäckig das Vorurteil, dass gerade ältere Arbeitnehmer schwer fortzubilden sind und sich daher entsprechende Programme und Maßnahmen besonders kostenintensiv für den Arbeitgeber auswirken können.[767] Ebenfalls ist zu beobachten, dass zwar die Arbeitslosenquote von älteren Beschäftigten niedriger als die Durchschnittsquote aller Arbeitslosen ist, jedoch der Anteil langzeitarbeitsloser älterer Personen weit über dem australischen Durchschnitt liegt.[768] Dennoch sind Arbeitsvermittler – nicht zuletzt auf-

763 Business Council of Australia, Age Can Work (2003) 10.

764 *Catanzariti*, Age and employment (1999) 4 Employment Law Bulletin 92.

765 Business Council of Australia, Age Can Work (2003) 10.

766 *Encel*, Age Discrimination in: *Patrickson/Hartmann*, Managing an Ageing Workforce (1998) 45.

767 *Encel*, Age Discrimination in Law and Practice, (2004) Elder Law Review 7; *Murray/Syed*, Critical issues in managing age diversity in Australia (2005) 43(2) Asia Pacific Journal of Human Resources 215; vgl. auch *Waltermann*, Alternde Arbeitswelt – Welche arbeits- und sozialrechtlichen Regelungen empfehlen sich?, NJW 2008, 2529..

768 House of Representatives Standing Committee on Employment, Education and Workplace Relations, Parliament of Australia, Age Counts (2000), ii; vgl. auch *Patrickson/Hartmann*, Managing an Ageing Workforce (1998), 54 und 56ff.; *Stein/Rocco/Goldenetz*, Age and the University Workplace: a Case Study of Remaining, Retiring, Or Returning Older Workers (2000) 11 Human Resource Development Quarterly 61; *Bennington*, Prime Age Recruitment: The Challenges

grund der Vorgaben Ihrer Auftraggeber, möglichst jüngere Kandidaten zu finden – überaus zögerlich in der Aufnahme von älteren Arbeitssuchenden in ihren Vermittlungspool und empfehlen sie im Vergleich zu jüngeren Bewerbern erheblich seltener.[769]

> „...recruitment agencies are predominantly 'sales driven' organisations and their objective is to satisfy client briefs, whatever they may contain, in order to obtain repeat business. Their objective is not to find the candidate work or to source the best candidate for the role. Their objective is to put a shortlist up to the client that meets their stated or unstated specifications. This will impress the client and allow them to choose the best candidate for the role from the provided shortlist. The flow on is a level of satisfaction with the agency which will ensure them repeat business from that client."[770]

Der australische Verband der Personalbeschaffung und Unternehmensberatung (*Recruitment and Consulting Services Association, RCSA*) räumt selbst ein, dass Arbeitgeber gegen ältere Kandidaten regelrecht abgeneigt sind und solche Bewerber nur widerwillig für ein Vorstellungsgespräch einladen, so dass es dadurch für Personalvermittler schwierig ist, ältere Arbeitnehmer trotz ihrer ausgeprägten Fähigkeiten und Berufserfahrungen erfolgreich am Markt zu platzieren.[771]

Diesem Zustand muss wirksam gegengesteuert werden. Da dies allein durch die zahlreichen Diskriminierungsverbote im Age Discrimination Act 2004 (Cth), durch die Tätigkeit der Human Rights and Equal Opportunity Commission und auch durch die australische Rechtsprechung jedoch nicht immer wie gewünscht gelingt, ist es förderlich, wenn direkt am Ort des Geschehens angesetzt wird.[772] Daher sind insbesondere die Arbeitgeber und Unternehmen gefragt, gezielte Maßnahmen gegen Altersdiskriminierungen vorzunehmen sowie konkrete Programme und Strategien zur Verhinderung und Bekämpfung derartiger Diskriminierungen wegen Alters im Bereich der Arbeit und Beschäftigung aufzustellen.[773]

---

for Age Discrimination Legislagtion (2004) Elder Law Review 8; Australian Bureau of Statistics, Successful and Unsuccessful Job Search Experience (2000).

769 Vgl. mit Erfahrungsberichten von Arbeitnehmern und Beschäftigten aus der Praxis *Encel*, Older Workers-Can They Succeed in the Job Market?, (2004) 23 Australasian Journal of Ageing 34; Business Council of Australia, Age Can Work (2003) 10.

770 Vgl. *Bourke*, Are we having fun yet? Age discrimination in recruitment, unveröffentlicht, abrufbar unter http://adage.com.au/Files/Are%20we%20having%20fun%20yet%20%20CCH%2014.10.05.pdf.

771 Vgl. *Bourke*, Are we having fun yet? Age discrimination in recruitment, unveröffentlicht, abrufbar unter http://adage.com.au/Files/Are%20we%20having%20fun%20yet%20%20CCH%2014.10.05.pdf; *Ozdowski*, Adressing Age discrimination (2002) 81 Older People and the Law 12.

772 Wegen der Bedenken gegen die effektive Wirkweise des Age Discirmination Act 2004 (Cth) vgl. auch *Encel*, Ageing, Pensions and Employment in Australia: Recent Developments, (2004) 34 Geneva Association Newsletter 3.

773 *Bourke*, Moving ahead on diversity and equality: Results from the 2005 Australasian Diversity and Equality Survey, in: *Davis/Pratt*, Making the Link. Affirmative Action and Employment Relations (2005).

I. Die unternehmensinterne Antidiskriminierungspolitik zur Vermeidung und Beseitigung von Altersdiskriminierung im Bereich von Arbeit und Beschäftigung

Hierbei kann die Erstellung sowie Fortentwicklung einer unternehmensinternen Antidiskriminierungspolitik und die Lückenschließung zwischen der bloßen Personalpolitik vor dem Hintergrund der Altersdiskriminierung sowie die tatsächliche praktische Anwendung und Umsetzung eine maßgebliche Rolle spielen. Denn durch dieses beschäftigungspolitische Instrument könnte sowohl dem Arbeitgeber als auch dem Arbeitnehmer hinreichend die Problematik der altersbedingten Diskriminierung aufgezeigt und zumindest unternehmensintern gelöst werden.

Wie aber sollte eine solche erfolgreiche Personal- und Antidiskriminierungspolitik aussehen, um letztendlich nachhaltig Altersdiskriminierung vorzubeugen, zu verhindern oder aber zu beseitigen?

1. Die Hauptbestandteile einer Antidiskriminierungspolitik

Sofern der Arbeitgeber bereits eine schriftliche Antidiskriminierungspolitik erarbeitet hat, muss der nächste Schritt darin bestehen, deren Hauptbestandteile zu prüfen. Insbesondere zu beachten sind dabei die Erklärung der Verbindlichkeit und Verdeutlichung der Ziel- und Zwecksetzung, die Klarstellung und Abgrenzung einzelner Rechte und Pflichten sowie die Verdeutlichung der Rechtsfolgen einer Missachtung bzw. Nichterfüllung.[774]

a. Die Verbindlicherklärung und Zielsetzung

Um einer abgefassten Antidiskriminierungspolitik einen verbindlichen Charakter zu geben, sollte der Geschäftsführer/Vorstand/Firmenchef („*CEO*“) in bestimmter Art und Weise die bindenden Ziele der Personalpolitik aufzeigen und die damit verbundenen Werte auf die Verhinderung von Altersdiskriminierung ausrichten. Eine entsprechende Erklärung kann in etwa wie folgt aussehen:

> „Als der Geschäftsführer fühle ich mich persönlich zur Herstellung einer ausgewogenen Personalvielfalt und Personalgleichheit verpflichtet. Unsere Personal- und Antidiskriminierungspolitik beabsichtigt daher die Gleichberechtigung aller Beschäftigten, die Verhinderung und Beseitigung von ungerechten bzw. ungerechtfertigten Arbeitspraktiken sowie die Schaffung einer ausgewogenen Altersstruktur. Eine Altersvielfalt ist ausdrücklich willkommen. Diese Ziele unterstütze ich in meiner Position in vollem Umfang.“[775]

---

774 *Bourke*, Age Discrimination and Human Resource Management in Practice, in: Baker & McKenzie, Age Discrimination: Mitigating Risk in the Workplace, S. 113.

775 Vgl. *Bourke*, Age Discrimination and Human Resource Management in Practice, in: Baker & McKenzie, Age Discrimination: Mitigating Risk in the Workplace, S. 113.

b. Die einzelnen Rechte und Pflichten innerhalb der Richtlinien

Eine schriftlich manifestierte Antidiskriminierungspolitik soll grundsätzlich die Beschäftigten mit all ihren Rechten und Pflichten schützen. Damit dies jedoch wirkungsvoll geschehen kann, bedarf es einer trennscharfen Definition des Begriffes Altersdiskriminierung (in der Theorie sowie in der Praxis) und somit der Klärung des Anwendungsbereichs der aufgestellten Richtlinien, die im Allgemeinen wie folgt aussehen könnte:

„I. Altersdiskriminierung

Die Diskriminierung wegen Alters ist aufgrund zahlreicher Gesetze der Bundesstaaten und Territorien sowie auch aufgrund des Age Discrimination Act 2004 (Cth) im Commonwealth u.a. im Bereich von Arbeit und Beschäftigung (wie die Bewerbungsphase, Bedingungen und Voraussetzungen der Beschäftigung, Aus- und Weiterbildung etc.) untersagt. Eine Beschränkung auf ein bestimmtes Alter einer Einzelperson besteht dabei nicht. Auch werden bestimmte Altersgruppen geschützt. Daher soll in umfassender Art und Weise eine Diskriminierung aufgrund des Alters verhindert bzw. beseitigt und den bereits betroffenen Beschäftigten ein Mittel zur Hand gegeben werden, mit welchem sie sich gegen altersbedingte Diskriminierungen im Bereich von Arbeit und Beschäftigung zur Wehr setzen können.

II. Definition von Altersdiskriminierung

Eine Altersdiskriminierung ist grundsätzlich immer dann zu bejahen, wenn eine Person oder Personengruppe aufgrund ihres Alters im Gegensatz zu einer anderen Person oder Personengruppe nachteilig behandelt wird. Eine solche Diskriminierung kann dabei in direkter als auch in indirekter Form auftreten. Eine direkte Diskriminierung liegt etwa dann vor, wenn der beste Bewerber auf eine Stelle mit dem Argument abgelehnt wird, dass er zu alt sei. Dagegen ist von einer indirekten Diskriminierung z.B. dann die Rede, wenn ein älterer Arbeitnehmer einen Fitnesstest absolvieren muss, obwohl seine Tätigkeit gerade keine besonderen Anforderungen an die körperliche Fitness aufstellt.

III. Rechtfertigung/Ausnahmen von Altersdiskriminierung

Zur Rechtfertigung von Verhaltensweisen des Arbeitgebers, die ggf. eine altersbedingte Diskriminierung darstellen können, werden vom Gesetzgeber vor allem zwei Fälle hervorgehoben. Einerseits sind dies gesonderte Löhne und Gehälter für Arbeitnehmer, welche jünger als 21 Jahre sind. Andererseits zählen altersbedingte Kündigungen zu diesen Ausnahmen, sofern ein Arbeitnehmer aufgrund seines Alters bestimmte Anforderungen seiner Tätigkeit nicht mehr erfüllen kann. Allerdings verpflichten wir uns als Arbeitgeber, darauf zu achten, dass diese tätigkeitsspezifischen Anforderungen hinreichend konkretisiert werden und dem einzelnen Beschäftigten bei Bedarf die erforderliche Unterstützung gewährt wird, um diese Anforderungen tatsächlich auch erfüllen zu können...“[776]

---

776 Angelehnt an die Antidiskriminierungspolitik der ABC Trading, auszugsweise abgedruckt in *Bourke*, Age Discrimination and Human Resource Management in Practice, in: Baker & McKenzie, Age Discrimination: Mitigating Risk in the Workplace, S. 114.

Darüber hinaus sollte den Arbeitnehmern aber auch verdeutlicht werden, welche Rechtsfolgen die Missachtung einer derartigen Antidiskriminierungspolitik auslöst und welche Beschwerdemöglichkeiten dem einzelnen Arbeitnehmer zukommen.

> „...Jedwedes Verhalten, dass in irgendeiner Art und Weise wegen seines Bezugs zum Merkmal Alter diskriminierend sein könnte, lehnen wir ausdrücklich ab und möchten unsere Arbeitnehmer zugleich ermutigen, über ein solches unrechtmäßiges Verhalten zu sprechen und Kontakt zu uns zu suchen. Wir werden dann versuchen, den Vorfall bestmöglich aufzuklären. Gleichwohl bleibt es jedem Arbeitnehmer unbenommen, sich direkt an die die Diskriminierung verursachende Person zu wenden, um eine Klärung herbeizuführen. Ebenfalls besteht daneben aber auch die Möglichkeit sich an die zuständige Behörde zu wenden und diese um eine Stellungnahme sowie um Aufklärung und Verhandlung zu bitten.
>
> Unabhängig davon, ob sich der Arbeitnehmer für eine formelle oder informelle Lösungsalternative entscheidet, existieren vier Kernpunkte, die es innerhalb der Beschwerde zu beachten gilt:
>
> 1. Die Art der Beschwerde sowie die Begründung sollten gleich laufen und somit entweder beide einen formellen oder informellen Charakter aufweisen.
> 2. Zur Frage, ob der behauptete Verstoß zuvor bereits schon einmal aufgetreten ist, sollte Stellung genommen werden.
> 3. Eine etwaige Stellungnahme der anderen Partei ist in die Beschwerde einzubeziehen und entsprechend zu berücksichtigen.
> 4. Die eigenen Vorstellungen zur weiteren Vorgehensweise sollten zudem ebenfalls berücksichtigt werden.“[777]

2. Die Kommunikation zwischen Beschwerdeführer und Beschwerdegegner unter Beteiligung des Arbeitgebers

Die Vermeidung bzw. Beseitigung von Altersdiskriminierung durch eine Antidiskriminierungspolitik innerhalb eines Unternehmens wird jedoch nur dann wirkungsvoll sein, wenn sie von einer effektiven Kommunikation zwischen allen Beteiligten begleitet wird und dadurch weitere Sicherheitsvorkehrungen im Bereich von Arbeit und Beschäftigung eröffnet werden können. Dazu sollte das einzelne Unternehmen insbesondere berücksichtigen, dass die verwendete Sprache und Redeweise verständlich ist, alternative Kommunikationsmittel benutzt werden können und die Richtlinien der Antidiskriminierungspolitik entsprechenden Eingang in die Aus- und Weiterbildung der Beschäftigten finden. Folglich ist es sinnvoll eine einfache und allgemeinverständliche Formulierung, ohne fachbezogenen Rechts- und oder Technikbegriffe, zu wählen und dabei vor allem die Kernaussagen entsprechend hervorzuheben, u.U. eine sprachliche Anpassung je nach Beschäftigungssektor vorzunehmen oder sogar alternativ auf eine andere Sprache zurückzugreifen. Selbstverständlich ist zugleich darauf zu achten, dass möglichst jeder Beschäftigte im Unternehmen die Möglichkeit der Kenntnisnahme (z.B. über gesonderte Besprechungen, Aushänge, e-Mails oder Gehaltsabrechnungen)

---

777 Angelehnt an die Antidiskriminierungspolitik der ABC Trading, auszugsweise abgedruckt in *Bourke*, Age Discrimination and Human Resource Management in Practice, in: Baker & McKenzie, Age Discrimination: Mitigating Risk in the Workplace, S. 114.

und zur Stellungnahme hat. Am vorteilhaftesten wäre es selbstverständlich, wenn jedem Angestellten und Mitarbeiter eine Kopie der Richtlinien aus der Antidiskriminierungspolitik ausgehändigt werden würde.

3. Die Einbindung der unternehmensinternen Antidiskriminierungspolitik in die allgemeine Personalpolitik

Die zuvor aufgezeigten Bestandteile und Voraussetzungen einer unternehmensinternen Antidiskriminierungspolitik mögen an sich sicherlich erfolgreich sein, um eine altersbedingte Diskriminierung im Bereich von Arbeit und Beschäftigung durch umfassende Informationen grundsätzlich zu verhindern bzw. – sofern bereits vorgefallen – zu beseitigen. Allerdings beseitigt die bloße Existenz einer solchen Politik nicht die Verantwortlichkeit des Arbeitgebers für Altersdiskriminierungen in seinem Verantwortungsbereich.[778] Denn erst wenn der Arbeitgeber alle erforderlichen Maßnahmen zur Verhinderung der Diskriminierung unternommen hat, soll seine Verantwortlichkeit verneint werden können.[779]

Zudem erscheint es aufgrund der logischen Wechselwirkung zwischen der Personalpolitik eines Unternehmens und seiner Richtlinien gegen Altersdiskriminierung fraglich, ob die Umsetzung und Durchführung einer derartigen Antidiskriminierungspolitik tatsächlich effektiv sein kann, wenn sie nicht auch direkt mit der allgemeinen Personalpolitik in Zusammenhang steht bzw. in einen solchen gestellt wird. Kann altersbedingte Diskriminierung daher erfolgreich vermieden bzw. beseitigt werden, wenn die Auswirkungen der unternehmensinternen Personalpolitik auf die verschiedenen Altersgruppen nicht berücksichtigt werden oder wenn die Vorgaben der Personalpolitik teilweise oder gänzlich nicht im Einklang mit den Richtlinien der Antidiskriminierungspolitik stehen?

Vorzugsweise sollte allerdings versucht werden, zwischen der Personalpolitik eines Unternehmens und seiner Antidiskriminierungspolitik zur Vermeidung von Altersdiskriminierungen ein Zusammenspiel und eine entsprechende Abstimmung herzustellen. Denn nur so kann gewährleistet werden, dass alle beschäftigungspolitischen Bereiche – wie etwa die Bewerbungsphase, die Aus- und Weiterbildung, die Aufhebung bzw. Auflösung des Arbeitsverhältnisses sowie auch der Arbeitsschutz und die Arbeitssicherheit – gleichermaßen erfasst werden.

a. Die Bewerbungsphase

Unternehmen setzen immer mehr auf jüngere Beschäftigte und sind daher bemüht den Altersdurchschnitt niedrig zu halten. Eine Durchmischung der Altersstruktur ist dabei scheinbar nicht gewünscht. Zwar mag stellenweise ein rechtfertigender – betriebswirt-

---

778 *Bourke/Ronalds*, Discrimination Laws – Striving For Equality, in: *Macken*, The Law of Employment, 2002, 640.

779 *Bourke/Ronalds*, Discrimination Laws – Striving For Equality, in: *Macken*, The Law of Employment, 2002, 645.

schaftlicher – Grund hinter dieser unternehmerischen Entscheidung stehen. Allerdings hat sich gezeigt, dass es oftmals die eine vorteilhafteste Altersgruppe gerade nicht gibt. Denn häufig spricht eine ausgewogene Durchmischung der betrieblichen Altersstruktur eine größere Zahl von Kunden an und verhilft somit nicht zuletzt zur Erweiterung der Produktpalette.

Um im Bewerbungsverfahren nicht in die Gefahr zu geraten, in Bezug auf das Alter – aber auch hinsichtlich anderer Gründe – diskriminierend zu handeln, sollte der Arbeitgeber folgende Regeln beachten:

(1) Der Arbeitgeber sollte einen Fragenkatalog erstellen, der die wichtigsten Punkte für den jeweiligen Bewerber enthält. Dabei muss darauf geachtet werden, dass kein Diskriminierungsgrund – insbesondere nicht das Alter – berührt wird.
(2) Im Vordergrund des Fragenkatalogs sollten die Fähigkeiten und Qualifikationen des Bewerbers für die konkret zu besetzende Stelle stehen, anhand derer die abschließende Entscheidung getroffen wird.
(3) Der Fragenkatalog sollte für alle Bewerber gelten und daher unverändert übernommen werden können.
(4) Das Bewerbungsgespräch sollte vorzugsweise immer von zwei Personen aus dem Unternehmen geführt werden, die sich zudem auf gleicher Hierarchieebene befinden.
(5) Für alle Bewerber sollten die gleichen – transparenten – Bewerbungskriterien während des gesamten Bewerbungs- und Vorstellungsverfahrens gelten.
(6) Zum Nachweis der Orientierung anhand der Fähigkeiten und Qualifikation des jeweiligen Bewerbers sollten umfangreiche Notizen während der Bewerbungsphase und während des Vorstellungsgesprächs angefertigt werden.[780]

b. Die Aus- und Weiterbildung

Die Personalplanung sollte vor allem auch im Bereich der Aus- und Weiterbildung ausschließlich auf das Leistungsvermögen und die Sachkunde der Mitarbeiter und nicht auf das Alter abstellen. Daher sollte bereits jüngeren Beschäftigten ausreichend Gelegenheit zur Weiterbildung gegeben und nicht erst abgewartet werden, bis diese ein bestimmtes – zuvor intern festgelegtes – Alter erreicht haben. Umgekehrt muss dies aber auch für ältere Arbeitnehmer gelten. Sie sollten ebenfalls nicht vor dem Hintergrund ihres Alters, und der Annahme, jüngere Beschäftigte seien aufgrund ihres längeren Karriereweges förderungswürdiger, übergangen werden. Ein Arbeitnehmer ist niemals zu alt für Ausbildung.[781] Oftmals meint der Arbeitgeber ein Spannungsverhältnis könne vermieden werden, wenn der ältere Beschäftigte weitergebildet werde, da der jüngere Arbeitnehmer ihn leichter als Vorgesetzten akzeptieren könne, als andersherum. Zwar ist zuzugeben, dass es eine entsprechend gewachsene Praxis gibt und es tatsächlich zur Vermeidung von Rechtfertigungssituationen und Konflikten beitragen kann. Allerdings darf jedoch nicht übersehen werden, dass mit dieser Entschei-

780 *Bourke/Ronalds*, Discrimination Laws – Striving For Equality, in: *Macken*, The Law of Employment, 2002, 624.
781 *Richards v Webforge Australia Pty Ltd* [2004] WAIRComm 13209.

dung bewusst das Alter als Entscheidungsgrundlage herangezogen wird, ohne dass ein tatsächlich überzeugender Rechtfertigungsgrund ersichtlich ist. Folglich sollten solche Entscheidungen auf der Basis einer erfolgreichen Antidiskriminierungspolitik nicht allein in eine Richtung erfolgen, sondern die gleichmäßige Berücksichtigung aller Altersgruppen zum Fortkommen des Unternehmens beitragen. Daher ist es besonders ratsam, entsprechende Richtlinien über den Zugang und die Auswahl für die Teilnahme an Ausbildungs- und Weiterbildungsmaßnahmen aufzunehmen.

c. Die Aufhebung bzw. Auflösung des Arbeitsverhältnisses

Die Personalpolitik ist im Hinblick auf die Aufhebung bzw. Auflösung eines Arbeitsverhältnisses insbesondere darauf zu prüfen, ob gewährleistet ist, dass die Gefahr einer Diskriminierung aufgrund des jeweiligen Alters des – insbesondere älteren – Arbeitnehmers nicht besteht. Hierzu helfen Regelungen, die eine automatische Entlassung älterer Arbeitnehmer, die eine bestimmte Altersgrenze erreicht haben, vermeiden und ebenfalls eine ausgewogene Durchmischung der betrieblichen Altersstruktur gewährleisten.[782] So könnte beispielsweise anstelle starrer Altersgrenzenregelungen auch eine Regelaltersgrenze treten, bei deren Erreichen ein Anspruch auf Altersrente bestünde. Erklärt der Arbeitnehmer dann bis zu einem bestimmten Zeitpunkt vor Erreichen dieser Regelaltersgrenze, dass er danach weiterbeschäftigt werden möchte, dann wäre es denkbar, dass der Arbeitgeber die Weiterbeschäftigung nur aus Gründen einer ausgewogenen Alterstruktur ablehnen darf. Ebenso sollte es möglich sein, dass der Arbeitnehmer seinerseits verlangen könnte, dass sein Beschäftigungsverhältnis nicht mehr in Vollzeit, sondern nur noch im Rahmen eines Teilzeitarbeitsverhältnisses ausgeübt wird.[783] Somit bestünde zumindest die Möglichkeit, den durch allgemeine und starre Alters- bzw. Pensionsgrenzen verursachten Widerspruch gegen den Grundsatz der Gleichbehandlung aller Altersgruppen zu begrenzen, die Einschränkung der Berufsfreiheit abzubauen sowie das individuelle Leistungs- und Erfahrungspotenzial Älterer zu nutzen.[784]

> „Durch Begründung der Wahlfreiheit, den Arbeitsplatz oder den gewählten Beruf bis über den Zeitpunkt der Rentenberechtigung hinaus beibehalten zu können, und durch Schaffung eines Diskriminierungsverbotes während der Laufzeit des Arbeitsverhältnisses wird das allgemeine Schutzniveau für ältere Erwerbstätige angehoben, ...“[785]

---

782 *Bourke*, Age Discrimination and Human Resource Management in Practice, in: Baker & McKenzie, Age Discrimination: Mitigating Risk in the Workplace, S. 120 mit Verweis auf ausgewählte Beispiele aus der Rechtsprechung der USA.

783 *Waltermann*, Alternde Arbeitswelt – Welche arbeits- und sozialrechtlichen Regelungen empfehlen sich?, NJW 2008, 2534.

784 *Senne*, Auswirkungen des europäischen Verbots der Altersdiskriminierung auf das deutsche Arbeitsrecht, 294.

785 *Senne*, Auswirkungen des europäischen Verbots der Altersdiskriminierung auf das deutsche Arbeitsrecht, 319 mit Verweis auf die zutreffende Feststellung von *Schlachter,* Altersgrenzen angesichts des gemeinschaftlichen Verbots der Altersdiskriminierung, in: *Richardi/Reichhold*, Gedächtnisschrift Blomeyer, 2003, 373.

d. Der Arbeitsschutz und die Arbeitssicherheit

Zusätzlich ist zur Vermeidung von Altersdiskriminierung im Bereich von Arbeit und Beschäftigung eine Abstimmung der Personalpolitik mit den Vorschriften und Vorgaben zum Arbeitsschutz und zur Arbeitssicherheit („*Occupational health and safety*") erforderlich. Als besonders beispielhaft kann dabei angesehen werden, wenn der Arbeitgeber die Beschäftigungsbedingungen – insbesondere von älteren Arbeitnehmern – derart anpasst, als dass er zusätzliche Pausen bei schwerer körperlicher Arbeit gewährt oder aber etwa Unterstützung für Personen vorhält, die Schwierigkeiten im Umgang mit modernen Computer- und Arbeitstechniken haben und ihnen daher eine zusätzliche Hilfestellung anbietet.[786]

II. Die unternehmensinterne Antidiskriminierungspolitik zur Vermeidung und Beseitigung von Altersdiskriminierung im Bereich von Arbeit und Beschäftigung in der praktischen Anwendung

Während die Erstellung und Einführung einer unternehmensinternen Antidiskriminierungspolitik im Hinblick auf die Vermeidung und Beseitigung bereits aufgetretener Diskriminierungen wegen Alters einen lohnenswerten Beginn gegen Altersdiskriminierungen darstellt und zur Beseitigung der Verantwortlichkeit für unternehmensinterne Diskriminierungen wegen Alters zwingend erforderlich ist, bedarf es zur erfolgreichen praktischen Anwendung jedoch weit mehr als ihrer bloßen Existenz.[787] Denn bereits vor dem Inkrafttreten des Age Discrimination Act 2004 (Cth) hat die *National Diversity and Equality Survey* im Jahre 2003 ergeben, dass bei führenden australischen Unternehmen ein erhebliches Ungleichgewicht zwischen den in der unternehmensinternen Antidiskriminierungspolitik festgeschriebenen Rechten und Pflichten und deren praktischer Anwendung – also folglich ein erhebliches Umsetzungsdefizit – besteht.[788] Lediglich 15 % aller Arbeitnehmer und Beschäftigten sind der Meinung, dass eine effektive praktische Anwendung bereits erfolge.[789]

---

786 In Australien wird in diesem Zusammenhang vor allem Apsen Pharmacare als Vorbildunternehmen angeführt. Apsen Pharmacare beschäftigte im Jahr 2004 insgesamt 32 Außendienstmitarbeiter, wobei 30 dieser Beschäftigten älter als 45 Jahre waren und Apsen Pharmacare daher die erwähnten Leistungen zusätzlich anbot.

787 *Bourke/Ronalds*, Discrimination Laws – Striving For Equality, in: *Macken*, The Law of Employment, 2002, 645.

788 Vgl. *Bourke* in: Australasian Diversity and Equality Survey (ADES) 2003; *dies.* in: Australaisan Diversity and Equality Survey (ADES) 2005; ADES sowie die Hauptergebnisse der jeweiligen Untersuchung sind abrufbar unter http://www.eeona.org/initiatives.html; vgl. ebenso *Bourke*, Age Discrimination and Human Resource Management in Practice, in: Baker & McKenzie, Age Discrimination: Mitigating Risk in the Workplace, S. 123.

789 *Bourke*, Age Discrimination and Human Resource Management in Practice, in: Baker & McKenzie, Age Discrimination: Mitigating Risk in the Workplace, S. 136 mit Verweis auf

Da oftmals Abweichungen zwischen dem Ist-Zustand und der Notwendigkeit einer Neustrukturierung des Arbeitsplatzes, des Arbeitsumfeldes und der Arbeitsbedingungen für einzelne Altersgruppen auftreten sowie die Bedürfnisse der jeweiligen Altersgruppen kaum zutreffend erkannt werden, bedarf es zusätzlich einer umfassenden Analyse der am Arbeitsplatz konkret bestehenden und auf den Einzelfall bezogenen Verbesserungsmöglichkeiten unter gleichzeitiger Betrachtung der Hindernisse durch auf das Alter abzielende diskriminierende Einflüsse. Auch können sich zusätzlich besondere Pilotprogramme zur Verbesserung der diskriminierungsrechtlichen Situation am Arbeitsplatz anbieten und Befragungen der Beschäftigten über vorgenommene Maßnahmen und deren Wirkung sowie laufende Berichtserstattungen von Unternehmens- bzw. Personalverantwortlichen zur effektiven Wirkkraft der Antidiskriminierungspolitik verhelfen.[790]

1. Die Analysierung der bestehenden Beeinträchtigungen – des Ist-Zustands – und der entsprechenden Verbesserungsmöglichkeiten

Der Hauptzweck einer Analyse des Ist-Zustands besteht vor allem darin, die existenten Beeinträchtigungen und Altersdiskriminierungen aufzudecken und somit konkrete Lösungen zur Verbesserung des durch Diskriminierungen wegen Alters beeinträchtigten Arbeits- und Beschäftigungsumfeldes aufzuzeigen. Daher können bestehende altersbedingte Unterschiede und hieraus resultierende Beeinträchtigungen idealer Weise durch eine Betrachtung des Dienstalters bzw. der Dauer der Betriebszugehörigkeit, des Geschlechts und der Beschäftigungsart sowie einzelner Interessengruppen oder einzelner Themenbereiche aufgezeigt werden.[791] Dem Arbeitgeber wird durch eine solche Analyse zur Schaffung flexibler Reaktionsmöglichkeiten und von individuellen Arbeits- und Beschäftigungsmodellen für die jeweiligen Altersgruppen verholfen.[792] Bereits die

Leadership Management Australia and Quantum Market Research (2004) *The LEAD 2004/5 Survey Report. Leadership, Employment, Direction, Lead Management Australasia.*

790 *Bourke/Ronalds*, Discrimination Laws – Striving For Equality, in: *Macken*, The Law of Employment, 2002, 645; auf Ebene der europäischen Gemeinschaft sowie auch auf Ebene einzelner europäischer Mitgliedsstaaten wird im Rahmen einer Charta der Vielfalt durch freiwillige Maßnahmen der beteiligten Unternehmen versucht, die Vielfalt und Chancengleichheit am Arbeitsplatz zu fördern, vgl. zur in Deutschland im Dezember 2006 durch Daimler, die Deutsche Post, die Deutsche Bank und der Deutschen BP initiierten Charta der Vielfalt die Informationen unter http://www.vielfalt-als-chance.de/index.php, vgl. zur französischen Charta de la diversité die detaillierten Angaben unter http://www.charte-diversite.com/.

791 Eine Untersuchung in den USA hat ergeben, dass speziell für ältere Arbeitnehmer eine ausschließliche Vollzeitbeschäftigung ein nicht unerhebliches Beschäftigungshindernis darstellt und mithin altersdiskriminierend wirkt. Denn mehr als die Hälfte der Arbeitnehmer zwischen 45 und 74 Jahren bevorzugt eine Teilzeitbeschäftigung; vgl. hierzu *American Association of Retired Person (AARP) 2002,* Staying Ahead of the Curve, abrufbar unter www.aarp.org; vgl. auch *Productivity Commission 2004 Economic Implications of an Ageing Australia,* Draft Research Report, Abbildung 8, S. 28.

792 *Bourke*, Implementing flexibility in the legal profession: Myths and realities, (2005) 43 Law Society Journal 54.

entsprechende Berücksichtigung von Teilzeitbeschäftigung, der Einrichtung eines Tele- bzw. Heimarbeitsplatzes sowie die Gewährung flexibler Arbeitsbeginn- und Arbeitsschlusszeiten kann zur praktischen Umsetzung der unternehmensinternen Antidiskriminierungspolitik führen und die gefundenen Verbesserungsmöglichkeiten direkt umsetzen.[793] Zur Umsetzung einer derartigen Analyse des Ist-Zustands bieten sich eine taggenaue Betrachtung des jeweiligen Arbeitsablaufs sowie ein Vergleich mit externen Daten, Statistiken und sonstigen Untersuchungsergebnissen an.[794]

2. Die Einführung von Pilotprogrammen zur Umsetzung der Verbesserungsmöglichkeiten

Die Umsetzung einzelner Verbesserungsmöglichkeiten zur Unterbindung und Beseitigung von Altersdiskriminierung sollte in Einzelfällen jedoch nur als Pilotprogramm für einen Teilbereich des Unternehmens erfolgen. Denn so kann in bestimmten Unternehmensbereichen die Wirkweise und der Erfolg der Umstellung ohne größeren organisatorischen Aufwand und mit einem überschaubaren Risiko getestet werden. Darüber hinaus ist es einfacher, ein Wechselspiel zwischen einer aktiven Beteiligung der Beschäftigung an den Neuerungen und einer passiven Umsetzung zu handhaben sowie entsprechende Trainings- und Unterstützungsmöglichkeiten anzubieten. Der Arbeitgeber bleibt flexibel.

Als Pilotprogramm kann in einer Abteilung des Unternehmens etwa die Umstellung einer Vollzeitstelle auf zwei Halbtagsstellen für ältere Arbeitnehmer, die bei einer Vollzeittätigkeit ansonsten in den Ruhestand gewechselt hätten, geschaffen werden, ohne sogleich alle Arbeitnehmer ab einem gewissen Alter auf eine Teilzeittätigkeit verweisen zu müssen. Denn oftmals wird erst durch die verallgemeinerte Umstellung eine Diskriminierung wegen des Alters bestimmter Beschäftigter verursacht.

3. Die Umfrage unter den Beschäftigten

Direkt nach der Umsetzung der einzelnen Verbesserungsmöglichkeiten sollte unter den betroffenen Beschäftigten eine Umfrage stattfinden, um festzustellen, ob die Altersdiskriminierung tatsächlich verhindert bzw. beseitigt werden konnte oder ob die Effektivität der jeweiligen Maßnahme gesteigert werden kann. Ebenso kann durch eine regelmäßige Rückmeldung aus dem Kreise der Arbeitnehmer die Umstellung und die eingeführte Maßnahme je nach Erfolg beibehalten, entsprechend modifiziert oder gar zeitnah wieder abgeschafft und durch eine wirkungsvollere ersetzt werden.

---

793 *Bourke*, Age Discrimination and Human Resource Management in Practice, in: Baker & McKenzie, Age Discrimination: Mitigating Risk in the Workplace, S. 124.

794 *Bourke/Ronalds*, Discrimination Laws – Striving For Equality, in: *Macken*, The Law of Employment, 2002, 646; vgl. auch *Bourke*, Job redesign: A strategic approach to implementing flexible work practices (2001), August (121) CCH Australia and New Zealand Equal Opportunity Law and Practice 10.

4. Die regelmäßige Berichterstattung durch die Unternehmensführung bzw. die Personalverantwortlichen

Um sicherzustellen, dass die unternehmensinterne Antidiskriminierungspolitik in der Praxis tatsächlich ihre bestmögliche Wirkung entfalten kann, müssen vor allem die Unternehmensführung und die Personalverantwortlichen zu einem höheren Maß an Verantwortlichkeit für deren Umsetzung verpflichtet werden. Denn die Untersuchung des *National Diversity and Equality Survey* aus dem Jahr 2005 hat ergeben, dass im Durchschnitt tatsächlich nur etwa 72 % aller Führungsverantwortlichen in Unternehmen für die erfolgreiche Umsetzung der internehmensinternen Antidiskriminierungsrichtlinien verantwortlich sind.[795] Idealerweise sollte die Verantwortlichkeit in einer Person gebündelt werden und diese wiederum mit der regelmäßigen Berichterstattung an den Vorstand bzw. die Geschäftsführung beauftragt sein. Denn ist ein Hauptverantwortlicher bestimmt, so kann eine Berichtsstruktur, die sie sich durch sämtliche Aufgabenbereiche des jeweiligen Unternehmens zieht, aufgebaut werden und somit eine Verantwortung sowie ein entsprechendes Bewusstsein zur Mitwirkung an der tatsächlichen Umsetzung der unternehmensinternen Antidiskriminierungspolitik hergestellt werden.[796]

795 Im Jahr 2003 waren es dagegen lediglich 57 % der Führungsverantwortlichen.

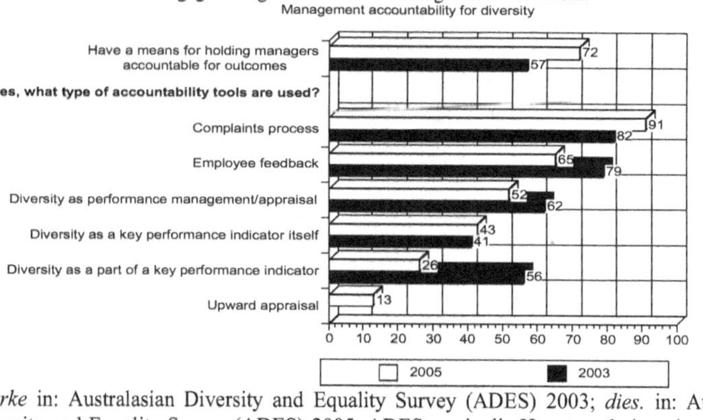

Vgl. *Bourke* in: Australasian Diversity and Equality Survey (ADES) 2003; *dies.* in: Australaisan Diversity and Equality Survey (ADES) 2005; ADES sowie die Hauptergebnisse der jeweiligen Untersuchung sind abrufbar unter http://www.eeona.org/initiatives.html; vgl. ebenso *Bourke*, Age Discrimination and Human Resource Management in Practice, in: Baker & McKenzie, Age Discrimination: Mitigating Risk in the Workplace, S. 125.

796 Vgl. *Bourke* in: Australasian Diversity and Equality Survey (ADES) 2003; *dies.* in: Australaisan Diversity and Equality Survey (ADES) 2005; ADES sowie die Hauptergebnisse der jeweiligen Untersuchung sind abrufbar unter http://www.eeona.org/initiatives.html.

J. Wesentliche Ergebnisse und Schlussbetrachtung

In diesem Schlussteil der Arbeit werden die erarbeiteten Grundelemente der australischen Rechts- und Gesetzeslage zum Altersdiskriminierungsrecht rekapituliert und mit eigenen Überlegungen zur Gewährleistung einer Mitarbeitervielfalt unterlegt, um einen ganzheitlichen Überblick auf die vorangegangen Ausführungen zu gewährleisten.

I. Wesentliche Ergebnisse der Arbeit

Die vorangegangenen Ausführungen haben gezeigt, dass nicht nur die Änderung der Altersstruktur in der australischen Bevölkerung und Arbeitswelt sowie die damit verbundenen Herausforderungen und Probleme im gesellschaftlichen Leben, aber insbesondere auch im Bereich von Arbeit und Beschäftigung bereits frühzeitig erkannt worden sind, sondern ebenfalls eine zunehmende Altersdiskriminierung als negative Auswirkung dieser Entwicklung zu Tage getreten ist. Insbesondere ist auch festzustellen, dass der Einstieg und Verbleib älterer Arbeitnehmer in die Arbeitswelt zunehmend erschwert wird und der Anteil der Langzeitarbeitslosen mit fortschreitendem Alter zunimmt. Mit dem Age Discrimination Act 2004 (Cth) hat sich der australische Gesetzgeber dem grundsätzlichen Problem der Diskriminierung wegen Alters angenommen, um durch zahlreiche Diskriminierungsverbote und entsprechende Rechtsschutzmöglichkeiten einen wirksamen Schutz vor Altersdiskriminierungen bieten zu können.

Dem Erlass des Age Discrimination Act 2004 (Cth) auf Ebene des Commonwealth ist ein mehr als dreißigjähriger Entwicklungsprozess auf bundesstaatlicher Ebene vorausgegangen. Dem ersten australischen Antidiskriminierungsgesetz gegen Diskriminierungen aufgrund der Rasse im Bundesstaat *South Australia* im Jahre 1966 folgten zahlreiche weitere Antidiskriminierungsgesetze in den einzelnen Bundesstaaten in kurzer zeitlicher Abfolge. Mit dem Erlass des Racial Discrimination Act 1975 (Cth) und der anschließenden Gründung der Human Rights Commission im Jahre 1981 wurde der Grundstein für die Gesetzgebung gegen Diskriminierungen im Commonwealth gelegt. Die Altersdiskriminierung selbst war erstmalig 1977 Gegenstand eines Gesetzgebungsverfahrens im Bundesstaat *New South Wales*, bevor im Zeitraum von 1984 bis 1999 eine umfassende Kodifizierung der Altersdiskriminierung in allen australischen Bundesstaaten und Territorien stattfand. Auf der Basis der Erfahrungen aus den bundesstaatlichen und territorialen Gesetzeswerken wurde ein Regelwerk für das gesamte Commonwealth geschaffen, welches am 22. Juni 2004 in Kraft trat. Dabei steht der – verfassungsrechtlich insbesondere durch die Annexkompetenz der *external affairs power* legitimierte – Age Discrimination Act 2004 (Cth) mit seinen antidiskriminierungsrechtlichen Regelungen im Wechselspiel mit den bundesstaatlichen oder territorialen Antidiskriminierungsgesetzen und der jeweiligen Rechtsprechung.

Mit dem Erlass des Age Discrimination Act 2004 (Cth) und durch die Regelung zahlreicher Diskriminierungsverbote sollen Altersdiskriminierungen beseitigt und auch das Bewusstsein, dass Menschen jeden Alters dieselben Rechte genießen können sollen, geschärft werden. Sofern erforderlich sollen in einem bestimmtem Alter Vorteile und Unterstützungen gesetzlich sichergestellt werden, die Wahrnehmung und Akzeptanz der unterschiedlichen Altersstrukturen innerhalb der Gesellschaft verstärkt sowie Hindernisse von Beteiligungsmöglichkeiten und etwaige Vorurteile bestimmter Altersgruppen ausgeräumt werden. Im Vordergrund der australischen Gesetzgebung gegen Altersdiskriminierung steht die Gleichstellung von Menschen unterschiedlichen Alters bzw. unterschiedlicher Altersgruppen. Daher greift der Age Discrimination Act 2004 (Cth) zahlreiche Diskriminierungsverbote auf und ist hinsichtlich der betroffenen Normadressaten, aber auch im Hinblick auf die zu schützenden Personen und Personengruppen sehr weit ausgestaltet. Der australische Gesetzgeber überlässt einen nicht unerheblichen Teil der konkreten Inhalts- und Begriffsbestimmung der Rechtsprechung. Feststeht jedoch, dass der Anwendungsbereich immer dann eröffnet ist, wenn eine direkte oder indirekte Diskriminierung wegen Alters – neben weiteren Diskriminierungsgründen – zumindest eine maßgebliche Rolle spielt. Auch die in ihrer Fülle im Age Discrimination Act 2004 (Cth) enthaltenen Diskriminierungsverbote sind klar geregelt und bestimmt, gelten jedoch nicht absolut. Vielmehr existieren zahlreiche Ausnahmen von den Diskriminierungsverboten wegen Alters, die zu einer Gleichberechtigung unabhängig vom jeweiligen Alter beitragen sollen. Um den umfassenden Schutz durch den Age Discrimination Act 2004 (Cth) aber nicht zu gefährden, legt die Rechtsprechung diese Ausnahmen grundsätzlich sehr eng aus.

Eine wesentliche Rolle unter den einzelnen Ausnahmen von den einzelnen Diskriminierungsverboten wegen Alters kommt den speziellen Befreiungen und Ausnahmen im Bereich von Arbeit und Beschäftigung zu. So sind die Grundsatzentscheidungen im Fall *Qantas Airways Limited v Christie* in der australischen Rechtsprechung insbesondere zu Fragen im Zusammenhang mit der Ausnahme der einer Beschäftigung anhaftenden Voraussetzungen bzw. Anforderungen (*„inherent requirements"*) ergangen. Die Rechtsprechung hat bei der Überprüfung von altersbedingten Kündigungen (*„compulsory retirement"*) diese per se als diskriminierend beurteilt, aber zugleich auch im Lichte der aus der konkreten Beschäftigung resultierenden Anforderungen als gerechtfertigt angesehen, um einen grundsätzlichen Ausschluss von altersbedingten Kündigungen durch das Antidiskriminierungsrecht zu verhindern und einen interessengerechten Ausgleich zwischen den arbeitsrechtlichen Mechanismen und dem Schutzzweck des Age Discrimination Act 2004 (Cth) herzustellen bzw. zu gewährleisten. Dies versucht die Rechtsprechung vor allem durch einen sehr weiten Beurteilungsmaßstab hinsichtlich der *„essential elements"* und für die Beantwortung der Frage, ob im Einzelfall die aufgestellten Anforderungen auch tatsächlich erfüllt werden können. Zugleich wird deutlich, dass eine Abstimmung der gesetzlichen Regelungen zur Diskriminierung wegen Alters mit dem Arbeitsrecht im Allgemeinen, aber auch mit arbeitsrechtlichen Schutzbestimmungen im Konkreten, erforderlich ist. Neben der Rechtsprechung versucht der Gesetzgeber durch zahlreiche spezialgesetzliche Arbeitsrechtsvorschriften dazu beizutragen, dass insbesondere arbeitsvertragliche Regelungen vermieden werden, die sich altersdiskriminierend auswirken könnten.

Daneben können sich Überschneidungen mit anderen Antidiskriminierungsgesetzen aber nicht zuletzt auch aufgrund des weiten Anwendungsbereichs des Age Discrimination Act 2004 (Cth) ebenso außerhalb des Arbeitsrechts ergeben. Derartige Überschneidungen sind insbesondere aufgrund von physischen oder psychischen Behinderungen denkbar, die mit einem bestimmten Alter zusammenhängen. Zwar soll bei einem solchen Fall durch den Erlass des Age Discrimination Act 2004 (Cth) weder eine zusätzliche Rechtsschutzmöglichkeit für andere Diskriminierungsgründe geschaffen werden, aber ebenso ist es vom Gesetzgeber auch nicht gewollt, eine Verkürzung der Schutzmechanismen in ihrer Gesamtheit herbeizuführen. Daher wird zur Beurteilung der Anwendbarkeit von etwaigen spezialgesetzlichen Regelungen des Disability Discrimination Act 1992 (Cth) ein behinderungsrelevanter Sachbezug gefordert. Ist die Ursache für die Diskriminierung jedoch maßgeblich bzw. überwiegend im Alter der diskriminierten Person zu finden, so verbleibt es bei der Anwendbarkeit des Age Discrimination Act 2004 (Cth). Dieser Anwendungsvorrang des Age Discrimination Act 2004 (Cth) im Sinne des *dominant reason test* gilt dabei auch bei Vorliegen anderer bzw. mehrerer weiterer Diskriminierungsgründe. Dieser *dominant reason test* findet sich in anderen australischen Antidiskriminierungsgesetzen nicht und steht aufgrund der Gefahr, dass der Rechtsschutz gegen Altersdiskriminierungen eingeschränkt wird, in der Kritik.

Um den zahlreichen Diskriminierungsverboten zu maximaler Wirkkraft zu verhelfen, werden zu Gunsten des Diskriminierungsopfers im Age Discrimination Act 2004 (Cth) vielfältige Ausgleichsmaßnahmen vorgesehen. Diese reichen von Schadensersatz- und Entschädigungszahlungen, der Abgabe von Unterlassungserklärungen, der Anstellung in einem Beschäftigungsverhältnis bzw. der Wiederanstellung in einem solchen bis hin zu Modifizierungen im Einzelfall und der Verpflichtung zur Vornahme bestimmter Handlungs- und Verhaltensweisen zur Beseitigung der aufgetretenen Altersdiskriminierung. Zusätzlich wurde neben der Möglichkeit zur gerichtlichen Durchsetzbarkeit eine weitere Rechtsschutzmöglichkeit für das Diskriminierungsopfer in Form des Beschwerdeverfahrens vor der Human Rights and Equal Opportunity Commission geschaffen, um eine bestmögliche Chancengleichheit durch Aushandlung einer Einigung zwischen den Parteien des jeweiligen Diskriminierungsfalles zu erzielen. Dieses außergerichtliche Beschwerde- und Anhörungsverfahren („conciliation“) zur Konfliktlösung stand und steht wegen der ursprünglich fehlenden Vollstreckbarkeit des Verfahrensergebnisse und der Abhängigkeit von der Freiwilligkeit der beteiligten Parteien in der Kritik. Die Diskussionen um die Effizienz einer derartigen außergerichtlichen Lösungsmöglichkeit und zahlreiche weitere Kritikpunkte dauern an, wobei nicht zu verkennen ist, dass eine Vielzahl von Argumenten für das conciliation-Verfahren zunehmend an Bedeutung gewinnen und die außergerichtliche Konfliktlösungsmöglichkeit in der Praxis an Bedeutung zunimmt.

II. Abschließende Überlegungen und Vorschläge zur Beseitigung von Altersdiskriminierung im Bereich von Arbeit und Beschäftigung

1. Die aktuelle Situation der Altersdiskriminierung in der täglichen Praxis

Das gesetzliche Instrument des Age Discrimination Act 2004 (Cth) ist in der Gesamtschau wegen seiner Vielzahl an Diskriminierungsverboten und der Sonderregelungen für den Bereich von Arbeit und Beschäftigung wirksam und effektiv, um gegen Diskriminierungen wegen Alters – insbesondere im Verhältnis von Arbeitgebern und Beschäftigten – vorzugehen. Vor dem Hintergrund des stetig zunehmenden Belastungsdrucks in der Arbeitswelt sind – wie zuvor bereits angedeutet – als besonders positiv für Angestellte und Beschäftigte der weite (für das gesamte Commonwealth definierte) Anwendungsbereich, der Schutz sowohl gegen direkte als auch gegen indirekte Diskriminierung wegen Alters und insbesondere das grundsätzliche Verbot von altersbedingten Kündigungen hervorzuheben.

In zahlreichen Fällen zeitigen die gesetzlichen Regelungen des Age Discrimination Act 2004 (Cth) jedoch keinen Einfluss auf die Einstellungs- und Beschäftigungspolitik von Arbeitgebern. Mit anderen Worten – trotz der gesetzlichen Verbote von diskriminierenden Verhaltensweisen wegen des Alters einer Person setzen viele Arbeitgeber ihre unrechtmäßigen Praktiken fort.[797] Daher dürfen die Augen nicht vor der Tatsache verschlossen werden, dass ältere Arbeitnehmern trotzdem weiterhin wegen ihres Alters (direkt und indirekt) diskriminiert werden, indem sie gegenüber jüngeren Kollegen seltener eingestellt werden und dafür aber vermehrt primär beim Stellenabbau betroffen sind.[798]

Die Altersdiskriminierung im Bereich von Arbeit und Beschäftigung beruht zu einem Großteil auf altersspezifischen Vorurteilen und Klischees. Obwohl wissenschaftliche und praktische Untersuchungen das Gegenteil mehrmals hinlänglich bewiesen haben, werden Arbeitnehmer über 45 Jahre als neuen Techniken gegenüber ablehnend, unflexibel und nicht für Änderungen und wechselnden Anforderungen bereit beschrieben.[799] So haben Arbeitgeber das ideale Durchschnittsalter ihrer Beschäftigten nicht

---

797 *Encel*, Age Discrimination in Law and Practice, (2004) Elder Law Review 7; *Patterson*, The Eradication of Compulsory Retirement and Age Discrimination in the Australian Workplace: A Cause for Celebration and Concern (2004) 3 Elder Law Review 7.

798 *Patterson*, The Eradication of Compulsory Retirement and Age Discrimination in the Australian Workplace: A Cause for Celebration and Concern (2004) 3 Elder Law Review 7 mit Verweis auf diversen wissenschaftliche Studien und Reports; vgl. nur *Encel*, Age Can Work: The Case for Older Australians Staying in the Workforce (2003) Australian Council of Trade Unions and the Business Council of Australia; Senate Select Committee on Superannuation, Planning for Retirement (2003) Australian Parliament.

799 *Laurent*, Time to listen (1990) 86 Nursing Time 20; Victorian, South Australian and Western Australian Equal Opportunity Commissioners, Age Limits: Age-Related Discrimination in Employment Affecting Workers Over 45 (2001) m.w.N.; vgl. auch The National Strategy for An Ageing Australia, Employment for Mature Age Workers, Issues Paper (1999) 31; *Sheen*, Older

selten im Bereich von 25 bis 35 Jahren angegeben.[800] Dieser Umstand führt dazu, dass zahlreiche Arbeitgeber bewusst nach Beschäftigten dieser Altersgruppe suchen und somit bereits Bewerber über 40 Jahre im Vorfeld aussortiert werden.[801]

Die Verbreitung der Altersdiskriminierung im Bereich von Arbeit und Beschäftigung in Australien findet ihre Ursache zugleich aber auch in der immer früheren Pensionierung von Arbeitnehmern und dem damit verbundenen Ausscheiden aus der Arbeitswelt. So lag das durchschnittliche Renteneintrittsalter australischer Angestellter im Jahr 2003 bei 61 Jahren.[802] Die bereits vorgenommenen Ausführungen zum hohen Anteil älterer Arbeitsloser in der Langzeitarbeitslosenstatistik spiegeln wider, dass Entscheidungen für ein frühzeitiges Ausscheiden aus der Arbeitswelt nur selten freiwillig passieren und dagegen gerade auch auf Nachdruck des Arbeitgebers – unter Bedienung der zuvor aufgezeigten altersspezifischen Vorurteile – gefällt werden.

> „Morgan and Banks´s 1998 national employment survey of 3,500 employers showed that about a third of the companies had replaced workers over 45 with younger staff. A growing number of workers are being forced out of their jobs. An employment agency for mature workers, DOME (Don´t Overlook Mature Expertise), said: „We´re told that when companies are looking to downsize, it´s the mature age people who put their hands up. But that´s not our experience. We find that these people are edged out. They are pressured into taking a package.“[803]

Zugleich ist zu berücksichtigen, dass die Entscheidung zu Gunsten einer früheren Pensionierung gegenüber der Alternative der Altersarbeitslosigkeit einen positiveren Stand bedeutet und für das eigene Selbstwertgefühl nicht zwingend nachteilig sein muss. Denn die psychologische Wirkung, nicht entlassen worden zu sein, sondern (freiwillig) eine Entscheidung zum Ausstieg aus der Berufswelt getroffen zu haben, ist wesentlich vorteilhafter.

Australians: Working for the future (1999); *Murray/Syed*, Critical issues in managing age diversity in Australia (2005) 43(2) Asia Pacific Journal of Human Resources 215 m.w.N..

800 *Peetz*, Retrechment and Labour Market Disadvantage: The Role of Age, Job Tenure and Casual Employment, in: Reflections and New Directions: AIRAANZ Conference 2003, Volume 2: Non-Refereed Papers, Association of Industrial Relations Academics of Australia and New Zealand; vgl. auch die auf bestimmte Branchen bezogene Übersicht von *Drake Executive Survey National Findings* in: House of Representatives Standing Committee on Employment, Education and Workplace Relations, Parliament of Australia, Age Counts (2000), 104.

801 House of Representatives Standing Committee on Employment, Education and Workplace Relations, Parliament of Australia, Age Counts (2000), 102.

802 *Fels*, Now is the Time to Raise the Retirement Age (2003), abrufbar unter http://www.theage.com.au/articles/2003/12/25/1072308626614.html.

803 *Patterson*, The Eradication of Compulsory Retirement and Age Discrimination in the Australian Workplace: A Cause for Celebration and Concern (2004) 3 Elder Law Review 7.

2. Anlass zum weiteren Handeln und Vorgehen gegen Alters diskriminierung – Was wird getan? Was sollte getan werden?

Trotz der Reaktion des Gesetzgebers und der Verankerung zahlreicher Diskriminierungsverbote im Age Discrimiation Act 2004 (Cth) bedarf es aufgrund der anhaltenden Diskriminierung wegen Alters – von sowohl jungen als auch älteren Menschen – eines weiteren aktiven Vorgehens. Denn allein scheint der Age Discrimination Act 2004 (Cth) für eine verbesserte Sensibilisierung der Gesellschaft, ältere Menschen und Arbeitnehmer über 45 Jahren als ein Bestandteil der Altersstruktur anzuerkennen und zu achten, nicht ausreichend genug zu sein. Nicht zuletzt die enorme Zeitdauer vom Erlass des ersten Anti-Diskriminierungsgesetzes auf Ebene des australischen Commonwealth – des Racial Discrimination Act 1975 (Cth) – bis zum Age Discrimination Act 2004 (Cth) von nahezu 30 Jahren ist Beleg für einen nur langsam voranschreitenden Wandlungsprozess innerhalb der australischen Gesellschaft und Arbeitswelt.

a. Was wird getan?

Daher sollte neben dem gesetzlichen Zwang zum Unterlassen von diskriminierenden Verhaltensweisen durch zusätzliche – öffentlichkeitswirksame Maßnahmen – das Bewusstsein in der Gesellschaft ausgeprägt und gestärkt werden, dass es Altersdiskriminierung in Australien (im Bereich von Arbeit und Beschäftigung) gibt, dieses Problem hochaktuell ist, jeden Einzelnen treffen kann und Altersdiskriminierung eine beklagenswerte Verletzung von subjektiven Rechten der Betroffenen in nicht unerheblicher Art und Weise zur Rechtsfolge hat sowie darüber hinaus moralisch verwerflich ist.[804] Denn nicht immer ist die Verwirklichung eigener Interessen ausschlaggebendes Motiv für einen Gesetzesverstoß. Denn oft ist es das bloße fehlende Verständnis, moralisch nicht einwandfrei zu handeln.[805] Zusätzlich ist es erforderlich, die Vorurteile gegenüber älteren Beschäftigten sowie aber auch gegenüber den jüngeren Mitarbeitern abbauen zu helfen und sie als festen Bestandteil der Arbeitswelt mit besonderen – der jeweiligen Altersgruppe entsprechenden – Fähigkeiten und speziellem Erfahrungspotential anzuerkennen.[806]

Parallel zum Age Discrimination Act 2004 (Cth) hat die Regierung des Commonwealth ein Begleitprogramm ins Leben gerufen, um das Bewusstsein um die Problematik der Altersdiskriminierung in der australischen Bevölkerung zu verbessern und

---

804 Australian Bureau of Statistics, Australian Social Trends 2004: Mature Age Workers (2004).

805 *Tyler*, Why People Obey the Law (1990) 107.

806 *Birren/Schiae*, Handbook of the Psychology of Ageing (1996), 296; *Spriduso/MacRae*, Motor Performance and Ageing, in: *Birren/Schiae*, Handbook of the Psychology of Ageing (1996), 183; *Schiae*, The Impact of Longitudinal Studies on Understanding Development from Young Adulthood to Old Age (2000) 24 International Journal of Behavioural Development 257; *Murray/Syed*, Critical issues in managing age diversity in Australia (2005) 43(2) Asia Pacific Journal of Human Resources 215.

entsprechende Bildungs- und Informationsquellen angeboten.[807] Das Programm *„National Strategy for an Ageing Australia"* setzt sich mit der zunehmend alternden Bevölkerungsstruktur auseinander und verdeutlicht dabei, dass die Hindernisse zur Beteiligung von älteren Arbeitnehmern in der Berufswelt beseitigt werden müssen und es für die Weiterentwicklung und Nutzung wertvoller Kenntnisse und Berufserfahrungen bedeutsam ist, ältere Beschäftigte anzustellen bzw. weiter zu beschäftigen. Die hierfür von der – damaligen – australischen Regierung vorgesehenen konkreten Maßnahmen lassen sich wie folgt zusammenfassen: Bildung von Partnerschaften zwischen Arbeitgebern und Arbeitsvermittlern zur Steigerung der Beschäftigungschancen für ältere Arbeitnehmer, Verbesserung der Weiterbildungs- und Spezialisierungsmöglichkeiten für ältere und jüngere Arbeitnehmer durch verstärkte Berücksichtigung der jeweiligen konkreten Interessen und Bedürfnisse, Verbesserung der Arbeitsbedingung durch Verstärkung der persönlichen Mitwirkung der Beschäftigten verschiedener Altersgruppen, Unterstützung bei der individuellen Lebens- und Karriereplanung für sämtliche Altersgruppen, Beseitigung der Anreize für ein frühzeitiges Ausscheiden aus der Berufs- und Arbeitswelt und Wechsel in den Ruhestand, Verdeutlichung der Erforderlichkeit der Beteiligung unterschiedlicher Altersgruppen innerhalb einer Personalstruktur und deren positiver Einflüsse für die Produktivität und das Unternehmenswachstum, Unterstützung beim Wiedereintritt in die Arbeitswelt älterer Arbeitnehmer durch Verbesserung der Verdienst-, Karriere und Arbeitsplatzsuchmöglichkeiten etc..[808]

Mit der Durchsetzung der vorgenannten Ziele und mit der Umsetzung der aufgeführten Maßnahmen hat das australische Commonwealth durch die gesetzliche Regelung in § 53 Abs. 1 des Age Discrimination Act 2004 (Cth) die Human Rights and Equal Opportunity Commission betraut. So führt die Human Rights and Equal Opportunity Commission wissenschaftliche Untersuchungen durch und initiiert Bildungs- und Informationsprogrammen, um die Einstellung gegenüber bestimmten Altersgruppen in der australischen Gesellschaft zu verbessern und gegen bestehende Vorurteile anzukämpfen, die Diskriminierungen wegen Alters nach sich ziehen können.[809]

b. Was sollte getan werden?

Es hat sich also gezeigt, dass der Kern der Altersdiskriminierungsproblematik im Bereich der Arbeit und Beschäftigung vor allem darin liegt, dass älteren Arbeitnehmern und Beschäftigten nicht mit dem erforderlichen Respekt gegenüber getreten wird. Daher muss maßgeblich an der Einstellung vieler Menschen gearbeitet werden, bevor

---

807 *Andrews* (Minister of Ageing), A Changing Workplace (2001) National Strategy for an Ageing Australia: An Older Australia, Challenges and Opportunities for All; abrufbar unter http://www.longevity-international.com/assets/National%20Strategy%20for%20an%20Ageing%20Australia.pdf.

808 *Andrews* (Minister of Ageing), A Changing Workplace (2001) National Strategy for an Ageing Australia: An Older Australia, Challenges and Opportunities for All; abrufbar unter http://www.longevity-international.com/assets/National%20Strategy%20for%20an%20Ageing%20Australia.pdf.

809 Vgl. überblicksartig die Darstellung auf de offiziellen Webseite der Human Rights and Equal Opportunity Commission: http://www.hreoc.gov.au/age/index.html.

verlangt werden kann, dass sie Menschen aus verschiedenen Altersgruppen mit dem Respekt behandeln, den diese verdienen. Denn erst wenn das bestehende ethisch-moralische Missverständnis beseitigt ist, können praktische Veränderungen stattfinden.[810] Die Befolgung der ethischen Pflicht zur Gleichbehandlung aller Altersgruppen kann den durch den Age Discrimination Act 2004 (Cth) kodifizierten Pflichten zu ihrer bestmöglichen Wirkkraft verhelfen.

Daneben müssen die in der Gesellschaft bestehenden Vorurteile gegen unterschiedliche Altersgruppen bestmöglich im Rahmen von Aufklärungskampagnen abgebaut werden. Die tatsächlichen Fakten gehören ans Tageslicht und bedürfen einer vermehrten Kommunikation in die Außenwelt: Zwar nimmt insbesondere die geistige Leistungsfähigkeit bis zum Ende der späten dreißiger bzw. frühen vierziger Lebensjahre stetig zu, aber sie verbleibt zumindest bis zum Beginn der frühen sechziger Lebensjahre in der Regel konstant auf diesem hohen Niveau.[811] Auch das Hör- und Sehvermögen nimmt altersbedingt nicht vorher so stark ab, als dass die Berufsausübung darunter merklich leiden würde. Wissenschaftliche Studien belegen diesen Umstand überwiegend bei Menschen, die bereit achtzig Jahre oder älter sind.[812] Auch gravierende Defizite in der Fähigkeit der Gedächtnisleistungen sind mit zunehmendem Alter nicht wissenschaftlich belegbar.[813] Außer in körperlich belastenden Berufen nimmt die Leistungsfähigkeit und Produktivität mit fortschreitendem Alter und gewonnener Berufserfahrung zu, wobei selbst Einschränkungen in der körperlichen Belastungsfähigkeit durch andere alters- und erfahrungsspezifische Kenntnisse und Fähigkeiten ausgeglichen werden können und somit kein grundsätzliches Manko darstellen.[814]

Die Beseitigung von existierenden und sich in den Köpfen der Menschen festgesetzten Vorurteilen bedarf eines nicht unerheblichen Zeitraums, der für Informationen für die Gesellschaft und zur Aufklärung dieser genutzt werden kann. Nur die umfassende Aufklärung darüber, dass insbesondere ältere Arbeitnehmer zumindest ebenso produktiv, lernfähig und flexibel wie ihre jüngeren Kollegen sein können, vermag einen Bewusstseinswandel herbeizuführen.[815]

Trotz des nicht zu vernachlässigenden Zeitfaktors wird sich aufgrund der sich schnell verändernden Anforderungen in der Unternehmens- und Arbeitswelt zeigen, dass Unternehmen und Institutionen, die sich gegen die Diskriminierung wegen Alters

810 *Tyler*, Why People Obey the Law (1990) 107.

811 *Schaie*, Intellectual Development in Adulthood, in: *Birren/Schaie*, Handbook of the Psychology of Ageing (1996), 296.

812 *Fozard/Gordon-Salant*, Changes in Vision and Hearing with Age, in: *Birren/Schaie*, Handbook of the Psychology of Ageing (1996), 349.

813 Vgl. etwa *Madden*, Speed and Timing of Behavioural Response, in: *Birren/Schaie*, Handbook of the Psychology of Ageing (1996), 349.

814 *Ketchman/Stelmach*, Age-Related Declines in Motor Control; in : *Birren/Schaie*, Handbook of the Psychology of Ageing (1996), 313; *Pickersgill/Briggs/Kitay/Keeffe/Gillezeau*, Productivity of Mature and Older Workers: Employers´ Attitudes and Experiences (1996), 9; vgl. auch *Ranzijn*, Discrimination against older worker: psychology and economics (2005), abrufbar unter http://www.hreoc.gov.au/age/workingage/speeches/ranzijn.html.

815 Vgl. auch die Initiative der Australian Human Rights and Equal Opportunity Commission *„Mature workers mean business"*,
Informationen abrufbar unter http://www.hreoc.gov.au/matureworkers/index.html.

stellen und sich aktiv an der Beseitigung und Verhinderung von Altersdiskriminierung beteiligen, besser vorankommen und erfolgreicher entwickeln werden. Denn sie sind es, die von einer ausgewogenen Altersstruktur und dem Ausgleich der Fähigkeiten und Kenntnisse zwischen jüngeren und älteren Beschäftigten profitieren können.

> „There is a whole range of misconceptions about older workers, yet evidence from a number of countries across the world indicates that there are very real benefits in having a balanced work force ... we should be aiming for a balanced work force, where we have older workers who can act as mentors for younger workers coming in and who provide a stable work force and who provide an example of good work habits for young people coming into the work force.“[816]

Nicht zuletzt werden auch die Arbeitnehmer von einer fairen Behandlung persönlich profitieren und bereit sein, für den Erfolg des sie beschäftigenden Unternehmens vollen Einsatz zu bringen.

Ebenso gut können zur Beseitigung der Altersdiskriminierung im Bereich von Arbeit und Beschäftigung insbesondere die Verbesserung der unternehmensinternen Arbeitsorganisation und die altersspezifische Modifizierung der zu erzielenden Arbeitsweise und -ergebnisse wirkungsvoll beitragen. Im Bereich der Organisation der Arbeit besteht ein immer größeres Bedürfnis nach einer flexiblen Arbeitsweise, um – je nach Altersgruppe – die Verantwortlichkeiten aus der Erwerbstätigkeit mit familiären Verpflichtungen, wie z.B. der Kindererziehung oder Pflege von Familienangehörigen, zu verbinden.[817] Wird dieses Bedürfnis vom Unternehmen erkannt und entsprechend durch Vereinbarung von Teilzeitarbeit, Job-Sharing oder Einrichtung eines Heimarbeitsplatzes darauf eingegangen, so werden der Arbeitgeber als auch der Arbeitnehmer zu gleichen Anteilen profitieren können. Denn der Ausbau und die Förderung von Eigenverantwortung lassen sich nicht nur im privaten Bereich vorteilhaft einsetzen, sie ist auch eine kostbare Fähigkeit für die Weiterentwicklung des Unternehmens.[818] Zusätzlich muss sichergestellt werden, dass Beschäftigten aller Altersgruppen ein Gleichmaß an Zugang zu Fort- und Weiterbildungsmöglichkeiten gewährt und seitens des Arbeitsgebers das lebenslange Lernen aktiv unterstützt wird. Dazu gehört vor allem die Beseitigung bestimmter Altersgrenzen für die Teilnahme an Schulungen und Seminaren. Wird dieser Umstand entsprechend von jedem einzelnen Unternehmen berücksichtigt, so wird sich zeigen, dass gut ausgebildete und fortlaufend geschulte Arbeitnehmer unabhängig von ihrem Alter in der Lage sind, sich auf neue Anforderungen im Beruf einzustellen.

Unabhängig davon kann zugleich durch staatliche Maßnahmen in die gleiche Richtung gesteuert werden. Zu denken sei in diesem Zusammenhang insbesondere an die Sicherung einer Anstellung bis zum 65. Lebensjahr, an Förderungen zur Wieder-

---

816 House of Representatives Standing Committee on Employment, Education and Workplace Relations, Parliament of Australia, Age Counts (2000), 102 m.w.N..

817 *Shergold*, Balancing Work and Family Conference – Different Lives, Different Needs, Key Note Adress (1999).

818 The National Strategy for An Ageing Australia, Employment for Mature Age Workers, Issues Paper (1999) 21.

einstellung älterer Menschen sowie aber auch an Förderungen von sozialer Partizipation älterer Arbeitnehmer und Beschäftigter.

III. Vom Diskriminierungsverbot zur Mitarbeitervielfalt im Rahmen eines Age Diversity Managements

Auch wenn das Bewusstsein bei den australischen Unternehmen für die Erstellung und Anwendung einer firmeninternen Antidiskriminierungspolitik zwar stellenweise aktiviert werden konnte, so bedarf es zur nachhaltigen Verbesserung der aktuellen Situation jedoch weiterer wirksamer Maßnahmen. Fraglich erscheint jedoch, ob und welche Regelungsmechanismen hilfreich sein können. Ein nicht zu vernachlässigender Störfaktor ist dabei in jedem Einzelfall die Abhängigkeit vom autonomen Willen zur Erstellung der Antidiskriminierungspolitik.[819] Solange es keine verbindliche – gesetzliche – Verpflichtung zur Entwicklung von unternehmensinternen Richtlinien gegen Altersdiskriminierung und zur wirkvollen Umsetzung, Anwendung sowie Weiterentwicklung gibt, besteht die Gefahr, dass die gewünschte Nachhaltigkeit nicht erreicht werden kann und selbst schon erstellte Antidiskriminierungsrichtlinien mangels kodifizierter Überwachungsregelung und -verpflichtung wieder – ohne Konsequenzen – aufgehoben werden können.

Reine Sensibilisierungs-, Aufklärungs- und/oder Informationskampagnen ersetzen gesetzliche Regelungen nicht, da sie keine verbindliche Handlungsanordnung beinhalten und zudem keine Rechtsfolgen für weitere Untätigkeit bei der Verhinderung und Beseitigung von Altersdiskriminierung regeln. Daher stellen sie keinen Ersatz für Gesetze dar, sondern ergänzen diese allenfalls sinnvoll. Nur die Macht der Gesetzgebung kann zu einer dauerhaften Durchbrechung der Barrieren gegen aktive Bekämpfung von Diskriminierungen wegen Alters verhelfen und zu einer Umsetzung von unternehmensinternen Antidiskriminierungsrichtlinien führen. Zum Wohle aller Altersgruppen und zur effektiven Erreichung des gesetzgeberischen Ziels („*equality*") muss der australische Gesetzgeber angehalten werden, den Age Discrimination Act 2004 (Cth) – zumindest soweit – zu ergänzen. Denkbar wäre in einem ersten Schritt aber auch, die Organisationspflichten des Arbeitgebers entsprechend zu erweitern und etwa durch Rechtsfortbildung in der Rechtsprechung die Förderung vom unternehmensinternen Diversity-Management anzustoßen.[820]

---

819 *Smith*, Australian Anti-Discrimination Laws – Framework, Developments and Issues, New Developments in Employment Discrimination Law – The 9 JILPT Comparative Labour Law Seminar (2008) 6.

820 Vgl. zu den Erfahrungen aus dem European Year of Equal Opportunity for All – EYEO 2007 und den daraus resultierenden Maßnahmen der Europäischen Kommission – wie etwa die Förderung der Vielfalt und Chancengleichheit am Arbeitsplatz – die Mitteilung der Kommission an das Europäische Parlament, den Rat, den Europäischen Wirtschafts- und Sozialausschuss und den Ausschuss der Regionen, Nichtdiskriminierung und Chancengleichheit: Erneuertes Engagement, 2. Juli 2008, abrufbar unter http://eur-lex.europa.eu/LexUriServ/LexUriServ.do?uri=COM:2008:0420:FIN:DE:HTML.

Auch wenn es vor dem Hintergrund einer möglichen Begrenzung der Handlungsfreiheit, der Meinungsfreiheit und im Hinblick auf anfallende Kosten notwendig ist, sich mit Kritikpunkten an der vorgenannten Lösung auseinander zu setzen, so vermögen diese aber kein abweichendes Ergebnis zu begründen. Denn einerseits müssen im Interesse des Allgemeinwohls die Individualinteressen der einzelnen Unternehmer, Arbeitgeber bzw. Personalverantwortlichen oder aber auch kurz, der diskriminierenden Person, zurückgestellt werden. Weiterhin würde lediglich eine äußere Verhaltensverpflichtung eingeführt werden, die jedoch nicht zum Verbot der Äußerung einer autonom gebildeten Meinung führt. Es steht jedem Einzelnen frei, den vorgenannten Lösungsweg zu kritisieren oder – unter Modifikationen – zu befürworten. Auch der Einwand erhöhter Kosten durch den Zwang zur Erstellung, Umsetzung und Überwachung einer unternehmensinternen Antidiskriminierungspolitik vermag nicht zu überzeugen. Denn die Durchmischung der Altersstruktur der Beschäftigten führt zu einer Bündelung der Stärken der unterschiedlichen Altersgruppen und zu einer Regulierung der individuellen Schwächen, so dass sich in der Regel durch eine ausgewogene Personalstruktur eine nicht unerhebliche Produktivitätssteigerung erreichen lässt. Die durch administrative Tätigkeiten verursachten Kosten werden so in der Regel schnell amortisiert.

Um Diskriminierungen wegen Alters in der Beschäftigungspraxis nachhaltig abzubauen und die zuvor genannten Vorteile einer ausgewogenen Mitarbeitervielfalt nutzen zu können, sollte sich die Abbildung der gesellschaftlichen Vielfalt auch im Bereich von Arbeit und Beschäftigung diskriminierungsfrei wieder finden. So könnte auch unter den sich wandelnden demografischen Verhältnissen versucht werden, Altersdiskriminierungen gegenüber jüngeren Beschäftigten zu vermeiden und zugleich die Berufsfreiheit im Alter zu schützen. Der Age Discrimination Act 2004 (Cth) steht dem nicht entgegen, sondern er bietet dafür in rechtlicher Hinsicht die entsprechenden Voraussetzungen.

K. Anhang

Complaint Form

(Version 2/09)

Part A – About you (the complainant) Enquiry reference no:

Name: Mr/Mrs/Miss/Ms:..

Ad-
dress:..

Post code: ....

Contact numbers: Home: .... Business:. .... Fax: ....

Mobile: .... TTY: .... Email: ....

Only fill out this box if you are complaining on behalf of someone else
Name of that person: .... What is your relationship to that person?..

Only fill out this box if someone is assisting you with the complaint – for example a solicitor or union representative
Name of representative: .... Organisation: .... Postal address: .... Contact numbers: Home: .... Business: .... Fax:..................... Mobile: .... TTY: .... Email: ....

**If you need help to fill in this form please contact one of our Complaint Information Officers on 1300 656 419 (local call charge) or (02) 9284 9600.

Part B – Your complaint

Who are you complaining about? (the respondent)

1. Name/organisation:..

Address:...

Post code:...............

Contact numbers: Home:............................Business:............................Fax:....................

Mobile:..............................TTY:....................................Email:...

What is this person's/organisation's relationship to you?..

....

....

2. Name/organisation:..

Address:...

Post code:..................................

Contact numbers: Home:.......................... Business:.......................... Fax:............................

Mobile:............................. TTY:............................. Email:...

What is this person's/organisation's relationship to you?..

....

....

If you are complaining about more than two people or organisations, please provide this additional information on an extra page.

Why are you complaining to the Commission?

I am complaining because I believe:

☐ I have been discriminated against because of my sex

(incl pregnancy, marital status, family responsibilities);

☐ I have been sexually harassed;

☐ I have been discriminated against because of my race;

(incl descent, national / ethnic origin, colour, immigrant status, racial hatred);

☐ I have been discriminated against because I have a disability

(incl physical, intellectual, psychiatric, learning, work related, medical condition, disease such as cancer or HIV, associates and carers of a person with a disability);

☐ I have been discriminated against because of my age;

☐ My human rights have been breached by a federal government agency; or

☐ I have been discriminated against in my employment because of my *(please tick which one)*:

☐ sexual preference

☐ trade union activity

☐ criminal record

☐ religious belief

☐ political opinion

☐ I have been treated unfairly for another reason.

Please state the reason:

....

....

....

When did this happen? (Day/month/year) ....

What happened?

Describe the events that you want to complain about. We need to know what you say happened, where it happened and who did it. Please give us all the dates and other details that you can remember. If you are complaining about employment, please tell us when you commenced employment, your job title and whether you are still employed.

....

....

....

....

....

....

....

....

....

....

....

....

....

....

....

....

....

....

....

....

....

....

....

....

....

....

....

....

Signature: .... Date: ....

Part C – Further information

Supporting evidence

Please attach copies of any documents that may help us investigate your complaint (for example, letters, pay slips, doctor's certificates or references). If you cannot do this, please tell us about the documents or other evidence and how this evidence can be obtained.

....

....

....

....

How has this affected you?

Please tell us how what you are complaining about has affected you?

....

....

....

....

What outcome are you seeking?

....

....

....

....

....

....

....

....

....

....

Have you made a complaint about this to another agency?

(For example a state anti-discrimination or equal opportunity agency, a workers compensation agency, an ombudsman or an industrial relations commission.)

If so, you must provide details of the complaint, the agency it was made to and any outcome. You should also attach copies of any letters you have received from the agency.

....

....

....

....

Have you tried to resolve your complaint in any other way?

(For example through an internal complaint process or your trade union.)

If so, please give details:

....

....

....

....

Remember

- to sign and date page 6 of this document; and
  attach copies of any relevant documents.

Send your completed form to:

Director, Complaint Handling
Australian Human Rights Commission
GPO Box 5218
SYDNEY NSW 2001

Kolibri 360 GmbH
Ferdinand-Jühlke-Straße 7
99095 Erfurt, Deutschland
produktsicherheit@kolibri360.de